Measuring History

Cases of State-Level Testing Across the United States

a volume in
Research in Curriculum and Instruction

Series Editor:
O. L. Davis, Jr., *The University of Texas at Austin*

Research in Curriculum and Instruction

O. L. Davis, Jr., Series Editor

Wise Social Studies Teaching in an Age of High-Stakes Testing:
Essays on Classroom Practices and Possibilities (2005)
edited by Elizabeth Anne Yeager and O. L. Davis, Jr.

Deep Change: Cases and Commentary on Schools and
Programs of Successful Reform in High Stakes States (2005)
edited by Gerald Ponder and David Strahan

Exposing a Culture of Neglect: Herschel T. Manuel and
Mexican American Schooling (2005)
edited by Matthew D. Davis

Narrative Inquiries of School Reform: Storied Lives,
Storied Landscapes, Storied Metaphors (2003)
edited by Cheryl J. Craig

Measuring History

Cases of State-Level Testing
Across the United States

edited by

S. G. Grant
University at Buffalo,
The State University of New York

INFORMATION AGE
PUBLISHING

Greenwich, Connecticut • www.infoagepub.com

Library of Congress Cataloging-in-Publication Data

Measuring history : cases of state-level testing across the United States / edited by S.G. Grant.
   p. cm. -- (Research in curriculum and instruction)
 Includes bibliographical references.
 ISBN 1-59311-480-X (hardcover) -- ISBN 1-59311-479-6 (pbk.)
 1. History--Study and teaching. 2. Achievement tests--United States--States. I. Grant, S. G. II. Series.
 D16.3.M43 2006
 907.1'273--dc22

                      2006002399

Printed in the United States of America

CONTENTS

FOREWORD

The idea of "measuring history" can only be ludicrous. History has no weight even if much of history deals with important, even "weighty" matters. Similarly, history has no length or depth although it calls attention to dimensions and variations of activities within and across periods of time. How bizarre to think of history in terms of ounces or yards or, yes, rulers and cups and gauges.

That realization—the impossibility of measuring history—is exactly one of the key points of this book.

Still, *Measuring History* really has very little to do with the nature of history, even historical inquiry and presentation. Rather, it properly focuses attention on a particular and a rather recent phenomenon characteristic of contemporary offerings of school history. This phenomenon is the testing of achievement following instruction, but it is not just any type of achievement testing. It is much more. It is state-wide achievement testing that is premised on the conviction that such testing truly and accurately *measures* both the nature and the extent—the quality and the quantity—of the historical contents of students' minds.

Such an ideological conviction about achievement testing is not new to American schooling. Previously, however, this conviction played out in only some classrooms on some occasions and was directed by only some educational leaders of schools in different parts of a state or the nation. What is new is the popular if misguided belief that curriculum emphases and instructional procedures appropriate for one hypothetical student are equally appropriate for all actual students in all schools throughout a state. Moreover, this belief is powered by a political enthusiasm for the benefits of what military planners call command and control. Consequently, interlocking systems of emphases (standards) in the history curriculum, instructional procedures, and achievement tests consistent with the standards have been mandated by state legislatures and developed and enforced by state-level bureaucrats.

In these circumstances, state-wide achievement testing is established at great distance from what most conventional teaching has ever known. This testing of history achievement deliberately does *not* develop from the informed choices and emphases of serious-purposed planning undertaken by committed individual teachers. It deliberately rejects as important or even as relevant the prior historical knowledge of students as well as the substantive historical strengths and/or weaknesses of individual teachers in particular schools and, also, of students' engagements with or studies of important and different types of historical knowledge.

Regardless of the possible benefits predicted for this dawning culture of accountability, the new state-wide achievement testing in school history has real and present costs. Strikingly, the costs of this testing have attracted little attention. Both the advocates and the critics of the new accountability largely have been silent. So, also, have teachers and school leaders and boards of education as well as editorial writers and columnists. Whatever the explanations of this regrettable circumstance, failure to deal directly with these costs represents a very serious shortcoming. As Arthur W. Foshay has explained so persuasively, actual and/or anticipated costs constitute one of the critical elements of curriculum decision making.

S. G. Grant and his associates have taken seriously the concern about *costs* of the current state-level testing in school history. In fact, they very well may be the first group in any curriculum area to focus on testing's costs. As such, they merit the applause of all educators.

These scholars, to be sure, focus attention on classroom cases in which some of the very important costs of state-level history testing initially appear. Their ordinarily rich portrayals reveal not just some of the impacts of this testing, they illuminate the nature and variety and specificity of a number of costs to students and teachers ... and to history and its teaching. On the other hand, Grant and his colleagues have not focused on some other important costs. For example, they have not estimated or ferreted out the monetary costs of this testing. Those costs, although mainly now hidden from public view, surely will be the object of other researchers' concerns and, when revealed, likely will stagger the imagination even of the most ardent advocates of the current testing. That Grant and his associates chose to focus on classroom cases rather than on monetary costs is altogether appropriate. Their accomplishment is certain.

I join the editor and authors in an invitation to readers to visit and to observe mindfully in the several real and usually recognizable American history classrooms that are portrayed in this book. In this invitation, we also encourage readers to think with the portrayals and with other data, to challenge the authors' assumptions and findings, as well as to wonder with them about not only the visible costs of state-wide achievement testing, but also about the tacit, even obscured costs of that testing. Additionally, I offer another invitation to a number of readers. That invitation is to join the editor and authors of *Measuring History* in the pursuit of additional research on matters of costs, research that builds and expands on the presently available findings and interpretations.

O. L. Davis, Jr.
Catherine Mae Parker Centennial
Professor of Curriculum and Instruction
The University of Texas at Austin

CHAPTER 1

INTRODUCTION

Measuring History

S. G. Grant

National and state-level policymakers have invested considerable faith in testing as a lever for positive educational change. As former U.S. Assistant Secretary of Education Chester Finn (1995) notes, national educational reforms will fail without "a meaningful examination or assessment system" (p. 121). State-level reformers apparently concur: New York State Education Commissioner Richard Mills asserts, "instruction won't change until the tests change" (Grant, 1997, p. 271).

Policymakers' faith in testing finds little support in academic research, however. As the first decade of the recent wave of educational reform crested, Stake and Rugg (1991) reported, "in sixty years of vast international research on school testing, the policy of emphasizing test performance in order to improve education has never been validated" (p. xx).

In the 10 years since this charge, the picture is no clearer (Amrein & Berliner, 2002; Camilli, Cizek, & Lugg, 2001; Cimbricz, 2002; Clarke, Madaus, Horn, & Ramos, 2000; Dorn, 1998). For example, controversy continues to swirl around the initial reports trumpeting the "Texas miracle" of increasing test score (Haney, 2000; Klein, Hamilton, McCaffrey, &

Measuring History: Cases of State-Level Testing Across the United States, 1–8
Copyright © 2006 by Information Age Publishing
All rights of reproduction in any form reserved.

Stecher, 2000; McNeil, 2000; Toenjes & Dworkin, 2002). With the passage of the No Child Left Behind legislation, the press continues for more tests and more consequences of those tests. Yet this press perseveres despite the absence of occasions for "independently evaluating a testing program before or after implementation, or for monitoring test use and impact" (Clarke et al., 2000, p. 177).

Literacy and mathematics teachers are used to standardized testing—school, district, state, national—and the publicity that goes along with the publication of scores. Most history/social studies (I will use these terms interchangeably) teachers, by contrast, have escaped both tests and the scrutiny attached to them. Students have been tested regularly on matrix-sampled history and geography exams developed by the National Assessment of Educational Progress (NAEP), and those results have been made public (e.g., Ravitch & Finn, 1987). Until recently, however, few state-level social studies exams existed. Of those, most incorporated history into a broad mix of subjects tested, and typically the students' scores were reported in the aggregate. Only a few states such as New York and California developed separate social studies exams, made students' scores public, and attached meaningful consequences to students' performance.

As national waves of reform have broken over the states, however, interest in the social studies curriculum and assessment has grown such that today 34 of the 50 states conduct some sort of annual social studies assessment (Buckles, Schug, & Watts, 2001). Those tests have generated a considerable response as supporters and opponents of the exams have volleyed back and forth. Lost in much of the shouting is the empirical study of what happens in classrooms as history teachers and students read and respond to new or revised state-level, and increasingly high-stakes, history tests. If tests drive teaching as so many policymakers seem to believe, then what does that relationship look like, and more importantly, do new tests ensure more ambitious teaching and learning?

These questions are hard to answer, in part, because the research literature exhibits gaps. First, most of the research to date has focused on students rather than on teachers. Second, the emphasis has been on students' test performance rather than on how students and their teachers make sense of the state exams and whether or not those exams assess meaningful teaching and learning. Finally, the research base on reading and mathematics testing far exceeds that on social studies. The focus on reading and mathematics in No Child Left Behind may mean that attention to social studies testing declines further in the next few years. Unless and until that action occurs, however, tracking the growth of state-level, high-stakes history tests seems useful. Given this background, the authors featured in *Measuring History: Cases of State-Level Testing Across the United*

States make a powerful contribution to the research literature on state-level testing within social studies and beyond.

It is of some concern that only three book-length treatments of testing in history exist. One, Diane Ravitch and Chester Finn's (1987) text, *What Do Our Seventeen Year Olds Know?*, presents an analysis of students' performance on the 1986 NAEP history exam. Ravitch and Finn argue that students' understandings are weak, at best. With no data on classroom practices, however, they can make no substantive claims about the relationship between testing and teaching and learning.

Linda McNeil's (2000) analysis of the influence of state tests on teachers and students in Texas, *Contradictions of School Reform: Educational Costs of Standardized Testing*, does look at the consequences of state tests on teaching and learning. McNeil deftly describes and analyzes the development of the Texas social studies exams through the classroom lives of several teachers and their students and, in so doing, she undercuts both the enthusiasm of those who believe that tests represent a panacea and the lamentation of those who believe that testing will drive all life and creativity from classrooms.

As I began the final editing of this book, a new volume was published. In *Wise Social Studies Teaching in an Age of High-Stakes Testing*, Elizabeth Yeager and O. L. Davis, Jr (2005) offer an edited collection of essays on teachers' classroom practices. Based in the experiences of real social studies teachers across a range of state and classroom contexts, Yeager and Davis demonstrate the diversity in teachers' practices.

Measuring History complements the cases presented in *Wise Social Studies Practices* (Yeager & Davis, 2005). Yeager and Davis highlight the rich and ambitious teaching that can occur in the broad context of state-level testing. In this book, the chapter authors and I bring the particular state history tests more to the fore and examine how teachers are responding to them. At the heart of *Measuring History* are cases of classroom teachers in seven states (Florida, Kentucky, Michigan, New York, Texas, Mississippi, and Virginia) where new social studies standards and new, and generally high-stakes, state-level history tests are prominent. In these chapters, the authors describe and analyze the state's testing efforts and how those efforts are being interpreted in the context of classroom practice. The results both support and challenge prevailing views on the efficacy of testing as a vehicle for educational reform.

Catherine Horn (University of Houston) and I lay the groundwork for the case studies through a set of introductory chapters that examine the current environment, the research literature, and the technical qualities of history tests. In chapter 2, "The State of State-Level History Tests," Catherine and I describe the particulars of how state-level history testing developed by noting the current status, types, and uses of contemporary exams. I review the empirical literature on social studies testing in chapter 3, "Research on History Tests." Then, Catherine offers a useful perspective on the nature of history test questions in chapter 4, "The Technical Realities of Measuring History." The ensuing case study chapters feature the most up-to-date research on several prominent state-level social studies exams. In each case, the author is among the very first to analyze the effects of standardized history tests on teachers and students.

In chapter 5, "Paradox of Practice: Expanding and Contracting Curriculum in a High-Stakes Climate," Letitia Fickel (University of Alaska, Anchorage) reports on field study data she collected on nine teachers in a Kentucky high school history department. Highlighting the paradox of both more and less ambitious teaching coming after the introduction of a high-stakes state exam, Letitia illustrates the power of case studies to detect subtle and unexpected results.

Avner Segall (Michigan State University) examines the influence of the Michigan state social studies test on five secondary school teachers in chapter 6, "Teaching History in the Age of 'Accountability': Measuring History or Measuring Up to It?" Avner's interview study examines teachers' perceptions of standardized tests and how those perceptions reflect various discourses around the exams. In particular, he looks at how the state tests influence teachers' stances, dispositions, and commitments toward history teaching and what it is they do and no longer do with students in classrooms as a result of the exams.

In the first of two cases of New York classrooms, Jane Bolgatz (Fordham University) reports on an action research project she conducted with urban elementary students in chapter 7, "Using Primary Documents With Fourth-Grade Students: Talking About Racism While Preparing for State-Level Tests." Jane describes the sets of primary sources she developed and used with the classroom teacher to help students understand concerns related to economics, race and gender relations, and the question of who participates in history. Jane argues that providing access to substantive issues need not be at the expense of preparation for state-level exams.

Jill Gradwell (Buffalo State College) looks at the practices of a middle school New York social studies teacher in chapter 8, "Teaching in Spite of, Rather than Because of, the Test: A Case of Ambitious History Teaching in New York State." Jill's case presents a useful contrast to Jane's in that her teacher questions rather than embraces the push to use historical documents in the form of the Document-Based Question (DBQ) on the state test. The teacher uses historical documents extensively and teaches her students to be thoughtful readers of the past. She believes, however, that the state test in general, and the DBQ in particular, poorly reflect both her and her students' efforts.

A richly complex story of false starts and missed opportunities characterizes Cinthia Salinas's (University of Texas) study of 11 Texas high school teachers' responses to the Exit Level Texas Assessment of Knowledge and Skills (TAKS) in chapter 9, "Teaching in a High-Stakes Testing Setting What Becomes of Teacher Knowledge?" By examining both the early (and changing) messages broadcast to teachers about the nature of the exam and the teachers' ensuing interpretations, Cinthia describes the many ways that teachers can appear to cooperate with testing dictates while holding on to the dimensions of their teaching practice they feel are most important.

Stephanie van Hover (University of Virginia) examines the experiences of novice Virginia teachers as they negotiate the state standards of learning and the attendant high-stakes state tests. In chapter 10, "Teaching History in the Old Dominion: The Impact of Virginia's Accountability Reform on Seven Secondary Beginning History Teachers," Stephanie looks at the influence (or not) of the state policies on teachers' content, instruction, and assessment decisions.

In chapter 11, "Negotiating Control and Protecting the Private: Accountability, History Teachers and the Virginia Standards of Learning," Ann Marie Smith (Northern Virginia Community College) reports on her ethnographic study of five veteran history teachers in a Virginia high school as they respond to the new state Standards of Learning. Not unlike the beginning teachers Stephanie describes, Ann Marie portrays teachers whose test-based responses vary considerably, both confirming and challenging the views of those who praise and pan state-level tests.

The final case study chapter, "'Does Anybody Really Understand This Test?' Florida History School Social Studies Teachers' Efforts to Make Sense of the FCAT," is noteworthy, in part, because social studies is *not* an explicit part of the Florida Comprehensive Assessment Test. As Elizabeth Yeager and Matthew Pinder (University of Florida) point out, however, the mere presence of a state exam can influence history teachers' practices, though to different degrees and in different ways.

In chapter 13, "The Impact of a High School Graduation Examination on Mississippi Social Studies Teachers' Instructional Practices," Kenneth Vogler (University of South Carolina) takes the study of teachers' responses to state history tests in a different methodological direction as he presents results from his survey of 107 Mississippi high school teachers. Ken argues that, although these teachers continue to use some open-ended instructional practices, the correlation between the new, high-stakes test and more traditional teaching strategies in strong.

Measuring History concludes with two chapters, one that synthesizes the patterns and themes emerging from the cases and a second that looks to the future of standards and high-stakes tests. In chapter 14, "Measuring

History Through State-Level Tests: Patterns and Themes," I review the findings of the case chapters by highlighting the salient similarities and differences, patterns and themes. I conclude with the argument that the construct of *ambitious teaching* offers a more useful lens for capturing the range and diversity of teachers' test-related practices than previous constructs. Finally, William Gaudelli (University of Central Florida) offers a perspective on the prospects and problems of state-level social studies tests in chapter 14, "The Future of High-Stakes History Assessment: Possible Scenarios, Potential Outcomes," Bill presents three visions of the direction state-level history testing might take and the implications each offers for teachers, students, and fate of American schools.

Rooted in the contemporary social studies testing scene, but with an eye toward the future, *Measuring History* extends and expands on Linda McNeil's case of history tests in Texas and on Elizabeth Yeager and O. L. Davis's cases of wise teaching. We may not know well what the future holds for history testing, but in these chapters we see the outlines.

ACKNOWLEDGMENTS

At a conference a few years ago, Steve Thornton accused me of creating a "cottage industry" around the study of state-level history standards and assessments. It was a funny remark, but it also felt quite true: While lots of researchers were studying policy effects in other school subjects, few seemed as interested as I was in social studies. This book, then, represents not only the latest in history testing scholarship, but it also marks the emergence of a group of colleagues to whom I am much indebted.

My list of thanks, then, begins with the chapter authors. On a substantive level, I applaud their fine research and thoughtful analyses for it is these qualities that what make this book work. On a rhetorical level, I thank them for their patience and good humor with the fussiness as first-time editor. Crafting a piece of research that is as well-written as it is informative is hard work and I can not imagine a group of scholars more concerned about the quality of their work. It has been a treat to work with them.

On behalf of the authors, I extend an enormous thank you to the nearly 150 teachers who participated in the research projects described. Simply put, this book would still be a dream without their willingness to help us understand their responses to the state-level exams.

Others whose efforts merit mention include O. L. Davis, Jr., whose keen insights into the general issues of curriculum, instructional, and assessment issues in general and the particulars of social studies are both long-standing and invariably on-target. I am particularly indebted to O.

L. for his willingness to support this book as series editor for Information Age Publishing. I also want to thank Jill Gradwell for the good humor and sharp insights she brings to our joint research projects and to her careful editing of these number of these chapters. I add to the acknowledgement list a host of folks whose ears I have bent at one time or another about this project: Fenice Boyd, Catherine Cornbleth, Scott DeWitt, Kathleen Lesniak, Martha Sanfilippo, and Bruce VanSledright. Finally, much thanks, as always, to Anne, Alexander, and Claire for their good thoughts, kind words, and plentiful hugs.

REFERENCES

Amrein, A., & Berliner, D. (2002). High-stakes testing, uncertainty, and student learning. *Educational Policy Analysis Archives, 10*(8). Retrieved from http://epaa.asu.edu/epaa/v8n10.html

Buckles, S., Schug, M., & Watts, M. (2001). A national survey of state assessment practices in the social studies. *The Social Studies, 90*(4), 141-146.

Camilli, G., Cizek, G., & Lugg, C. (2001). Psychometric theory and the validation of performance standards: History and future perspectives. In G. Cizek (Ed.), *Setting performance standards: Concepts, methods, and perspectives* (pp. 445-476). Mahwah, NJ: Erlbaum.

Cimbricz, S. (2002). State testing and teachers' thinking and practice: A synthesis of research. *Educational Policy Analysis Archives, 10*(2). Retrieved from http://epaa.asu.edu/epaa/v10n2.html

Clarke, M., Madaus, G., Horn, C., & Ramos, M. (2000). Retrospective on educational testing and assessment in the 20th century. *Journal of Curriculum Studies, 32*(2), 159-181.

Dorn, S. (1998). The political legacy of school accountability systems. *Educational Policy Analysis Archives, 6*(1). Retrieved from http://epaa.asu.edu/epaa/v6n1.html

Finn, C. (1995). Who's afraid of the big, bad test? In D. Ravitch (Ed.), *Debating the future of American Education: Do we need national standards and assessments?* (pp. 120-144). Washington, DC: Brookings Institution.

Grant, S. G. (1997). Opportunities lost: Teachers learning about the New York state social studies framework. *Theory and Research in Social Education, 25*(3), 259-287.

Haney, W. (2000). The myth of the Texas miracle in education. *Educational Policy Analysis Archives, 8*(41), Retrieved from http://epaa.asu.edu/epaa/v8n41.html

Klein, S., Hamilton, L., McCaffrey, D., & Stecher, B. (2000). What do test scores in Texas tell us? *Educational Policy Analysis Archives, 8*(49), 1-15. Retrieved from http://epaa.asu.edu/epaa/v8n49.html

McNeil, L. (2000). *Contradictions of school reform: Educational costs of standardized testing.* New York: Routledge.

Ravitch, D., & Finn, C. (1987). *What do our seventeen year olds know?* New York: Harper & Row.

Stake, R., & Rugg, D. (1991). Impact of the classroom. In R. E. Stake (Ed.), *Advances in program evaluation* (Vol. 1, pp. xix-xxii). Greenwich, CT: JAI Press.

Toenjes, L., & Dworkin, A. G. (2002). Are increasing test scores in Texas really a myth, or is Haney's myth a myth? *Educational Policy Analysis Archives, 10*(17). Retrieved from http://epaa.asu.edu/epaa/v10n17.html

Yeager, E., & Davis Jr., O. L. (Eds.). (2005). *Wise social studies teaching in an age of high-stakes testing.* Greenwich, CT: Information Age.

CHAPTER 2

THE STATE OF STATE-LEVEL HISTORY TESTS

S. G. Grant and Catherine Horn

The No Child Left Behind (NCLB) legislation has put the nation on alert: Standardized testing is the coin of the educational realm. State-level protests against NCLB notwithstanding, the Bush education plan rests squarely on tests. But not all testing counts the same at the national level. Reading and mathematics tests have clear preference as measures of student and school success. Testing in science and social studies merits mention in the NCLB guidelines, but more as afterthought than as essential.

The focus on reading and mathematics is not new. Policymakers and the public have long noted student performance on reading and mathematics testing. Teachers, especially those at the elementary level would seem to agree. Surveys consistently show that teachers give far more classroom attention to reading and mathematics than to science and social studies (Mathison, 2003). Most states require some number of science and social studies courses at the high school level. But while virtually every state tests students' reading and mathematics abilities, state-level science and social studies tests are not a given.

That said, attempts to assess students' historical knowledge are not new. Whether surveys commissioned by newspapers, tests constructed by

Measuring History: Cases of State-Level Testing Across the United States, 9–27
Copyright © 2006 by Information Age Publishing
All rights of reproduction in any form reserved.

national organizations, or interviews with people on the street conducted by late night talk show hosts, Americans regularly have asked what students know about history (Paxton, 2003). The answer—"not much"—is as distressing as it is consistent. The rhetoric of an educational golden age appears to be just that: Assessments conducted from 1917 through 2001, although different in sample and in approach, have yielded reliable results—students know, at best, half of the expected correct answers. As expected, responses to this dismal news stretch from "shameful" to "abysmal" to "shocking" and most every synonym in between (Paxton, 2003).

If assessments of students' historical knowledge and the "shocking" results are not new, the number of new, state-level tests created and the uses to which these tests are put is. Although the No Child Left Behind legislation has created a degree of uncertainty by putting social studies testing to the side, there are today far more, and more consequential, state-level history tests than in the past. National tests and surveys of historical knowledge may result in banner headlines and best-selling books. State-level history tests, however, are influencing what and how teachers teach and which students graduate from high school. The difference, then, is both one of degree and kind.

In this chapter, we survey the state-level history test scene along three dimensions. First, we chart the growth of state social studies tests, particularly those with high stakes attached, over the last several years. Second, we describe the content the new history tests cover. And finally, we outline the uses to which history tests are linked.

Preceding the rise of state-level history testing, however, was the rise of state-level social studies standards. Studies of those standards are numerous (Buckles, Schug, & Watts, 2001; Grant, 2003) so we will not spend much time describing them. But before looking at issues of state-level testing, we present a short history of the standards movement in social studies by contrasting the development of the New York and California curriculum frameworks.

THE RISE OF HISTORY STANDARDS

As in other subject areas, social studies standards have surfaced at both the national and state levels. Unlike the other subject areas, however, the enduring battles over social studies versus history (Evans, 2004; Jenness, 1990) engendered competing standards at the national level, such that there are no less than five sets of standards in play. When combined with the various curriculum policies created by state policymakers, the standards landscape for history/social studies is a complicated one.[1] Some state-level standards bear strong resemblance to one or another set of national standards, other state standards draw on a range of standards documents, and still others represent a unique array of ideas. The active interest in social studies curriculum standards means that there is some intersection between state and national standards. Consistency between and among different sets of standards can not be assumed, however.

Social studies standards development began in earnest during the mid-1980s at the state level. Most states had state-level curriculum of one sort or another, although these documents varied considerably. North Carolina, for example, produced detailed K–12 curriculum guides of more than 200 pages. By contrast, Maine's state social studies guidelines consisted of a single paragraph. As the fallout from the *Nation at Risk* report (National Commission on Excellence in Education, 1983) developed, state policymakers around the U.S. initiated curriculum revisions across school subjects. In social studies, that work gained particular notoriety as policymakers in two states, California and New York, took very different tacks (Cornbleth & Waugh, 1993). Ever-present, however, is the long-simmering, occasionally erupting battle between advocates of history and social studies.

In the 1800s, school curricula often included history courses. Those courses typically focused on worlds beyond the United States. Course titles like "Ancient History," "British History," and "The Modern World" predominated; "U.S. History" did not become a mainstay in the school curriculum until the late 1800s. Even then history courses were far from students' favorites. Students routinely decried the heavy emphasis on facts and dates and the leaden pedagogy of endless lecture and recitation. The rationale behind the move from a straight history curriculum to "social studies" in the early 1900s included both curricular and instructional hope: The curriculum was to be more attuned to the social realities of the day and teachers were to embrace different forms of teaching. Wide applause greeted proponents of social studies as they "fulminated against the mere imposition, the enforced memorization, of facts" (Jenness, 1990, p. 72).

Widely embraced, the new social studies curriculum became instantiated through courses such as "Problems of Democracy" at the high school level and later, in the early grades, in the "expanding horizons" model. Problems of Democracy courses epitomized the social studies initiative in that the content focused on analyzing the contemporary world surrounding students through various social science and historical perspectives. The notion of students actively examining their worlds also surfaced in the emerging elementary school social studies curriculum. Teachers typically included stories of the past and lessons in geography, but little in the way of formal curricula existed before 1900. With the new social studies curriculum, reformers saw the elementary years as an opportunity. Advocates of the expanding horizons approach (Haas, 1977) assumed that, although students have the ability to think and reason, their interests and abilities are fundamentally egocentric. The curriculum, then, began in kindergarten with a focus on self and family. Moving steadily outward, students studied other families, neighbors, communities, their states, and then the United States through Grade 5.

Some critics of the expanding horizons model rightly have pointed to the unfounded assumption that students' social awareness progresses in an orderly geographic fashion (LeRiche, 1987). More vocal, however, have been advocates of history who argue that the social studies curriculum eliminates serious historical study in favor of "tot sociology" (Ravitch, 1987). This later claim seems odd on two levels. First, the widespread adoption of a K–12 social studies curriculum means that attention to political, economic, social, and global issues is far more prevalent in schools than it ever was pre1900. One may critique the content of some social studies curricula, but the growth in content, including history content, can not be denied. Moreover, the explicit attention to history, and U.S. history in particular, increased dramatically in the new social studies curriculum. Aside from the fact that the K–5 curriculum is almost exclusively U.S.-based, formal coursework in U.S. history became firmly fixed in Grades 5, 8, and 11 under the social studies mantle (Gehrke, Knapp, & Sirotnik, 1992).[2] These two points aside, critics continue to denounce social studies as ahistorical.[3]

Criticism of social studies crested in the mid1980s with the publication of Diane Ravitch and Chester Finn's analysis of the "shameful" 1986 National Assessment of Educational Progress test results in history. Ravitch and Finn (1987) conclude that the national sample of 11th graders are "ignorant of important things it should know, and that it and generations to follow are at risk of being gravely handicapped by that ignorance upon entry into adulthood, citizenship, and parenthood" (p. 201). Ravitch and Finn's book reignited the history versus social studies debate in ways that have shaped curriculum standards across the U.S. into the present.

One of the first places the debate became realized was in California. Standards work in social studies began in California in the 1970s when state policymakers introduced their first state-wide curriculum. That document caused little stir: Although it served as the basis for the state social studies textbook adoption process, no state-level test was created and public reaction was minimal. All of that changed in the mid1980s, however, when California officials under the leadership of then Superintendent of Schools, Bill Honig, initiated a new round of curriculum policy revisions. Much influenced by Ravitch and Finn's (1987) critique, Honig invited Ravitch to serve as a consultant to curriculum development process.

The result of that process, the *History/Social Science Framework for California Public Schools* (California Board of Education, 1988), announced the resolution of the history versus social studies debate in its title. Not only does "social studies" not appear in the title, but it is virtually absent the entire 120 page document. Superintendent Honig puts the point on this effort: "This framework places history at the center of the social sciences and humanities, where it belongs" (p. viii). To that end, the California framework allots 6 years of the K–12 curriculum specifically to historical study. U.S. history is featured at three grade levels (Grades 5, 8, and 11) as is world history (Grades 6, 7, and 10).[4] The effect of this action, the authors contend, "departs from current practice by significantly increasing the time allocated to chronological history" (California Board of Education, 1988, p. 29).[5] Arguably, the biggest curricular change, however, is the injection of history into the elementary curriculum. According to one of the principal authors, "returning history to the elementary school curriculum is one of the decade's major movements for school reform" (Crabtree, 1989, p. 173). From kindergarten on, students are directed to use biographies, stories, legends, and folktales to begin thinking about the past. Summing up the California reform, Superintendent Honig (California Board of Education, 1988) mixes his metaphors, but emphatically states the case for a history-based curriculum: "History is the glue that makes the past meaningful, the lens through which children and adults can come to understand the world that they live in and understand how it was shaped" (p. vii).[6]

Like California's Honig, Commissioner of Education Thomas Sobol initiated a reform of the state's social studies curriculum in New York. And as in California, history plays a dominant role in the resulting policy. Different, however, were the circumstances under which the new curriculum developed and the nominal commitment to the language of social studies.

In the early 1990s, Commissioner Sobol[7] initiated an ambitious reform agenda under the umbrella of the *New Compact for Learning* (New York State Education Department, 1991). The *Compact*, according to Sobol, represented a "comprehensive strategy for improving public elementary, middle, and secondary education results in the 1990s" (p. 1). More specifically, the *Compact* proposed to "change the system" (p. 2) along two lines. One line redefined the relationship between state and local education authorities exemplified by the phrase, "Top down support for bottom up change" (p. 4). The second line of change involved the development of new curriculum, instruction, and assessment frameworks in all curricular areas. These frameworks were intended to "state more specifically the skills, knowledge, and values students should acquire as a result of elementary and secondary education" (p. 4).

The *Compact* provided the *raison d'être* for curriculum framework development in all school subjects. Concern about the state social studies curriculum, however, predated the *Compact*. After taking office in 1987, Commissioner Sobol constituted a group to review the existing social studies curriculum. The ensuing report, *A Curriculum of Inclusion* (New York State Minority Task Force, 1989), was heavily criticized by social conservatives as an extreme form of multiculturalism (Committee of Scholars in Defense of History, 1990; Schlesinger, 1991). Seemingly sensitive to some of these critiques, Sobol nevertheless took seriously the perceived need to revise the existing social studies curriculum. He impaneled a second committee in 1990 whose report, *One Nation, Many Peoples* (Social Studies Review and Development Committee, 1991) also inflamed conservatives. The proposal, according to one observer, was little more than "a repackaging of multicultural extremism as moderate academic reform" (MacDonald, 1992, p. 9).

New York state has published state curriculum or syllabi since the late 1800s. The authors of *One Nation, Many People* critiqued the existing syllabi, but they did not offer a new curriculum. With the release of the *New Compact for Learning* in 1991, Commissioner Sobol appointed yet a third committee, the Social Studies Curriculum and Assessment Committee, charging this group to develop "desired learning outcomes" and recommend "elements" of a state-wide assessment (Cornbleth, 1995, p. 177).

Almost 3 years later, as the committee-produced draft document was about to go to the state Board of Regents, Commissioner Sobol recalled it. The timing of this move was noteworthy: The 1994 Republican congressional victory and the conservative outcry over release of the U.S. history standards developed by the National Center for History in the Schools (1994) meant that new state social studies curriculum was certain to be closely scrutinized. Sobol acknowledged that his decision to recall the committee draft and to employ a consultant (Tom Ward and Associates) to revise it reflected his sense of being "still bruised from our own social studies content battles" (Diegmueller, 1995, p. 9).

In June 1995, the revised draft framework entitled, *Curriculum, Instruction, and Assessment Preliminary Draft Framework for Social Studies* (Ward, 1995), was reviewed and accepted for dissemination by the state Board of Regents. Commissioner Sobol characterized this draft as a "balanced, moderate but progressive middle ground" (Diegmueller, 1995, p. 9). Some reviewers agreed, but most added only qualified support. For example, the president of the New York State Council for the Social Studies said, "There is no question that there are people who are going to think it is a cop-out" (p. 9). Although applauding the lack of "radical multiculturalism" she believed evident in previous drafts, the first vice president of the New York State United Teachers worried that the new framework "lacks the grist to have a really good debate over social studies" (p. 9).

State-level attention to and activity around school curriculum hit full stride in the mid1990s under current Commissioner Richard Mills. As the language of "standards" gained prominence, working groups of state policymakers, teachers, and administrators produced two new social studies documents reflecting key elements of the 1995 *Draft Framework*. The *Learning Standards for Social Studies* (New York State Education Department, 1996) organizes the K–12 social studies curriculum around broadly-expressed U.S. and New York history, world history, geography, economics, and civics/citizenship/government standards. The *Resource Guide for Social Studies* (New York State Education Department, 1999) offers far more specificity, detailing people, places, events, and concepts grade by grade.

Compared with the previous round of curricular revisions in the mid-to-late 1980s, the the *Standards* and *Resource Guide* represent virtually no changes in the K–5 grades curriculum (which follows an expanding horizons model), in the 7th and 8th grade U.S. and New York State history courses, or in the 12th grade participation in government and economics courses. Modest changes are evident in other grades, such as the emphasis on geography in the 11th grade U.S. history and government course. Major changes are localized at 6th grade, where the course of study expanded from Western and Eastern Europe and the Middle East to the entire Eastern hemisphere, and at 9th and 10th grades, where the emphasis changes from a cultural approach as represented in the title, global studies, to a chronological study expressed as Global History and Geography.

Although the routes taken differ, California and New York emerged with curricula largely centered on the study of history. Many other states have followed suit, although the resultant standards vary considerably in quality if the reports of the Fordham Foundation (Stern, 2003) and *Education Week* (2003) can be believed.[8] The former gives top grades to 11 states' social studies standards and failing grades to 25 based on the qualities of historical content, sequential development, and balance. Using a different measure, *Education Week* analysts rate the social studies standards of 34 states to be "clear, specific, and grounded in content." [9]

Lurking in the background of the curriculum standards movement has been state-level testing (Smith & O'Day, 1991). Operating under the common sense assumption that new standards ought to drive the creation of new tests, state-level policymakers began generating new exams in earnest once state standards were in place. Although this work began at the state-level, support and encouragement from both the Clinton and Bush administrations has been evident.[10]

THE GROWTH OF STATE-LEVEL HISTORY TESTS

Understanding the growth of state-level history tests is problematic as the number of exams has proven to be a moving target. Although the percentage of states with history tests has hovered around 50% since 1999, that figure represents a large increase over the preceding years. Moreover, the states that do or do not test students' historical knowledge continue to change.

Key to the uncertainty around the importance of social studies/history as a tested subject comes is the marginal position it occupies within the No Child Left Behind legislation. Reading and mathematics tests typically receive more publicity than social studies tests. NCLB confirms that priority. History (not social studies) is listed as a core academic subject, but the call for history testing is vague. Even supporters of NCLB worry that this mixed message may decrease attention to history teaching and learning. Chester Finn (2003) notes that "without intending to, however, NCLB may actually worsen the plight of U.S. history. By concentrating single-mindedly on reading, math, and science, it will likely reduce the priority that states, districts, and schools assign to other subject matters" (p. 5). Finn and others are right to worry. For every state like Washington that is developing a new test, states like Michigan are scaling back the scope of their social studies testing, and others such as Maine and Minnesota are eliminating history tests all together. As Burroughs (2002) notes, "state legislatures repeatedly pass and rescind laws that mandate [social studies] tests and/or define their use" (p. 315).

Complicating an understanding of the growth of state-level history testing is the fact that sources vary. For example, based on their 1999 survey of state education departments, Buckles, Shug, and Watts (2001) report that 34 states[11] had or expected to have state-level social studies tests. Compare that with the *Education Week* survey of the same year which listed only 22 states as having tests aligned with state standards. Key to the difference is the phrase "aligned with state standards." That is, a number of states include social studies as part of their general assessment package, but the tests may not be specific to a state's standards and thus have few consequences for teachers and/or students. As an example, Burroughs (2002) reports that, although 30 states have mandated social studies tests, only 22 of these states have or plan to develop high-stakes exams.

Table 2.1.   Number of States With Standards-Based History Tests, 1998–2004

Year	Number of Standards-Based State History Tests
1997–1998	17
1998–1999	22
1999–2000	22
2000–2001	23
2001–2002	22
2002–2003	24
2003–2004	23

The most reliable numbers around testing, come from the annual survey of state education departments conducted by the staff of *Education Week* under the series entitled *Quality Counts*. Since 1999, the number of states reporting standards-based history tests has held steady at just under 50%. (See Table 2.1.) The seeming stability of the 22–24 state-level history tests belies two kinds of fluctuation. One is the jump in the number of states reporting standards-based testing from 1997 when 17 states reported administering standards-based exams to 1998 when another 5 states added tests. This increase is most likely explained as a result of a peaking standards-setting period. The relatively stable number of state history tests since 1998 suggests that NCLB may not have as much effect on decisions to test as some (e.g., Finn, 2003) might believe.

The second source of fluctuation, however, may be a more direct result of NCLB. For although the overall number of states testing history is little changed, there has been considerable movement by states onto and off from the list each year. For example, the 2004 *Quality Counts* survey shows that, over the preceding year, three states—Kansas, Maine, and New Hampshire—dropped their state social studies assessments while two states—Tennessee and West Virginia—added new ones. As we write this chapter, then, 23 states have state-level history tests tied to their state standards.[12] (See Table 2.2.) Fluxuations aside, recent trends show a stable number of history tests and far more tests than were administered seven years ago.

A couple of patterns surface across the data in Table 2.2. First, history tests are far more common in the south than in the other parts of the United States: Only a handful of states in the west, midwest, and north/east require state-level exams compared with a dozen or so states (depending on how one counts) located in the south. This pattern is of little surprise since state-level testing has long been a more pervasive phenomena in the south than in the rest of the country. The second pattern is

Table 2.2.   States With State-Level History Tests, 2004

State	Elementary-Level Test	Middle-Level Test	High School-Level Test
Alabama			*
California		*	*
Delaware	*	*	*
Georgia	*	*	*
Illinois	*	*	*
Kentucky	*	*	*
Louisiana	*	*	*
Maryland			*
Michigan	*	*	*
Mississippi			*
Missouri	*	*	*
New Mexico	*	*	*
New York	*	*	*
North Carolina			*
Ohio	*	*	*
Oklahoma	*	*	*
South Carolina	*	*	
South Dakota	*	*	*
Tennessee	*	*	
Texas		*	*
Virginia	*	*	*
West Virginia	*	*	*
Wisconsin	*	*	*

that most states administering standards-based history tests do so at all three levels of schooling. The difference is interesting—15 states test at all three levels versus 8 states that skip one or more level—but more useful is the assumption that policymakers believe that success on high school exams is dependent, at least in part, on early testing experience.

Critics of history testing may have thought they had an unlikely ally in NCLB. It appears they were wrong. Some states have dropped their history exams in response to the heavy NCLB pressure for reading and mathematics testing. But as they do, other states have stepped in and initiated their own history tests. State-level history testing may never develop in more than half of the states, but neither do the trends suggest any substantial cut-back in the number of tests administered.

THE CONTENT OF STATE-LEVEL HISTORY TESTS

Among the states currently implementing a history test, a vast range of topics, divisions of information, and item types are evident. Even at the level of grades tested, the differences across the states are stark. As noted above, 15 states test at all three levels of schooling, but 12 of those states test students 4 or more times across those grades. In fact, three states—Georgia, Louisiana, and West Virginia—test students at 8 or more levels between 3rd and 12th grades. Compare this commitment to testing with Illinois, for example, that tests students across all three levels of schooling but does so only 3 times (i.e., at Grades 5, 8, and 11). As one might expect from these differences in grades tested, the level of specificity of content assessed on each exam also varies. The Georgia Criterion-Referenced Competency Test of Social Studies, for example, tests students on five broad content areas in Grades 3–8: geography, history, economics, civics, and core skills. Within those areas, the history strand serves as an example of how the specific content tested changes notably from grade to grade:

- Third grade—U.S. and Georgia history
- Fourth grade—The historical development of the New World, including the exploration of the New World through the causes for the Civil War
- Fifth grade—The U.S. from the Civil War to the present
- Sixth grade—The Americas, Europe, and Oceania
- Seventh grade—Asia, the Middle East, and Africa
- Eighth grade—The Americas and Georgia

Because history tests are administered frequently across many grades, each Georgia exam tests a relatively narrow band of information.[13] Looking across the entire testing program, however, Georgia children are tested over a wide range of curriculum.

Compare the content of Georgia tests with that in Illinois. There, Grades 5, 8, and 11 students take tests across four content areas: political systems, economics, geography, and history. Looking again at the history strand, whereas each of the Georgia tests covered fairly discrete information, each of the Illinois Standards Achievement Tests (and Prairie State Achievement Exam of Social Studies at Grade 11) contain test questions on U.S., world, environmental, and Illinois history. Consequently, the depth to which any one of these subtopic areas can be tested is limited because of time, space, and testing frequency constraints. Whether Georgia's children know more history than do their Illinois peers is a debatable question. Comparing these two states, however, serves to bring into focus the possible differences in information states gather about their students' history knowledge.

Perhaps more importantly, Georgia and Illinois also highlight the variation in what is meant by the term "history" or "social studies" across the states. While several states administer specific subject area tests, for example, government (e.g., Maryland) or U.S. history (e.g., Tennessee),[14] many more employ broad-based social studies tests at various grades. Yet what tests of "social studies" cover can vary tremendously. Consider the differences between Oklahoma's fifth grade Core Curriculum Test of Social Studies and Kentucky's fifth grade Core Content Test of Social Studies. The former includes questions on early exploration, colonial America, the American Revolution, the early federal period, and geographic skills. The Oklahoma test blueprint suggests a heavy weighting toward history over other components of the typical social studies curriculum. Kentucky's exam, by contrast, looks much more like a broad-based social studies exam because it includes items about government and civics, culture and society, economics, geography, and U.S. and Kentucky history.

One other complication to understanding the content tested under the umbrella term "social studies" is the fact that three states—Montana, New Mexico, and Utah—currently utilize "off the shelf" nationally-normed tests to assess their students' social science knowledge. These exams rely on a broadly-defined set of standards, typically drawn from national sources. For example, Montana administers the Iowa Test of Basic Skills in Social Studies at Grades 4 and 8 and the Iowa Test of Educational Development in Social Studies at Grade 11. The content on these tests is selected from the National Council for Social Studies' 10 thematic strands and covers four broad areas:

- History—Culture, time, continuity, and change
- Geography—People, places, and environments; global connections
- Economics—Production, distribution, and consumption; science, technology, and society; global connections
- Government and society—Power, authority, and governance; civic ideals and practices; individual development and identity; individuals, groups, and institutions

"Off the shelf" assessments may provide information about how students in a state are performing relative to similar test takers across the country, but they do not reflect how much students know and can do relative to the state's specific curriculum standards nor do they necessarily represent what different states even mean by the term "social studies" itself.

Considered carefully, it becomes clear that what the term "social studies" or "history" means and what is measured in the exams administered can differ sometimes substantially from state to state. Although a set of concepts—history, economics, civics, and sometimes geography—frequently appears among the content standards assessed, the variation across states is sometimes striking and raises the question of how, if at all, such results might be compared. These differences also serve as a reminder that the extent to which such exams rely on fact-based or recall types of items may further exacerbate the dissimilarities. This is not to argue that we should have a national exam of social studies (NAEP tests notwithstanding) or to say that less specific tests such as the Iowa Test of Basic Skills serve a better purpose. As federal mandates such as NCLB begin to draw attention to history (even tangentially), though, any national accountability structure that sets up comparisons across states must be considered carefully.

The Uses of State-Level History Tests

As with the content of the state-level history tests, the uses to which the scores are put vary dramatically across the states. Currently, 10 states make some sort of student-level, high-stakes decision, in part, on the basis of a history test (see Table 2.3). Most of these decisions take the form of a graduation sanction: Students are required to pass the social studies assessment (typically in combination with tests of reading, math, and sometimes others) to receive a high school diploma. In Texas, for example, 11th grade students must receive a passing score on the Texas Assessment of Knowledge and Skills (TAKS) Social Studies Test to graduate. The TAKS exam tests students' knowledge of U.S. history from the colonial era to the late twentieth century, geography, economic and social influences, political influences, and social studies skills. Similarly, test performance on the Wisconsin Knowledge and Concepts Exam of Social Studies at Grades 4 and 8 is considered in making student promotion decisions. These exams test proficiency in geographic perspectives, historical and cultural perspectives, civics and government perspectives, and economic perspectives, taking items from the off-the-shelf Terra Nova exam and supplementing them with state specific questions (Office of Educational Accountability, n.d.).

For the majority of states that implement a history exam, student-level accountability is inconsequential. That is not to say, however, that the test results carry no effect. Increasingly, schools and districts are being held responsible for the performance of their students on such exams. As discussed earlier, despite the fact that NCLB does not target history or social studies as a primary accountability lever, states are utilizing the data to measure progress and, in some cases, issue sanctions or rewards. In Cali-

**Table 2.3.   Existence of Student-Level Consequences for
Performance on State Exams**

State	Consequences for Students Attached to Performance at One or More Grades
Alabama	*
California	
Delaware	
Georgia	*
Illinois	
Kentucky	
Louisiana	*
Maryland	
Michigan	
Mississippi	*
Missouri	
New Mexico	*
New York	*
North Carolina	
Ohio	*
Oklahoma	
South Carolina	
South Dakota	
Tennessee	
Texas	*
Virginia	*
West Virginia	
Wisconsin	*

Note: Data sources for this table are each individual state's Department of Education Web site.

fornia, for example, the California History Test scores at Grades 10 and 11 are used in calculating a school's Academic Performance Index (API), which measures academic performance and growth across multiple subject areas. Schools that meet API standards are eligible for monetary and other rewards; schools that fall short of growth targets and are ranked in the lower half of the state distribution may be identified for intervention programs or other sanctions (California Department of Education, n.d.).

Some analysts conclude that tests that carry high-stakes consequences for teachers, schools, or districts, may also carry high stakes for students by virtue of the fact that pressure is placed on the students to perform well (Pedulla, Abrams, Madaus, Russell, Ramos, & Miao, 2003). Additionally, policymakers have begun to embrace the idea that placing stakes beyond the student level will leverage educational improvement for the students. Perhaps most notably at the K–12 level, NCLB requires that every school make adequate yearly progress (AYP) toward 100% proficiency on reading and mathematics assessments among all of its students within 12 years. Such progress is based on the assumption that a system of test-based accountability will "create performance pressures for schools to improve student proficiency ... and narrow achievement disparities based on student background characteristics" (Kim & Sunderman, 2004, p. 9). Both NCLB and state-mandated high-stakes testing work under the premise that they will leverage the intended outcome: increased educational achievement for all.

Such test-based accountability structures are likely to heighten the attention to and preparation for the particular standardized assessments being administered. Further, such tests may be drawing useful attention to the disparate educational opportunities of traditionally underserved students and identifying schools in need of help (Kim & Sunderman, 2004). To the extent that such consideration results in improved K–12 education, and, ultimately, in a more prepared college applicant pool, then, tests will have had their intended consequence. Equally important, however, are the unintended consequences that such exams may bring, including a narrowing of the curriculum and increased retention and dropout rates. The accumulating evidence, then, suggests that test-based "accountability" may take a number of forms and have a number of intended audiences (Grant & Salinas, in press). Moreover, it is clear that history or social studies tests may, in fact, be increasing in their importance for accountability discussions at various levels, at least among the roughly half of the states currently utilizing them.

CONCLUSION

Large-scale state assessments purportedly serve many purposes. Some of those purposes, proponents claim, serve important and positive aims including "gauging student learning, signaling worthy goals for students and teachers to work toward, and providing useful feedback for instructional decision making" (Chudowsky & Pellegrino, 2003, p. 75). Critics of such tests have much evidence to draw on, arguing that the drawbacks of testing far exceed the benefits. Those drawbacks—a narrowing curriculum, pedantic teaching, and increasing disparities among students—become even more profound as the stakes associated with tests increase (Linn, 2000; McNeil, 2000; Smith, 1991). These presumably unintended consequences have some researchers wondering if the move toward high-stakes testing can ever function as a real lever for educational reform

(Camilli, Cizek, & Lugg, 2001; Clarke, Madaus, Horn, & Ramos, 2000; Firestone & Mayrowetz, 2000; Grant, 2003).

Neither the uncertain research evidence nor the uncertain place of social studies in the NCLB legislation has resulted in the abandonment of history testing. True, the number of states testing students' history knowledge has not grow much of late, but neither has it declined. While no where near as prevalent or as influential as reading and mathematics tests, history tests are not going away.

Despite the best hopes and the direst predictions, we actually know very little about how history teachers and their students are responding to state-level tests (Grant, 2003). The cases in this book are intended to address the apparent lack of research and led to deeper, if no less complex, understandings.

NOTES

1. We use "standards" and "curriculum policies" as synonyms, but that translation, like the one between "social studies" and "history" can be problematic when states like New York adopt both *standards* for social studies and a state *curriculum*. Presumably the latter flows from the former, but given the specificity of curriculum documents, reasonable people can disagree as to whether the more globally expressed standards are faithfully enacted in the more specific curriculum guidelines.

2. In New York, U.S. history is the curriculum at Grades 5, 7, 8, and 11.

3. Criticism of social studies shows no sign of abating. The most recent attack was launched by the Fordham Foundation (Leming, Ellington, & Porter, 2003)

4. The curriculum for Grade 9 consists of several elective courses which range from social sciences such as anthropology, psychology, geography, and sociology to ethnic and area studies to law-related education.

5. Although beyond the scope of this chapter, one wonders why the traditional pattern of U.S. history at Grades 5, 8, and 11 was maintained and why world history is taught for 2 years in Grades 6 and 7 and then not again until Grade 10.

6. For a comparative analysis of the relative attention to history in the California framework on the *Final Report* history curriculum in Great Britain, see Grant (1995). For different, but equally interesting analyses of the California history wars, see Cornbleth and Waugh (1995) and Nash and Dunn (1995).

7. Sobol resigned as Commissioner effective July 1, 1995. His successor is Richard Mills, former Commissioner of Education in Vermont.

8. Two states, Iowa and Rhode Island have resisted the push to produce social studies standards

9. A neat comparison of the two quality lists is impossible given their different rating scales, but there are some obvious and profound differences. For example, Fordham gives grades of D or F to 18 sets of standards, while

Education Week assigns passing scores. The watchword, as with all ratings, is caution.

10. A notable difference: Following the lead of the first Bush administration, Clinton-era policymakers pushed for voluntary national exams. G. W. Bush, drawing on his purported "Texas miracle," pushed through the NCLB act which requires state-level testing.

11. Most reports of state-level testing include the District of Columbia.

12. Just to add one more bit of complexity, two states, Montana and Utah, do not have state-level tests tied to state history standards, but they do administer norm-referenced social studies tests. Since those exams do not produce any individual student data, however, they are not considered standards-based tests.

13. By contrast, the Grade 11 Georgia High School Graduation Test of Social Studies test covers a wide scope: world studies (world history and geography), U.S. history, map and globe skills, and information processing skills.

14. Ohio administers a proficiency test in citizenship at Grades 4, 6, and 9, but the content—American heritage (including U.S., North American, and Ohio history), people and societies, world interactions, decision making and resources, democratic processes, and citizenship rights and responsibilities—is similar to that of many states' social studies exams.

REFERENCES

Buckles, S., Schug, M., & Watts, M. (2001). A national survey of state assessment practices in the social studies. *The Social Studies, 90*(4), 141–146.

Burroughs, S. (2002). Testy times for social studies. *Social Education, 66*(5), 315–319.

California Board of Education. (1988). *History-social science framework for the California public schools.* Sacramento, CA: California Department of Education.

California Department of Education. (n.d.). *API description.* Retrieved May 31, 2004, from http://www.cde.ca/gov/ta/ac/ap/apidescription.asp

Camilli, G., Cizek, G., & Lugg, C. (2001). Psychometric theory and the validation of performance standards: History and future perspectives. In G. Cizek (Ed.), *Setting performance standards: Concepts, methods, and perspectives* (pp. 445–476). Mahwah, NJ: Erlbaum.

Chudowsky, N., & Pellegrino, J. (2003). Large-scale assessments that support learning: What will it take? *Theory Into Practice, 42*(1), 75–83.

Clarke, M., Madaus, G., Horn, C., & Ramos, M. (2000). Retrospective on educational testing and assessment in the 20th century. *Journal of Curriculum Studies, 32*(2), 159–181.

Committee of Scholars in Defense of History. (1990). Statement of the Committee of Scholars in Defense of History. *Perspectives, 28*(7), 15.

Cornbleth, C. (1995). Controlling curriculum knowledge: Multicultural politics and policymaking. *Journal of Curriculum Studies, 27*(2), 165–185.

Cornbleth, C., & Waugh, D. (1993). The great speckled bird: Education policy-in-the making. *Educational Researcher, 22*(7), 31–37.

Cornbleth, C., & Waugh, D. (1995). *The great speckled bird: Multicultural politics and education policy making.* New York: St. Martins.

Crabtree, C. (1989). Returning history to the elementary schools. In P. Gagnon (Ed.), *Historical literacy: The case for history in American schools* (pp. 173–187). New York: Macmillan.

Diegmueller, K. (1995, June 21). Controversy predicted over N.Y. social-studies framework. *Education Week,* p. 9.

Evans, R. (2004). *The social studies wars: What should we be teaching the children?* New York: Teachers College Press.

Finn, C. (2003). Foreward. In S. Stern (Ed.), *Effective state standards for U.S. history: A 2003 report card* (pp. 5-8). Washington, DC: Fordham Foundation.

Firestone, W., & Mayrowetz, D. (2000). Rethinking "high stakes": Lessons from the United States and England and Wales. *Teachers College Record, 102*(4), 724–749.

Gehrke, N., Knapp, M., & Sirotnik, K. (1992). In search of the school curriculum. In G. Grant (Ed.), *Review of research in education* (pp. 51–110). Washington, DC: American Educational Research Journal.

Grant, S. G. (1995). Teaching history: Curricular views from California and the United Kingdom. *Journal of Social Studies Research, 19*(2), 17-27.

Grant, S. G. (2003). *History lessons: Teaching, learning, and testing in U.S. high school classrooms.* Mahwah, NJ: Erlbaum.

Grant, S. G., & Salinas, C. (in press). Assessment and accountability in social studies. In L. Levstik & C. Tyson (Eds.), *Handbook of research in social studies education.* Mahwah, NJ: Erlbaum.

Haas, J. (1977). *The era of the new social studies.* Boulder, CO: ERIC Clearinghouse for Social Studies/Social Science Education and Social Science Education Consortium.

Jenness, D. (1990). *Making sense of social studies.* New York: Macmillan.

Kim, J., & Sunderman, G. (2004). *Large mandates and limited resources: State response to the No Child Left Behind Act and implications for accountability.* Cambridge, MA: The Civil Rights Project at Harvard University.

Leming, J., Ellington, L., & Porter, K. (2003). *Where did social studies go wrong?* Washington, DC: Fordham Foundation.

LeRiche, L. (1987). The expanding environments sequence in elementary social studies: The origins. *Theory and Research in social education, 15*(3), 137–154.

Linn, R. (2000). Assessments and accountability. *Educational Researcher, 29*(2), 4–16.

MacDonald, H. (1992). The Sobol report: Multiculturalism triumphant. *The New Criterion, 10*(5), 9–18.

Mathison, S. (2003). Constraining elementary teachers' work: Dilemmas and paradoxes created by state mandated testing. *Educational Policy Analysis Archives, 11*(34). Retrieved from http://epaa.asu.edu/epaa/v11n34.

McNeil, L. (2000). *Contradictions of school reform: Educational costs of standardized testing.* New York: Routledge.

Nash, G., & Dunn, R. (1995). History standards and culture wars. *Social Education, 59*(1), 5-7.

National Center for History in the Schools. (1994). *National standards for United States history.* Los Angeles: Author.

National Commission on Excellence in Education. (1983). *A nation at risk.* Washington, DC: U.S. Government Printing Office.

New York State Education Department. (1991). *A new compact for learning.* Albany, NY: Author.

New York State Education Department. (1996). *Learning standards for social studies.* Albany, NY: Author.

New York State Education Department. (1999). *Social studies resource guide with core curriculum.* Albany, NY: Author.

New York State Minority Task Force. (1989). *A curriculum of inclusion.* Albany, NY: New York State Education Department.

Office of Educational Accountability. (n.d.). *Wisconsin student assessment system knowledge and concepts examinations.* Retrieved June 20, 2004, from http://www.dpi.state.wi.us/dpi/oea/socst97.html

Paxton, R. (2003). Don't know much about history—Never did. *Phi Delta Kappan, 85*(4), 264–273.

Pedulla, J., Abrams, L., Madaus, G., Russell, M., Ramos, M., & Miao, J. (2003). *Perceived effects of state-mandated testing programs on teaching and learning: Findings from a national survey of teachers.* Chestnut Hill, MA: National Board on Educational Testing and Public Policy.

Ravitch, D. (1987). Tot sociology or what happened to history in the grade schools. *American Scholar, 56*, 343–353.

Ravitch, D., & Finn, C. (1987). *What do our seventeen year olds know?* New York: Harper & Row.

Schlesinger, A., Jr. (1991). *The disuniting of America.* Knoxville, TN: Whittle.

Smith, M., & O'Day, J. (1991). Systemic school reform. In S. Fuhrman & B. Malen (Eds.), *The politics of curriculum and testing* (pp. 233–267). New York: Falmer.

Smith, M. L. (1991). Put to the test: The effects of external testing on teachers. *Educational Researcher, 20*(5), 8–11.

Social Studies Review and Development Committee. (1991). *One nation, many peoples: A declaration of cultural independence.* Albany, NY: New York State Education Department.

Stern, S. (2003). *Effective state standards for U.S. history: A 2003 report card.* Washington, DC: Fordham Foundation.

Ward, T. (1995). *Curriculum, instruction, and assessment preliminary draft framework for social studies.* Albany, NY: New York State Education Department.

CHAPTER 3

RESEARCH ON HISTORY TESTS[1]

S. G. Grant

Testing has been a part of the American education landscape for well over 100 years. And, if anything, its presence is increasing: Central to George W. Bush's No Child Left Behind legislation is more testing. Even states with well-established testing programs such as Maryland, New York, and Michigan are adding exams in order to meet new federal guidelines. Although the many problems associated with testing have not diminished, neither has policymakers' faith in testing as a means of educational change.

Just as testing advocates line up their rationales, so too do testing critics line up theirs. Some of these rationales are based in empirical studies, but most are not. So in this chapter, I focus on the available research in order to address three questions that lie close to the heart of the testing debate. The first asks what tests can tell us about students' understandings of history. The news here is not good, especially if one looks only at the national testing data. A couple of issues complicate this assessment, however. The second question centers on whether testing drives teaching. Although this assumption is largely accepted in some faculty rooms and in most state departments of education, I argue that the research literature offers little direct support for this claim. The final question explores the relationship between increasing the stakes for students and teachers and increasing educational standards and more ambitious teaching. Poli-

Measuring History: Cases of State-Level Testing Across the United States, 29–56
Copyright © 2006 by Information Age Publishing

cymakers, and a good portion of the public, pin much hope on the common sense premise that more tests and higher stakes will yield better academic outcomes. The research evidence undercuts this optimism. Tests do matter to teachers and students as they construct their classroom lives, but whether tests matter in ways that promote higher standards and better teaching is unclear.

Were I to focus only on research related to history tests this would be a short chapter for only a small measure of the testing literature is research-based. Although it is now over 10 years old, Dana Kurfman's (1991) caution that, "there has been far more argumentation about test effects than there has been actual research" (p. 310) remains true. Of the large literature on testing in social studies, little directly investigates the impact of testing on teachers' practices and on students' historical knowledge and understanding. So while I will focus on the research related to history tests, I will include relevant findings from other school subjects as seems appropriate.

As the level of state testing increases, understanding what effects these tests have becomes critical. In the following sections, I examine what tests tell us about students' understandings of history, whether or not testing drives teaching, and to what extent high-stakes tests seem to support higher standards. Tests like the TEKS in Texas, the MEAP in Michigan, and the Regents exam in New York are intended to promote ambitious teaching and higher levels of student achievement. But what does this intent look like in schools and classrooms? The empirical literature is far from clear here, but we can draw some tentative conclusions about how tests affect students and teachers.

TESTING AND STUDENTS

American schooling without tests? It is hard to imagine. Kindergarten readiness tests, classroom tests in every subject from English to physical education, standardized IQ and aptitude tests, general achievement tests, college entrance tests, and school, district, and state-level graduation tests—the list is lengthy. These tests have a variety of purposes: Some involve placement in appropriate classes, grades, and programs, others entail ranking students and making decisions about the colleges they can attend, and still others include judgments about what students know and can do. It is this last set of purposes that I am most interested in for it is the area that generally concerns students, teachers, parents, and the public. More specifically, I am interested in exploring what tests can tell us about students' understanding of history.

To find out what children know, we give them tests. The logic of this proposition seems so obvious as to be beyond question. Yet problems surface when we look at the kinds of questions asked, the number of opportunities students have to convey what they know, and the circumstances under which they are tested. Interpreting the scores that tests produce can be problematic as well. Before discussing the problems, however, let us look at the research literature findings on what students know about history.

WHAT DO STUDENTS KNOW?

What do students know? It seems like a simple question. Teachers teach, students learn, and tests confirm what they know, or so common perception would have it. And yet, the complex, contextualized, and messy worlds of teaching, learning, and testing yield little in the way of hard conclusions. Part of the problem is figuring out what we want to hold students responsible for knowing; another part is figuring out how to assess them accurately.

Understanding What Students Know

Bad news abounds. Reports detailing student performance on national assessments of historical knowledge (Beatty, Reese, Persky, & Carr, 1996; Lapp, Grigg, & Tay-Lim, 2002; Ravitch & Finn, 1987) suggest students know little history and understand less. Diane Ravitch and Chester Finn term "shameful" the performance of a national sample of 11th graders on the 1986 National Assessment of Educational Progress (NAEP). This sample of students, they argue, is "ignorant of important things it should know, and that it and generations to follow are at risk of being gravely handicapped by that ignorance upon entry into adulthood, citizenship, and parenthood" (p. 201). A different group of students and a different NAEP test in 1994 yielded distressingly similar results: "Simply put, students are not performing as well … as the [National Assessment of Educational Progress] Governing Board and the many panelists and reviewers think these students should perform" (Beatty et al., 1996, p. 31). The preliminary results from the 2001 NAEP history exam show no significant changes from the 1994 test: Scores of students in Grades 4 and 8 rose slightly, but the Grade 12 results are virtually unchanged (Lapp, Grigg, & Tay-Lim, 2002).

Students know some things quite well. Most 11th graders can identify the contributions of Thomas Edison, George Washington, and Adolph

Hitler, they can locate the former Soviet Union and Italy on a map, and they can recognize the importance of the Underground Railroad and the assembly line (Ravitch & Finn, 1987). Twelfth graders can interpret William Jennings Bryan's "Cross of Gold" speech, compare Franklin Roosevelt's 1933 and 1937 inauguration speeches, and explain differences between White and Native American attitudes toward land ownership (Beatty et al., 1996).

Other test items prove more challenging. Most 11th graders can not correctly connect the Puritans with the founding of Boston, Betty Friedan and Gloria Steinem with the women's movement of the 1970s, or Abraham Lincoln with the decades of his presidency (Ravitch & Finn, 1987). Similarly, 12th graders struggle to interpret documents around FDR's New Deal, identify the Brown versus Board of Education decision, and recognize rights protected by the 14th amendment (Beatty et al., 1996).

A limited number of qualitative studies confirm these quantitative results. For example, in a pair of studies, Bruce VanSledright (1995a, 1996b) finds that students' knowledge of historical events is spotty, even after direct instruction. Before their classroom unit on colonial America, six eighth grade students demonstrate that their knowledge of explorers, early colonists, and early governmental structures is relatively weak, that their sense of what a colony is is pretty keen, and that, although they often express highly opinionated views, they only occasionally demonstrate the ability to understand multiple perspectives (VanSledright, 1996b). VanSledright's analysis of the students' understandings after the unit reveals no large knowledge increases and, in a few students, even more confusion. VanSledright concludes, however, that despite a unit heavy on "information overload," students do pick up on central elements of the European and Native American colonial experience.

And yet, when 79% of 11th graders fail to recognize the role of Reconstruction and when 59% of 12th graders can not identify the purpose of the Monroe Doctrine, it is easy for those who hold history dear to shake their heads and ask how can they not know these simple ideas and how can they forget so much of which they just learned?

The fact of the matter is that we really do not understand *why* students know (or do not know) what they do. A big part of the problem is that, as educators and as a society, we have yet to decide *what* we want students to know. Rhetorically, the old argument about whether students should know basic facts or what those facts mean (as in concepts and generalizations) is over: They need to know both. Ravitch and Finn (1987) put the matter bluntly:

> A knowledge of disconnected facts that are joined, related, or explained by no concepts is obviously without significance; we learn particular facts in

order to grasp ideas and develop generalizations. At best, concepts explain the facts of a given situation, while facts provide examples with which to illustrate or test concepts. (p. 16)

The authors conclude, "in order for history to make sense, concepts and facts must be blended. It is not necessary to choose between them" (p. 17). Kathryn and Luther Spoehr (1994) agree, making the argument that facts are to generalizations as the alphabet is to reading:

Facts (and letters) are essential building blocks; without them you cannot do history (or read). But, just as reading necessitates looking at how the letters and words stand in relation to one another ... thinking historically requires going beyond chronology or chronicle and looking at the relations that the facts bear to one another. (p. 71)

Okay, so students need to know facts, concepts, and generalizations. But which ones? States like Massachusetts, Virginia, and most recently, Minnesota, have tailored their state curricula around very specific lists of people, places, and events. The New York state curriculum for 11th grade U.S. history is 33 single-spaced pages. Is every item on that list of such importance that students will be "gravely handicapped" if they can not recall it? And if not all, which of those facts, concepts, and generalizations do students have to know in order to function as good citizens?

Assessing What Students Know

The problem of what students need to know is compounded by how we assess their knowledge. Here, I want to point to the problems that three issues—incommensurate data, the validity of test items, and stability in test scores—pose for answering the question of what students know.

One problem is the incommensurate nature of test data. Part of the issue here is one of moving targets. The testing literature reflects several trends—from low-stakes to high-stakes tests, from minimal competency to higher-order thinking, and from generic to standards-based testing parameters. Assessing complex learning is difficult enough; doing so under differing conditions and across differing contexts presents myriad problems (Linn, 2000, 2003). This general issue of incommensurate data becomes magnified in the special case of testing historical knowledge and understanding. Only recently has national data concerning students' history test performance begun to employ similar testing conditions. Comparing state-level tests with this national data or with one another only magnifies the problem of drawing coherent conclusions based on incommensurate measures. Moreover, since the kinds of questions asked heavily influence the kinds of responses that ensue (Nuthall & Alton-Lee, 1995), even if we did have multiple test results on the same group of teachers and students, drawing any firm inferences would be dicey (Amrein & Berliner, 2002; Linn, 2000, 2003).

An example of incommensurate data can be seen when comparing older and newer NAEP exams. A series of test administrations over time could provide a set of useful data points for understanding student historical knowledge. Unfortunately, two problems emerge: The 1987 and 1994 tests were given to different age groups (11th graders took the 1987 exam; 12th graders took the 1994 test) and the 1987 exam assessed only basic factual knowledge, while the 1994 exam (and the one administered in 2001) was purposely constructed to be "challenging" (Beatty et al., 1996). Rather than assess straightforward who, what, when, and where information, the authors of the 1994 and 2001 exams created questions that pushed students into higher levels of thinking, asked students about the nature of history as well as about historical events, and demanded that students answer extended response questions as well as multiple-choice items. Once all the analyses have been done on the latest test, we can begin comparing the 1994 and 2001 results. Pushing our analysis of student knowledge back to 1987, however, is problematic.

Incommensurate data poses an even bigger problem when we try to compare NAEP results with those of the state testing programs. A good example of this problem developed when researchers attempted to verify the "Texas miracle" by comparing students' performance on the state-level literacy tests with their performance on the NAEP literacy exam. The hypothesis was simple: If Texas students' literacy skills really had improved as much as the state tests indicated, then those improvements ought to surface in the same students' NAEP results. In independent analyses, neither Haney (2000) nor Klein, Hamilton, McCaffrey, and Stecher (2000) could confirm that relationship. As Klein et al. note, the NAEP and Texas results "tell very different stories." Klein and his colleagues continue, making the point that what students "know" may depend on what kind of test they are given:

> The gains on the TAAS were several times greater than they were on NAEP. Hence, how much a Texas student's proficiency in reading and math actually improved depends almost entirely on whether the assessment of that student's skills relies on NAEP scores (which are based on national content frameworks) or TAAS scores (which are based on tests that are aligned with Texas' own content standards and are administered by the classroom teacher).[2]

No similar analysis has been done between the NAEP history tests and those of any of the states. Perhaps a different result might ensue, but equally possible is the prospect that different test data will produce different results. And if that is the case, how can we have confidence in the test scores at hand?

The issue of incommensurate data is related to a second problem: Even with similar tests and good baseline test data, the challenge of how well tests measure what students know remains.

Psychometricians, experts in the field of testing, are proficient at developing test items, cut scores, and the like. They are less able to guarantee that their tests assess knowledge worth knowing. Lee Cronbach (1963) puts the psychometrican's dilemma this way:

> Whenever it is critically important to master certain content, the knowledge that it will be tested produces a desirable concentration of effort. On the other hand, learning the answer to a set of questions is by no means the same as acquiring understanding of whatever topic that question represents. (p. 681)

In addition to the specific criticisms of multiple-choice items, many observers worry that state-level tests best measure trivial information. James Popham (1999), a long-time advocate of "measurement-driven instruction," now questions the potential for tests to assess significant learning. As tests are increasingly used as accountability measures, Popham concludes that "the most serious consequence" of state-level tests is that they "contribute only modestly, if at all, to the central mission of education—namely teaching children the things they need to know" (p. 14). Camilli, Cizek, and Lugg (2001) put the matter more bluntly: "There is, lamentably, little evidence currently available that suggests a causal link between assessment information and increased student learning" (p. 466).

Consider one additional wrinkle on the issue of test question validity. In their study of how students respond to standardized, test-like questions, Graham Nuthall and Adrienne Alton-Lee (1995) conclude that "students with the same scores on the achievement test were unlikely to know, or have learned, the same content" (p. 192). In short, gross errors in understanding what students know can develop when we only count right and wrong answers to a test question.

Evidence for this last point comes in Sam Wineburg's (1991) study of how high school students and college history professors interpret various kinds of text. The substantive differences in students' and professors' interpretations aside, Wineburg points to the fallibility of tests as a measure of knowing. Wineburg begins his study by giving students and professors the same short quiz asking them to identify elements of the American Revolution period—What was Fort Ticonderoga? What were the Townshend Acts?—that sort of thing. Although the students do not read the texts Wineburg gives them as wisely as the historians, they do almost as well as the historians on the quiz. In fact, two students outperform one of the eight historians, while another historian answers correctly about the same number of questions as do most of the students. Appropriately, Wineburg makes no wild claims about such findings, but this report underscores the problematic nature of deeply understanding what students know based on test questions alone.

One final problem with tests highlights the fairly stable pattern test scores exhibit over time. It tends to be true that when students are first tested, their scores rise (Grissmer & Flanagan, 1998). Linn (2000) cites long-term studies, however, showing that early gains soon level off. Moreover, the race and class differences that appear in most standardized testing situations remain: Affluent and white kids fare better than their poorer and Hispanic and African American peers. This tendency leads some (e.g., Horn, 2003; Kornhaber, Orfield, & Kurlaender, 2001; Mathison, 1997) to conclude that tests confirm rather than confront prevailing school patterns.

These last two problems of the mismatch between tests and learning and the stability of test results over time become magnified when state-level tests are used as evaluations. Many observers (Camilli, Cizek, & Lugg, 2001; Haladyna, Nolen, & Haas, 1991; Linn, 2000) believe state-level tests can be an effective component of an larger assessment plan: A test score on the Regents exam in New York or the Texas Essential Knowledge and Skills test may offer a useful snapshot of what students know and can do. But just as a snapshot can not replace a panoramic view, neither can a state-level test provide a rich assessment of a student's capabilities. And so, when state tests become one-shot measures of learning and as one-shot judgments of who graduates, the connection between tests and meaningful student achievement weakens.

Do not misunderstand: I outline the problems above not to minimize the issue of what students know or to argue that we should be sanguine about what little students seem to know about history. It is discouraging to see students struggle over seemingly basic information, especially if it has been recently taught to them. But in the face of all that that we do not understand about what students know, we ought to avoid making hasty and hard judgments.

TESTS AND TEACHERS

If a weak link exists between tests and student learning, what about the relationship between testing and teaching? Do tests, as is often thought, drive teaching? A flurry of popular books (e.g., Kohn, 2000; Rothman, 1995; Sacks, 1999) sharply criticize state-level testing both as a poor measure of student achievement and as a foul influence on teachers' class-room practices. Some researchers (e.g., Corbett & Wilson, 1991; McNeil, 2000; Noble & Smith, 1994; Segall, 2003; Smith, 1991), too, have pointed to pernicious effects of tests on teachers. Others (e.g., Firestone, May-rowetz, & Fairman, 1998; Grant, 2001b, 2005; van Hover & Heinecke, 2005; Webeck, Salinas, and Fields, 2005; Zancanella, 1992), however, are less sure that a direct relationship exists between standardized testing and teachers' classroom practices. Thus the research around teachers and tests shows no clear pattern of influence (Cimbricz, 2002). Tests seem to matter, but how and to what extent, is unclear.

Advocates of tests as a vehicle for driving educational change tend to cite general good effects rather than specifics. Some (Feltovich, Spiro, & Coulson, 1993; Finn, 1995; Ravitch, 1995; Shanker, 1995) make the all-purpose argument that good tests inevitably drive good instruction. With neither any more specificity nor any empirical evidence, Popham, Cruse, Rankin, Sandifer, and Williams (1985) suggest that whatever is being tested by definition is important and that good results equal good educa-tion. Advocates of systemic reform (Fuhrman, 1993; Smith & O'Day, 1991) believe that testing must be part of an overall strategy aimed at school change. Still other observers (English, 1980; Glatthorn, 1987; Heubert & Hauser, 1999) assert that because standardized tests are a real-ity in most school districts, they should be used as a fundamental part of curriculum planning. Chester Finn (1995) makes the general case for testing this way: Forecasting a dismal end to the national education goals the first President Bush and the nation's governors endorsed in 1990, Finn asserts, "a sizable part of the reason will be the refusal to construct any sort of meaningful examination or assessment system tied to those [national] goals" (p. 121).[3]

While some critics of testing (Kohn, 2000; Ohanian, 1999) rely more on principle than on research, many back up their claims with empirical evidence. George Madaus (1988) argues that teachers teach to the test, that they adjust their instruction to follow the form of the questions asked (e.g., multiple choice, essay), and that tests transfer control over the cur-riculum to whoever controls the test. LeMahieu (1984), Koretz (1995), and Romberg, Zarinnia, and Williams (1989) are a bit more tentative, but they too conclude that teachers tailor their curricula to the content cov-ered on a test. More recent empirical work supports some of these claims. H. Dickson Corbett and Bruce Wilson (1991), for example, argue that testing, especially minimum-competency testing, has a harmful effect on teachers in that it causes them to narrow their sense of educational pur-poses and to focus on activities designed to raise test scores whether or not they think those activities are good for students (see also, Miller, 1995; McNeil, 2000; Noble & Smith, 1994; Smith, 1991). They conclude that squeezing teachers in this fashion encourages them to rebel against reform measures, both good and bad: "Statewide testing programs do control activity at the local level, but the subsequent activity is not reform" (Corbett & Wilson, 1991, p. 1). Mary Lee Smith (1991) makes the more specific claim that testing "significantly reduces the capacity of teachers to adapt to local circumstances and needs of pupils or to exercise any discretion over what to teach and how to teach it" (p. 10). She worries that tests "result in a narrowing of possible curriculum and a reduction of teachers' ability to adapt, create, and diverge" (p. 10). She concludes that multiple-choice testing leads to "multiple-choice teaching" (p. 10). Finally, Avner Segall (2003) makes the point that the presence of a state-level test, even if it is not tied directly to the state curriculum, can lead to pedantic teaching. The Michigan social studies test holds no particular stakes for teachers or students, and yet it "impacts teaching in mostly negative ways, reducing teaching to low levels of intellectual engagement and teachers to implementers of externally designed curricula and pre-packaged materials intended to help them teach to the test" (p. 321).

Still other researchers are less sure that any direct relationship exists between state-level testing and teachers' classroom practices. Earlier studies by Freeman, Kuhs, Porter, Knappen, Floden, Schmidt, and Schwille (1980), Salmon-Cox (1981), Kellaghan, Madaus, and Airasian (1982) and Mehrens and Phillips (1986) found little direct impact of standardized testing on teachers' daily instruction. A bit more recently, Rita O'Sullivan (1991) asserts that testing is "part of teaching but not really as immediate instructional reality … testing is the pale rider on the various educational trails" (p. 144). Her survey results show little explicit influence of tests on teachers' practices: Teachers do more reviewing and teaching of test-taking strategies, but few say that tests have any dramatic effect on their content selection, instructional practices, or classroom assessments. Bill Firestone, David Mayrowetz, and Jean Fairman (1998) also see weaker than expected testing influences on teachers' practices in both low and high-stakes settings. Teachers do make changes in their practices, especially in terms of the content they teach, but major changes in pedagogy do not surface. James Pellegrino (1992) makes the point explicitly: "[Standardized] test information is of little practical assistance to teachers and other individuals involved directly in the instructional process" (p. 277).

Tests do matter to teachers, but how they matter is uncertain. Consider the example of Paula, a third year global history teacher (Grant, 2005; Grant, Derme-Insinna, Gradwell, Lauricella, Pullano, & Tzetzo, 2002). Although she believes in promoting an active, engaging, and substantive pedagogy reflecting the tenets of "teaching for understanding" (Cohen, McLaughlin, & Talbert, 1993; Prawat, 1989), these views clash with the evaluation and accountability directions she perceives the state curriculum and test promote. "The message that I got," Paula said, "and this was not explicit, was that the objective was to get these kids to pass this test and that the state education people were using the test to change teaching."

The state's efforts, Paula believes, lie squarely at odds with her own sense of powerful teaching and learning:

> I think the curriculum should have gone in a very different direction, and maybe even if they wanted to change it from the more social science approach I would have liked to have seen it go to some kind of thematic approach where history, great themes of history, and teachers would be free to pick out examples of those themes and teach those themes, not necessarily in chronological order.... That seems to me more how history really is written, how historians write, and it seems more meaningful to me certainly and, I think, to kids as well.

With such convictions, one might conclude that Paula can substitute her own more ambitious inclinations for the state's. Paula complicates that impression. "Generally I think it's forced me to teach history in a way that I'm philosophically at odds with," she said, "and in a way that I don't think kids are going to remember or care about, and I feel obligated to do that because of this test at the end." Disposed toward more powerful instruction, Paula nevertheless feels "forced" to teach history in traditional ways:

> I just feel this sense of breathlessly running through a curriculum, never having an opportunity to relax enough to do that, to bring the materials (primary source documents) in and work with kids, take the time to work with kids through those materials. Because clearly it would take lots of time, and if I've got to get through World War II in two weeks, you know, I just don't know how to, how I could do that at this point.

In addition to racing through the curriculum, Paula feels a need to teach test-taking skills, especially for lower ability students. "I feel a pressure to drill certain kids on methods of passing a test," she said.

With the information above, one might see Paula as captive to the state policies: Paula's more ambitious intentions seem impotent next to the more conventional approaches she perceives advocated by the state. Paula's response could be read as an over-reaction to the policymakers' intent. After all, the rhetoric of the state policies seems to support the kind of pedagogy Paula espouses. What underlies her doubts about this rhetoric?

Paula's relative inexperience figures prominently. A newly-tenured teacher, Paula still considers herself a novice, both curious and uncertain about her teaching. Believing that students need provocative and substantial experiences to become thoughtful learners, she does not know if such instructional activities will, by themselves, help students on the state test. She finds herself in an awkward position: Trusting what she believes the state is telling her to do—that is, emphasizing content coverage and test-taking skills—until she knows otherwise. "I don't even know what [the test's] going to look like," she said, "So I'm going to take their word that this is going to work, I'm getting [the students] through the exam and, you know, do what I am supposed to, what they (the state) think I'm supposed to be doing."

Another dimension of Paula's seeming embrace of traditional practices is that it only explains part of her practice. For Paula has created, in effect, two teaching approaches: One is explicitly state curriculum and test-directed, while the other is explicitly self-directed. Paula's use of primary source documents is a case in point: "I use [documents] the way I thought I would use them. I think, well, I use them the way I would like to use them sometimes, and I use them the way I think the state would like me to use them sometimes." Paula describes how she uses documents to execute these different teaching objectives:

> And those are different. The way I use documents is for kids to make interpretations of them, of the documents, based on their knowledge of the topic. And that means that there may be a very wide variety of answers to whatever the question is. When I use them how I think the state wants to use them, there is probably not a wide variety of answers to the question. There's probably a pretty specific answer to the question that goes with the document that I'm presenting to them.

> I'm not sure I've ever used the same document two different ways....I used a political cartoon which showed a Red Army soldier helping a peasant plow a field. And the caption underneath it was, "How can I ever repay you?" And it wasn't clear who was saying it to whom. As I looked at it, I realized it could have gone either way. So that was the question I asked: "If the peasant was asking the soldier, what was the response? If the soldier was asking the peasant, what would the response be?" But I think if I were to use that same document for a DBQ essay, I would make it clear who was speaking to whom, and ask maybe a more direct, explicit question, like what kinds of, I'm not even quite sure what I would ask. But it would be a different kind of question, and it would not be as ambiguous to what was going on in the cartoon. I would not allow for that kind of ambiguity in the document.

> I think when I'm doing it (using documents) for the way I'd like to do it, I have an idea of the response I'm looking for, but if [the students] come up

with something that is different from what I was expecting but it makes sense and they can back up with some reasoning, then that's acceptable. But if I were using it for the state test-taking skill thing, then there would be one response, and if they didn't get that, then it would be wrong.

The tension this teacher feels resonates. On the one hand, documents such as the Red Army cartoon help push her students to think about the historical context of the situation, to draw from their prior knowledge, and to build both an argument and the evidence for that argument. Such actions are what some call powerful instruction (e.g., Wineburg & Wilson, 1991) and promote what the authors of the National Standards for American History call "real historical understanding" (National Center for History in Schools, 1994, p. 17). And yet, Paula feels compelled to use other documents that support more limited understandings, understandings from which students presumably will draw the right "state test-taking skill thing." Instead of crafting an instructional plan that coherently promotes ambitious teaching and learning, then, Paula constructs a wobbly mix of the rich and the dull, the engaging and the pedantic. The latter of these pairs reflects her sense that she can not afford not to; the former reflects her hope to offer something more than a superficial treatment of the subject matter. But here is the kicker: Paula's ambitious teaching comes in spite of rather than because of the new state test. Tests are driving a portion of Paula's teaching, but not the part that seems most beneficial to students. Rothman (1995) points to the apparent irony in this kind of situation:

> The emphasis on raising test scores has thrown into doubt the meaning of the higher test scores. If test scores go up because schools have focused extensively on preparing students for the test at the expense of other material, what does the increase signify? (p. 62)

Paula's case suggests that one reason tests may not have a dramatic influence on teachers' practices is that they can conflict with deeply-held beliefs. Teachers can hardly ignore tests, especially of the high-stakes variety, but tests are like many influences on teachers: They are more potential than direct (Grant, 1996, 2003; Romanowski, 1996; Sturtevant, 1996; van Hover & Heinecke, 2005).

Another reason for the diminished influence of tests is that they typically do not provide the kind of information teachers value (Kellaghan, Madaus, & Airasian, 1982). Testing advocates argue that exam scores provide insights into students' strengths and weaknesses; information that can then be used to modify instruction (Popham et al., 1985). Problems with getting test scores back in a timely fashion, with drawing direct parallels between test and instructional tasks, and with issues of "test score pollution" (Haladyna, Nolen, & Haas, 1991) undercut this argument. Ten years ago, Dana Kurfman (1991) noted that "there is little research evidence on one potentially positive instructional effect of testing: the diagnostic use of test results by teachers to modify their teaching practices to provide remediation for students who need it" (p. 317). Today, Camilli, Cizek, and Lugg (2001) observe little hope for improving the relationship between test results and positive changes in teachers' practices: "Performance standards embedded in high-stakes achievement tests have little, if any, formative value for individual students" (p. 466).

Whatever the reasons, the proposition that tests drive teaching and learning must be qualified. For while researchers detect some influence of tests on the content teachers choose to teach (Firestone & Mayrowetz, 2000; Firestone, Mayrowetz, & Fairman, 1998; Grant, Derme-Insinna et al., 2002; Grant, Gradwell, Lauricella, Derme-Insinna, Pullano, & Tzetzo, 2002; Smith, 1991; van Hover & Heinecke, 2005), far less evidence shows profound influences on teachers' instructional practices. Kellaghan, Madaus, and Airasian (1982) observe, "while the cooperation of teachers in administering the test program was good, their commitment to using test results, even on their own admission, was not great" (p. 128). Tests, then, influence how teachers construct their practices, but that influence is less direct, powerful, and predictable than most observers believe.

HIGH-STAKES TESTS AND HIGHER EDUCATIONAL STANDARDS

In this last section, we confront a common sense assumption: Increasing the pressure on students and teachers should make both more accountable, and ultimately improve education for all. Common sense fails us in this area, however, for the research literature undercuts the relationship between high stakes and high standards. High-stakes tests induce some changes in teachers' practices, but as Corbett and Wilson (1991) observe, change is not the same thing as reform.

The Cases For and Against High-Stakes Testing

The former president of the American Federation of Teachers, Al Shanker (1995) makes the case for high-stakes testing this way:

> School reformers who are working to solve the problem of students' low achievement levels have come up with all sorts of new and creative things, but as long as students are given no reason to work, it is hard to see how any

reform, however ingenious or creative, will achieve what is needed. The absence of stakes makes the whole system trivial. (p. 147)

Shanker, like many advocates of testing, argues that real educational reform demands high curriculum standards and high-stakes tests. This advocacy rests on two premises: that tests are a reasonable way to decide if schools are working, and that increasing the stakes represented by test scores will induce the desired kinds of changes, notably more ambitious teaching and learning for all students. "High stakes," then, refers to the twin notions that "examinations are associated with important consequences for examinees" and "examinations whose scores are seen as reflections of instructional quality" (Popham, 1987, p. 680). Amrein and Berliner (2002), Madaus (1988), and Koretz (1988) expand the definition of high stakes to include the publication of test scores. The conditions Popham describes highlight the efforts of students and teachers in the classroom; the condition that Amrein, Beliner, Madaus, and Koretz describe puts those efforts on public display.[4]

New York state policymakers, like their colleagues in Virginia, Mississippi, and elsewhere, have embraced the premises and conditions of high-stakes testing as a means to educational reform. The Regents tests have been revised, but so too has the context in which the Regents is administered and the implications of taking the test. First, the importance of state testing has been pushed into lower grades. Elementary and middle school teachers used to give program evaluation tests in social studies. These tests and the scores they produced were used by teachers and administrators to make content and instructional decisions; no individual student scores were generated. The exams were almost exclusively multiple-choice in format and the scores were reported only to local school and district offices. Today, fifth and eighth grade students take tests that mirror those given at the high school level, including document-based questions, and the school scores may be reported in local newspapers. Moreover, low scores now mark individual students for remedial work and even more testing. Increased stakes attached to the New York testing program also surface at the high school level. Passing a 10th grade global studies and an 11th grade U.S. history exam has been required in order to graduate. Students could opt, however, to take the less-demanding Regents Competency Test (RCT) and receive a local diploma or to take the more challenging Regents test and receive a higher-status Regents diploma. With the call for higher standards, state policymakers decided to phase out the RCT and to require that all students take and pass the newly-designed and presumably more rigorous Regents tests. Newspapers anxiously await the release of Regents scores and they publish them by school and district. One last indication of increased stakes is that, while no explicit state-level sanctions have been created for individual teachers whose students do not perform well, schools whose test performance lags for three years can be taken over by the state education department.

Although policymakers in New York and across the U.S. pin their hopes on the power of new tests to drive educational reform, those hopes seem to be falling on hard ground. Analysts continue to arrive at the same conclusion: Tests, even high-stakes tests, fail as levers of policy change (Clarke, Madaus, Horn, & Ramos, 2000; Darling-Hammond & Falk, 1997; Firestone & Mayrowetz, 2000; Grant, Gradwell et al., 2002; Popham, 1999). Robert Linn (2000) points to the lamentable chasm between the promise and problems of high-stakes tests:

> In most cases the instruments and technology have not been up to the demands that been placed on them by high-stakes accountability. Assessment systems that are useful monitors lose much of their dependability and credibility for that purpose when high stakes are attached to them. (p. 14)

Gregory Camilli and his colleagues (2001) concur, concluding that research evidence confirms the "diminishing returns of high-stakes assessment as an educational reform strategy" (p. 466)

The seeming exception to the consensus view on high-stakes testing is the state of Texas. The Texas Assessment of Academic Skills (TAAS) began in 1990 as a criterion-referenced test (like the New York Regents exam) designed to measure students' higher-order thinking skills and problem-solving abilities.[5] TAAS test results in reading and mathematics were dubbed the "Texas miracle" because they showed enormous gains in student achievement and demonstrated a reduction in average score differences among racial and ethnic groups. This latter point seemed especially important since African American and Hispanic American students have not done well on standardized tests in the past. Ecstatic, then governor Bush and state education department policymakers asserted that Texas teachers and students were fulfilling the promise of high-stakes testing.

That initial enthusiasm muted some of the criticism that the new exams promoted an unhealthy focus on test scores alone, which in turn promoted excessive teaching to the test and even cheating scandals. That criticism took a new turn, however, when researchers began comparing students' TAAS scores with their performance on the NAEP, which is generally considered the "gold standard" of standardized testing (Klein et al., 2000). As those research reports came in (Haney, 2000; Klein et al., 2000), the bloom began to fade on the Texas rose. In short, the huge gains registered on the TAAS failed to register on the NAEP exams.

Moreover, the gap between white students and students of color in Texas increased on the NAEP. Klein and his colleagues (2000) argue that not only is the Texas miracle suspect, but so too is faith in high-stakes tests as a means of reform:

> Our findings from this research raise serious questions about the validity of the gains in the TAAS scores. More generally, our results illustrate the danger of relying on statewide test scores as the sole measure of student achievement when these scores are used to make high-stakes decisions about teachers and schools as well as students.[6] (p. 2)

Discrepancies between TAAS and NAEP scores are not unrealistic since the two tests were developed by different groups (Linn, 2003). As noted above, the problem of incommensurate data begins with incommensurate tests. Important for the discussion of high-stakes testing, however, is the notion of how to understand and use different test scores, especially when they suggest inconsistent results. To put the point on this issue, note Barton and Coley's (1998) analysis which shows an inverse relationship between students' performance on the NAEP and those states that have high-stakes graduation exams: The higher the stakes, the lower the NAEP scores.

Bizarre as all this sounds, it points to a key realization: High-stakes tests may result in higher test scores, but strong doubts surface around what those scores mean and whether those scores represent real academic achievement. Evidence for this conclusion arises in work graduate students and I have done around the new New York global history test (Grant, 2001b; Grant, Derme-Insinna et al, 2002; Grant, Gradwell et al, 2002). State policymakers promote new exams as a means of elevating education standards. Teachers' reactions to and students' performance on the new global test, however, undercut that premise. The teachers we studied contend that the new exams are far less challenging and that the scoring process is far more generous than under the old system. Student test scores bear this out: Passing rates at all the schools in our study are either the same or above the rates for the old exams. More surprising, the recent state passing rates reflect a large increase over past rates: Whereas 60.9% of 10th graders passed the last global studies exam, almost 10% more students (68.5%) passed the new, presumably more difficult global history exam. This increase is even more astounding given the conditions of the test: Virtually all 10th graders took the new exam as schools moved to drop the RCT option. So not only did test scores rise dramatically, but they did so when many students who once would have taken the easier RCT now took the reportedly more challenging Regents test. An experienced teacher put the matter bluntly: "It's dumbing down the content so they (the state) get higher numbers.... You can do anything you want with numbers, it doesn't show that [the students] are gaining." Teachers scoff at policy-maker claims that the new, high-stakes test inspires higher educational standards. For example, one teacher notes, "we (the teacher's colleagues) sat there and chuckled and said, 'Oh yes! We are raising standards, aren't we?' A Billy goat can pass them, but that's okay."

Linn (2000) contends that high-stakes tests inevitably produce "inflated notions of achievement" (p. 7). Results on the new global history exam bear out this claim. Even so, the teachers we interviewed are not sanguine about their students' high scores. Their comments reflect Stake's (1991) conclusion that teachers "have essentially no confidence in testing as the basis of the reform of schooling in America" (p. 246).

Solutions to the Problems of High-Stakes Tests

So what is the solution? While some observers (Berliner & Biddle, 1995) question whether there is anything really wrong with America's schools, policymakers seem convinced otherwise. Is the answer even higher stakes? improved tests? more ambitious teaching? The first suggestion seems unlikely given the strong consequences already in place. Here, I examine the potential for new tests and ambitious teaching.

The Promise of New Tests?

Would improved tests help address some of the problems of high-stakes tests? The answer seems obvious, but may not be.

Although tests generally produce reliable results when students' performance is compared on the same exam,[7] the incidence of test score pollution undercuts some of this accomplishment. High-stakes testing, in the view of Thomas Haladyna and his colleagues (1991), is surrounded by activities, some ethical, some not, which damage the relationship between tests and student achievement.[8]

Haladyna's argument notwithstanding, some observers argue that test questions can be improved. For example, Stuart Yeh (2001) asserts that even multiple-choice questions can be designed to better assess critical thinking. His example of a question using the differing interpretations of the Vietnam War by Frances Fitzgerald and Neil Sheehan presents a genuine task that moves students beyond factual recall. Other observers are less optimistic. Setting out to determine whether radical changes in large-scale tests are possible and realistic, Eva Baker (1994) and her colleagues describe the DBQ-like activities they designed. Their efforts crashed, however, when teachers scored the students' essays:

> Four history teachers, handpicked on the basis of their excellent teaching reputations, shared neither explicit nor implicit sets of criteria to judge the quality of students' historical understanding. Judging 85 written explanations, they came to little agreement. (p. 100)

Baker argues that more and better training of scorers can mitigate some of this problem, but when one imagines the testing of hundreds of thousands of students by thousands of teachers, the potential for wild scoring fluctuations grows rather than diminishes.

Beyond the problems of achieving consistent scores is the authenticity of test questions. While multiple-choice items have long been suspect, Jill Gradwell, Sandra Cimbricz, and I (Grant, Gradwell, & Cimbricz, 2004) question the authenticity of tasks like the DBQ. Using Wiggins and McTighe's (1998) criteria for authentic assessments, we analyzed the DBQ on the first new global history exam. We conclude that, although the task has a patina of authenticity, it fails to reflect well the conditions of a genuine historical assignment.

Whether or not new and better test items emerge, the larger issue nags of how test scores are used. Assessment experts caution against using the results of one test to make any decisions about students, much less high-stakes decisions such as who graduates and who doesn't (Lapp, Grigg, & Tay-Lim, 2002; Linn, 2000). Wiggins (1993) puts the point directly: The key issue, he asserts, is "not whether we should use one kind of test or another but what role testing should play in assessment" (p. 14).

The (Better) Promise of Good Teaching

Designing better test questions and finding a spot for tests within the wider field of assessment makes sense. Yet these directions seem more like band-aids than a substantial boost toward higher standards and more powerful student learning. So if better tests are not the answer, is better teaching?

The answer seems to be, yes. Among researchers, a consensus is building that connects higher test scores with ambitious teaching. Pat Avery (1999), Fred Newmann and his colleagues (Newmann, Bryk, & Nagaoka, 2001; Newmann, Secada, & Wehlage, 1995), Julia Smith and Richard Niemi (2001), and Diana Hess (2005) offer evidence of a tight link between good teaching and improved student performance. The increased use of complex writing tasks, in-depth reading (meaning from sources outside the textbook), student discussion, and learning tools (such as outside speakers, film, computers) strongly correlate with higher scores on the NAEP exams in U.S. history (Smith & Niemi, 2001). Smith and Niemi (2001) conclude that "in history as well as elsewhere, active involvement promotes student achievement" (p. 34). Especially interesting is their finding that good instruction is an even better predictor of strong student test performance than are family and social characteristics. Fred Newmann (1996) concurs: Socioeconomic factors matter, but teachers' pedagogy matters more. "If faced with a choice of only one 'solution' to raise history scores," Smith and Niemi make the point plainly that "it is clear that instructional changes have the most powerful relationship to student performance" (p. 38).

The Consequences of High-Stakes Testing

The good news, then, is that ambitious teaching pays off. Teachers can play a powerful role in what their students learn and the evidence of their learning appears in higher test scores. If we could be sure that high-stakes state-level testing promoted more ambitious teaching, then the anxieties surrounding the high-stakes environment might be worth it. Unfortunately there is no evidence for this hope. In fact, cases like that of Paula suggest it's just the opposite: Teachers offer ambitious instruction in spite of rather than because of high-stakes tests (Grant, Gradwell et al., 2002; McNeil, 2000).

This last point is key because it suggests that the gamble on high-stakes tests yields important, if unintended, consequences. Those consequences can include the narrowing of curriculum, the reduction of instruction to test preparation, and the continued disadvantaging of minority and low income students. The work my students and I have done points to yet another consequence: The undermining of ambitious teachers (Grant, Gradwell et al., 2002). Although the mounting evidence connects good teaching with good student test scores, many teachers sense that state tests promote recall learning and drill and practice teaching (Grant, Derme-Insinna et al., 2001; Grant, Gradwell et al., 2002; Segall, 2003). Teachers understand the irony in this situation and they face a steady sapping of their energies. New teachers like Paula juggle competing demands (Grant, 2005; Grant, Derme-Insinna et al., 2002). Her students do well on the state tests, but the press of high-stakes conditions feels more enervating than invigorating. Veteran teachers, by contrast, are angry that the new global history exam fails to live up to its advanced billing. A teacher active in New York state social studies circles sums up the frustrations of many:

> I think teachers throughout the state were appalled when they saw the exam.... I heard that many teachers wrote, when they filled out the evaluation sheet, and they put down comments, that it (the test) was almost like an insult. (Grant, Gradwell et al., 2002, p. 507)

Another veteran teacher recalls her surprise at the exam's simplicity as she distributed it to her students: "You pass them out, and then while they're working on it, you're standing there and going through it and thinking, 'You've got to be kidding me. I mean you (the state) made me nervous for four years prior to this?'" (p. 507).

Rather than promoting more ambitious teaching, then, state-level exams in New York and other states (McNeil, 2000; Segall, 2003) may be inspiring a sharp skepticism in teachers about the relationship between high-stakes tests and high educational standards. An experienced teacher sums up the frustrations of virtually all we interviewed:

> I think it's a sad, sad case that after two years of studying in great detail and depth that we do, that you have 50 questions and two simple, little essays that someone not even taking the course probably could watch the Discovery Channel a couple of weeks, and get through the essays. I'm not impressed with it at all. (Grant, Gradwell et al., 2002, p. 509)

Such comments inspire a scenario where state and national policymakers increasingly distrust teachers and where teachers increasingly distrust those policymakers. McLaughlin (1991) observes that "ironically, accountability schemes that rely on existing testing technology trust the system (the rules, regulations, and standardized procedures) more than they trust teachers to make appropriate, educationally sound choices" (p. 250). Percolating through a number of recent studies is a corresponding mistrust. Accused of failing to meet high standards, teachers are aggravated by state efforts that seem to undercut their more ambitious efforts. Ironically, then, high-stakes testing may ultimately drive out the very teachers who are most responsible for their students' academic success.

CONCLUSION

High-stakes testing advocates like the late Al Shanker (1995) argue that "without stakes, reform will not go anywhere: The kids will not take it seriously and neither will the teachers" (p. 149). The common sense logic embodied in such claims can be powerfully persuasive: Witness the fact that recent legislation proposed by the Bush administration and overwhelmingly embraced by Congress puts a premium on more testing. Common sense is not always the best sense, however, as the research evidence fails to support testing as lever of ambitious reform. High-stakes testing, Linda Darling-Hammond (1997) argues, has "failed wherever it has been tried" (p. 238). The good news is that powerful teaching pays off for students. The tricky part is how to support the ambitious teaching is occurring and how to nurture that capacity in the classrooms where it is not.

NOTES

1. Portions of this chapter draw on chapters 4 and 6 in Grant (2003).

2. For a dissenting perspective on the relationship between the NAEP and Texas tests, see Toenjes & Dworkin (2002).

3. Sandra Cimbricz (2002) reviewed all the research literature related to the effects of testing on teachers' thinking and practice. She first determined that the bulk of the literature consists of advocacy, theoretical, and historical pieces rather than research. She also determined that not a single piece of empirical work supported claims of testing as a positive influence on teachers' thinking and practice. See Libresco (2005) as a recent example that challenges this claim.

4. See Amrein and Berliner (2002) for a thorough analysis of high-stakes testing practices and effects.

5. The TAAS has been revised and is now known as the Texas Assessment of Knowledge and Skills (TAKS).

6. See Toenjes and Dworkin (2002) for an alternative perspective.

7. There are glitches, however, such as the CTB/McGraw-Hill's mis-scoring of almost 9000 New York City students' tests which resulted in huge numbers of students sent to summer school for remediation. The classic case, however, is the "Lake Woebegon effect" (Koretz, 1988). In nosing around, a West Virginia physician observed that the results on norm-referenced national standardized tests indicated that students in every state were above average. Since norm-referenced tests are predicated on the notion that 50% of the scores must lie below the median, such results smelled funny (Cannell, 1988).

8. Examples of ethical activities include teaching test preparation skills and developing a curriculum that reflects test objectives. Unethical activities include using programs designed only to boost students' test scores and dismissing low-achieving students on test days. Whether ethical or not, the point Haladyna, Nolen, and Haas (1991) stress is that these activities diminish the potential for using high-stakes tests as accurate and useful measures of students' learning.

REFERENCES

Amrein, A., & Berliner, D. (2002, March 28). High-stakes testing, uncertainty, and student learning. *Educational Policy Analysis Archives, 10*(18). Retrieved from http://epaa.asu.edu/epaa/v10n18.html

Avery, P. (1999). Authentic assessment and instruction. *Social Education, 63*(6), 368–373.

Baker, E. (1994). Learning-based assessments of history understanding. *Educational Psychologist, 29*(2), 97–106.

Barton, P., & Coley, R. (1998). *Growth in school: Achievement gains from the fourth to eighth grade*. Princeton, NJ: Educational Testing Service.

Beatty, A., Reese, C., Persky, H., & Carr, P. (1996). *U.S. history report card* . Washington, DC: U.S. Department of Education, Office of Educational Research and Improvement.

Berliner, D., & Biddle, B. (1995). *The manufactured crisis: Myths, fraud, and the attack on America's public schools*. Reading, MA: Addison-Wesley.

Camilli, G., Cizek, G., & Lugg, C. (2001). Psychometric theory and the validation of performance standards: History and future perspectives. In G. Cizek (Ed.), *Setting performance standards: Concepts, methods, and perspectives* (pp. 445–476). Mahwah, NJ: Erlbaum.

Cannell, J. (1988). Nationally normed elementary achievement testing in America's public schools: How all 50 states are above the national average. *Educational Measurement: Issues and Practices, 7*, 5–9.

Cimbricz, S. (2002, January 9). State testing and teachers' thinking and practice: A synthesis of research. *Educational Policy Analysis Archives, 10*(2). Retrieved from http://epaa.asu.edu/epaa/v10n2.html

Clarke, M., Madaus, G., Horn, C., & Ramos, M. (2000). Retrospective on educational testing and assessment in the 20th century. *Journal of Curriculum Studies, 32*(2), 159–181.

Cohen, D., McLaughlin, M., & Talbert, J. (1993). *Teaching for understanding: Challenges for policy and practice*. San Francisco: Jossey-Bass.

Corbett, H. D., & Wilson, B. (1991). *Testing, reform, and rebellion*. Norwood, NJ: Ablex.

Cronbach, L. (1963). Evaluation of course improvement. *Teachers College Record, 64*, 674–683

Darling-Hammond, L., & Falk, B. (1997). Using standards and assessments to support student learning. *Phi Delta Kappan, 79*(3), 190–199.

English, F. (1980). *Improving curriculum management in the schools*. Washington, DC: Council for Basic Education.

Feltovich, P., Spiro, R., & Coulson, R. (1993). Learning, teaching, and testing for complex conceptual understanding. In N. Frederikson, R. Mislevy, & I. Bejarq (Eds.), *Test theory for a new generation of tests* (pp. 181–217). Hillsdale, NJ: Erlbaum.

Finn, C. (1995). Who's afraid of the big, bad test? In D. Ravitch (Ed.), *Debating the future of American education: Do we need national standards and assessments?* (pp. 120–144). Washington, DC: Brookings Institution.

Firestone, W., & Mayrowetz, D. (2000). Rethinking "high stakes": Lessons from the United States and England and Wales. *Teachers College Record, 102*(4), 724–749.

Firestone, W., Mayrowetz, D., & Fairman, J. (1998). Performance-based assessment and instructional change: The effects of testing in Maine and Maryland. *Educational Evaluation and Policy Analysis, 20*(2), 95–113.

Freeman, D., Kuhs, T., Porter, A., Knappen, L., Floden, R., Schmidt, W., & Schwille, J. (1980). *The fourth grade mathematics curriculum as inferred from textbooks and tests* . East Lansing, MI: Institute for Research on Teaching, Michigan State University.

Fuhrman, S. (1993). *Designing coherent education policy: Improving the system*. San Francisco: Jossey-Bass.

Glatthorn, A. (1987). *Curriculum leadership*. Glenview, IL: Scott, Foresman.

Grant, S. G. (1996). Locating authority over content and pedagogy: Cross-current influences on teachers' thinking and practice. *Theory and Research in Social Education, 24*(3), 237–272.

Grant, S. G. (2001a). An uncertain lever: The influence of state-level testing in New York State on teaching social studies. *Teachers College Record, 103*(3), 398–426.

Grant, S. G. (2001b, October 3). When an "A" isn't enough: Analyzing the New York state global history exam. *Educational Policy Analysis Archives, 9*(39). Retrieved from http://epaa.asu.edu/epaa/v9n39.html

Grant, S. G. (2003). *History lessons: Teaching, learning, and testing in U.S. high school classrooms*. Mahwah, NJ: Erlbaum.

Grant, S. G. (2005). More journey than end: A case study of ambitious teaching. In O. L. Davis & E. Yeager (Eds.), *Wise social studies teaching in an age of high-stakes testing* (pp. 117–130). Greenwich, CT: Information Age.

Grant, S. G., Derme-Insinna, A., Gradwell, J. M., Lauricella, A. M., Pullano, L., & Tzetzo, K. (2001). Teachers, tests, and tensions: Teachers respond to the New York state global history exam. *International Social Studies Forum, 1*(2), 107–125.

Grant, S. G., Derme-Insinna, A., Gradwell, J. M., Lauricella, A. M., Pullano, L., & Tzetzo, K. (2002). Juggling two sets of books: A teacher responds to the new global history exam. *Journal of Curriculum and Supervision, 17*(3), 232–255.

Grant, S. G., Gradwell, J. M., & Cimbricz, S. (2004). A question of authenticity: Examining the document based question on the New York state global history and geography Regents exam. *Journal of Curriculum and Supervision, 19*(4), 309–337.

Grant, S. G., Gradwell, J. M., Lauricella, A. M., Derme-Insinna, A., Pullano, L., & Tzetzo, K. (2002). When increasing stakes need not mean increasing standards: The case of the New York state global history and geography exam. *Theory and Research in Social Education, 30*(4), 488–515.

Grissmer, D., & Flanagan, A. (1998). *Exploring rapid achievement gains in North Carolina and Texas*. Washington, DC: National Educational Goals Panel.

Haladyna, T., Nolen, S., & Haas, N. (1991). Raising standardized achievement test scores and the origins of test score pollution. *Educational Researcher, 20*(5), 2–7.

Haney, W. (2000, February 24). The myth of the Texas miracle in education. *Educational Policy Analysis Archives, 8*(41). Retrieved from http://epaa.asu.edu/epaa/v8n41.html

Hess, D. (2005). Wise practice in an innovative public school. In E. A. Yeager & O. L. Davis, Jr. (Eds.), *Wise social studies teaching in an age of high-stakes testing* (pp. 131–152). Greenwich, CT: Information Age.

Heubert, J., & Hauser, R. (1999). *High stakes: Testing for tracking, promotion, and graduation*. Washington, DC: National Academy Press.

Horn, C. (2003). High-stakes testing and students: Stopping or perpetuating a cycle of failure. *Theory into Practice, 42*(1), 30-41.

Kellaghan, T., Madaus, G., & Airasian, P. (1982). *The effects of standardized testing.* Boston: Kluwer-Nijhoff.

Klein, S., Hamilton, L., McCaffrey, D., & Stecher, B. (2000, October 26). What do test scores in Texas tell us? *Educational Policy Analysis Archives, 8*(49), 1–15. Retrieved from http://epaa.asu.edu/epaa/v8n49.html

Kohn, A. (2000). *The case against standardized testing: Raising the scores, ruining the schools.* Portsmouth, NH: Heinemann.

Koretz, D. (1988). Arriving in Lake Woebegon: Are standardized tests exaggerating achievement and distorting instruction? *American Educator, 12*(2), 8–15; 46-52.

Koretz, D. (1995). Sometimes a cigar is only a cigar, and often a test is only a test. In D. Ravitch (Ed.), *Debating the future of American education: Do we need national standards and assessments?* (pp. 154–166). Washington, DC: Brookings Institution.

Kornhaber, M., Orfield, G., & Kurlaender, M. (2001). *Raising standards or raising barriers? Inequality and high-stakes testing in public education.* New York: Century Foundation Press.

Kurfman, D. (1991). Testing as context for social education. In J. Shaver (Ed.), *Handbook of research on social studies teaching and learning* (pp. 310–320). New York: Macmillan.

Lapp, M., Grigg, W., & Tay-Lim, B. (2002). *The nation's report card: U.S. History 2001, NCES 2002-483.* Washington, DC: U.S. Department of Education, Office of Educational Research and Improvement, National Center for Education Statistics.

LeMahieu, P. (1984). The effects on achievement and instructional content of a program of student monitoring through frequent testing. *Educational Evaluation and Policy Analysis, 6*(2), 175–187.

Libresco, A. (2005). How she stopped worrying and learned to love the test ... sort of. In E. A. Yeager & O. L. Davis, Jr. (Eds.), *Wise social studies teaching in an age of high-stakes testing* (pp. 33–50). Greenwich, CT: Information Age.

Linn, R. (2000). Assessments and accountability. *Educational Researcher, 29*(2), 4–16.

Linn, R. (2003, September 1). Performance standards: Utility for different uses of assessments. *Educational Policy Analysis Archives, 11*(31). Retrieved from http://epaa.asu.edu/epaa/v11n31

Madaus, G. (1988). The influence of testing on the curriculum. In L. Tanner (Ed.), *Critical issues in curriculum: 87th yearbook of the NSSE, Part 1* (pp. 83-121). Chicago: University of Chicago Press.

Mathison, S. (1997). Assessment in social studies: Moving toward authenticity. In E. W. Ross (Ed.), *The social studies curriculum* (pp. 213–224). Albany, NY: SUNY Press.

McLaughlin, M. (1991). Test-based accountability as a reform strategy. *Phi Delta Kappan, 73*(3), 248-251.

McNeil, L. (2000). *Contradictions of school reform: Educational costs of standardized testing.* New York: Routledge.

Mehrens, W., & Phillips, S. E. (1986). Detecting impacts of curricular differences in achievement test data. *Journal of Educational Measurement, 23*(3), 85–96.

Miller, S. (1995). Teachers' responses to test-driven accountability pressures: "If I change, will my scores drop?" *Reading Research and Instruction, 34*(4), 332–351.

National Center for History in the Schools. (1994). *National standards for United States history.* Los Angeles: Author.

Newmann, F. (1996). *Authentic achievement: Restructuring schools for intellectual quality.* San Francisco: Jossey-Bass.

Newmann, F., Bryk, A., & Nagaoka, J. (2001). *Authentic intellectual work and standardized tests: Conflict or coexistence?* Chicago: Consortium on Chicago School Research.

Newmann, F., Secada, W., & Wehlage, G. (1995). *A guide to authentic instruction and assessment: Visions, standards and scoring.* Madison, WI: Wisconsin Center for Educational Research.

Noble, A., & Smith, M. L. (1994). Old and new beliefs about measurement-driven reform: "Build it and they will come." *Educational Policy, 8*(2), 111–136.

Nuthall, G., & Alton-Lee, A. (1995). Assessing classroom learning: How students use their knowledge and experience to answer classroom achievement test questions in science and social studies. *American Educational Research Journal, 32*(1), 185–223.

O'Sullivan, R. (1991). Teachers' perceptions of the effects of testing on classroom practices. In R. Stake (Ed.), *Advances in program evaluation* (Vol. 1B, pp. 145–161). Greenwich, CT: JAI Press.

Ohanian, S. (1999). *One size fits few: The folly of educational standards.* Portsmouth, NH: Heinemann.

Pellegrino, J. (1992). Commentary: Understanding what we measure and measuring what we understand. In B. Gifford & M. O'Connor (Eds.), *Changing assessments: Alternative views of aptitude, achievement, and instruction* (pp. 275–294). Boston: Kluwer.

Popham, W. J. (1987). The merits of measurement-driven instruction. *Phi Delta Kappan, 68,* 679–682.

Popham, W. J. (1999). Where large scale assessment is heading and why it shouldn't. *Educational Measurement: Issues and Practice, 18,* 13–17.

Popham, W. J., Cruse, K., Rankin, S., Sandifer, P., & Williams, P. (1985). Measurement-driven instruction: It's on the road. *Phi Delta Kappan, 66*(9), 628–634.

Prawat, R. (1989). Teaching for understanding: Three key attributes. *Teaching and Teacher Education, 5,* 315–328.

Ravitch, D. (1995). *National standards in American education: A citizen's guide.* Washington, DC: Brookings Institution.

Ravitch, D., & Finn, C. (1987). *What do our seventeen year olds know?* New York: Harper & Row.

Romanowski, M. (1996). Issues and influences that shape the teaching of U.S. history. In J. Brophy (Ed.), *Advances in research on teaching* (Vol. 6, pp. 291–312). Greenwich, CT: JAI Press.

Romberg, T., Zarinnia, A., & Williams, S. (1989). *The influence of mandated testing on mathematics instruction.* Madison, WI: University of Wisconsin, National Center for Research in Mathematical Sciences Education.

Rothman, R. (1995). *Measuring up: Standards, assessment, and school reform*. San Francisco: Jossey-Bass.

Sacks, P. (1999). *Standardized minds: The high price of America's testing culture and what we can do to change it*. Cambridge, MA: Perseus.

Salmon-Cox, L. (1981). Teachers and standardized achievement tests: What's really happening? *Phi Delta Kappan, 62,* 631-634.

Segall, A. (2003). Teachers' perceptions of the impact of state-mandated standardized testing: The Michigan Educational Assessment Program (MEAP) as a case study of consequences. *Theory and Research in Social Education, 31*(3), 287–325.

Shanker, A. (1995). The case for high stakes and real consequences. In D. Ravitch (Ed.), *Debating the future of American education: Do we need national standards and assessments?* (pp. 145–153). Washington, DC: Brookings Institution.

Smith, J., & Niemi, R. (2001). Learning history in school: The impact of course work and instructional practices on achievement. *Theory and Research in Social Education, 29*(1), 18–42.

Smith, M., & O'Day, J. (1991). Systemic school reform. In S. Fuhrman & B. Malen (Eds.), *The politics of curriculum and testing* (pp. 233–267). New York: Falmer.

Smith, M. L. (1991). Put to the test: The effects of external testing on teachers. *Educational Researcher, 20*(5), 8–11.

Spoehr, K., & Spoehr, L. (1994). Learning to think historically. *Educational Psychologist, 29*(2), 71–77.

Stake, R. (1991). The teacher, standardized testing, and prospects of revolution. *Phi Delta Kappan, 73*(3), 243–247.

Sturtevant, E. (1996). Lifetime influences on the literacy-related instructional beliefs of experienced high school history teachers: Two comparative case studies. *Journal of Literacy Research, 28*(2), 227–257.

Toenjes, L., & Dworkin, A. G. (2002, March 21). Are increasing test scores in Texas really a myth, or is Haney's myth a myth? *Educational Policy Analysis Archives, 10*(17). Retrieved from http://epaa.asu.edu/epaa/v10n17.html

van Hover, S., & Heinecke, W. (2005). The impact of accountability reform on the "wise practice" of secondary history teachers: The Virginia experience. In E. A. Yeager & O. L. Davis, Jr. (Eds.), *Wise social studies teaching in an age of high-stakes testing* (pp. 89–116). Greenwich, CT: Information Age.

VanSledright, B. (1995a). "I don't remember—the ideas are all jumbled in my head" Eighth graders' reconstructions of colonial American history. *Journal of Curriculum and Supervision, 10*(4), 317–345.

VanSledright, B. (1995b). The teaching-learning interaction in American history: A study of two teachers and their fifth graders. *Journal of Social Studies Research, 19*(1), 3–23.

Webeck, M. L., Salinas, C., & Field, S. (2005). A good teacher in Texas: Conversations about wisdom in middle school social studies practice. In E. A. Yeager & O. L. Davis, Jr. (Eds.), *Wise social studies teaching in an age of high-stakes testing* (pp. 69–88). Greenwich, CT: Information Age.

Wiggins, G. (1993). Assessment: Authenticity, context, and validity. *Phi Delta Kappan, 75*(3), 200–214.

Wiggins, G., & McTighe, J. (1998). *Understanding by design*. Alexandria, VA: ASCD.

Wineburg, S. (1991). On the reading of historical texts: Notes on the breach between school and academy. *American Educational Research Journal, 28*(3), 495–520.

Wineburg, S., & Wilson, S. (1991). Subject matter knowledge in the teaching of history. In J. Brophy (Ed.), *Advances in research on teaching* (Vol. 3, pp. 305–347). Greenwich, CT: JAI Press.

Yeh, S. (2001). Tests worth testing to: Constructing state-mandated tests that emphasize critical thinking. *Educational Researcher, 30*(9), 12–17.

Zancanella, D. (1992). The influence of state-mandated testing on teachers of literature. *Educational Evaluation and Policy Analysis, 14*(3), 283–295.

CHAPTER 4

THE TECHNICAL REALITIES OF MEASURING HISTORY

Catherine Horn

Although a range of assessments is utilized in educational settings (e.g., classroom tests, diagnostic measures, formative exams), this chapter focuses on large-scale standardized exams. Use of such mandated testing to evaluate programs (e.g., Title 1) and to hold students accountable has been part of the public educational landscape in the United States for more than 30 years (Haney, Madaus, & Lyons, 1993; Heubert & Hauser, 1999), and almost exclusively, such judgments have been made on the basis of reading and math scores.

Because history exams traditionally have not been considered among the tests necessary for graduation, promotion, or school- or district-evaluation (D'Agostino, 2000; Farrar, 1972; Pipho, 1978), there has been relatively less public attention paid to the technical underpinnings of their construction, administration, and validation. However, the complexities of creating a large-scale standardized exam that captures student knowledge of a historical genre are worthy of examination.

In this chapter, I begin with a discussion of the broad framing question—What is the pragmatic value of large-scale standardized testing, writ large, and of history exams, in particular? I then explore three method-

Measuring History: Cases of State-Level Testing Across the United States, 57–74
Copyright © 2006 by Information Age Publishing

ological issues surrounding history assessments: (a) the challenges of item development (among them, the question of "whose history" is represented); (b) the ways in which scaling these exams is impacted by the often factual nature of the assessment of history; and (c) the ways in which student knowledge may and may not be appropriately represented given such constraints. As the implementation of the No Child Left Behind Act continues to focus attention primarily on math and literacy exams and to reinforce the expectation that all standardized exams are an accurate measure of both aggregated school and individual student achievement, it is increasingly important to turn a critical lens onto the technical realities of these tests.

LARGE-SCALE TESTING AND ITS VALUE

Testing is, by definition, a sociocultural phenomenon (Madaus & Horn, 2000) and a potentially valuable but incomplete tool that can provide important information about a student's progress toward or achievement of a defined standard or objective. At their best, standardized assessments give the stakeholders involved—e.g., students, teachers, parents, schools, districts, the community, the state—a snapshot of how individuals or groups are performing relative to a set of predetermined standards or objectives. Depending on the intent, design, and construction of tests, the attendant results can highlight strengths and flag areas where growth is needed at various instructional levels of interest, thus acting as one component in the diagnosis and ultimately the improvement of educational achievement for all students. Some observers have also argued that large-scale standardized tests allow policy makers to infuse a level of accountability not otherwise present in schooling (e.g., Haycock & Gerald, 2002). Although the extent to which increased test-based accountability actually translates into increased learning remains largely tenuous,[1] such mechanisms have been widely embraced and implemented at the state and national level. In sum, the assumption is that well-crafted, well-implemented, well-used assessments can be developed.

To understand the potential value of assessing historical knowledge specifically, one must first establish the educational importance of history more broadly. John Dewey (1938) describes the benefits of including history as part of the educational curriculum taught in schools:

> Intelligent insight into present forms of associated life is necessary for a character whose morality is more than colorless innocence. Historical knowledge helps provide such insight. It is an organ for analysis of the warp and woof of the present social fabric, of making known the forces, which

have woven the pattern. The use of history for cultivating a socialized intelligence constitutes its moral significance. It is possible to employ it as a kind of reservoir of anecdotes to be drawn on to inculcate special moral lessons on this virtue or that vice. But such teaching is not so much an ethical use of history as it is an effort to create moral impressions by means of more or less authentic material. At best, it produces a temporary emotional glow; at worst, callous indifference to moralizing. The assistance which may be given by history to a more intelligent sympathetic understanding of the social situations of the present in which individuals share is a permanent and constructive moral asset. (pp. 254–255)

As Dewey describes, the study of history can benefit students intellectually and socially as the purpose of understanding history is to "enrich and liberate the more direct and personal contacts of life by furnishing their context, their background and outlook" (p. 247). Measuring the acquisition of such skills seems a natural outflow of an interest in ensuring all students are prepared to become fully contributing members of society.

The extent to which standardized measurements actually meet that goal, however, is complicated both by the nature of current accountability structures and by methodological constraints. The nature of the current test-based accountability structures burgeoning across the country potentially limits the extent to which history tests can provide useful information to various stakeholders. Specifically, a growing body of research shows that the curriculum becomes more narrowly focused on the subject areas tested to the disregard of other topics as stakes on the former increase (Clarke, Shore, Rhoades, Abrams, Miao, & Li, 2003; Pedulla, Abrams, Madaus, Russell, Ramos, & Miao, 2003). Moreover, given that literacy and mathematics assessments continue to dominate the accountability structures at state and national levels, there is an increased likelihood that the study of history, especially in elementary school classrooms, is being reduced (von Zastrow & Janc, 2004). Recognizing this potential restriction, the importance of reiterating the broader value of history education is paramount; teaching, learning, and measuring historical knowledge carries with it potential immediate and long-term worth. That said, I now turn to the methodological challenges of producing tests that meet such goals.

METHODOLOGICAL COMPLEXITIES

In understanding the utility of large-scale standardized tests in general and of history tests in particular, it is important to look closely at their limitations. Crocker and Algina (1986) note four measurement problems common to all assessments: (a) no single approach to large scale assessment is collectively accepted; (b) assessments are typically based on a limited sample of content; (c) the measurement obtained is subject to error; and (d) measurement scales lack well-defined units. These limitations provide a useful framework in which to discuss the complexities, including the issues of validity and reliability, that befall standardized assessments of history.

No Single Approach Is Collectively Accepted

The issue of how to test is universally discussed, but it becomes particularly salient when thinking about the limitations of history testing. There are long-standing debates about the ways in which to measure students' mastery of a subject that, in turn, have implications for the method of testing used. Perhaps most clearly defining this challenge is the dispute over whether multiple-choice or alternative assessments (sometimes referred to as authentic or performance assessments) more accurately capture or reflect student knowledge. Supporters of traditional multiple-choice items argue that asking test takers to select from limited choices across a range of topics and many levels of abstraction can, in fact, adequately provide important information about student learning (e.g., Loadman & Thomas, n.d.). Proponents of alternative assessments believe that requiring a student to generate a response rather than simply select from a predefined set of choices more fully represents what a student knows and can do (e.g., Wiggins, 1989).

Regardless of one's view, suffice it to say that different approaches provide different types of information, and the choice of measurement method can have serious implications for the conclusions drawn about a student's competency. Depending on need and definition of the skill to be measured—in the case of this chapter, history broadly conceived—the tradeoffs (e.g., the breadth versus depth of coverage, the reality of the costs of test administration) might incline states to use one form over another. Recently, however, many states have implemented tests that incorporate multiple measurement methods. For example, 25 states have been involved with the Council of Chief State School Officers' (CCSSO) Comprehensive Social Studies Assessment Project. This multiyear endeavor has developed a series of assessment tools that include selected and constructed response items as well as a series of performance tasks, and is now focused on encouraging and supporting educators' use of those tools (Council of Chief State School Officers, 2003-2004). By utilizing several approaches to assessing student competency within the same exam, the test ideally provides a fuller picture of student achievement. As Sanders and Horn (1995) note, however, "the issue is not whether one form of assessment is intrinsically better than another. No assessment model is suited for every purpose. The real issue is choosing appropriately among indicator variables and applying the most suitable model to render them" (p. 13). A test can include different measurement approaches, but without the inclusion of appropriate content in conjunction with careful attention to the best methods by which to measure that content, the results are rendered useless. It is to this latter point, the choice of indicator variables for a test and the inherently limited capacity to measure the full skill set of interest, that I now turn.

Tests Are Based on a Limited Sample of Content

The second methodological problem Crocker and Algina (1986) identify highlights the relationship between subject matter content and the representation of that content on standardized tests. In administering a test of history knowledge, the assumption is that the results will reflect the test-taker's level of competency across the entire area of interest. No test, however, can directly measure or include enough items to fully represent a construct (Osterlind, 1998). As such, test writers are forced to assemble and sample from a pool of questions that, ideally, adequately reflects the test's purpose and specifications and capture the construct of interest through indirect means.

This is no simple task. In constructing a history exam, perhaps one of the most fundamental struggles may come in the naming of the constructs themselves. The discussion over what subject matter, broadly defined, ought to be included means a resurrection of the contest between "history" and "social studies." As part of a larger study of what key concepts and ideas in the social sciences should be tested at the secondary level, House and Lawrence (1990) found that "there is a fundamental disagreement over whether social studies tests should cover history or the social sciences, reflecting perhaps a schism between history and social sciences in the academic disciplines themselves" (p. 19). The inclusion or exclusion of subjects such as geography, economics, sociology, and civics in the construct of "history" or "social studies" knowledge varies greatly across both state and national assessments and makes it difficult to generalize performance.

Further, the choice of the broader areas of interest (e.g., world history, economics, civics) marks only the beginning of the narrowing process for test construction. Much more detailed test specifications have to be formed that lay out the content and processes to be measured (Osterlind, 1998). In the case of state-mandated exams, such guidelines are typically defined by the curriculum learning standards that have been established.

Question 23:   How did the French Revolution Affect the Latin American Independence Movements?

1. It encouraged the British to meet the demands of the people.

2. It promoted regional cooperation to solve economic problems.

3. It provided ideas for making political changes.

4. It was a model for peaceful solutions to political conflicts.

Question 28:   Which Situation led to the Defeat of China in the Opium War (1839–1842)

1. A civil war on the Sino-Tibetan border

2. The technological advantages of the European powers

3. A famine that weakened the Chinese military

4. The lack of support for the Manchu government from Chinese scholars

Question 29:   A Common Goal of the Salt March in India, the Boxer Rebellion in China, and the Zulu Resistance in Southern Africa was to

1. Overthrow totalitarian leaders

2. Force upper classes to carry out land reform programs

3. Remove foreign powers

4. Establish Communist parties to lead the governments

Source: New York Regents Global History and Geography Test Sampler Draft (1999). http://www.emsc.nysed.gov/osa/socstre/socstudarch/ghist1.pdf

Figure 4.1.

For example, New York state outlines five learning standards for social studies upon which students are assessed: U.S. and New York history, world history, geography, economics, and civics, citizenship, and government. Across these standards, several subcategories of interest (e.g., historical eras such as the ancient world, expanding zones of exchange, global interactions) have been identified, and within each of the shared cells (e.g., geography and the ancient world), test questions have been constructed (New York State Education Department, 1999). Three questions from the 1999 test sampler draft of the New York Regent's 10th grade global history and geography exam provide an example of how this complex relationship is operationally defined (see Figure 4.1). These items are indicated in the test specification grid as the measure of the world history standard for the Age of Revolution.

Three important observations can be made. First, the technical realities of measuring a construct as broad as global history and geography limits the number of questions that can be dedicated to any particular area of interest. Most observers would argue that relying on three questions to assess a student's knowledge of world history during the Age of Revolution is insufficient. Time, space, and resource constraints, however, make this type of choice both common and necessary.

Second, the subject matter of the questions themselves speaks to a broader issue common to history tests. In measuring the construct—global history knowledge—item development becomes a manifestation of some aspects of history to the exclusion of others. As Bigelow (1999) points out, "given the broad scope of the standards and the resulting randomness of the test questions that are generated, an infinite number of facts could appear on future social studies tests" (p. 37). More pointedly, the question becomes whose history is being represented in the tested items? Jackson (2000) found that, of the 57 questions on the 2000 10th grade Massachusetts Comprehensive Assessment System (MCAS) world history and social sciences test, 40 referred to Europe, five were about capitalism, and the remaining 12 covered the rest of the world. Grant (2001) found similar patterns on the New York Global History and Geography Regents exam: "Questions related to western nations (i.e., Europe, including Russia/USSR) dominate the test: Twenty-four questions assess issues relevant to the west, while only 10 questions each are assigned to India/Asia and to the rest of the world (Africa, Latin America, Caribbean, South America, and the Middle East)" (p. 6). Such patterns are troubling in light of the increased curricular interest in providing a multicultural curriculum (Bigelow, 1999) as well as the changing demographics of the country's school-age population (Orfield & Lee, 2004). They are also methodologically problematic in that they may create systematic error that biases results.

Finally, history tests are often super-saturated with fact-based items. In his study of the New York Regents exam, Grant (2001) concludes, "the real issue related to significance is the type of questions asked rather than the content. In short, test makers aimed at low-level knowledge questions rather than at higher-order thinking questions" (p. 6). Beyond the potential limitations the reliance on fact-based questioning may put on the breadth of historical vantage points that can be represented, it also may impact students' performance. Because the content of an exam can have a direct impact on performance (House & Lawrence, 1990), it is reasonable to assume that both the historical leanings and the knowledge-based understanding measured from those confines may skew test scores in a way that has nothing to do with how much an examinee knows about the construct in question, "history." John Dewey (1938) offers an important warning related to the decision about content sampling in constructing history exams:

> The words "history" and "geography" suggest simply the matter, which has been traditionally sanctioned in the schools. The mass and variety of this matter discourage an attempt to see what it really stands for, and how it can be so taught as to fulfill its mission in the experience of pupils. But unless

the idea that there is a unifying and social direction in education is a farcical pretense, subjects that bulk as large in the curriculum as history and geography, must represent a general function in the development of a truly socialized and intellectualized experience. The discovery of this function must be employed as a criterion for trying and sifting the facts taught and the methods used. (pp. 246–247)

Without careful attention to the ways in which history, as a construct, is operationally defined—including whose history is represented and the ways in which an understanding of that knowledge are captured—first in the classroom and then on the state-mandated tests that follow—such exams will ultimately provide little fruitful information for interested students, teachers, and communities. Embedded within this concern is the fundamental testing principle of validity, to which I now turn.

Validity

Relevant to Crocker and Algina's (1986) notion of the problematic nature of test content is the issue of validity. Validity represents the meaningfulness, adequacy, and accuracy of the inferences being made from test scores. Validity is not an all or nothing scenario; it is a matter of degree. As is the case with reliability, many factors, some of which overlap, may influence the various components of validity. Those factors include unclear directions and ambiguity, inadequate time limits, inappropriate item difficulty, poorly constructed items, and teaching to the test.

Messick (1989) outlines four kinds of validity evidence that are needed—construct, content, criterion, and consequential—and notes that any responsible use of test scores requires that inferences being drawn for the intended purpose with such evidence are justifiable. Validity is a unified concept: Each of these validity types is necessary unto itself, but the overall extent to which validity exists is more than simply the sum of the parts. Confirmation of all components alone and in conjunction must be considered when determining the appropriateness of any conclusions drawn. Although a full discussion of validity is beyond the scope of this chapter, I offer a series of questions that demand attention if inferences from history exams are to be correctly made and interpreted.

The notion of *construct validity* is important when "the test user desires to draw an inference from the test score to performance that can be grouped under the label of a particular psychological construct" (Crocker & Algina, 1986, p. 218). In the case of history tests, assessing construct validity determines the extent to which a test accurately and adequately captures how much a student knows or can do related to the specific areas of interest such as U.S. or world history being measured. Without assurances of such validity, stakeholders may incorrectly assume that a test accurately measures a particular construct and, ultimately, may make important decisions on that incorrect assumption. The National Research Council (1999) lists four questions to be asked when evaluating construct validity: Are the right things being measured in the right balance? Is the scoring system consistent with the structure of the domains about which inferences or predictions are being made? Are the scores reliable and consistent across the different contexts for which they are used, as well as across different population groups? What are the short-term and long-term consequences of score interpretation and use?

In focusing specifically on tests of history knowledge, several more pointed questions might be asked: How is a competent student of history defined? How does the test define what a competent student will demonstrate during the test to show that she or he is indeed competent? Do the scores on the history exam correlate with other measures of a similar construct such as course GPA or scores on a different standardized test of history? Are there counterfactual reasons for students' performance on the history test (e.g., content on the test not covered in coursework)? If no relationship is found between the test and the hypothesized construct, the problem may lie with a poorly developed instrument and/or a poorly defined attribute of interest, which is of particular importance to history exams. As discussed earlier, creators of such assessments may struggle to fairly and fully name and define the construct of interest and then to balance a breadth versus depth of information needed to measure that construct once identified.

Along with construct validity is the idea of *content validity*, which assesses the extent to which items included on the test sufficiently represent the domain or construct of interest (Crocker & Algina, 1986; Messick, 1989). Content validation is evaluated after an initial form of the instrument has been developed.

Again, many important questions need to be asked when determining the extent to which a history test has a high degree of content validity: Does the content tested match the curriculum and instruction provided in the social studies courses? Do students have an equitable opportunity to learn the material covered? To what extent do history and social studies experts agree that the content covered on the test corresponds to the curriculum? To what extent do experts agree that the content covered on the test corresponds to a reasonable measure of a student's history competency? Is the content biased (e.g., racially/ethnically, on the basis of gender)? Are all items on the test essential or are some items superfluous? Is a student historically incompetent if she or he cannot answer a question or set of questions correctly? Content validity is especially important in the interpretation of test scores, particularly as it pertains to high-stakes decision-making. If a student is denied a diploma based on a test score that shows she or he did not have mastery of an assessment of world history, for example, it is critical to understand the extent to which the exam content actually measures knowledge of that subject area, fully defined.

The third form of validity, *criterion validity*, deals with the extent to which inferences may be drawn from test scores on some performance criterion not directly measured on the exam (Crocker & Algina, 1986). Such information reveals how well a test score may relate to actual characteristics of interest such as an ability to think critically about current political events or to apply lessons learned in history to contemporary problems.

In thinking about the criterion-related inferences being made on the basis of history exam scores, one might ask: How valid is the cut score in classifying distinct groups (e.g., passing or failing)? Are those students who achieve a passing score really historically competent? Are those scoring below the passing score truly incompetent? To what extent does the strength of the relationship between the test score and the criterion of interest exist? To what extent does a score predict "real world" performance on a task related to tested area of interest? The presence of criterion validity better ensures that test scores are being used appropriately, confirming that performance on an exam reflects important demonstrable skills, knowledge, or abilities that are desired. Without such information, misguided decisions may be made as to their practical utility.

Finally, *consequential validity* pertains to the intended and unintended results of the inferences made from test scores (Messick, 1989). Such validity is particularly important for tests that carry a substantial sanction or reward tied to performance.

Those assessing the consequential validity of history tests might ask the following questions: Is a reward or sanction (e.g., the denial of a diploma) made on the basis of a single history test score justifiable? Are there adverse consequences associated with bias in scoring and/or interpretation? Do the consequences attached to the test score adversely impact some stakeholders more than others? Is the particular test of history a test worth teaching to?

In essence, the issue of validity, holistically perceived, is largely one of fairness. And it is an issue that needs to be taken very seriously, especially in the case of high-stakes history testing. As the National Research Council (1999) notes, "fairness, like validity, cannot be properly addressed as an afterthought once the test has been developed, administered, and used. It must be confronted throughout the interconnected phases of the testing process, from test design and development to administration, scoring, interpretation, and use" (pp. 80–81). Without direct and active attention to the questions inherent in the issues of construct, content, criterion, and perhaps most importantly, consequential validity, tests of history will render unfair results that nonetheless carry potentially important consequences.

Measurement Is Subject to Error

Crocker and Algina's (1986) third category of methodological problems focuses on the issue of error. In measurement theory, there are two kinds of error that affect test scores: random and systematic. Systematic errors impact a score because of factors unrelated to the construct being measured (e.g., a hearing impairment, opportunity to learn, fluency in the tested language); random errors affect a student's score by chance (e.g., lack of adequate breakfast the morning of testing, content sampling, scoring problems) (Crocker & Algina, 1986). In understanding test scores from a technical perspective, it is the random errors that are most salient, and historically, two different models have dominated how such errors are calculated.

In the classical true score test model, an observed score on a test, X, is equal to a true score plus some error score: $X = T + E$. The assumption in classical true score theory is that a test-taker's true score remains constant over administrations while the observed score fluctuates due to error, which has no relationship to the true score. Because error is assumed to be random, the expected error score over multiple administrations for a particular test taker will be a constant subtracted from itself, or zero (Crocker & Algina, 1986). Although classical test theory is viewed by the measurement community as a more simplistic way of constructing and analyzing test data relative to the more sophisticated Item Response Theory discussed next, the language of Classical True Score theory and error still holds firmly in the discussion of test accuracy. That is, the fundamental measurement principle, reliability, is tantamount to any conversation of the technical realities of testing.

The item response theory (IRT) model in its simplest form—the one-parameter model—is an evolution of classical true score theory in that measuring a construct is done independently of the test by looking concurrently at the relationship between item difficulty and ability levels. The one-parameter model is represented by the statistical formula shown in the following equation:

$$P\{\chi_{vi} = 1 | \beta_v, \delta_i\} = \frac{e^{\beta v - \delta 1}}{1 + e^{\beta v - \delta 1}}$$

The values for the formula are defined as the following:

x_{vi} = response for person v on item i

e = exp = 2.71828

β_v = ability parameter for person v

δ_i = difficulty parameter of item I

This formula asserts that the probability of a correct response for a given person on a given item is equal to the exponential function of the difference between that person's ability estimate and the item difficulty for that question divided by that term plus one. These estimations also have standard error (Hambleton, Swaminathan, & Rogers, 1991; Wright & Stone, 1979). In IRT, the influence of error is actually discussed in the reciprocal term, information: "More information implies less error of measurement" (Item Response Theory, n.d.). Although more sophisticated, IRT in its general form produces the same main results as classical true score theory procedures (Holland & Hoskens, 2002), and, as such, reinforces the discussion of error in the language of reliability.

Before turning to a more detailed discussion of reliability, however, it is worth noting the important influence error can have when making high-stakes decisions about subject-area proficiency on the basis of a test score. In their study of cut score establishment and MCAS performance levels, Horn, Ramos, Blumer, and Madaus (2000) correlated students' scores on the state's standardized test to their performance on other commercially developed measures of a similar construct.[2] The authors explained that the error on the 1998 eighth grade MCAS math test was plus or minus 14.4 points for a student whose scale score was below 240. This meant that a student who scored 218 (a "Failing" performance) might have had a real score that was as low as 204 (also "Failing") or as high as 232 ("Needs Improvement"). Given that the 10th grade passing standard for graduation on the MCAS math and English/Language arts exams is "Needs Improvement," such distinctions are potentially critical. To this issue, Gene Glass (1978), a pioneer in the psychometric community, writes:

> Interpretations and decisions based on absolute levels of performance on exercises will be largely meaningless, since these absolute levels vary unaccountably with exercise content and difficulty, since judges will disagree wildly on the question of what consequences ought to ensue from the same absolute level of performance, and since there is no way to relate absolute levels of performance on exercises to success on the job, in higher levels of schooling or in life. (p. 259)

The arbitrary nature of cut score setting coupled with all tests' ever-present error makes the use of an absolute performance criterion for high-stakes decision making risky. As evidenced above, stakeholders must be careful to acknowledge the real impact error can have.

Reliability

Let me now turn to a discussion of reliability. Reliability is the consistency between two measures of the same phenomena. Many factors can affect the reliability of a test. For example, all other things being equal, a test that is longer, not rigidly limited by time, bound by cut scores away from the center of the test score distribution, and administered to a heterogeneous group will produce more reliable results than one that neglects one or more of these criteria. Especially important for standardized tests purported to assess students' mastery of standards is assurance that the content domain taught matches the content domain measured. For tests that include essay exams, reliability is improved when readers use a rubric to score responses, when each response is scored by more than one reader, and when all responses to one item are scored by a reader before moving to the next (Crocker & Algina, 1986; Osterlind, 1998).

Depending on the aspect of error and the dimension across which consistency is defined (e.g., time, raters, test forms, test conditions), the calculated reliability coefficient will differ (Crocker & Algina, 1986). For example, the test-retest method, usually represented by a Pearson's r, assesses the stability of test scores over time. An equivalent forms method tests the consistency of the test scores over different forms of the test. The reliability of a composite score is typically expressed as Cronbach's alpha. A standard error of measurement indicates the amount of error around individual test scores. For any test used to determine competency, reliability typically is discussed in terms of how consistently multiple administrations categorize test takers as passing or failing. The reliability of performance-based assessments typically is determined by the degree of agreement between two or more judges who rate the performance independently. Across all of these forms of reliability estimation, the central tenet remains assessing the extent to which a score consistently represents student performance.

For history tests, this issue is particularly significant in the context of the potential technical complications that have already been raised in the chapter. As an example, the extent to which the specific content sampled on one form of a test varies from that on another form may directly impact student performance. Given the often-factual nature of history tests, such variation may be a prominent problem. As with the other methodological concerns highlighted throughout this chapter, without reliability, a test score is essentially worthless.[3]

Measurement Scales Lack Well-Defined Units

Crocker and Algina's (1986) final methodological constraint burdening standardized assessment is the definition, labeling, and interpretation of the values derived from a test score. As DeVellis (1991) writes, "we develop scales when we want to measure phenomena that we believe to exist because of our theoretical understanding of the world, but which we cannot assess directly" (pp. 8–9). Such scales allow inferences to be made about the level of understanding a test taker possesses.

In developing scales, several approaches can be used. Subject-centered methods, for example, locate individuals where stimulus-centered methods position stimuli at different points on a continuum (Crocker & Algina, 1986). Regardless of method, the level of measurement scales—nominal, ordinal, interval, or ratio—impact both the reliability and validity of the measure. Specifically, numbers on a nominal scale have no order; numbers on an ordinal scale only have order (e.g., first, second, and third), but no fixed origin; numbers on an interval scale have order and equal distance between units, but no fixed origin; and numbers on a ratio scale have all real number properties (Crocker & Algina, 1986). As one can imagine, such scale levels directly impact the extent to which a student's test score can meaningfully or usefully place him or her at a point on a continuum. A test score that only provides the information that two students "Need Improvement," for example, might not prove as useful as knowing that one student scored a 220 where the second scored 240 out of 280 possible points. Even finer-grained scales might show that the first student had a strong mastery of economics but none of geography whereas the second student had minimal but consistent competency across both. Such distinctions allow stakeholders to make potentially better-informed decisions about what a test taker knows and can do relative to the objective of exam.

In creating a scale of history achievement, several specific issues arise. First, as has been discussed earlier, the act of determining what ought to be measured can be precarious for such tests. Second and related, it is often difficult to create items that accurately reflect the scale's purpose, particularly given the often-factual nature of the items generated. Third, the format of the items, which remains hotly debated within the history assessment community, should be considered and selected based on the purpose of the scale (DeVellis, 1991). Finally, the optimal scale length is complicated again by the factual nature of many of the items typically used to assess history knowledge. Although well-constructed scales can be incredibly useful, inappropriately constructed scales will only result in misguided information about student performance.

CONCLUSION

The technical realities of assessment burden history exams in much the same way that they encumber other large-scale standardized measures of achievement. Complexity of design, a limited ability to sample items to represent a construct of interest, error, and issues of scaling each contribute to the complexity of constructing a reliable and valid history tests. In his book, *Why Things Bite Back*, Edward Tenner (1996) discusses the revenge effects that often arise as a result of technological advances. Such effects certainly have emerged within the social technology of testing. Although history tests have been intended to focus attention on an important subject matter and better ensure learning, they are burdened by methodological constraints that limit their ability to do that. Tenner warns, "technology usually fails to solve chronic problems in the direct ... way we have been led to expect—or hope. This does not mean that technology fails; quite the contrary. It means that it requires skill and vigilance" (p. 233). With the technical vigilance Tenner describes, assessments of history can provide useful and prudent information to a variety of stakeholders. Unfortunately, the reality is often far different. Both the measurement and policy community too often have allowed testing technology to go largely unchecked.

Stephen Gould (1981) writes that

> [science] progresses by hunch, vision, and intuition. Much of its change through time does not record a closer approach to absolute truth, but the alteration of cultural contexts that influence it so strongly. Facts are not pure and unsullied bits of information; culture also influences what we see and how we see it. (pp. 53-54)

History exams are laden with such alterations, and both methodological and cultural influences ultimately affect the development, administration, and interpretation of test scores. Individual perceptions and beliefs bias useful test construction in unavoidable ways and throughout the process—from the definition of the construct to the identification of the test questions to the decision about how to utilize the results. Despite advances in measurement capabilities and accuracy standards, lurking revenge effects still exist. In order to maximize the utility of large-scale history tests, then, assessment specialists and stakeholders must heed Tenner's (1996) advice: They must vigilantly continue to question, critique, and improve on the task at hand.

NOTES

1. For a fuller discussion of the student, classroom, and school impacts of test-based accountability systems, particularly the recently implemented No Child Left Behind Act, see Koretz, Mitchell, and Stetcher (1996),

Clarke, Shore, Rhoades, Abrams, Miao, and Li, (2003), and Kim and Sunderman (2004).

2. The MCAS test reduces a scale score ranging from 200-280 to one of four MCAS performance levels (i.e., Failing (200-219), Needs Improvement (220-239), Proficient (240-259), and Advanced (260-280)). It is on the basis of that performance level that consequential decisions are made (e.g., high school graduation sanction).

3. Eva Baker (1994) offers a particularly salient illustration of how difficult reliable scores can be to obtain. In a study of how English and history teachers scored student responses to a Document-Based Question, Baker and her colleagues found far more agreement between some of the English and history teachers than among the history teachers themselves.

REFERENCES

Baker, E. (1994). Learning-based assessments of history understanding. *Educational Psychologist, 29*(2), 97–106.

Bigelow, B. (1999). Why standardized tests threaten multiculturalism. *Educational Leadership, 56* (7), 37–40.

Clarke, M., Shore, A., Rhoades, K., Abrams, L., Miao, J., & Li, J. (2003). *Perceived effects of state-mandated testing programs on teaching and learning: Findings from interviews with educators in low-, medium-, and high-stakes states.* Chestnut Hill, MA: National Board on Educational Testing and Public Policy.

Council of Chief State School Officers. (2003–2004). *Comprehensive social studies assessment project.* Retrieved from http://www.ccsso.org/projects/SCASS/Projects/Comprehensive_Social_Studies_Assessment_Project/1911.cfm

Crocker, L., & Algina, J. (1986). *Introduction to classical and modern test theory.* New York: Harcourt Brace Jovanovich.

D'Agostino, J. (2000). Achievement testing in American schools. In T. Good (Ed.), *American education: Yesterday, today, tomorrow. Ninety-ninth yearbook of the NSSEU* (pp. 313–337). Chicago: University of Chicago Press.

DeVellis, R. (1991). *Scale development: Theory and applications.* Newbury Park, CA: Sage.

Dewey, J. (1938). *Democracy and education.* New York: Macmillan.

Farrar, C. (1972). *The social studies curriculum and standardized achievement tests.* A paper presented at the Mid-South Educational Research Association, New Orleans, November 1972.

Grant, S. G. (2001). When an "A" is not enough: Analyzing the New York State global history and geography exam. *Education Policy Analysis Archives, 9*(39). Retrieved from http://epaa.asu.edu/epaa/v9n39.html

Glass, G. (1978). Standards and criteria. *Journal of Educational Measurement, 15*(4), 237–261.

Gould, S. J. (1981). *The mismeasure of man.* New York: W. W. Norton.

Hambleton, R., Swaminathan, H., & Rogers, H. J. (1991). *MMSS: Fundamentals of item response theory.* Newbury Park, CA: Sage.

Haney, W., Madaus, G., & Lyons, R. (1993). *The fractured marketplace for standardized testing*. Boston: Kluwer.

Haycock, K., & Gerald, C. (2002). Closing the achievement gap. *Principal, 82*(2), 20–23.

Heubert, J., & Hauser, R. (Eds). (1999). *High stakes: Testing for tracking, promoting, and graduation*. Washington, DC: National Academy Press.

Holland, P., & Hoskens, M. (2002). *Classical test theory as a first-order item response theory: Application to truescore prediction from a possibly nonparallel test*. Educational Testing Service Research Report RR-02-20. Retrieved May 14, 2004, from http://www.ets.org/research/dload/RR-02-20.pdf

House, E., & Lawrence, N. (1990). *Report on content definition process in social studies testing*. CSE Technical Report 310. Los Angeles: UCLA Center for Research on Evaluation, Standards, and Student Testing.

Horn, C., Ramos, M., Blumer, I., & Madaus, G. (2000, April). *Cut scores: Results may vary*. Chestnut Hill, MA: The National Board on Educational Testing and Public Policy, Boston College.

Item Response Theory. (n.d.). Retrieved March 20, 2004, from http://encyclopedia.thefreedictionary.com/Item%20response%20theory

Jackson, D. (2000, June 7). MCAS history test is not only silly, it's racist. *Boston Globe*, p. A19.

Kim, J., & Sunderman, G. (2004). *Large mandates and limited resources: State response to the No Child Left Behind Act and implications for accountability*. Cambridge, MA: The Civil Rights Project at Harvard University.

Koretz, D., Mitchell, B., & Stetcher, B. (1996). *The perceived effects of the Kentucky instructional results information system*. Santa Monica, CA: RAND.

Loadman, W., & Thomas. A. M. (n.d.) Standardized test scores and alternative assessments: Different pieces of the same puzzle. *ENC Online*. Retrieved March 20, 2004, from http://www.enc.org/features/focus/archive/assessment/document.shtm?input=FOC-001558-index

Madaus, G., & Horn, C. (2000). Testing technology: The need for oversight. In Filer, A. (Ed.). *Assessment: Social practice and social product* (pp. 47–66). London: Routledge Farmer.

Messick, S. (1989). Validity. In R. L. Linn (Ed.), *Educational measurement* (3rd ed., pp. 13–103). New York: Macmillan.

The National Research Council. (1999). *High stakes testing for tracking, promotion, and graduation*. Washington, D.C.: National Academy Press.

New York State Education Department. (1999, Spring). *Global history and geography Regents examination: Test sampler draft*. New York: The University of the State of New York. Retrieved from http://www.emsc.nysed.gov/osa/socstre/socstudarch/ghist1.pdf

Orfield, G., & Lee, C. (2004). *Brown at 50: King's dream or Plessy's nightmare?* Cambridge, MA: The Civil Rights Project at Harvard University.

Osterlind, S. (1998). *Constructing test items: Multiple-choice, constructed-response, performance, and other formats*. Boston: Kluwer.

Pedulla, J., Abrams, L., Madaus, G., Russell, M., Ramos, M., & Miao, J. (2003). *Perceived effects of state-mandated testing programs on teaching and learning: Find-*

ings from a national survey of teachers. Chestnut Hill, MA: National Board on Educational Testing and Public Policy.

Pipho, C. (1978). Minimum competency testing in 1978: A look at state standards. *Phi Delta Kappan, 59*(9), 585–588.

Sanders, W., & Horn, S. (1995). Educational assessment reassessed: The usefulness of standardized and alternative measures of student achievement as indicators for the assessment of educational outcomes. *Educational Policy Analysis Archives, 3*(6). Retrieved from http://epaa.asu.edu/epaa/v3n6.html

Tenner, E. (1996). *Why things bite back.* New York: Random House.

von Zastrow, C., & Janc, H. (2004). *Academic atrophy: The condition of the liberal arts in America's public schools.* Washington, DC: Council for Basic Education.

Wiggins, G. (1989). A true test: Toward more authentic and equitable assessment. *Phi Delta Kappan, 20,* 703–713.

Wright, B., & Stone, M. H. (1979). *Best test design.* Chicago: MESA Press.

CHAPTER 5

PARADOX OF PRACTICE

Expanding and Contracting Curriculum in a High-Stakes Climate

Letitia Hochstrasser Fickel

For the last 2 decades, the United States has been engaged in a national debate about the need for educational reform and about the vision toward which we should be working. Little (1993) identified five concurrent streams of educational reform: content area rigor, equity for a diverse student population, student assessment, school organization, and the professionalization of teaching. The confluence of these five streams presents school reform as a multifaceted and dynamic process of reconceptualizing schooling, teaching, and student learning. Yet, in the last few years, reform efforts at both the national and state level have coalesced around a focus on standards and accountability as expressed in high-stakes testing. Many members of the educational community are now questioning whether the reforms originally envisioned can be fully realized in narrowed focus on standards and testing (Thompson, 2001).

That said, the assumption that standards and testing will eventually lead to substantial, positive changes in schools and classrooms seems to

Measuring History: Cases of State-Level Testing Across the United States, 75–103
Copyright © 2006 by Information Age Publishing
All rights of reproduction in any form reserved.

be widely accepted. The reality is, however, that we are only beginning to understand how and in what ways these reform policies, including high-stakes testing, actually influence or effect changes in teaching and learning in the classroom. Critical, then, are more studies that "can capture in some detail how professionals attend to (or ignore) reforms, interpret the meaning of reform activity, engage in reform-related work, and adopt (or reject) reform ideas as part of their practice" (Knapp, Bramburg, Ferguson, & Hill, 1998, p. 408).

In this chapter, I try to capture this type of detail about the work of teachers in a high school department as they collaboratively negotiated Kentucky's educational reform mandates. The data are drawn from a larger case study designed to illuminate the form and content of the teacher culture within the department (Fickel, 1998). However, because the teachers were working within the context of statewide educational reform, including high-stakes testing, the data also reveal the ways in which the department culture served to mediate their individual and collective understanding of, and response to, the state policies. Most studies of the impact of high-stakes testing and accountability focus on individual teachers as the unit of analysis. By illuminating the complex and seemingly paradoxical ways the teachers collectively interpreted and responded to the state reform policies, this case study offers unique and important insights into the continuing dialogue regarding the influence of standards and testing on the teaching of history and the social studies, as well as the implications for students' opportunities to learn.

CURRICULUM INFLUENCES

Classrooms are the nexus of the educational enterprise, for it is there that teachers, students, instruction, and content converge. As Sarason (1980) reminds us "educational change depends on what teachers do and think. It is as simple and as complicated as that" (p. 193). The literature on educational change makes clear that teachers mediate reform by adapting innovations to fit their local context and existing understandings (Elmore, Peterson & McCarthy, 1996; Fullan, 1982). It is unrealistic to view teachers as automatons that unthinkingly act out preconceived programs with fidelity. Rather, we must understand that they are active curriculum agents (Miller & Seller, 1985) who engage in creative, purposeful actions of their own design based on their talents, needs, beliefs, ideas, and professional socialization (Sarason, 1980; Tabachnick, Popkewitz, & Zeichner, 1980). Teachers' subjective realities, the meaning they make of the policies and reforms, can be not only powerful motivations for engaging in change, but can serve as powerful constraints or potential protections against undesirable or thoughtless changes (Cornbleth, 2002). This body of literature helps us better understand teaching as a contextually situated activity, and paints a more nuanced picture of the multiple and overlapping influences that policy, organizational, and personal factors have on teacher curriculum decision making (Grant, 1996, 2003; McLaughlin & Talbert, 1993; Segall, 2003).

Empirical and theoretical research help us understand schools as both formal organizations and as sociocultural systems situated in multiply-embedded contexts (McLaughlin, 1990; McLaughlin & Talbert, 1990). The school itself is situated within a broad arena of policy influences that includes school reform initiatives (McLaughlin, 1990), curriculum frameworks and standards (Grant, 1996), and issues of testing and assessment (Corbett, & Wilson, 1991; Whitford & Jones, 1999). In many states and districts, curriculum frameworks have become more and more explicitly connected to the content of the assessments, and to the high stakes that often accompany the outcomes of such tests (Hoffman, Assaf, & Paris, 2001; Whitford & Jones, 1999). In fact, Elmore, Abelmann, and Fuhrman (1996) have argued that the intent of this move toward using testing for accountability purposes is to "focus schools' attention less on compliance with rules and more on increasing learning for students" (p. 65). Although testing may focus schools and teachers on student learning, researchers suggest that it more often leads them to focus on teaching the structure and format of the test (Grant, 1996; Linn, 2000; McNeil, 2000; Smith, 1991; Stecher, Barron, Kaganoff, & Goodwin, 1998; Whitford & Jones, 1999).

Educational reform policies and expectations provide a contextual framework within which teachers work, and certainly influence their practice. However, policies are not the only influences, nor necessarily the most salient. The local school context, such as organizational structures, culture, and norms (Hargreaves, 1994; Little, 1982; Sarason, 1980), and departmentalization and resources (McLaughlin & Talbert, 1993) can also influence teachers' thinking and decision making. Within high schools not all these organizational structures impact professional practice in the same way. Researchers suggest that in comprehensive high schools with large numbers of faculty members, subject-specific departments may be the most important professional context for teachers (Grossman & Stodolsky, 1995; Johnson, 1990; Siskin, 1994). As Talbert (1995) notes, "the intersection of subject cultures and high school department organization is a powerful frame for teachers' professional identities and communities" (p. 88).

Teachers in high schools seem to identify most strongly with their departmental colleagues. This affiliation is not unexpected given that through extended course work in a subject-matter discipline during their preservice preparation, secondary teachers learn not only the content knowledge, but also the habits of mind, and ways of knowing and doing associated with their chosen academic discipline. In fact, Bernstein (1971) has argued that such learning experiences should be understood as induction into a disciplinary culture and its accepted assumptions and supporting beliefs about what constitutes knowledge and the appropriate learning and teaching of that knowledge. This induction surfaces in the literature on teacher socialization. Zeichner and Gore (1990) note that studies consistently show "distinct differences in teachers' theories of knowledge, beliefs, practices, and patterns of socialization into teaching that are related to particular academic disciplines" (p. 335). Other studies also identify subject specialty as a key factor in teacher action (Hargreaves, 1988; Siskin, 1991), and suggest that these socialization patterns can lead to the development of discipline-based subcultures within high schools, most frequently manifested as departments (Grossman & Stodolsky, 1995). We could expect, then, that, for colleagues within a department, shared disciplinary-based beliefs about content and teaching, may influence how they make sense of and respond to reform policies and initiatives.

Grant (1996, 2003) points out, however, that while school organization and policy influences interact to pull and lead teachers in various ways, there are no predictable or identifiable patterns. This is to be expected, he argues, because teachers inevitably interpret the organizational and policy contexts in which they are situated through their own knowledge, beliefs, and experiences. Clearly teachers' beliefs and their personal practical theories and knowledge (Elbaz, 1983; Clandinin, 1985; Sanders & McCutcheon, 1986) serve as mediating lenses through which teachers define, understand, and perceive these contexts.

A teacher's theories, then, enable him or her to negotiate the myriad issues of organizational structure, student prior knowledge and attributes, and local needs. In this way, the personal theories teachers hold, both individually and collectively as department members, about pedagogy and the nature of their content area subject-matter can be understood as influences on teacher decision making about curriculum and instruction. Furthermore, these beliefs and theories are lenses through which teachers make sense of educational policies and reform efforts, and as such they are mediating forces in the implementation of educational change.

METHOD OF INQUIRY

The data for this case study are drawn from a larger, ethnographic study designed to illuminate the form and content of the teacher culture within a high school department (Fickel, 1998). I met the teachers in the department in the late summer of 1995 when I was involved with a professional development session at Wilson County High School.[1] One of the teachers in the social studies department had been my colleague during my teacher education program and introduced me to his eight department colleagues. Their easy rapport, conversation topics, and seemingly open relationship intrigued me, as it ran counter to so much of the literature on teacher culture. To learn more about the form and consequences of their seemingly collegial culture, I initiated a research study with the teachers at the beginning of that same school year.

Setting and Participants

Wilson County High is a comprehensive, departmentalized school located a suburban/rural county in central Kentucky. The school curriculum is typical of comprehensive high schools, offering students a wide range of required and elective courses in the core discipline areas—humanities, vocational-technical, agricultural, and business. During the years of the study, the school enrolled approximately 1100 students in grades 9–12, and had a certified staff of nearly 70 teachers, as well as three administrators, and three full-time counselors. The student body was fairly representative of the general population demographics in the community—predominately White, middle to upper-middle class students with approximately 8% African American students, and a recent influx of immigrant Mexican families. The county was also home to a custodial-care facility for troubled youth that enrolled about 10–15 students a year at the high school.

The social studies department had a full complement of history and social science specialists in its nine members. Although the student population closely mirrored the community demographics, the department more closely reflected the school's predominately White, male teaching staff: six men and three women, all of whom were White. The two most senior department members were 22 and 13 year veterans, who had spent their entire careers at this school. The 13-year veteran served as the department chair and was completing her third year in this leadership role during the study. The other seven members had been teaching from 2 to 8 years and had all joined the department since 1991. Some of the newer members of the department came to the teaching profession as a second career. Their previous careers included the military, real estate agent, childbirth education, and manufacturing sales. Seven of the department members had attended the same university for either their teacher preparation program or for advanced degrees and had worked with the same social studies educator there. The other two completed their teacher education programs at small private colleges in the state. Two of the teachers commuted daily from the nearby metropolitan area, while the remaining seven lived in Wilson County.

Data Collection

Data collection took place over a 2-year period from the end of September 1995 through the 1996–97 school year, with one final visit in November 1997 to conduct exit interviews. I spent a total of 44 full days on site with the teachers observing in their classrooms, conducting informal and semistructured interviews, and attending department and school faculty meetings.

I planned my visits to coincide, as much as possible, with the regularly scheduled department meetings. During my visits, I observed in classrooms taking field notes on the form and substance of the lessons, trying to capture as much verbatim dialogue as possible. On these days, I also ate lunch with the teachers, and attended department and school faculty meetings. On the days when there were no meetings after school, I usually remained to talk and listen, or do some meaningful "hanging out" with whoever stayed around. Part of this "hanging out" included informal, unstructured, field-based ethnographic interviews (Spradley, 1980). The data from these conversations were captured in field notes. In the spring term of 1996–97, I spent 2-weeks of daily visits during which I shadowed five of the nine teachers for a whole day, and two others for half a day each. I did not shadow two of the department members because, as two of my three key informants, I had previously spent a great deal of time in their classrooms. Finally, I conducted two audio taped, semiformal interviews with each of the department members. The first round of interviews focused on the collegial culture by capturing the department members' individual perceptions of being a teacher in the department. The exit interviews centered around exploring further their perceptions on how the departmental culture affected them as teachers and their individual and collective practice.

Data Analysis

Analysis of the data was on-going and consisted of both contextualizing strategies (Maxwell, 1996) and categorizing strategies. I used contextualizing strategies to analyzed data from the field notes looking for relationships within each text (i.e., each individual field note entry) in order to understand it as a coherent whole. I did this with each subsequent text. Then, I looked across the texts using a categorizing strategy in order to identify patterns and themes across time. This sort of continuous data analysis allowed for the identification of new or alternative categories or themes, as well as the identification of disconfirming data. Such an inductive process is typical of a grounded approach (Glaser & Strauss, 1967), and is frequently used in qualitative case studies (Merriam, 1988).

The purpose of the participant interviews was to capture the insiders' perspectives. Therefore, when I analyzed the interviews I did not use any themes or patterns I had devised from the analysis of the field notes. I followed the same analytic process of first using contextualizing strategies with each interview making marginal notes, which I then used to identify categorical themes and patterns across the texts. I then integrated the themes from the field notes and interviews and reanalyzed the transcripts using these synthesized categories. I found that using categorization and contextualizing strategies together provided a well-rounded account of the data (Maxwell, 1996) and served as a form of triangulation.

Because the teachers were working within a high-stakes policy context, the ethnographic approach captured how they collectively tried to make sense of the various policy mandates, as well as how they collectively responded. The case presented here was crafted by selecting out from the larger ethnographic study data that would provide a snapshot in time to illuminate the complex ways in which the teachers sought to make sense of and responded to Kentucky's policy context of standards, accountability and high-stakes testing from 1995–1997.

POLICY AND ORGANIZATIONAL CONTEXTS: STATE REFORM AND DEPARTMENTAL CULTURE

Educational reform in Kentucky has been, and continues to be, a sweeping and complex effort that embodies and entwines the five streams identified by Little (1993). And, as with most developmental work, it continued to evolve over time (Lusi, 1997). Therefore, what I present here is not an exhaustive examination of the full scope of the reform. Rather, I describe two critical aspects of the policy context during the years in which the ethnographic case study was conducted. I begin by describing the broad and sweeping changes brought about by the Kentucky Educational Reform Act from its inception in 1990 through 1998 when the study ended and follow that with specific details and examples of the content and format of social studies testing.

STATE POLICY: THE KENTUCKY EDUCATION REFORM ACT

For decades, Kentucky consistently ranked in the bottom fifth of states on national educational achievement measures. Such rankings reflected the overall state trend of high drop-out rates, low per-pupil funding, below average scores on national standardized tests, and the low rate of Kentucky residents going on to postsecondary education. Painted with a broad brush, the emerging portrait made these educational issues appear to be uniform statewide. So, these patterns represented a fairly accurate picture of many areas of the state, they hid the few counties, districts, and schools that often met or exceeded the national norms on educational quality indicators. In effect, they masked the inequity in the state's education system.

In the fall of 1985, this inequity surfaced when a lawsuit challenged the equity and adequacy of the state funding provided for education. Four years later, the Kentucky State Supreme Court issued its opinion on the suit, ruling that the existing state system of common schools was unconstitutional. The justices argued that the state had the responsibility of providing sufficient funding so as to provide each child in the state an adequate education. The Court's opinion was that the General Assembly had an "absolute duty ... to re-create, re-establish a new system of common schools in the Commonwealth" (Legislative Research Commission, 1997, p. 8). The resulting state statutes established a new funding structure, provided for a revenue increase, set education goals for students, set requirements for a state assessment and accountability system, and detailed a plan for restructuring the governance of the education system statewide. This sweeping, multifaceted reform became law in July of 1990 with the passage of the Kentucky Educational Reform Act (KERA).

KERA was conceived as a statewide, systemic approach to school reform to recreate the educational system. The three prongs of the reform focused simultaneously on issues of school finance, school governance, and curriculum in an attempt to explicitly interconnect the multiple facets of schooling so as to raise student achievement levels. Part of the curriculum enhancement piece was an assessment system devised as the leveraging agent that would drive the reform and bring about improved student learning under the assumption that what is emphasized on the test influences what gets emphasized in the classroom and thus what students learn. As McDonnell (1994) reports, state policy makers made clear their intention: They wanted "the assessment system and the policies linked to its use to shape not just student outcomes, but also what and how students are taught" (p. 406). Therefore, the format of the assessment system originally focused on performance events, open-ended response items, and writing and mathematics portfolios, so as to force changes in instructional methods and practices at the classroom level that would promote complex thinking, problem-solving and improved communication skills in writing.[2] Advocates of this carrot and stick approach to accountability argued that it was needed in order to compel schools to change fundamentally so as to improve educational quality in Kentucky (Whitford & Jones, 1999).

At this time, Kentucky schools were held accountable for student progress toward the state-defined six learner goals and 75 corresponding academic outcomes that characterize student achievement of the goals. These outcomes were the identified standards of achievement for students and were stated as broad generalizations rather than specific content topics. School and student achievement of these expectations was measured by the state assessment system known as the Kentucky Instructional Results Information System (KIRIS).[3] The KIRIS index was a mathematical model of continual growth toward the state's goal of all students scoring in the proficient category on the various components of the assessment. The target time to reach 100% proficient student achievement was set at 20 years, with progress determined in biennial increments. Thus, every 2 years a school was expected to meet its state-defined threshold score on the index to demonstrate successful progress. Based on progress toward the biennium threshold score, or lack there of, a school was deemed to be in one of four performance levels: success, improving, decline, or in crisis. Schools that met or exceeded their biennium threshold were considered to be successful and the teachers in the school received a financial reward based on the number of students in the school. Schools in the improving category demonstrated progress toward their threshold during one or the other years of the biennium. However, a school that failed to show progress during both years of the biennium was considered to be in decline and those schools that showed no progress or fell below their baseline score or previous biennium threshold were designated in crisis. Schools considered in decline and in crisis could be sanctioned by the state. Sanctions depended on the performance designation and duration of the designation, and included the implementation of a state-mandated improvement plan, the assignment of a "highly skilled certified educator" to oversee the implementation of the plan and potentially taking control of the school.

Assessing Social Studies: Academic Outcomes, Core Content, and Test Items

The academic outcomes established by the state for the social studies were framed as broad cross-disciplinary generalizations rather than as discipline-based topics. The eight social studies outcomes were as follows:

- Students recognize issues of justice, equality, responsibility, choice, and freedom and apply these *democratic principles* to real-life situations.
- Students recognize varying *forms of government* and address issues of importance to citizens in a democracy, including authority, power, civic action, and rights and responsibilities.
- Students recognize varying *social groupings and institutions* and address issues of importance to members of them, including beliefs, customs, norms, roles, equity, order, and change.
- Students interact effectively and work cooperatively with the *diverse ethnic and cultural groups* of our nation and world.
- Students make *economic decisions* regarding production and consumption of goods and services to real-life situations.
- Students recognize the *geographic interaction between people* and their surroundings in order to make decisions and take actions that reflect responsibility for the environment.
- Students recognize continuity and change in *historical events, conditions, trends, and issues* in order to make decisions for a better future.
- Students observe, analyze, and interpret human behaviors to acquire a better understanding of self, others, and *human relationships*. (Kentucky Department of Education, 1993, p. 7; emphasis in original).

Although these academic outcomes provided a general sense of the fundamental understandings students should learn from school in a high-stakes testing environment, they did not provide teachers, schools, or districts with clear indications of the specific history and social studies content that would appear on the state exam. From 1991 until 1996 the only guidance provided to districts regarding tested content ended up being whatever they could deduce from the released test items.

This lack of specificity was intentional. In deference to local school-board control, the state initially tried to steer clear of producing a state curriculum, and so created and distributed a curriculum framework called *Transformations: Kentucky's Curriculum Framework* (Kentucky Department of Education, 1993). This framework was designed to help schools develop local curriculum aligned with the learner goals and academic expectations assessed by the state. However, the high-stakes nature of the assessment and accountability process led to the eventual development of content standards outlining the core knowledge for each content area—mathematics, science, social studies, arts and humanities, practical living and vocational studies, reading, and writing. These documents, known collectively as the *Core Content for KIRIS Assessment*, were provided as working drafts to schools in January 1996 to serve as a foundation for preparing students for the state test.

Rather than flow directly from the eight Academic Outcomes for social studies, the final version of the *Core Content for Social Studies Assessment* was organized in a more traditional discipline-based manner. The five assessment areas included government and civics, culture and society, economics, geography, and history. Each of these areas was "organized around three to four assertions or broad content statements" that were used across the grade level clusters (elementary, middle, high) with bulleted information that highlighted the grade level differences (Kentucky Department of Education, 1999, p. 1). For each assertion, there were several bulleted descriptions of the content that illuminated the assertion and demonstrated how it aligned across the grade levels to create a spiral curriculum for that concept. For example, in the area of history, the second assertion states, "the history of the United States is a chronicle of a diverse people and the nation they formed." One of the grade level descriptions provided for this assertion was as follows:

- Elementary—Native America cultures, both in Kentucky and the United States, had similarities (e.g., gender roles, family organization, religion, values) and differences (e.g. language, shelter, tools, foods, clothing);
- Middle—America's diverse society began with the "great convergence" of European, African, and Native American people beginning in the last fifteenth century;
- High—Disagreements over how Reconstruction should be approached and its various programs led to conflict, constitutional crisis, and limited success (p. 21).

Just as the content of the test continued to evolve over the first few years of implementation, so did the format of the test (Lusi, 1997). Initially the assessment system consisted of performance events (i.e., group problem-solving tasks) and open-ended questions requiring short, on-demand written responses, both of which were given under timed and controlled circumstances, as well as writing and mathematics portfolios. Over time, persistent concerns related to scoring reliability for the performance events and the portfolios led to changes. Eventually, policymakers removed the performance events altogether and reduced the weight of portfolio scores in the scoring index. Of the original assessment format, only the open-ended response questions survived. Thus, they accounted for the majority of a school's score in the content areas, although multiple-choice items eventually were added as well.

For the social studies portion of the test, students were generally expected to answer 10 to 12 open-ended questions. Of these, approximately half were common items to which all students responded. The other half of the questions were divided between a variety of previously validated questions and new questions being test-run. Each year the state released approximately five of the common test items to districts along with the scoring guide and examples of student responses at each performance level. For each open-ended question, student answers were scored on a scale of 0–4, representing a range of performance levels. A score of 4 was considered a "distinguished" response, 3 a "proficient" response, 2 an "apprentice" response, and 1 a "novice" response. A question was given a zero if the student left it blank.

Open-ended questions were usually brief statements of a general social studies principle or concept with a prompt to the student to explain or describe the concept using specific factual information. Graphics or visuals, accompanying some questions, required students to interpret and explain the information. Examples of released items from the 1996–97 common test questions illustrate the more common question format:

> Historically, the North has been an industrial, urban area and the South has been a rural, agricultural area. In the latter part of the 20th century, however, the characteristics of both regions have been changing quickly. Explain reasons for these changes.

> Labor unions began to form in the United States during the late 1800s and early 1900s as the country became more industrialized.

> (a) Describe three conditions workers faced that led to the formation of labor unions in the United States.
> (b) Discuss how the newly formed labor unions changed those conditions.

Clear in the structure of these questions was the expectation that students provide answers drawing on specific historical content and facts, so it was no wonder that teachers and school districts continued to press the state to provide specific information about what would be tested. State educational officials eventually created and distributed the core content documents, but continued to maintain that these should not limit the local school curriculum. Nevertheless, since school test scores meant rewards or sanctions for schools, including the possibility of state takeover for continuous low-performing status[4] the high-stakes nature of the testing system meant that the *Core Content for Assessment* ultimately became a de facto state curriculum.

TEACHING AND LEARNING HISTORY AND
SOCIAL STUDIES IN A HIGH-STAKES CLIMATE

Schools are complex organizational systems comprised of multiple contexts of policy, organizational structures, and personal relationships. These overlapping contexts form the intricate web of the workplace in which teachers engage and participate. As such, these multiple contexts influence teachers, shaping their content and curriculum decision making, their choice of teaching strategies and, ultimately, their students' opportunities to learn. During the years of this study, the teachers in the social studies department at Wilson High School were fully engaged in trying to make sense of the elaborate state reform embodied by the shifting and seemly disparate policies of standards, testing, and accountability. Collectively, they used their shared beliefs about students, teaching, and content as a primary filter in this sense-making process. Together they struggled with the pressures they felt from themselves, the community, and the state accountability system, and worked collaboratively to negotiate a path through these pressures and the potential consequences they held for the curriculum and their practice. Through their struggle, we are offered a window into the complex and varied effects of a high-stakes climate on teachers' work and decision making.

Mediating Lens: Departmental Culture of Shared Beliefs and Principles of Practices

The teachers in the department shared a similar perspective regarding what the goal of the social studies curriculum should be for students. They believed that social studies was about the development of active citizenship and a critically-thoughtful mind. Although each of the department members made similar statements during the individual interviews, the veteran of the department best captured this shared sense of purpose: "I think there is a strong desire ... to produce independent learners who are reflective, critical thinkers ... [who engage in] reflection upon the social world in which they live." This shared understanding of social studies was further evidenced in the department's vision statement:

> We, the Social Studies Department, see social studies as applicable to the real world and a vital part of our students' lives. Our aim is not to provide all the answers, but to encourage students to raise the questions that will take us into the 21st century.

The teachers in the department understood the future to be a process of change in which students would have to be critical thinkers and questioners. Therefore, they thought that education, and social studies in particular, should prepare students for handling and dealing with change by providing a base of knowledge about the world and the intellectual sensibilities and processes for making sense of diverse information.

The teachers also believed that social studies education should focus on the whole student as an individual with cognitive, emotional, social, and moral dimensions. They recognized their work as being intimately involved in the development of human beings who would take on many roles in their life, as parents, neighbors, voters, and friends, as well as employees or workers. As one department member expressed it, "there are life lessons and other things that we try to work on with the kids." For this reason, the teachers in the department believed that students should be at the center of the instructional and learning process. They consistently talked about themselves as teachers who "have kids as their central focus," who are "student oriented." The department chair talked about this instructional orientation in terms of care:

> We care about kids as individuals. We recognize they are different. We appreciate the differences. We don't expect all the students to learn, perform, or behave in exactly the same ways. We all accept them for who they are and where they are. And, then, we try to help them get to wherever it is they need to get.

In recognition of their students' diverse needs, the teachers used multiple strategies to increase the likelihood that students would be active participants in the instruction and in the construction of knowledge about the world. Students' interests and prior knowledge helped guide the teachers as they shaped the curriculum. To get students actively involved in learning, the teachers used instructional strategies such as inquiry-based units, role plays, lectures, text-based and class discussions, independent investigations and research, mock trials, videos and film, primary document analysis, interpretation and creation of maps and visuals, and the infusion of literature into the curriculum. From these multiple forms of instructional strategies, the students produced skits, arts-based interpretations of social science concepts, research papers, letters to the local editor, letters to national or international political or social figures, and learning activities for primary school classes. More traditional assessments, such as quizzes and exams, were also part of the instruction in the department.

Active student participation in the department meant engagement not just with instructional activities. It also meant engaging students in complex ideas and having them use multiple perspectives when exploring an historical era, event, or social or political issue. The teachers did not shy away from having students investigate and grapple with what others might consider taboo topics—African American slavery, U.S. government genocide policy on Native Americans, Japanese internment camps, lynchings, economic inequities, changing women's roles. They saw these topics as fundamental to students' development of a complex worldview and as reflective of the concepts and issues which students themselves felt the need to understand, such as inequity, prejudice, and social stratification. It was with this high level of engagement in mind that one department member commented, "if the kids don't leave the classroom discussing what we talked about, if they don't leave excited, it's been a bad day."

These types of learning activities and assessments were a part of all of the teachers' repertoires, though they were used with varied frequency across the individual members. Over time, and through much discussion and sharing, the teachers had developed a remarkable degree of agreement about what constituted "good teaching." Thus, in effect, they created a context in which each teacher could construct his or her own practice with the tacit support of their colleagues. The only issues of continuing debate and discussion among the members had to do with finding the "right balance" in terms of the frequency of uses of various strategies, and the more contentious issue of whether a chronological or thematic approach to history was best for student learning (Fickel, 1998).

Curriculum Decision Making: Differences Between Required and Elective Courses

Although the department members shared a clear set of beliefs about the goals and best-practices for teaching social studies, a paradox emerged in their practices. The syllabi for the department course offerings showed a distinct difference between the descriptions of the content and curriculum of the *required* U.S. and world history courses and the *elective* social studies courses such as Global Issues, Geography, Cultural Diversity, and Law and Justice.[5] This difference in orientation was also noticeable in how the teachers described and explained their various curricula, as well as in observations of classroom practices in these two types of classes. Although each of the teachers drew from the diverse repertoire of instructional strategies mentioned above and looked for avenues to build on student interests, a stark difference surfaced in the degree to which these practices played out across the required and elective courses.

In practice, the required history courses tended to be organized in a sequential manner and tended to be fact and information-based. The teacher-developed syllabi described these classes as historical survey courses and identified a cursory introduction to historical eras and epochs as the objectives of the course. For example, the syllabus from the World Civilization stated that the purpose of the course was "to familiarize the student with world events from antiquity (1500 B.C.) to the present." There is no indication here that the course would do much more than skim across the historical eras under study in a chronological manner. The topics and periods to be covered included ancient empires (Persian and Greco-Roman), the Roman era, Reformation, Exploration—Africa and China, Industrialism, and the World Wars. This syllabus also suggested that the content of the course was generally Eurocentric, focused on events and history from a European rather than a global perspective; very little of the course content was devoted to exploring the history of cultures from Africa, the Americas, or Asia.

Meanwhile, the syllabi for the elective courses typically stated the objectives in terms of social studies concepts and presented a more holistic and multiple-perspective orientation. For example, the syllabus for the Cultural Diversity course identified the goals as: (1) stimulating positive attitudes in students about the role of cultural differences and (2) recognizing the functions of self and culture in fostering and inhibiting cultural awareness. Further, the syllabus listed five major social science concepts that formed the foundation of the course: perception, culture, discrimination, cultural conflict, and institutional racism.

Asked how they made decisions about the content and curriculum of the courses, the teachers' responses reflected a division between the required history courses and the social studies electives. Their responses also illuminated the complex interplay of teacher's personal beliefs and subject-matter socialization with their organizational and policy context. Like her colleagues in the department, Sara described her general approach to curriculum decisions as relying on her beliefs about what makes a good social studies curriculum, as well as pertinent national standards. However, the differences between the elective and required courses also figured prominently. Sara felt she had "more autonomy" to select the content in her elective courses. The required courses were taught by several teachers, however, and she felt more need to "be consistent" and to "cover more of the same things."

For example, in developing the Global Issues course, Sara relied "mainly on my training and the fact that I wanted the course to be more activity based." She selected the concept of geographical literacy as the course theme because it was a thematic standard released by the National Council for the Social Studies (NCSS) and because recent national studies that indicated students were geographically illiterate resonated with her personal experiences. Further, she felt conceptual knowledge and vivid experiences with geographic terms, ideas, and concepts would be an appropriate foundation for the students' learning in other social studies classes. Therefore, the students engaged in three major learning activities.

First, the students investigated how geographically illiterate they and their community were by conducting a global issues survey among the teachers and students in the school, their parents, and other community members. The students had to devise the survey, conduct it, tabulate it and analyze the results in order to construct their interpretation. From their evidence-based conception of geographic literacy, they began to explore the theme of human/environmental interaction. Second, the students identified and investigated environmental issues around the world through group research projects. Finally, they participated in a simulation of the United Nations where they took on foreign policy issues regarding environmental and population policies. All of these activities and the content selection grew out of Sara's initial decision to use the NCSS standards as a guideline for curriculum development. However, her selection of pedagogical strategies was greatly influenced by her existing professional beliefs about the ultimate goal of social studies and how students should be engaged in the learning process, including providing space for student interests to guide the curriculum content. Because she wanted the course to be activity-based, she explained, "I knew that I had to organize the curriculum around some major activities that would get them excited."

In contrast, Sara's curriculum decision-making process for the required World History course was quite different. She selected content for the course based on the shared sense that department needed to "start looking at what we were doing and making sure that all the world civ classes were covering similar things, and that we [individually] weren't out on the edge somewhere." One facet of this collective desire to be try to be more consistent with the content and topics covered in the course came from the shared sense of doing what is right for students. The department members recognized they had a tendency to teach the historical content and eras they personally knew the most about or enjoyed the most. By discussing the content, they negotiated a shared understanding of that most basic curriculum question, what knowledge is of most worth? However, this collective negotiation and deliberation did not take place in a vacuum. Sara explained that she and her colleagues were also concerned about the need to "be sure the students have the content for the [state] test." She noted that there were "lots of facts and information" on the test and she, like her colleagues, felt a responsibility to "cover the material" so that the students would be familiar with it.

An example of this coverage decision can be seen in one of Sara's lessons on the Middle Ages. On the blackboard she listed six characteristics that defined the era. She began class by asking students to close their eyes and "picture the time period," and then sharing their images. Knights, castles, and jousting abounded. Sara proceeded to give a 45 minute lecture while the students took notes. After the observation, she explained that the Middle Ages was not content that she used to cover in the course. However, this content had recently appeared on a released item from the state test. So, even though according to the district curriculum guideline the high school course in world civilizations was to begin in 1500, she was now including a review of the era in the course.

Clearly, the state test influenced the teachers' content decision making, but it was not the only factor. They still recognized themselves as active agents in the decision-making process. Kevin noted that while they often felt that external forces shaped their decisions, "it is probably really us." When together, he explained, teachers talked about "what we are going to cover, and by the time we've included everything that everyone thinks is important, we are bogged down again in content." As a result of this sense of needing to cover so much material, teachers tended to do more lecturing and direct instruction in the history courses than in the electives. Even so, the teachers enacted other practices in line with their beliefs by including some student-centered and project-based activities in the history courses, such as a group project on world religions in World Civilization and a mock-trail simulation of the Dred Scott Decision in U.S. History.

Expanding and Contracting Curriculum: Negotiating Competing Ends

It is important to note here that the state did not release the *Core Content for KIRIS Assessment* documents until the fall of 1996. So, from 1992 with the first administration of the test until the release of this document, the teachers in the department engaged in an elaborate guessing game, relying on "what we think kids ought to know" and hoping that would served students well on the test.

As noted above, their collective sense of "what students should know" was not the only rubric the Wilson teachers used to guide their curriculum decisions. They also considered the state test, especially the released test items, though on an individual or on an ad hoc basis. In the fall of 1995, the department members decided to conduct a systematic content analysis of the released state test items to get a sense of direction for what content to include in their courses, both the electives and required courses. Teresa explained that they felt the need to do this because the information provided in the state curriculum framework documents was "so disjointed and unconnected that it is really hard to come up with any plan."

During their analysis, the teachers found U.S. history content to be a major focus. This observation was not unexpected given the state's graduation requirement of one credit in U.S. history. The group also noted that test questions covered thousands of years of human history, including multiple civilizations and all the social science disciplines. Since the inception of the testing system, teachers had felt pressed to be sure their students could perform well on the test. Without state guidance about the likely tested content, however, the teachers became increasingly concerned about content coverage. They admitted that their response had been to make the history courses a "rush through time." Even so, they felt they hardly put a dent in it and were concerned that they rarely were able to deal with recent history, about which they thought students might have more interest. Thus, the item analysis only served to reinforce and exacerbate their sense of pressure to cover content, especially historical content.

At the same time, the teacher' analysis did help them resolve two issues. First, the pressure to cover large amounts of content in the history courses raised new concerns about consistency across sections and teachers. Within the department, five or six teachers typically taught the U.S. history course, and three or four teachers taught sections of world history. Creating consistency across course sections had been a lingering concern; they interpreted the wide content demands of the new state test as reason to even more carefully to coordinate the content they covered. To help with this alignment, they developed a course content guideline and a common final exam for the each of the two required courses. Second, the analysis of the released test items also brought at least a temporary resolution to the discussion about a thematic or chronological focus to history. In the history courses, George said, "we are not doing thematic stuff. We made a decision that for now we were going to go on the old fashioned march through time thing."

Resolving the lingering consistency and focus issues resulted in two different responses which reflected differing influences. In response to the perceived need for consistency, teachers revised the required history courses to emphasize chronology, focusing on the breadth of content rather than on deeply engaging students with ideas. At the same time, lectures increased and activity-based strategies decreased, especially in relation to the elective courses. The teachers did not allow their courses to become textbook-driven, but their content and instructional decisions demonstrated a triumph of the state test over their stated beliefs and goals for social studies.

Analyzing test items, however, also inspired innovation and expanded student opportunities to learn. With a proposed change to a block schedule for the 1996–97 school year, the total number of credits a student needed to graduate increased. As a consequence, administrators asked the school departments to expand their course offerings. The social studies department members' response—to create a new, required course for freshmen—drew simultaneously from their shared beliefs about good teaching and learning, as well as the analysis of the test items and their resulting concerns regarding meeting the expectations of state testing.

One influence on the teachers' thinking was the departmental goal of engaging students in social science inquiry, helping them to grapple with the complexity of social issues, and reading beyond the textbook. The teachers emphasized their professional responsibility to help students cultivate the critical and questioning mind so crucial to democratic citizenship. As George explained it, the department had "a strong desire to produce independent learners who are reflective, critical thinkers, [and who engage in] reflection upon the social world in which they live." The group knew that the development of the inquiry skills and critical thinking required cultivation through in-depth and focused study with concepts, themes, problems, or historical eras. Also influencing their thinking was the rise of "social studies groupies," students who, once they took a social studies course, got hooked and kept coming back for more. Every teacher's dream, these were students "willing to speak up in class to express an opinion or challenge an opinion" and who would "actively participate and engage with ideas." One last influence on the teachers was the recognition that the press to cover content in the U.S. history course meant that very complex and multifaceted historical events often came across as one-dimensional. Kevin believed the group had "hamstrung" themselves by trying to cover too much: "We've moved away from a conceptual focus that allows us to explore perspectives and the messiness."

With these considerations in mind, the teachers decided to use the administration request as an opportunity to create a required course for freshmen that allowed for this type of deeper, conceptual learning for all students, and serve as a common base for them to build on in subsequent courses rather than simply create more elective courses.

The department members first considered having the new course address all eight of the social studies academic expectations. However, their content analysis of the test had helped them identify the economic, geographic, and government concepts as the students' weak spots. They agreed that these were areas that they neglected in both the elective and required courses. Therefore, the new class featured these three thematic areas with the local community as the overarching focus. Together, the teachers developed a list of skills they wanted the students to learn along with the instructional activities that would help them develop the skills. Those activities included reading maps, interpreting graphs, reading and analyzing different sources of information, development of a social sciences vocabulary, conflict resolution, public speaking, and oral and written communication. Across the three units of this new course, students would engage in simulations, write a "defend a position" paper, write article abstracts, construct graphs and maps, make oral presentations, and have weekly vocabulary quizzes. The resulting syllabus emphasized the real-world possibilities of the course:

> Social Studies I is a course designed to help students recognize and understand the relationship between people and geography and apply their knowledge in real-life situations, as well as to give students an understanding of and practice in the American political, social, and economic systems. The goal of the course is to provide students with a knowledge base strong enough to help them be successful in other social studies classes and active participants in our community at large....All students will be expected to actively participate in a variety of activities designed to simulate our political, social, and economic systems. Students will work collaboratively on a culminating project that will utilize the thinking skills necessary to become contributing citizens.

This new, collaboratively-designed course reflected the areas of concern highlighted on the state test. Yet, at the same time, it was in keeping with the elective social studies courses in that it was more expansive and conceptually-focused than the required courses offered.

As implemented, the new course rotated students through each of three key content areas—economics, government, and geography—for a 6-week unit culminating in an integrated assessment. Each 6-week unit was taught by a department members with expertise in that area. The teachers engaged the students in various learning opportunities from community field trips to mapping projects. And in keeping with the outcome of helping students become "contributing citizens," the final assessment asked students to identify two aspects of the community that could be improved and to make a proposal for a specific change that could made toward that improvement. So while the required history courses reflected a considerable state test influence, the new freshman requirement reflected the more ambitious ideas of the department's goals.

Test Results: Examining Principles and Questioning Practices

In the fall of 1996, the new freshman course had been introduced and the department members were feeling positive about their collaborative efforts. In late October, however, the previous year's test scores were released and the teachers faced a significant drop in their students' scores. From the inception of the state test, student scores had risen steadily, had consistently been the highest of any Wilson academic department, and had been the highest social studies scores among schools in the surrounding counties. Teachers expected a drop because the state exam moved to the 11th grade from 12th grade, meaning the students had completed only about two-thirds of the U.S. history class before taking the exam. However, scores were even lower than expected.

The low test scores dominated the department meeting that week, and the teachers' disappointment was palpable. Moreover, they learned that the test would be changing yet again next year to a new format. The teachers were clearly tired of "flying the airplane as you build it," a metaphor often used by state education leaders. They expressed anger at having to "keep up with all the changes" and "being accountable when we don't know what for."

The department chair, Teresa, shared her summary of a recent state meeting on testing and the newly released *Core Content for Assessment in the Social Studies*. George commented on the revival of multiple-choice items and the suspension of the performance events, arguing that the state seemed to be "moving away from the original intent of the reform." Teresa reminded the group, "we are accountable" and "need to take a look at what we are doing" to identify areas for improvement. Examining the core content document, they noted that their course curricula seemed to be aligned with it, especially the U.S. and World History courses. However, they believed they were "going to have to make changes in [assessment] strategies."

George admitted that he used few of the open-response type questions like those on the state test. Although students did plenty of writing, in fact, more than ever, they were not doing the "quick, response type" writing, characteristic of the open-response items on the test. His colleagues agreed that they needed to help students become familiar with the exam format. Kevin suggested that the drop in scores might indicate that they were not meeting the needs of their "clients." Maybe, he noted, they were not making the work relevant and engaging for the students. As the conversation bounced around the room Donald, the senior member of the department, quietly asked, "don't you feel that at some point you don't want to compromise or give up our goals, our beliefs about what makes good social studies, what we want for students? Do we agree with this [the test as the goal]?"

Donald's comment brought the conversation to a halt as it pushed the group to consider if they were losing sight of their stated beliefs about social studies education. The near perfect unison of their gentle, affirming nods made it obvious he had struck a chord. However, the silent, reflection on this question was momentary; soon the teachers were back to discussing how to respond to the declining test scores and generating ideas for changes in instructional practices and curriculum materials. Eventually, they agreed to purchase a new U.S. history curriculum series they thought focused on critical thinking, was interactive and engaging for students, offered a well-articulated content strand, while leaving them latitude to supplement the materials with local events that connected to the historical eras. They also decided to give students in each section of the new freshman and the U.S. History courses an open-response question once a week.

During the following spring semester, the department expanded on their plans. They required that all the students in the U.S. History course complete the same open-response question, one of the released test items. During a subsequent department meeting, they scored the responses and discussed their rationale for their scoring. In this way they tried to develop some sense of shared norms about the quality of the responses. They also looked for patterns across and within the students' writing. They noted two main features in the writing. First, students did not write their responses for an unknown audience, but rather responded as if the question was an item for discussion taking place orally in a classroom. Second, because of this more conversational tone in the writing, some students tended toward tangential issues. Therefore, the teachers decided to teach students how to organize a cohesive single-paragraph response by drawing a parallel to the five-paragraph essay format. They also decided to model aloud their own thinking processes as a means to help students write open-ended responses. Finally, they decided to provide individualized feedback to a few students with unique needs.

THE INTERACTING INFLUENCES OF BELIEFS, ORGANIZATION, AND POLICY ON CURRICULUM

Teaching is a highly-complex and situated activity that takes place within the contexts of national, state and local policy, diverse community settings, and various organizational structures. At the center of these multiple contexts, teachers confront and seek to make sense of the different demands placed on them by using their personal practical theories and beliefs as filters to construct an understanding of the context and to make decisions about their practices.

Although researchers have begun to help us better understand the interactive nature of these influences on individual teachers, this chapter provides insight into the ways in which a department collaboratively negotiated these interacting influences of beliefs, organizational structures, and policy. It highlights the ways in which the multifaceted nature of the policy context of state reform, especially the state assessment and accountability system, served as an important context of curriculum influences and change for the teachers in this department.

Thompson (2001) has highlighted the tendency within the current educational rhetoric to conflate what he calls "authentic, standards-based reform," with "high-stakes, standardized, testing-based reform." It is fair to say that this duality existed within the initial years of Kentucky's reform (Jones & Whitford, 1997). In its broadest sweep, policymakers conceived of KERA as an authentic, standards-based reform effort dedicated to changing classroom practice by focusing on performance-based learning and assessment and critical thinking. On the other hand, KIRIS, the accountability system, included a high-stakes test that moved toward standardization. The teachers in the department continuously grappled with this dichotomy, trying to make sense of what it meant for their instructional practices.

In their conversation after the release of the test scores, the teachers confronted this dichotomy head on. They understood KERA as a philosophical framework that encouraged teachers to engage students in more authentic learning activities with the goal of developing life-long learners. That orientation fit with their own deeply held beliefs about teaching and learning social studies. Moreover, the set of assumptions about good teaching embodied in the broader reform publicly validated and supported the instructional practices that these teachers were already using. KERA legitimized their practices in ways that they had not necessarily felt before. Their interpretation and use of the academic expectations as a set of common goals for all students provided supported their individual and collaborative efforts.

In developing the freshman class, the Wilson teachers negotiated the mixed messages they perceived in the state curriculum and assessment policies in a way that enabled them to create a cohesive and interconnected set of learning experiences. The state test influenced their decision making in this instance. At the same time, the teachers interpreted the test through their shared goals for the social studies and the fit with their sense of good practice. We can see here the interactive nature of beliefs and policies, and the ways these influences intersect (Grant, 1996, 2003). Managing the state test expectations together with their strong beliefs about teaching and learning social studies, the teachers revamped their practice in ways that created expanded opportunities to learn for students.

And yet, while crafting this middle road, the teachers faced consequences arising from the high-stakes testing context of the reform. Even before the release of the *Core Content for Assessment* document, the teachers in the department felt pressed to cover content in their required history courses. The growing sense of pressure within a high-stakes climate affected their decisions around content as they focused on chronological coverage. The test also led them to make changes in their assessment practices. Over time the teachers in the department began slowly shifting the writing tasks, especially in the required history courses, to match the testing format. This was evident in their decision to use more open-ended response prompts and to explicitly teach the students how to answer these types of questions. In other words, they began to highlight test-taking strategies, rather than the real-life, authentic application of knowledge that was advocated in the broader statement of KERA reform goals. It seems that the longer they worked within the high-stakes climate, the more acutely they felt that their pedagogical decision making was being proscribed and limited. As Kevin explained, he and his colleagues were "really struggling" because they felt "confined by it [the test].... We're bogged down in content. Even though we say we should be skills based and are going to deal with concepts and themes, we can't.... By the time we've got it all in [content] it's too much for the time we are allotted."

Within this context of interacting influences of state and local reform policy and school organization, these teachers developed a collaborative departmental culture with a shared set of beliefs about teaching generally, and teaching history and social studies in particular. This sense of collegiality meant that the individuals need not go it alone. Rather, their collaborative departmental relationship allowed them to approach reform as a group problem to be discussed, questioned, and dealt with collectively. Their shared beliefs about social studies and teaching served as a filter for both interpreting and deciding how to respond to the various aspects of state reform. In this way, they came to understand that state reform offered professionally liberating opportunities, as well as constraints to their practice (Cornbleth, 2002).

FINAL THOUGHTS

The teachers in the Wilson social studies department are highly committed professionals with clear educational aims and a vast knowledge base about sound instructional practices. However, the state policy context began to hinder the department's shared vision of cultivating thoughtful classrooms that foster critical citizenship through inquiry and collective grappling with historic and modern ideas, issues, and problems. At the least, the pressure to perform on the test began to curtail somewhat the use of innovative practices and divergent curriculum content. At its most detrimental, this pressure threatened to undercut such instructional strategies and result in narrowing and limiting students' access to knowledge.

After all, one might ask, "how will these activities and content knowledge help the student perform well on the state exam?"

Within the national rhetoric about standards and accountability, the stated goal has consistently been that of providing educational experiences that prepare students for the complex and unknown situations they are likely to encounter throughout their lives. However, the findings of this case study suggest that state testing used for high-stakes accountability ultimately may divert teachers and the educational community from that goal. High-stakes testing appears to press teachers to focus on preparing kids for test-taking in ways that limit not only the subject-matter content, but the intellectual manner in which students engage with content. Thus, rather than expanding students' access to knowledge, standards and testing may have the unintended consequence of limiting students' knowledge and their opportunities to learn.

NOTES

1. Pseudonyms have been used for participant names and locations.
2. The test has undergone numerous changes in the last decade. In 1998 performance events and the math portfolio were removed, and content-area multiple-choice tests were added.
3. The accountability system has since been renamed Commonwealth Accountability Testing System (CATS).
4. In 1999, the Kentucky Department of Education also released a Program of Studies for high school social studies. The document reflects similar content found in the Core Content for Assessment document. At the time of the study presented here, this regulatory document had not been released.
5. The Commonwealth of Kentucky requires students to complete three credits in social studies for graduation. Wilson County required students to complete four credits. At Wilson, World History and U.S. History were both year-long, one-credit required courses. The other two credits required for graduation could be accrued by taking any combination of the year-long, one-credit A.P. courses or the half-credit, semester-long elective courses offered by the department.

REFERENCES

Bernstein, B. (1971). On the classification of educational knowledge. In M. F. Young (Ed.), *Knowledge and control: New directions for the sociology of education* (pp. 47–69). New York: Collier Macmillan.

Clandinin, D. J. (1985). Personal practical knowledge: A study of teachers' classroom images. *Curriculum Inquiry, 15,* 261–385.

Corbett, H., & Wilson, B. (1991). *Testing, reform, and rebellion*. Norwood, NY: Ablex.

Cornbleth, C. (2002). What constrains meaningful social studies teaching. *Social Education, 63*(3), 186–190.

Elbaz, F. (1983). *Teacher thinking: A study of practical knowledge*. London: Croon Helm.

Elmore, R., Abelmann, C., & Fuhrman, S. (1996). The new accountability in state education reform: From process to performance. In H. F. Ladd (Ed.), *Holding schools accountable: Performance-based reform in education* (pp 65–98). Washington, DC: The Brookings Institute.

Elmore, R, Peterson, P., & McCarthy, S. (1996). *Restructuring in the classroom: Teaching, learning, and school organization*. San Francisco: Jossey-Bass.

Fickel, L. H. (1998). *Teacher culture and community: An ethnographic case study of a high school social studies department*. Unpublished doctoral dissertation, University of Louisville, KY.

Fullan, M. (1982). *The meaning of education change*. Toronto: OISE Press.

Glaser, B. G., & Strauss, A. L. (1967). *The discovery of grounded theory*. Hawthorn, NY: Aldine de Gruyter.

Grant, S. G. (1996). Locating authority over content and pedagogy: Cross-current influences on teachers' thinking and practice. *Theory and Research in Social Education, 24*, 237–272.

Grant, S. G. (2003). *History lessons: Teaching, learning, and testing in U.S. high school classrooms*. Mahwah, NJ: Erlbaum.

Grossman, P., & Stodolsky, S. (1995). Content as context: The role of school subjects in secondary school teaching. *Educational Researcher, 24*(8), 5–11.

Hargreaves, A. (1994). *Changing teachers, changing times: Teachers' work and culture in the postmodern age*. New York: Teachers College Press.

Hargreaves, A. (1988). Teaching quality: A sociologic analysis. *Journal of Curriculum Studies, 20*(3), 211–231.

Hoffman, J., Assaf, L., & Paris, S. (2001). High-stakes testing in reading: Today in Texas, tomorrow? *The Reading Teacher, 54*(5), 482–494.

Johnson, S. M. (1990). The primacy and potential of high school departments. In M. W. McLaughlin, J. E. Talbert, & N. Bascia (Eds.), *The context of teaching in secondary schools: Teachers' realities* (pp. 167–184). New York: Teachers College Press.

Jones, K., & Whitford, B. L. (1997). Kentucky's conflicting reform principles. *Kappan, 79*(4), 276–281.

Kentucky Department of Education. (1993). *Transformations: Kentucky's curriculum framework* (Vols. I & II). Frankfort, KY: Author.

Kentucky Department of Education. (1999). *Core content for social studies assessment*. Retrieved from www.education.ky.gov/KDE/Instructional+Resources/ Curriculum+Documents+and+Resources/Core+Content+for+Assessment/ default.htm

Knapp, M. S., Bramburg, J. D., Ferguson, M. C., & Hill, P. T. (1998). Converging reforms and the working lives of frontline professionals in schools. *Educational Policy, 12*(4), 397–418.

Legislative Research Commission. (1997). *Kentucky Education Reform Act: A citizen's handbook*. Frankfort, KY: Author.

Linn, R. L. (2000). Assessments and accountability. *Educational Researcher, 29,* 4–16.

Little, J. W. (1982). Norms of collegiality and experimentation: Workplace conditions of school success. *American Educational Research Journal, 19*(3), 325-340.

Little, J. W. (1993). Teachers' professional development in a climate of educational reform. *Educational Evaluation and Policy Analysis, 15*(2), 129–151.

Lusi, S. (1997). *The role of state departments of education in complex school reform*. New York: Teachers College Press.

Maxwell, J. A. (1996). *Qualitative research design: An interactive approach*. Thousand Oaks, CA: Sage.

McDonnell, L. M. (1994). Assessment policy as persuasion and regulation. *American Journal of Education, 102,* 394–420.

McLaughlin, M. W. (1990). The Rand Change Agent Study revisited: Macro perspectives and micro realities. *Educational Researcher, 19*(9), 11–16.

McLaughlin, M. W., & Talbert, J. E. (1990). The contexts in question: The secondary school workplace. In M. W. McLaughlin, J. E. Talbert, & N. Bascia (Eds.), *The context of teaching in secondary schools: Teachers' realities* (pp. 1–14). New York: Teachers College Press.

McLaughlin, M. W., & Talbert, J. E. (1993). *Contexts that matter for teaching and learning*. Stanford, CA: Stanford University Press.

McNeil, L. (2000). *Contradictions of school reform: Educational costs of standardized testing*. New York: Routledge.

Merriam, S. B. (1988). *Case study research in education: A qualitative approach*. San Francisco: Jossey-Bass.

Miller, J. P., & Seller, W. (1985). *Curriculum perspectives and practices*. New York: Longman Press.

Sanders, D., & McCutcheon, G. (1986). The development of practical theories of teaching. *Journal of Curriculum and Supervision, 2,* 50–67.

Sarason, S. (1980). *The culture of school and the problem of change* (2nd ed.). Boston: Allyn and Bacon.

Segall, A. (2003). Teachers' perceptions of the impact of state-mandated standardized testing: The Michigan Educational Assessment Program (MEAP) as a case study of consequences. *Theory and Research in Social Education, 31*(3), 287–325.

Siskin, L. S. (1991). Departments as different worlds: Subject subcultures in secondary schools. *Educational Administration Quarterly, 27*(2), 134–160.

Siskin, L. S. (1994). *Realms of knowledge: The academic department*. Philadelphia: Falmer.

Smith, M. L. (1991). Put to the test: The effects of external testing on teachers. *Educational Researcher, 20*(5), 8–11.

Spradley, J. P. (1980). *Participant observation*. New York: Holt, Rinehart and Winston.

Stecher, B. M., Barron, S., Kaganoff, T., & Goodwin, J. (1998). *The effects of standards-based assessment on classroom practices: Results of the 1996-97 RAND survey of Kentucky teachers of mathematics and writing* (CSE Tech. Rep. No. 582). Los

Angeles: University of California, Center for Research on Evaluation, Standards, and Student Testing (CRESST).

Tabachnick, B. R., Popkewitz, T., & Zeichner, K. (1980). Teacher education and the professional perspectives of student teachers. *Interchange 10*(4), 12–29.

Talbert, J. E. (1995). Boundaries of teachers' professional communities in U.S. high schools: Power and precariousness of the subject department. In L. S. Siskin, & J. W. Little, (Eds.), *The subjects in question: Departmental organization and the high school* (pp. 68–94). New York: Teachers College Press.

Thompson, S. (2001). The authentic standards movement and its evil twin. *Kappan, 82*(5), 358–362.

Whitford, B. L., & Jones, K. (1999). Assessment and accountability in Kentucky: How high stakes affects teaching and learning. In A. Hargreaves, A. Lieberman, M. Fullan, & D. Hopkins, (Eds.), *International handbook of educational change* (pp. 1163–1178). Dordrect, Netherlands: Kluwer

Zeichner, K. M., & Gore, J. M. (1990). Teacher socialization. In R. W. Houston, M. Huberman, & J. Sikula (Eds.), *Handbook of research on teacher education* (3rd ed., pp. 329–348). New York: Macmillan.

CHAPTER 6

TEACHING IN THE AGE OF ACCOUNTABILITY

Measuring History or Measuring Up to It?

Avner Segall

I came to Michigan State University as a new faculty member in 1999, the same year the state-mandated social studies test—the Michigan Evaluation Assessment Program (MEAP)—was administered for the first time. Coming from Canada, a country that allows its teachers much more freedom than that allowed their counterparts in the United States, I was confused, if not overwhelmed by the phenomenon called the MEAP and the discourse about state standards and benchmarks that went along with it. The very idea that better practice would be achieved by regulating and monitoring teachers and holding them accountable to students' results on unauthentic tests designed by outsiders was, in many ways, antithetical to the new social studies curriculum guide produced by Ministry of Education in British Columbia, Canada only a year before I moved south of the 49th parallel. In Canada, a more traditional curriculum was being replaced by an open-ended, thematic curriculum guide; the trend in the United States seemed very much the reverse. Indeed, trusted to make

Measuring History: Cases of State-Level Testing Across the United States, 105–132
Copyright © 2006 by Information Age Publishing
All rights of reproduction in any form reserved.

curricular choices even in light of provincial end-of-school tests, Canadian teachers appeared to have more freedom and autonomy in their classrooms than their colleagues in the United States.

What is intended to implicate teachers, I quickly learned, also implicates colleges of education that prepare future teachers. The first department meeting I attended as a faculty member was devoted largely to state-mandated standards and testing and the ways we, as a department of teacher education, ought to respond. Although it was easy to engulf oneself in this kind of discourse, a discourse that, on the one hand strongly opposed the new wave of imposed standardization and, on the other hand, recognized the need to abide by it—I chose to simply ignore it and concentrate on my own work. This was partly due to my hope that, as with most imposed initiatives in education, this one would soon pass. But my attempt to ignore (Felman, 1982) this discourse mostly reflected my belief that by participating in it—in either of its manifestations—I was rewarding those who had the power to raise that particular conversation to the top of the educational agenda, participating in a game not only whose results were troubling to me but one in which mere participation, I believed, would legitimize its creators and the agendas promoted by them. I strongly believed that what was being advanced in the guise of accountability and higher standards was a mechanism to distract the educational community from focusing on what actually matters. In a way, I saw it as laying a minefield in front of educators at all levels, who, once in it, could do little more than find a way to get out of it safely or be blown up by it. Preoccupied with finding the mines and attempting to dismantle them required that other, more pressing thoughts—for example, how to make education more meaningful, accessible, equitable, democratic, and just—must be suspended in that process.

Yet, as the cacophony of federal and state imperatives grew louder, and as the consequences became more real and immediate, I could no longer avoid examining their implications: The MEAP minefield seemingly surrounded me. So in 2001–2002, with the support of a small seed grant from my university, I conducted a study of the impact of the MEAP on social studies teachers and teaching. Having explored much of the existing literature dealing with the issue (e.g., Finn, 1995; Firestone & Mayrowetz, 2000; Haney, 2000; Hursh, 2000; Kohn, 2001; Linn, 2000; Meier, 2000; Ravitch, 1995), it appeared to me that what was missing from the testing discussion was the voice of classroom teachers—the ones most impacted by state mandated standards and testing. The need to incorporate such voices became increasingly clear to me through my work with practicing teachers. Part of my responsibility at Michigan State University has been to head the internship year of our social studies secondary teacher education program. In that capacity, I have worked closely with mentors—practicing teachers in whose classrooms our student teachers intern during their fifth year of teacher preparation. Those mentor teachers have pointed to the MEAP as the factor most negatively impacting their practice. That state-mandated testing has an impact on teaching is beyond question (Grant, 2000). What was of interest to me, however, was how this impact came into being, how it operated, and with what consequences.

Incorporating teachers' voices as I attempted to answer these questions meant one more thing: I did not wish to simply conduct research *on* or *about* teachers; I wanted to do so *with* and *for* them. Coming from a critical perspective, I believe that in order for research to matter it needs to be praxical (Lather, 1986), to take a stand, to advocate something and/or for some body. Although this may sound radical for those not in the critical camp, its radical nature is merely the result of being overt about such issues. All research is inherently ideological in the sense that it advocates something, even if that something is the idea that advocacy is unacceptable—a means to preserve the appearance and status of research as scientific, removed, and objective. The ideological nature of more traditional, "scientific" studies is not called into question since they comply with the acceptable, mainstream paradigm of research. As Derrida (1979) noted, scholarly communities are willing to bear more readily the most apparent revolutionary "content," as long as that content does not touch upon the accepted and acceptable borders of method and language and all the juridico-political contracts they guarantee. Part of my intent, then, was to move beyond much of the existing research about testing, a research literature that examines what takes place in classrooms without implicating it in the broader structures and discourses that give rise and meaning to such practice, a research literature that calmly addresses policy responses yet avoids an engagement with the ethical ramifications of policy on the lives of those it most impacts. (For exceptions, see, e.g., Corbett & Wilson, 1991; Firestone, Mayrowetz, & Fairman, 1998; Grant, 2000, 2001; Mathison & Freeman, 2003; McNeil, 2000; Smith, 1991).

METHODOLOGY

This chapter combines findings from my initial study (Segall, 2003) and those generated by a smaller, follow-up study a year later. The first study was conducted (2001–2002) with five practicing secondary social studies teachers: Susan, Debbie, Seth, Matt, and Kevin.[1] Participants self-selected to participate in this study following a general announcement that I was interested in exploring teachers' perceptions of the MEAP and its impact during a meeting I regularly conduct with a group of about 30 social studies teachers affiliated with my university's teacher education program. Of the five participants, three taught high school, the other two taught middle school. At the time of the study, four of the teachers were tenured with 5 or more years of teaching experience; Kevin was in his first year of teaching. Three of the teachers had a masters degree either in education or in one of the disciplines comprising the social studies and one was in the process of completing course work toward that degree. Other than Kevin, all others had administered the MEAP in their classrooms at least twice.

Data Collection

In the original study, 2 to 3-hour, in-depth, semistructured interviews were conducted with each participant. Questions guiding these interviews focused on exploring teachers' perceptions of the MEAP and its impact on their teaching and on them as teachers as well as on how teachers responded to the test and its imperatives in their classrooms. In the follow-up study, conducted late in 2003, I conducted another round of interviews with Kevin, Matt, and Seth, three of the original participants.[2] The intent of the second study was to elicit participants' responses to the first study and the theories generated by it as well as to provide data that might extend my understandings, especially with regard to the impact of the MEAP on history education. Teachers' ability to separate history education from social studies in relation to the MEAP, however, was more difficult than I had expected. This argument has two sources: First, the MEAP is a social studies test; it is not separated into tests for each subject area. Second, and more importantly I would argue, the impact of the MEAP is more profound at the level of teachers as professionals than at the level of their actual subject matter teaching. That is, its impact is primarily ontological—affecting teachers' sense of being in their classrooms—rather than the content and/or pedagogy in those classrooms. Consequently, a history teacher need not be impacted any differently than a teacher of world cultures.

Data Analysis

In both parts of the study, my primary concern was not with what social studies teachers do and no longer do in classrooms as a result of the MEAP. Rather, I tried to avoid the "fetish of experience" by examining how teachers came to perceive the MEAP as a phenomenon that is broader than the test itself, a phenomena that tests students' content understandings at the same time that it works to sanction preferred ways of thinking and being as it includes/excludes certain meanings and secures or marginalizes particular ways of behaving (Giroux, 1996, p. 48). Of interest to me were teachers' perceptions (Goodman & Adler, 1985; Heilman, 2001; Richardson & Placier, 2001; Ross, 1987) of the MEAP and how such perceptions then surfaced in teachers' views of themselves as teachers. Consequently, this study did not involve observations in classrooms. Instead, teachers were interviewed outside of their classrooms, providing a space for critical reflection about their practice in those classrooms and its relation to broader issues influencing it. I did so because I believe that although the MEAP is "real"—an external measure mandated by the state that is of a particular format, comes at specific, predetermined intervals, and is accompanied by certain rewards and punishments—what the MEAP means to teachers and how they respond to it are largely dependent on teachers' perceptions. These perceptions are not constructed by the test itself but are given definition and body through teachers' experiences with the test and the broader discourses and practices surrounding it that they encounter within the various communities in which they work (Corbett & Wilson, 1991; van den Berg, 2002).

THE MEAP AND ITS CONTEXTS

Like any educational phenomena, the MEAP is broader that the sum of teachers' and students' experience with it. That is, although the test is administered in classrooms, its meaning and significance are constructed in contexts well beyond the classroom walls—in the operations of the state, in the media, and in the larger school culture. In this section, I explore how the MEAP has been constructed in and through these arenas and how that construction gives the test its particular substance.

The State

Following a growing trend in the United States for more standardization and accountability in education, the Michigan Department of Education (MDE) adopted a set of content standards and benchmarks in social studies (see Appendix A) and in other subject areas with the purpose of describing what students should know and be able to do at each grade level. Designed to operate in conjunction with the standards and benchmarks is the MEAP—a tool intended to measure the extent to which each student has mastered the presumably significant state standards in each subject area. Although the MEAP has been administered since 1989, the first social studies test was administered in 1999. Michigan students currently take the 90-minute social studies test three times, in Grades 5, 8, and 11.

What began as a rather ineffective measure—more than 20% of students across Michigan and 90% of students in some of the more affluent districts exempted themselves from the MEAP prior to 1999—has become a comprehensive, all-encompassing test that leaves few students untested. Several actions account for this shift. Prominent among them is a system of state-initiated rewards and punishments attached to the MEAP. Each year, every school receives a report card reflecting its MEAP results. Schools with low MEAP scores must submit a report to the MDE detailing a plan ensuring that students learn what is expected at each grade level. Low MEAP scores can lead to state takeover of a school and/or district as was the case with the Detroit Public Schools system in 1999.

Accompanying these sticks are some carrots. Using portions of its annual $325 million share of a multistate tobacco settlement, the MDE established two awards to be given to schools and individual students who do well on the MEAP. The Michigan Merit Award, in the form of $2500 scholarships to institutions of higher education for high school students and $500 for middle school students, is given to students who pass the MEAP in reading, writing, math, and science. Social studies is excluded from the formula and students' scores on the social studies test do not count toward that award. MDE also rewards schools whose students do well on the MEAP in all subject areas, including social studies. Schools that achieve high scores or that make major improvements in scores can win the governor's Golden Apple award worth at least $50,000 toward school improvement.

The Media

The impact of the MEAP on teachers and teaching, however, goes well beyond the sticks and carrots dished out by state government. Indeed, the largest impact of the MEAP may be that outside of education proper (Segall, 2003). This impact emerges largely from the media reporting on the MEAP and its results. With no direct power over curriculum and instruction, this discourse nevertheless plays an important role in defining the MEAP. Test results appearing on the front pages of newspapers and in television newscasts build a sense of its importance. The media, as Haladyna, Haas, and Allison (1998) note, matters: "Legislators talk about the test scores. School board members either break out the champagne to celebrate high scores or blame the superintendent who, in turn, blames

the teachers for low scores" (p. 262). And poor scores can "prompt editorial writers to lament the sorry state of schools, often criticizing the quality of teaching, as if nothing else contributed" (p. 262). Such media
publicity not only builds or breaks a district's reputation, but often pits
one district against the other. "When those things come out in the
media," said Matt, "it's a personal slam. It's like I'm not doing my job
right. And nobody wants that in his evaluation. I just don't think it's fair."
Confirming Haladyna et al.'s (1998) findings, Matt added:

> We never have a reporter come into our room and just sit down and say,
> "Hey, that was the coolest project I've seen about Michigan history. I'm
> going to go write an article about that in the [local paper]." All we get from
> journalists, following the state report card is, "Why is this a C school?" Well,
> because our MEAP scores are low. We don't teach very well to the MEAP.
> And it comes from all angles, not just the press but what the press writes
> gets to the superintendent and the superintendent says, "Well, I need to
> raise my MEAP scores because if I don't fewer parents will be sending their
> kids to this school—with school choice and everything—and that will mean
> budgetary problems because of less state funding which depends of the
> number of students in each school."

Matt's point is simple: In the conversation around standards and tests,
the media's voice is loud and pervasive.

Schools and Teachers

Although policymakers' and media voices are important, the impact of
the MEAP cannot be understood without an examination of what the test
entails in the culture of schools. With imperatives and incentives coming
from within the education system and outside of it, the adoption of the
MEAP seems an offer teachers, administrators, and parents could not
refuse. For beyond the issue of relating school accreditation to MEAP
scores and proposals to reward schools whose students do well on the
MEAP and punish those that do not, there is the persistent issue of reputation and public perception when results are published in the media.
Before delving deeply into the teachers' responses to the test, I explore
the larger context in which such responses are embedded. I thus begin by
outlining the larger issues of the school-wide social studies curriculum in
the age of the MEAP.

The administration of the new MEAP at defined intervals that do not
necessarily correspond to existing curricula sequences means that schools
have reorganized their courses. Seth describes the curricular changes he
and his colleagues have made:

> We were told [by a representative of the MDE] that the scope and sequence of the MEAP would require that students take government in the 9th grade. We used to give that course in 12th grade, but in order to allow students to answer questions on government in the MEAP they will be taking in 11th grade, the course had to be moved to 9th grade which I thought was silly, because seniors are the people you really need to encourage to study government because at that age they are a little bit more worldly; they've been out in the world and they've maybe experienced some government ... and they're going to be voting. History would have to be moved from the 11th grade to the 10th grade for the same reasons.

Susan notes that curricular changes within courses are also necessary:

> Geography and economics needed to be emphasized since they are both a very big part of the MEAP. We were teaching economics at the senior level, but that meant it would be too late for students taking the MEAP in 11th grade. So, pretty much everyone in Michigan had to adjust their curriculum.

Impacting most every school in Michigan, these curricular changes—not a result of pedagogical decisions to enhance learning, but of an imposed directive in order to accommodate a test—have become a point of contention with teachers. Believing that such changes are educationally counter-productive (or, as Seth put it, "silly"), teachers resent the intrusion into their professional domain. Kevin describes a brewing resentment of the state's influence:

> There is some resentment from teachers, especially those who've been in the system for a while because they feel that the MEAP test, and the social studies MEAP in particular, was a way for the state to dictate curriculum which normally it wouldn't be able to. This is a way for them to indirectly dictate what is going to be taught and how it's going to be taught. I think some people feel that, as a teacher, you go through a certification process that is more rigorous now than it's probably ever been, with the certification tests and all, so you're a qualified person, you're a professional. So why not let me do what you hired me to do? It's all as if there's some distrust going on and has to do with issues of respectability or the lack thereof. I think it's almost that the attitude of the state is, we don't trust you to educate people on your own so we're going to tell you what to do. And that causes resentment for teachers: You don't respect us, you don't think we're good enough because you obviously don't think that on our own we can get these thing accomplished. And so I think that that's where a lot of the tension comes from. I think it's a respect issue.

Coupled with the notions of imposition, distrust, and the lack of respect, is the idea, much emphasized in the literature (e.g., Gibson, 1999;

McNeil, 2000; Smith, 1991) and, at times in the local press, that although the MEAP attempts to evaluate educational progress, it mostly evaluates socio-economic factors. Despite Smith and Niemi's (2001) compelling argument that results of standardized tests correlate more strongly with good teaching than with socioeconomic factors, teachers like Seth, Susan, and Matt who teach in blue-collar and/or urban districts see the MEAP results as inextricably linked to students' social class. Seth notes the distinct patterns between students' performance in high and low SES schools:

> All the rich areas do well. But how about Detroit, a large city with a high minority population and struggling public schools? Does it surprise anybody that kids there aren't scoring well? And does it surprise anybody that in the majority of schools in the wealthy areas kids are getting high scores on the MEAP and then getting the scholarships?

In Seth and his peers' eyes, the MEAP evaluates teachers on factors such as SES over which they have little control. Still, the demand to improve MEAP scores regardless of students' SES is conveyed to teachers on a regular basis by school and district administrators. As Matt puts it, "There is constant push, pull, pressure, whatever term you want to put on it, to do things in a way that will make them more successful on that test." The degree and manner in which this message surfaces varies. In more affluent districts, where students tend to do well on the MEAP, expectations to improve are conveyed explicitly. According to Debbie, who teaches in such a district, her school principal emphasizes MEAP scores "big time!"

> We get the transparencies thrown up on the overhead projector and take a look at how we did this year compared to other years. And, of course, they're in the newspaper all the time. It's plastered all over and schools' reputations depend on that.

As for the district level, Debbie recalls memos to teachers announcing that "there are all kinds of workshops dealing with [the tests]" and carrying the message of "you will do this [for the MEAP]." Kevin, who also teaches in an affluent district, reports similar pressures. Interactions with the social studies department chair in his school often consist of MEAP-related directives:

> He'll say, "you have to be here by this time, you have to do this and you have to do this," and a lot of it is all MEAP stuff.... It's all, "You have to have the kids do six practice MEAP extended response essays by this time. You have to do this MEAP economics packet. You have to do this MEAP civics packet." He sends all this stuff to me [saying], "you have to give them a quiz

on the map of the United States," all things that we normally wouldn't do if it wasn't for the MEAP. So, there's pressure…so that when students take the MEAP they won't only have the knowledge down, but they'll also understand the format of the test and be good MEAP test-takers.

In smaller, primarily blue-collar districts, where students tend not to score well on the MEAP, the expectations of and pressure from building administrators are more implicit. Susan describes the tacit pressure that accompanies media reports:

I have not had anybody come to me and say, "your students are not meeting up to the standards." But when the scores are published in the paper, and although we do better than the state average, when you compare our scores to those of the richer districts around us, we still look poor.

Compounding Susan's frustration is the lack of administrative direction or support for her efforts:

There's no monies or time allowed for you to extend or advance yourself in learning these [MEAP related] things. Any workshop or anything I go to has to be totally driven from within my own self—not by directives from anybody else. They basically just say, "make sure the kids pass the MEAP," and that's it.

As Susan's experience illustrates, the lack of direct pressure from administrators does not mean an absence of pressure. School time and resources for teachers' professional development are denied at the same time that teachers are told, "make sure the kids pass the MEAP." This contradiction shifts responsibility for MEAP preparation from the institution to individual teachers. It also denies teachers the resources to fulfill that responsibility, relying instead on teachers' self-motivation—their desire to help out their students, the fear of "looking poor," not to mention their own time and pocketbook—to fill the void.

Although the different stories teachers tell illustrate that the school and district-level discourses and practices surrounding the MEAP are by no means universal, none leave their authors content. Whether by explicit or implicit language, through denial of resources or being bombarded with them, teachers seem frustrated, confused by knowing too little or too much. In short, the MEAP appears to undermine rather than support teachers' confidence in their ability to teach social studies in meaningful ways. Yet, as the next section of this chapter illustrates, the relationship between the MEAP and good teaching (or any kind of teaching, for that matter) is more complex than initially meets the eye.

TEACHERS, TEACHING, AND THE MEAP

Most of my conversations with teachers centered around the kind of changes—real or perceived—they believed the MEAP required of them as teachers in classrooms. Although teachers often spoke of deep curricular and pedagogical changes necessitated by the MEAP, the significance of the changes teachers asserted did not seem to pan out upon analysis of their responses. Teachers might be making some changes with regard to the content of their courses, but few pedagogical changes seem apparent (Firestone et al., 1998; Grant, Gradwell, Lauricella, Derme-Insinna, Pullano, & Tzetzo, 2002). This does not mean that their teaching has not been impacted by the MEAP. What it does mean is that the impact has been generated more at the ontological than at the pedagogical level. In other words, the clearest impact of the MEAP is on how teachers understand their teaching of social studies—their level of investment, commitment, and sense of professionalism—rather than on their pedagogical decisions. I make that claim not only by examining what teachers did say, but also by what they did not say implicating the explicit with that which was null in their statements. To do so, however, one must first begin with what teachers did disclose.

The MEAP and Teachers' Content Decisions

Under pressure from district and school administrators as well as from the media and parents, the teachers in this study view the MEAP as a force they cannot afford to ignore. At the broad level, this means that teachers constantly think of the MEAP as they plan for and teach. "Every time we step into the classroom to start the school year," Susan explains, "one of the end results needs to be: Are these kids going to be ready to take the MEAP? And are they going to do well?" Although this sense does not mean teachers spend the year simply teaching to the MEAP, she adds, "you always teach with the pressure of the MEAP hovering over you."

At a more specific level, not being able to ignore the MEAP means that teachers feel a need to emphasize or de-emphasize particular topics within existing courses. As an example, Seth explains that teachers of world history courses must eliminate deep discussions about topics like the Middle Ages, the Crusades, the Renaissance, or the Reformation in order to make room for current issues, such as the Middle East that often appear on the test. "There's a lot of pressure," Seth claims, "to get to current issues because they're on the MEAP. You've got to get to the Middle East!"

Kevin offers a different example, of reshuffling topics within a course rather than abandoning them. He explains why he and other eighth grade teachers in his school can no longer teach early American history in chronological order:

> We have to start with the Constitution, because there are a lot of constitutional principles on the MEAP. We're afraid that if we do it in order, by the time we get to the Constitution, it's going to be so close to the MEAP that we may not focus as much on that as we should. So we start with that at the beginning and then go backwards: Do the Constitution, the Core Democratic Values, then backtrack to the colonial times and work our way forward from there.

In these examples, teachers speak of the MEAP and its curricular mandates as instruments that require or seem to require them to teach some topics rather than others or to order topics differently than they might otherwise. They see a test that dictates curriculum decisions rather than simply assessing what is taught—a test that drives rather than reflects teaching.

But more than requiring certain content in a certain sequence, teachers see the test as a restricting force, as something that prevents them from doing certain things in their classrooms. Examples offered by participants in the initial part of the study included not being able to invite in guest speakers, go on field trips, engage students in time consuming projects like mock trials, and the like. To do such things, Kevin explains, "requires me to either cut something or shorten something or speed something up because the MEAP is coming on January 29, whether I have covered the material or not.... We just don't have the time for that. I mean, we have to be through the War of 1812 by January 29th—that's what the MEAP covers."

Two Puzzles

Although Kevin's dilemma fits well within teachers' description of curricular changes mentioned above, two issues regarding the examples teachers provide and the explanations they offer for them seem puzzling. The first issue deals with the nature of the examples of MEAP influence the teachers describe; the second issue concerns the idea of what, in Kevin's words, "the MEAP covers." I explore each puzzle in turn.

The Puzzle of MEAP Influence

Looking at the experiences teachers describe, one realizes that they are not central to teaching social studies. This realization puzzled me in light of teachers' recurring statements that the MEAP has had significant impact on their *teaching*. My first reaction was to assume that I did not ask the right questions or did not pursue the questions I did ask long enough to understand the the idea that the MEAP had caused major changes in their instruction. So I decided to return to this issue in the second round of the study. Yet, in spite of my persistent questions on the issue, none of the teachers offered any examples beyond those initially provided—that is, *content* decisions pointing to topics they no longer teach, topics they spend less time on, or activities they have reconfigured, but not to influences on their *instructional* decisions.

How can this contradiction be reconciled? In my analysis of the first study (Segall, 2003), I argued that the impact of the test was less pedagogical than ontological. That is, the MEAP had less of an impact on what teachers did in their classroom than on their perceptions of themselves as teachers, as professionals. I argued that confining the idea of how one teaches to methods of instruction neglects other important factors. *How* one teaches, I suggested, also includes the perceptions, beliefs, understandings, commitments, and investments one brings to one's teaching, regardless of the methods used.

The Puzzle of What the MEAP Covers

That teachers see the test as a major impediment to their teaching and yet produce little evidence of how it impedes their teaching is the result of a conundrum of social studies/history education in Michigan in the age of accountability. This conundrum, a second puzzle, is a consequence of what teachers see as the disconnect between the MEAP and the state standards and benchmarks it supposedly evaluates. This disconnect occurs at multiple levels and has ramifications that underlie teachers' perceptions of the test *and* their responses—indeed their inability to respond—to it. Addressing this puzzle means paying attention to the issue of "what the MEAP covers" and to the need felt by teachers to teach particular topics because "that's what the MEAP asks." As we will see, however, this issue proves puzzling for the MEAP does not ask teachers to teach particular topics. In fact, it requires very little of them in the form of curriculum mandates.

The social studies MEAP comprises 42 multiple-choice questions generally organized in sets of five, four constructed response questions, and two extended responses or essays in which students take a position on a public issue. All questions, regardless of the kind of response required, correspond to provided prompts—a reading passage, chart, graph, map, or photograph. Students are asked to read the prompt and answer the questions following it. The extended responses pertain to what is normally considered civics or government content. History and geography questions appear largely in the multiple-choice section with a rare appearance in a constructed response question. Students' answers to the multiple-choice questions are scanned; their constructed and extended responses are graded by subject-area teachers assembled in a central Michigan location, not by the students' classroom teacher him/herself.

Although some argue that multiple-choice questions are not the best way to assess understanding and deep knowledge, what troubles teachers is not the *kind* of questions asked—after all, they use multiple-choice questions on their own tests—but what such questions ask students to do and what they need to know in order to respond. In contrast with mandated tests in other states (e.g., Virginia) that ask students to recall information learned in the social studies classroom, the MEAP is a very different test. It is, in many ways, a self-contained test whereby little external knowledge beyond the ability to read and reason is necessary (see Appendix B). Students are not questioned directly about the social studies curriculum, but instead are asked to read a provided prompt and respond to multiple-choice questions about that text. Although the preamble to each set of questions advises students to use prior knowledge in their responses, such knowledge is not always, or even often, required to be able to answer the questions. A student can pass the test, even do well on it, simply by carefully reading the texts and knowing how to respond to such texts. In many ways, this format renders social studies education provided in schools unnecessary (see also, Grant et al., 2002)

"What the MEAP asks," Matt notes, "doesn't evaluate students' knowledge in social studies." Instead, it gives students various charts and graphs and short scenarios and then "tests students on their skill level, their reading and writing ability, their overall intelligence, maybe." "You could take a kid with a very high I.Q. who has never been in a social studies classroom," Seth adds, "and give him the social studies MEAP and he'll do very well." Matt, Seth, and the other participants do not mean that topics covered in the curriculum are not addressed in the MEAP, but rather that the way the MEAP deals with such topics makes the process of learning them in the classroom unnecessary. By having answers to test questions evident in the text itself, Matt points out, the MEAP becomes a test of reading comprehension rather than of social studies. "It's almost like you can have a kid do really well on the MEAP and not know history at all," adds Kevin. Debbie expresses her frustration with a test that seems to devalue the content of social studies:

[The MEAP] really makes me mad—there is like nothing! Oh, my gosh! It's like our whole year is not necessary at all. That just blows me away....I mean it's nice to be able to reason things and look at something and pull out information from that, but I'd like to see more of a balance. I would like to see more, you know … have you learned some basic facts here? It's almost as if we don't even need to teach the curriculum if we can teach them how to read a graph or look at a map. It almost makes you feel like, why bother, they don't have to know this stuff anyway. I mean, they do, just to be intelligent human beings, but not for the MEAP.

The teachers' frustration is not simply a result of the test not validating their individual choices as teachers. Although this notion of invalidation ties into the idea of lack of respect for teachers as professional (recall Kevin's quote at the beginning of the chapter) and the idea that students' scores on the social studies MEAP play no role in determining whether students receive the Merit award toward college, its roots lie primarily elsewhere—with the state and the contradictory messages it conveys to teachers about social studies/history education. The MEAP is intended to work in conjunction with the state standards and benchmarks for social studies education. Having established a set of standards and specifications as to what students need to know and be able to do at each grade level in order to master those standards, the MEAP is intended to evaluate the degree to which students have mastered the state standards. But the MEAP, according to teachers, has very little to do with the state standards and benchmarks and, thus with what teachers do (and feel they are required by the state to do) in their classrooms.

The result: Teachers believe they are caught in a catch 22—damned if they follow the state standards and damned if they don't. They are, they believe, in a no-win situation, torn between these two contradictory imperatives of the state government and never able to fulfill either without failing the other. This is the essence of the conundrum. If they follow the state standards and benchmarks, their students might gain better knowledge and understanding on subject matter, but may do poorly on the MEAP. And if they teach students how to pass the test—that is, through teaching previously unseen prompts followed by sets of multiple choice questions—students may do better on the test, but leave their classroom with very little knowledge and understanding of the subject matter.

Perceiving the standards and benchmarks and the MEAP as coming from two irreconcilable domains of the same agent, teachers believe they cannot choose both simultaneously. To do so, Kevin explains, would require "double teaching"—teaching the content once and in one way to "cover" the standards and benchmarks, and teaching it again, and differently, to ensure students are able to answer a question on the test. Double teaching would require double contact hours, and as Seth exclaims, "there just isn't enough time to do all of this in the time we have with students." With no option to add more time, teachers feel they must choose either of the two approaches, not both. Their decision to side with the

standards is unanimous.[3] That choice is both understandable and surprising. It is understandable, because these teachers fundamentally agree
with the state standards and benchmarks, which represent the traditional
conceptions of social studies as a set of concepts, skills, and information
students are to acquire as they move from one grade to another. Including concepts such as sequencing of and within historical eras, comparing
narratives about major historical eras and events, evaluating key decisions
made in the past and assessing their implications (to use only the example of history), the standards and benchmarks are mostly a reflection of
the kind of social studies teachers have always taught. It is thus easy to see
why teachers have a favorable response to them and are comfortable
using them. Indeed, teachers note that they use the standards and benchmarks at times to guide their planning and at times to find validation for
what they have already planned. For example, Seth sees the standards
and benchmarks as clear and useful guides to his curriculum planning:

> When I construct my curriculum in history, the first thing I do is pull out
> the [state] standards and benchmarks. And it works out fine. It's not like I
> have to make major adjustments; it's not like I have to go out of my way. So
> for each unit we say: "Here are the chapters that apply, these are the bench-
> marks that we hit, here's the assessment, and here are the resources." For
> everything we do there has to a benchmark that goes with it and there can't
> be a benchmark that we're not addressing. But that's not usually a problem
> because the benchmarks are pretty good and we would have covered them
> anyway.

Solving the Puzzle of What the MEAP Covers

The choice to embrace the standards and benchmarks, as understandable as it may be, is also surprising. For teachers are not evaluated on the
degree to which they have incorporated state standards and benchmarks;
they are mostly (in some cases, only) evaluated on their students' MEAP
scores. Recognizing an inherent difference between the test and that
which it supposedly evaluates, could result in one of two solutions.

The first, a "liberating" solution, would have teachers say: "If the test
has nothing to do with the curriculum, I don't have to spend any time
preparing students for it and can in a sense, have more freedom in my
classroom to do what I think is important." This view, as my earlier study
illustrates, is not a route chosen by any of the participants. Instead, every
time they see their students' normally low MEAP scores, teachers echo
Matt's reaction: "I need to change things and make the curriculum more
responsive to the standards and benchmarks. I need to follow those more
closely if I want students to do better on the test." This second "solution"
seems odd, if not counterproductive. For as teachers' experience with the
MEAP since 1999 has illustrated time and again, adhering more closely to

the standards, while at the same time claiming the test has little correlation to those standards, will only produce one result: a closer relationship between the curriculum and the standards. It will not help students achieve higher scores on the test since standards, according to teachers, are not "covered" in the test. What is intriguing, then, is why teachers choose a path that they inherently know will not produce the results they seek? Kevin clearly articulates the disconnect between the curriculum and the state test:

> You take the benchmarks given to you, you try to align the curriculum as best you can, you try to give the students the knowledge and, hopefully, that will be enough to get them by....We're doing everything we can do. Unfortunately, we don't feel that the test is reflective of that.

If higher test scores are the goal, it might make more sense for teachers to use the test, not the standards, as the basis for teaching. At the most rudimentary level, that would require reconceptualizing teaching as providing students with texts in the form of those used by the MEAP about the particular topic being learned and having students engage the material through a set of multiple-choice questions, similar to those given on the test. As *sensible* as this approach might seem on first inspection, none of the teachers participating in this study, indeed none of the many teachers I work with on a regular basis chose this option. Asked why not, Kevin voices the common preference for teaching ideas rather than teaching the test:

> There may be a time when we'll have to do that—if scores get really low—but it'll be unfortunate to have to waste valuable class time to do so, to teach students how to take a test.... I mean, I can do this, but if I do, are students learning anything? Are they getting anything out of it?... So I choose learning over teaching them how to take a test. It's difficult though. I mean you want them to do well on the test, but you want to make sure they get something out of your class. So I don't really feel comfortable with just giving in and saying, "you know what, this is the way it has do be: We're going to do really well on the test and everybody's going to think we're great, but when students leave they won't necessarily know as much as they could have." I don't know if I feel very good about that.

Echoing Kevin's conviction, Matt adds that using tests as the basis for teaching is unacceptable:

> I'd quit the profession. I would hate that. It would drive me absolutely nuts. I'm not going to be a teacher that just does that. I'm not going to teach that way. I couldn't do it. I could not do it.... I don't want to be a cookbook. I want my job to be of importance, not just a cookbook of "Here's the stuff.

Do it and I'll grade it." I want them to get something out of it that I think is
going to be important for them as a life skill.

Although Matt's comment illustrates the dilemmas the MEAP poses for
teachers in relation to their practice and the degree to which its mandates
do and do not coincide with their beliefs about teaching, teachers' tendency to align themselves with the standards rather than the MEAP also
opens the door for an alternative—even ironic—explanation for their
choice. This is especially the case if we consider the relationship Matt
mentions between social studies as cookbook teaching on the one hand,
and providing students with a life skill on the other. Although Matt positions classroom teachers as pursuing the latter and the MEAP as requiring the former, such a depiction is problematic when one considers what
the MEAP asks of students. As illustrated earlier, the MEAP does not
require students to recall dates and facts or any of the other cookbook
learning Matt and other participants attribute to the test. In fact, by asking students to read a text and analyze it, the MEAP requires that students demonstrate a life skill, a practice they presumably will use as
citizens following the completion of their schooling. As such, the MEAP
asks students to do something with what they have learned, to apply it
rather than simply recall it. Whereas most observers, and all of the participants in this study, tend to blame standardized testing for emphasizing
pedantic, just-the-facts kinds of content, the MEAP asks questions that
seem more like the "real world"—for example, interpreting social texts.
So in a curious irony, it is the teachers rather than the test makers who
seem rooted in and supportive of a more conventional, facts-only
approach to social studies.

Understanding the Solutions

The different solutions offered provide insights into teachers' complex
relationship with the MEAP and illustrate the relationship between teachers' ontological and pedagogical beliefs, on the one hand, and their
responses to the test, on the other. Pedagogically, teachers' rejection of
the MEAP tells us much about the degree to which they are willing to let
outsiders dictate curriculum and pedagogy. It also illustrates the point
that in spite of teachers' willingness to modify parts of their curriculum
and pedagogy, they are not ready to institutionalize practices that are
counter to their beliefs about what social studies education should be.

This unwillingness to bend as far as the test requires, however, goes
beyond teaching. It has much to do with teachers' sense of being, as professionals, in the age of the MEAP. Inherent in their responses is teachers'
management of the MEAP and its imperatives. They recognize the reality
of the MEAP as a measure that will not go away by simply wishing it. At

the same time, teachers are unwilling to embrace it. Rather, their attempts—through what they do and no longer do in classrooms, through conversations with themselves, their colleagues, and outsiders like me—are fundamentally directed toward creating a modus vivendi with the test, learning to live with but not by it. This form of cohabitation does not require them to sacrifice that which they believe is essential to social studies education or to the core of their professional identity. Managing the MEAP, it appears, means doing what is absolutely necessary for the test, but nothing more. And it is in this space between doing and not doing, between passive acceptance and active resistance, that the relationship between teachers and the MEAP plays out. It is an active game where teachers play some cards, but refuse to play others. Although teachers' ultimate goal would be, no doubt, to win this game and have the MEAP disappear, they know that this is no more than wishful thinking. Winning, then, means not losing. It means playing by the rules and doing what is required in order to maintain the appearance of preparing students for the test but, at the same time, taking no real action in that direction. From their position, teachers can only hope to maintain "industrial calm" by ensuring the game always ends with a draw, where there are no clear winners or losers and all can save face for having done something though never really doing too much. In some ways, this form of being and teaching resembles what McNeil (1986) termed "defensive teaching."

The need teachers feel to manage the MEAP is constant. And although such actions could be defined as teacher resistance to an instrument imposed from the outside, viewing these actions as teacher activism alone misses a key point. Indeed, their management of the MEAP is not something teachers seek out; it is, by and large, a form of life imposed upon them, a reaction to the various, conflicting messages conveyed by the state. Every teacher, no doubt, wants to be considered successful—by him/herself as well as by others. But how might one achieve success, teachers seem to ask, when the system positions them for failure? Further, if failure and success are positioned not as opposites where one can attain either, but as two components intertwined in the very context underlying one's teaching, what do either of those terms mean? When one puts the MEAP in its broader context, one soon realizes, as did teachers in this study, that failure is no longer something teachers can avoid by working harder, by doing more or better, or even by doing something completely different. Rather failure has become unavoidable, something to learn to live with regardless of what one does as a teacher.

A Recipe for Failure

Several elements combine to produce the sense of unavoidable failure on the part of teachers. The first is the disconnect between the state-mandated standards and benchmarks and the state-mandated MEAP. Teachers are required to adhere to the standards and benchmarks, but are ultimately evaluated on how well their students do on the MEAP as if the two measures are indeed congruent. Requiring teachers to do one thing, but evaluating them on another is a recipe for failure. Regardless of how well teachers construct their curriculum with state standards in mind, their students will not do well on an instrument measuring something all together different. And if teachers choose to teach their curriculum in a manner that emulates the kind of questions asked on the MEAP, they believe they will be failing their students for not teaching the concepts underlying the state standards—a classic no-win situation.

Further, teachers are evaluated, collectively rather than individually, through media reports, by school administrators, and by the state through its annual report cards on how well students performed on the MEAP. Indeed, students who pass the MEAP receive state scholarships to institutions of higher education, that is, students who pass the MEAP in reading, writing, math, and science, but not in social studies. Herein lies the second recipe for failure. For while the state evaluates schools and teachers based on students' MEAP performance, it sends a message to students that they need not bother trying too hard on the social studies MEAP since their scores do not count toward the scholarships. In other words, the state maintains MEAP scores as the measure by which to evaluate social studies teachers, but removes any incentive for students to take the test seriously. That scores on the social studies test are traditionally lower than those in other subject areas where scores do matter toward scholarships should come at no surprise. But this important element is not factored in to how MEAP scores are read; MEAP scores are used to evaluate social studies teachers in exactly the same manner in which they are used to evaluate teachers in other subject areas.

That the test scores on the social studies MEAP do not count toward students' scholarship sends a message to students; it also sends a powerful message to teachers about the value of their subject area and their own value as teachers of it. Such a message implies two classes of classroom teachers—those who teach important subject areas and those who do not. And social studies teachers define this second category according to Michigan policymakers. How might one expect social studies teachers to excel when the state deems them and what they teach as insignificant? Teacher failure then, has little to do with how well their students do on the test; it is inherent in the status bestowed upon them, a priori, by their own employer—the state.

Underlying social studies teachers' response to the MEAP is a complex combination of the ontological and the pedagogical. Feeling disrespected as professionals, teachers want neither to be defined nor identified with the MEAP. Matt summarizes the dilemma teachers face:

> I think I do a good job as a teacher—teaching what I think students should know, turning them on, getting them interested in the world. But when I look at the [MEAP] scores I say, "what in the heck?!" I mean, I think I'm doing a good job. I bust my tail. I work hard and I do everything that I think is right by kids. And then we get results and I'm like, we're not even close, we're 30%.... So if I stick to my kind of social studies, it looks like I'm a terrible teacher who doesn't care. But I do care. I want to be looked upon as one of the best teachers we have. I want my principal to say to anyone who comes to the school, "he's one of the best teachers I have and if you don't believe me, walk down to his room right now and see for yourself." That's how I want to be known, not as "he's got the highest MEAP scores in this building and year-in and year-out his kids are just outstanding on the MEAP." That's not how I want to be remembered.

Matt's stance points to the inherent dilemmas teachers face in the age of standardized testing. First, and regardless of whether one believes the MEAP promotes "real life" or conservative teaching, Matt's point illustrates the dichotomy between the kind of social education teachers believe in and that which they believe is promoted by the test. But more than pointing to that dichotomy, this example demonstrates that keeping that dichotomy alive acts as a mechanism for teachers to differentiate between and disassociate themselves from the test and its results. Second, it is the very dilemma of one's legacy—how a teacher is remembered—that points to the many, complex issues underlying teaching in the age of accountability: Accountability to whom? For what? Under what conditions? For what and whose benefit? At what and whose cost?

More than informing us about what one teaches or how one engages students, answers provided by teachers to these and other questions point to the idea that standardized testing and the various imperatives that go along with it, engage or violate teachers' sense of being. Bringing the intersection of the ontological and the pedagogical to the surface, indeed helping conflate the two, standardized testing, while perhaps not radically altering what takes place in classrooms, nevertheless impacts teachers' understandings of themselves as professionals, as decisions makers, as autonomous beings in charge of what happens in their classrooms. Although levels of teacher investment, commitment, and passion often seem peripheral in research compared to that which unfolds in classrooms, these issues and their attendant ramifications deserve attention. If social education, at least in part, is about empowering students to author and act in the world, we might consider the MEAP's implicit curriculum—the disempowerment and disenfranchisement of teachers—as possibly more dangerous than its explicit curriculum. For as they learn content so, too, do students learn attitudes in their social education classes. And it may be increasingly hard for teachers to convey a sense of ownership, autonomy, and passion to their students when they feel disempowered, disillusioned, and often defeated. So although teachers' responses to the MEAP may not dramatically alter what they do in classrooms, those responses reflect how they come to their teaching and the degree of commitment and passion they invest in it. It thus might be that teachers' sense of disempowerment may have more of an impact on the kind of messages students ultimately receive than the kind of classroom activities with which those same teachers engage their students.

NOTES

1. All names used in this chapter are pseudonyms.
2. By the time of the second study, Susan had already retired from teaching. And, since my hope, in line with the substance of this book, was to focus the follow-up study on history, I did not include Debbie in this round of interviews since she only teaches geography.
3. The other side of that is a unanimity in "blaming" the MEAP rather than the standards for the ills of social studies/history education. One continuously hears teachers claim "It's because of the MEAP!' but never "It's because of the standards!"

APPENDIX A

MICHIGAN FRAMEWORK FOR SOCIAL STUDIES EDUCATION: CONTENT STANDARDS

1. Historical Perspective:

    1.1   Time and Chronology
    1.2   Comprehending the Past
    1.3   Analyzing and Interpreting the Past
    1.4   Judging Decisions from the Past

2. Geographic Perspective:

    2.1   People, Places, and Cultures
    2.2   Human/Environment Interaction
    2.3   Location, Movement, and Connections

2.4   Regions, Patterns, and Politics
2.5   Global Issues and Affairs

3. Civic Perspective:

3.1   Purposes of Government
3.2   Ideals of American Democracy
3.3   Democracy in Action
3.4   American Government and Politics
3.5   American Government and World Affairs

4. Economic Perspective:

4.1   Individual and Household Choices
4.2   Business Choices
4.3   Role of Government
4.4   Economic Systems
4.5   Trade

5. Inquiry:

5.1 Information Processing
5.2 Conducting Investigations

6. Public Discourse and Decision Making:

6.1   Identifying ands Analyzing Issues
6.2   Group Discussion
6.3   Persuasive Writing

7. Civic Involvement:

7.1 Responsible Personal Conduct

APPENDIX B

A SAMPLE QUESTION FROM THE MICHIGAN EDUCATIONAL ASSESSMENT OF PROGRESS

What follows is a released sample of the Social Studies grade 8 MEAP. For additional released items see, http://www.meritaward.state.mi.us/mma/released.htm

Directions: Read the following passage and use it with what you already know to answer the questions that follow.

THE AFRICAN AMERICAN PRESENCE IN THE AMERICAN REVOLUTION

African Americans served on both sides in the Revolutionary War in a variety of traditional military roles, such as soldiers, scouts, guides, and guards. In the earliest battles of the Revolution, African American minutemen Lemuel Hayes and Peter Salem helped drive the British back from Concord Bridge. At Bunker Hill, Peter Salem, again, along with Salem Poor earned praise for their leadership and valor.

In spite of these contributions, conflict arose about whether to allow slaves, or even free African Americans to bear arms. During the Second Continental Congress and for several years to come, southern delegates in states where slaves outnumbered whites were afraid of possible uprisings. Due to southern objections, General Washington terminated all black enlistments in October of 1775. In 1776, Congress approved the reenlistment of free African American veterans, and by the end of the year, Washington succeeded in getting the acceptance of black enlistments, eventually including slaves. With the war dragging on and with manpower short, fears of slave owners were less important to Washington that winning freedom from England.

The first all African American regiment was the Black Regiment of Rhode Island. The new regiment proved itself at the Battle of Rhode Island where it inflicted casualties of six to one on the professional soldiers who fought for the British.

In 1781, African American soldiers took part in the defeat of Cornwallis at Yorktown, Virginia. James Armistead Lafayette, who was born into slavery, assumed a key intelligence role. The valuable reports he furnished enables the Americans to check the troop advances of British General Cornwallis, setting the stage for Washington's victory at Yorktown.

The 1786 General Assembly of Virginia freed Lafayette and, much later, gave him a pension.

During and after the war, African Americans continued their political struggle for liberty. In January of 1777, African Americans sent a petition to end slavery to the Massachusetts House of Representatives. They argued that the same principles that led America to break with England should be applied.

1. Why did Washington end all black enlistments?

    (a) States with large slave populations were against having African American soldiers.
    (b) African Americans did not have a chance to prove themselves in battle.
    (c) The patriots no longer needed more soldiers.
    (d) Washington knew the patriots would win the war.

2. Why did Washington eventually approve of African American enlistments?

    (a) African Americans would fight only in northern states.
    (b) African American could help win the patriot cause.
    (c) He wanted to gain political support from the southern states.
    (d) He knew that slaves would never fight for the American cause.

3. What does the petitioning to the Massachusetts government by African Americans illustrate?

    (a) Whites were ready to treat them as equals.
    (b) They wanted to serve as leaders of the government.
    (c) They tried to fight discrimination within the legal system.
    (d) They spent most of their time during the war dealing with the abolitionist movement.

4. Which of the following is suggested by the passage?

    (a) After the war, African Americans made great political gains.
    (b) Throughout the war, African Americans participated in battle and exhibited bravery.
    (c) The African Americans made great strides in eliminating discrimination during the war.

    (d)   The British held African Americans in higher esteem than other Americans.

  5. What is the significance of the Black Regiment of Rhode Island and the African American soldiers listed in the passage?

    (a)   Their contributions were not known until after they died.

    (b)   They were prevented from entering the war sooner, when they could have made a difference.

    (c)   They were exposed to disease and thereby prevented from reaching their potential.

    (d)   Their actions made a difference in many battles.

REFERENCES

Corbett, H. D., & Wilson, B. L. (1991). Two state minimum competency testing programs and their effect on curriculum and instruction. In R. Stake (Ed.), *Advances in program evaluation: Effects of mandated assessment on teaching* (Vol. 1., pp. 7–40). Greenwich, CT: JAI Press.

Derrida, J. (1979). Living on: Border lines. In H. Bloom, P. de Man, J. Derrida, G. Hartman, & J. H. Miller (Eds.), *Deconstruction and criticism* (pp. 75–176). New York: Continuum.

Felman, S. (1982). Psychoanalysis and education: Teaching terminable and interminable. In B. Johnson (Ed.), *The pedagogical imperative. Yale French Studies, 63*, 21–44.

Finn, C. (1995). Who's afraid of the big, bad test? In D. Ravitch (Ed.), *Debating the future of American education: Do we need national standards as assessments?* (pp. 120–144). Washington, DC: Brookings Institute.

Firestone, W. A., & Mayrowetz, D. (2000). Rethinking "high-stakes": Lessons from the United States and England and Wales. *Teachers College Record, 102*(4), 724–749.

Firestone, W. A., Mayrowetz, D., & Fairman, J. (1998). Performance-based assessment and instructional change: The effects of testing in Maine and Maryland. *Education Evaluation and Policy Analysis, 20*(2), 95–113.

Gibson, R. (1999). The impact of testing in Michigan. *FairTest Examiner.* Retrieved July 12, 2005, from http://www.faitest.org/examarts/spring99/impactontesting.html

Giroux, H. A. (1996). Is there a place for cultural studies in colleges of education? In H. A. Giroux, C. Lankshear, P. McLaren & M. Peters (Eds.), *Counter narratives: Cultural studies and critical pedagogies in postmodern spaces* (pp. 41–58). New York: Routledge.

Goodman, J., & Adler, S. (1985). Becoming an elementary social studies teacher: A study of perspectives. *Theory and Research in Social Education, 13*(2), 1–20.

Grant, S. G. (2000, February). Teachers and tests: Exploring teachers' perceptions of changes in New York state's testing program. *Education Policy Analysis Archives, 8*(14). Retrieved from http://olam.ed.asu.edu/epaa/v8n14.html

Grant, S. G. (2001). An uncertain lever: Exploring the influence of state-level testing in New York State on teaching social studies. *Teachers College Record, 103*(3), 398–426.

Grant, S. G., Gradwell, J. M., Lauricella, A. M., Derme-Insinna, A., Pullano, L., & Tzetzo, K. (2002). When increasing stakes need not mean increasing standards: The case of New York state global history and geography exam. *Theory and Research in Social Education, 30*(4), 488–515.

Haladyna, T., Haas, N., & Allison, J. (1998). Continuing tensions in standardized testing. *Childhood Education, 74*(5), 262–273.

Haney, W. (2000, August). The myth of the Texas miracle in education. *Education Policy Analysis Archives, 8*(41). Retrieved from http://epaa.asu.edu/epaa/v8n41.html

Heilman, E. E. (2001). Teachers' perspectives on real world challenges for social studies education. *Theory and Research in Social Education, 29*(4), 696–733.

Hursh, D. (2000). Neoliberalism and the control of teacher, students, and learning: The rise of standards, standardization, and accountability. *Cultural Logic, 4*(1). Retrieved from http://eserver.org/clogic/4-1/hursh.html

Kohn, A. (2001). Fighting the tests: A practical guide to rescuing our schools. *Cultural Logic, 4*(1). Retrieved from http://eserver.Org/clogic/4-1/kohn.html

Lather, P. (1986). Research as praxis. *Harvard Educational Review, 56*(3), 257–277.

Linn, R. L. (2000). Assessment and accountability. *Educational Researcher, 29*(2), 4–16.

Mathison, S., & Freeman, M. (2003). Constraining elementary teachers' work: Dilemmas and paradoxes created by state mandated testing. *Education Policy Analysis Archives, 11*(34). Retrieved from http://epaa.asu.edu/epaa/v11n34

McNeil, L. M. (1986). *Contradiction of control: School structure and school knowledge.* New York: Routledge.

McNeil, L. M. (2000). *Contradictions of school reform: Educational costs of standardized testing.* New York: Routledge.

Meier, D. (2000). *Will standards save public education?* Boston: Beacon Press.

Ravitch, D. (Ed.). (1995). *Debating the future of American education: Do we need national standards and assessments?* Washington, DC: Brookings Institute.

Richardson, V., & Placier, P. (2001). Teacher change. In V. Richardson (Ed.), *Handbook of research on teaching* (pp. 905–947). Washington, DC: American Educational Research Association.

Ross, E. W. (1987). Teachers perspective development: A study of pre-service social studies teachers. *Theory and Research in Social Education, 25*(4), 225–243.

Segall, A. (2003). Teachers' perception of the impact of state-mandated standardized testing: The Michigan Educational Assessment Program (MEAP) as a case study of consequences. *Theory and Research in Social Education, 31*(3), 287–325.

Smith, M. L. (1991). Put to the test: The effects of external testing on teachers. *Educational Researcher, 20*(5), 8–11.

Smith, J., & Niemi, R. G. (2001). Learning history in school: The impact of course work and instructional practices on achievement. *Theory and Research in Social Education, 29*(1), 18–42.

van den Berg, R. (2002). Teachers' meanings regarding educational practice. *Review of Educational Research, 72*(4), 577–625.

CHAPTER 7

USING PRIMARY DOCUMENTS WITH FOURTH-GRADE STUDENTS

Talking About Racism While Preparing for State-Level Tests

Jane Bolgatz

Despite all the attention paid to race in our culture and despite the fact that racist oppression occurs on many levels, race and racism have not been easy topics for many schools to address. Moreover, the current focus on preparing students for standardized tests has led to less emphasis on multicultural education and an increased pressure on teachers to concentrate on decontextualized skill development (Smith, 1991). I want to argue that it is possible to open conversations with children about the racial history of the United States while at the same time preparing them for standardized and high-stakes tests.

In this chapter, I first explore the argument that using primary source materials that focus students' analytical and interpretive skills upon issues of race and racism can enable students to critically engage the past. I then

Measuring History: Cases of State-Level Testing Across the United States, 133–156
Copyright © 2006 by Information Age Publishing
All rights of reproduction in any form reserved.

describe how—while addressing provocative historical controversies—students in a fourth grade class were able to practice skills that are required by the state tests for which they must be prepared. The students addressed issues of economics, race and gender relations, and the question of who participates in history. They also practiced the skills of critical thinking, reading for meaning, vocabulary building, deciphering figurative language, and making intertextual connections. In conclusion, I argue that social studies teachers need not sacrifice teaching historical content—multicultural content, in particular—for teaching skills or vice versa. Indeed, the two are mutually beneficial.

LEARNING ABOUT HISTORY AND RACE

The National Assessment of Educational Progress (NAEP) often provides a bleak portrait of American students' knowledge of history, yet there was a ray of hope in the 2001 report card. NAEP data indicated that "eighth graders whose teachers reported using primary historical documents such as letters, diaries, or essays written by historical figures, on a weekly basis had higher average scores than those whose teachers did so less frequently" (National Assessment of Educational Progress, 2001, p. 14). At the eighth-grade level, instruction using primary documents is correlated with students' higher test performance. Although the NAEP analysts found that teachers' use of primary documents was not related to student performance on the fourth grade test, research shows that elementary students' encounters with historical documents can elicit historical thinking skills (VanSledright, 2002). As students-cum-historians study old letters, diary entries, political cartoons, and other primary sources, they engage in analysis and interpretation of the documents (Stearns, Seixas, & Wineburg, 2000; Wineburg, 2001).

Beyond the research on history learning with primary sources, I locate this study within previous research on students' encounters with the racial history of the United States and North America. Seixas (1993) argues that history instruction connected to students' ethnic backgrounds holds potential for simultaneously building on students' particular group experiences, while providing "a common public forum for the discussion of divergent historical experiences" (p. 322). Wills (1996) claims that learning about the history of racial hierarchy and conflict offers students an understanding that race conflict is not "'their problem' but 'our problem'" (p. 386).

In research comparing African American and European American students' perspectives on U.S. history, Epstein (1998) finds that African American students regard teachers and textbooks as presenting, for the most part, a "White" version of history disconnected from their understandings of the past and present (see also Almarza & Fehn, 1998). By contrast, Epstein finds that most White students' understandings cohere with teacher and text versions of U.S. history, which emphasize progress in the extension of equal opportunity to everyone. Like Seixas, Epstein argues that multicultural history holds potential for meaningfully connecting both marginalized and majority students to the common experience of racial hierarchy and White privilege. Levstik and Barton (1998) assert that middle school students—regardless of racial or ethnic background—characterize the United States as a land of increasingly extending rights and opportunities for all. They suggest that teachers expose students to "the complexity and diversity of perspectives that have always existed" (p. 501).

Significant for the findings discussed here, researchers have shown teachers to be reluctant to engage students in discussion about the history of race. Race and racism are all but ignored in traditional texts (Anderson, 1994). Even when using materials that are explicitly racial in content, teachers often avoid engaging elementary students in conversations about race or racism (Ladson-Billings, 2003). Although several studies indicate students are interested in race and other dimensions of difference and identity (e.g., Bolgatz, 2005; Kuklin, 1993), school curricula, school culture, classroom context, and teachers themselves have all been implicated in the failure to examine the history of race relations (Chapman, 2003; Dipardo & Fehn, 2000; Ladson-Billings, 2003). Indeed, I began this study because I was confounded by my own White preservice teachers' objections to raising controversial issues with their elementary students.

Scholars who study secondary and higher education have shown that race and racism can be complex and emotionally risky issues to talk about (Davis, 1992; Ellsworth, 1989, 1997). Theorists describe, in the abstract, the ways educators soften, simplify or avoid conversations about race and racism (Poplin, 1999; West, 1994). There are, however, few fine-grained analyses of interactions in which students and teachers engage complicated issues of prejudice and oppression, particularly in elementary classrooms. Although some research has opened the door to looking at the links between multicultural theories and teachers' practices (Epstein, 1998; Hatcher & Troyna, 1993), many questions remain. In this study, I ask what it looks like when teachers try to engage elementary students in conversations about race: How does the use of primary documents impact teacher-student discussions? And is it possible to study racial history while simultaneously preparing students for standardized tests?

THE NEW YORK STATE CONTEXT

In New York state, fourth-grade students take state-wide standardized exams in English language arts (ELA), math, and science. In the fall of fifth grade, students take a state-level social studies exam. All the exams are required, however, scores from the social studies test are not part of the data reported on the New York City Board of Education or New York State Department of Education (n.d.) Web sites.[1] In some schools, scores from the social studies test are not part of the criteria used to determine whether students are promoted to the next grade level. Teachers are encouraged to focus on social studies, particularly at the beginning of the fifth grade year, as the test is administered in November, but the stakes attached to the social studies test are not as high as for the ELA and math exams.

On the social studies exam, students answer multiple choice and short answer questions about social studies concepts (such as rural, suburban, and urban), events (e.g., the Revolutionary War), and skills (e.g., map reading). They also write an essay in response to a Document-Based Question (DBQ) based upon interpretation of several historical documents (e.g., cartoons, photographs, drawings, newspapers, or other primary documents, often accompanied by a short explanation) and short sections from secondary sources such as encyclopedias or children's history books. In 2002 and 2003, the essay portion of the test counted for 4 points out of 58 and 59 total points respectively.

Although external pressure often can distort teachers' ability to make informed pedagogical decisions with regard to his or her particular students, the existence of the New York state fifth grade social studies test provides a justification to teach social studies, and the inclusion of the Document-Based Question can represent a positive development in the area of standardized testing. Students must make sense of at least some historical documents.[2] Moreover, although the questions do not require evaluation or historiographical analysis, the students must synthesize their analytical and interpretive insights into a coherent narrative. On the 2002 exam, for instance, students had to "discuss four kinds of contributions made by Native American Indians, the Dutch, and/or the English to our culture today" (http://www.emsc.nysed.gov/osa/scostei/socstudeiarch/ss5bk2no02.pdf). And on the 2003 test, they were asked to "describe how New Yorkers and others worked for women's rights" (http://www.emsc.nysed.gov/osa/scostei/socstudeiarch/ss5bk2no03.pdf).

Unlike the social studies exam, the fourth grade ELA and mathematics tests were high-stakes tests: Students' scores determine whether they will go on to the next grade level. In addition, scores from these exams were used to establish how well a school is faring academically. Teachers, particularly those in low-performing schools, face a great deal of pressure to prepare their students for these tests. The ELA exam tests students' ability to read, write, and listen for information and understanding, for literary response and expression, and for critical analysis and evaluation, and these are the topics teachers are expected to cover in preparation for the exams. The mathematics test includes many word problems, and teachers are expected to help students practice reading and comprehending such problems. Although the social studies test scores are not used for promotion of students or evaluation of schools, the teachers expect that they will be soon. Therefore, the social studies test is considered practice for the time when more serious consequences are attached to students' performances on the test. Teachers are often strongly encouraged to do considerable test prep, but currently the stakes for social studies are less than those surrounding the ELA and math tests.

RESEARCH SETTING

To examine what happens when students talk about race, and to test my belief that primary sources about the history of race relations can generate productive discussions about the racial history of the United States as well as be used to help students prepare for standardized tests, I took my research into a test- and textbook-driven public elementary school in New York City. In 2001, the school met neither the expected level of performance established by the state and nor the school-specific adequate yearly progress (AYP) target in English language arts. Less than a quarter of the students in the school met the English language arts standards as measured on the city-wide reading test and the state-wide language arts test. On these exams about a quarter of the students tested far below the standard (performance level 1 on a scale of 4). By test measurement alone, these were not successful students. There was a constant threat that the school would be taken over by the New York City School Chancellor, which meant administrators' and teachers' jobs were in jeopardy. Not surprisingly, then, I was able to attain entrée to the research site by offering to help prepare students for the standardized exams.

I conducted participant observation research with the same group of students beginning in the fourth grade and continuing into the fifth grade. The class had approximately 25 students; attendance fluctuated because students were frequently added to and removed from the class by school administrators. The class reflected the general make-up of the school: The approximately 750 students in the school were almost 57% Hispanic, almost 43% Black, and less than 1% Asian or Native American; almost 98% of the students were eligible for free lunch. In the class there were, however, a disproportionate number of students (20%) who used special education services: One student was being mainstreamed, three students were in an inclusion program, and another student received resource room assistance. (Overall only 4.4% of the students in the school were in special education part time.)

Lorenza Agosto,[3] the teacher in the class, had been teaching for 4 years, all of them at the school. She had a MA degree in education and a reputation in the school for being tough and effective in working with students. She identified herself as Puerto Rican or Hispanic.

My role in the class was one of participant observer: I took the lead in introducing materials to the whole class on several occasions, I observed while the teacher conducted read-alouds and discussions with the whole class, and I led smaller groups in the analysis of documents and work sessions (brainstorming, editing, and sharing) for their various written assignments. I am a White university professor. The students called me Ms. Bolgatz. They described me as a cross between a teacher and a friend.

Helping a teacher and her students prepare for New York State's DBQ questions represented an excellent site for exploring the connection between multicultural history and the development of youngsters' historical thinking skills. When our collaboration began, Agosto said that she wanted help improving students' higher- level thinking skills because they were not performing well on state test questions requiring interpretation and inference-making. I suggested that scrutinizing primary sources would exercise students' higher order thinking skills and potentially improve students' performance on parts of the New York State tests.

Data Collection

During the students' fourth grade year, I went to the class once a week during a 100 minute communication arts block. In that time, Agosto and I taught lessons connected to the multicultural history of New York and the United States. At first, I introduced primary documents to supplement conventional text-based history instruction. For instance, when studying the early history of New York State, students read parts of Verrazano's letter to the King of France and analyzed drawings of slaves in New Amsterdam. Later, when Agosto wanted students to study Martin Luther King and African American history, I selected documents connected with the U.S. civil rights movement and the contemporary debate over affirmative action. While there, I also team taught with Agosto using secondary sources such as children's historical fiction books and excerpts from monographs and Web sites dealing with history.

In order to generate a range of perspectives, I included a variety of data sources. I audiotaped and videotaped whole class and small group discussions. I kept a researcher's journal in which I described participants and their interactions, the setting, and my reflections on the class activities. Informally during and after class, and in formal sessions during the lunch and free periods, I interviewed students individually and in small groups. The interviews often began with prepared questions based on what had happened in the class, but evolved into unstructured discussions about the topics behind the initial questions. I also interviewed Agosto after class and during her free periods about herself, the students, the class in general, and specific topics and events in the class. We also brainstormed regularly as we decided what and how we wanted to teach. Interviews with students and teacher lasted from 10 minutes to an hour. Finally, I collected student work related to the topics studied. I made notes from all of the above and transcribed the portions of those classes, interviews, and assignments that related most directly to race, multiculturalism, test preparation, and the use of primary documents.

Data Analysis

To make sense of the data, I organized portions of the transcripts and individual statements into categories related to my research questions. I cross-referenced the categories for common themes and coded the transcripts using the common themes. I drew tentative conclusions and then went back and searched for counterexamples to those conclusions. For the purposes of this chapter, I focused on units about the Montgomery bus boycott and affirmative action. I chose the former because transcripts of the classroom discussions were loaded with references to racism and sources of learning. I chose the affirmative action unit because it offered insights into the ways that the teacher helped students learn a variety of skills needed on the standardized exams, and because the unit was heavily influenced by the teacher's attention to preparation for the exam.

PRIMARY SOURCES AND LEARNING
SOCIAL STUDIES CONTENT

In the class I studied, primary source documents from the history of race relations in the United States open up conversations about race and racism in United States history and deepen students' understandings of this history. When talking about primary documents, students' assumptions and questions come into focus and are open for discussion and debate.

Students' discussion of the Montgomery bus boycott illustrates the opportunities primary documents offer for students to grapple with economics, race and gender relations, and the role of ordinary people in history. In this section, I describe how students talked about these issues, but first I describe the class in which the students studied the immediate impetus for the boycott.

I first give students the text of the notice that Jo Ann Gibson Robinson, the president of the Women's Political Council (WPC) in Montgomery, Alabama, wrote on the night police arrested Rosa Parks in 1955. The notice, copies of which are posted around town the morning following Parks' arrest, read:

> Another Negro woman has been arrested and thrown in jail because she refused to get up out of her seat on the bus for a White person to sit down.... This has to be stopped. Negroes have rights, too, for if Negroes did not ride the buses, they could not operate. Three-fourths of the riders are Negroes, yet we are arrested or have to stand over empty seats. If we do not do something to stop the arrests they will continue. The next time it may be you, or your daughter, or mother. This woman's case will come up on Monday. We are, therefore, asking every Negro to stay off the buses Monday in protest of the arrest and trial. Don't ride the buses to work, to town, to school, or anywhere else on Monday. (Banks, 1996, p. 341)

During class, I facilitate an extended role play to illustrate the circumstances surrounding the posting of the fliers. I assign several tables of 3–4 students to roles as Black families deciding whether or not they would join the boycott. I assign two tables of students to roles as White families who employed Black workers deciding how they wanted to respond to the strike. In particular, I ask one student, Diana, to pretend to be a rich White woman who had invited several "very important people" for dinner for Monday night, and she did not know what she would do without another student, Sharona, who is playing the role of her cook.

After giving them a chance to talk with their pretend family members, I tell the students to pretend that they are talking with their neighbors and friends after church on the Sunday morning before the boycott was scheduled to begin. I designate one area of the room for the Black church and one for the White church. At first the students engage in two simultaneous larger group discussions. On several occasions, however, one group is silent as they become interested in listening to what is going on in the other "church." In the Black church scenario, students talk about whether or not the boycott will be effective, and if it is worth losing their jobs. In the White church scenario, the students talk about the consequences of the strike and how they might respond to the possibility. With some prompting, Diana figures out that she could pick up Sharona in her car so that she could still hold her dinner party.

Although our dialogue is improvised, the fact that we are working with a primary document gives the exercise an authenticity and vividness typically lacking in textbook readings: The role play engages students in ways that do not occur when they simply read from a text. Students actively participate in both the small group and larger class discussions. Diana, whose attention often drifts during class discussions, listens to her peers' suggestions so she can act out her part. All students focus on the dialogue. They are captivated, for instance, when their teacher, pretending to be the president of the bus company angrily responds to the threat of a boycott.

In an interview later, Devonte explains that "everybody was focused because we knew we had to do something, an assignment." He continues, still excited about the topic: "Everybody wanted to go [on the boycott]... because it wasn't fair that Black people wasn't treated the same as White people." Meaningful to students, issues of racial equity provoke inspired discussion.

STUDENTS CRITICALLY ENGAGE THE PAST

After the whole-class discussion, I talked with students individually about the Robinson document. Below I use interview excerpts to demonstrate the potential of document-based teaching. Students' responses to the document illustrate how they probe the past. With the help of guided questions, the students analyze the subtext of the document to assess authorship for bias and perspective, a skill that Wineburg (2001) argues is an important historical thinking skill.

Opening Discussion of Economics

After rereading the boycott notice, several students ask why White people hated Black people so much, or why the former were so unfair. This questioning leads to a deeper exploration of racial history. Tiffany, for example, speaks to larger notions of economics:

JB: Do you have any questions for me?
Tiffany: Why White people hate Black people in the past?
JB: What do you think?
Tiffany: Because probably the Black people were ugly to them and probably they would get mad at them and tell them to do

> their chores. Because if they [Whites] would be their friends then they would have to do the chores. Probably those people were lazy.

Here, Tiffany explores the economic underpinnings of racism by focusing on the master-servant dimension of past White-Black economic relations. She raises an interesting point—that certain conditions must be maintained in order for a system of domination to be perpetuated. Whites, according to Tiffany, have to see Blacks as ugly and to not be their friends if they are going to be able to have Blacks work for them. Because Whites are so interested in having Blacks do their work—"those people were lazy"—Whites are responsible for fostering hostility; they can not be friendly. This is an astute perception of the human consequences—on the part of the privileged as well as the oppressed—of a racist system.

Like Tiffany, Ebony explains that Whites were not interested in equal treatment of Blacks, and alluded to Whites' historical tendency to economically exploit African Americans:

> JB: Who wrote [the flyer]?
> Ebony: I have no idea. I guess it was like a Black person.
> JB: Why?
> Ebony: Because it says, "Negroes have rights too." Whites didn't think Negroes should go on the bus.
> JB: Could it have been that a White person wrote it?
> Ebony: (shaking her head "no") Cause a White person doesn't agree with Negroes. They think that they should not be treated equally. They think they don't get along with the Blacks and they're supposed to be their slaves.

Conflating slavery and Jim Crow opens the door for a discussion of whether or not there was much difference in the way Whites treated African Americans under systems of slave and free wage labor. The dehumanization of Blacks in the antebellum United States facilitated and justified slave owners' use of Blacks as chattel slaves. Inhuman treatment and perceptions of African Americans continued long after the war as well. During the discussion of the boycott, I explain that a bus driver might take a fare from a Black rider at the front door of the bus, tell the rider to get out and enter through the back door, and then drive off before the rider was able to get back on the bus. This humiliating treatment, however, was not the same as the experience of slavery. Why did Ebony connect the two?

Wills and Mehan (1996) describe a "discontinuity trap" in which many students learn little about African Americans beyond their experience of slavery: "The only injustices these students thought African Americans experienced were associated with their enslavement. To these students, moreover, slavery was a problem that was 'solved' many years ago" (p. 64). The students in this school learn about famous African Americans like Mary McCloud Bethune and Mae Jemison, but they learn little about the century of Jim Crow oppression before the Civil Rights Movement. It makes sense, therefore, that students like Ebony assume that the abusive conditions Blacks faced in Montgomery in 1955 were those of slavery.

Opening Discussion of Race and Gender Relations

In addition to promoting critical exploration of economics, the bus boycott flyer provokes questions of how and why individuals and groups built, or failed to build, cross-race alliances and questions of who plays significant roles in history.

Most students think that a Black person wrote the flyer. Although there is textual evidence for thinking this (e.g., the use of the word "we" in the phrase "we are arrested or have to stand over empty seats"), students do not refer to this fact. Rather, they offer several explanations that related to race relations. Hector, for example, thinks that, because Blacks would not believe Whites, a Black person must have written the notice:

JB: Who do you think wrote it?
Hector: I think now it was the Negroes.
JB: Why?
Hector: Because they're the one that are warning them. If the White [people] warned them, they [the Negroes] wouldn't believe them.

Here, Hector articulates an assumption of inherent distrust between Blacks and Whites. Tiffany explains that the writer must have been Black because she was so concerned about the situation. Tiffany recognizes how strongly the writer voiced her concern and concludes that the writer must have been a Black person:

JB: Who do you think wrote this?
Tiffany: One of the Negroes.
JB: What makes you say that?
Tiffany: Because it says, "Negroes have ... operate."
JB: Why?
Tiffany: (reads) "Another ... stopped." Probably a Negro said "this has to be stopped." Probably that person was Black, too.

> "This has to be stopped" (emphatically). It says thrown in
> jail—they don't want it to happen to them.

Like Hector, Tiffany reveals her view that one is more likely to care about members of one's own group than another. In the notice, there is evidence for this response: ("The next time it may be you, or your daughter, or mother"). Tiffany and the other students do not entertain the idea that one might fight for the rights of someone other than a person in one's racial group. This assumption has implications for understanding racial history and the potential for cross-racial alliance building. Questioning the document enables students to ponder how Whites, (and potentially Blacks), historically have cultivated such divisions.

Much of the students' analyses come as a result of my asking, "who do you think wrote this document?" This deceptively simple question is powerful because it enables students to attend to issues of bias, motivation, and attribution. Studying the boycott notice and other documents such as photographs of city streets, statistics of school district spending, and political pamphlets written by trade organizations also helps students broaden their sometimes simplistic notions about historical actors. The boycott notice, for instance, leads one student to interrogate the role of women in history. Calvin seems surprised that women could have been responsible for such a significant social development:

JB: What did you learn from reading this that was new to you?
Calvin: What's their names again, the people who wrote that?
JB: The Women's Political Council.
Calvin: Yeah. I didn't know they wrote that.
JB: When you found out they wrote what did you think? What was your reaction?
Calvin: I thought that men wrote it.
JB: What did you think when you found out women wrote it?
Calvin: When I found out they wrote it, I felt confused.
JB: Why did you feel confused?
Calvin: Because I was confused because that little note could take a lot of people to do a boycott. It could take a lot of people to start helping them. To stop the buses so the bus could change their ideas.... They wrote the note and a lot of Black people started helping them with the boycott and it was only from a little note.
JB: Sounds like you were surprised.... Why did you think it was men that had written it? (Calvin shakes his head to show that he doesn't know.)

Compared to the conventional historical explanation of Martin Luther King as hero that students learn about every January, Calvin begins to see from the document that King did not act alone. Rather, King's work would not have been possible without the sacrifices of many people. In particular, through studying the boycott notice, Calvin comes grips with the power African American women organized and wielded during the civil rights movement.

Researchers argue that attention to social history and to the lesser-known actors in events such as the Montgomery bus boycott is not common in the teaching and learning of history (Levstik & Barton, 1998; Noddings, 1997). In particular, the focus on heroes and holidays in the teaching of multicultural history leads to a distorted view of the past (Anderson, 1994; Banks, 1996; Wills & Mehan, 1996). The lesson alone however, does not magically transform students' understanding of how ordinary people contribute to history. In an interview, I ask Tina what would happen if similar civil rights violations happened today. She responds, "no one would be able to stop it because Martin Luther King is dead." Even after we had stage the role play where many students discuss the personal sacrifices required to win civil rights, Tina, one of the most articulate students in the class, sees King as a savior acting alone.

PRIMARY SOURCES AND PRACTICING THE SKILLS TESTED ON STANDARDIZED EXAMS

In addition to opening important conversations about race and racism, studying primary documents offers a viable route to learning skills required on various standardized tests. In particular, the primary documents related to the nation's multicultural heritage offer students meaningful ways to learn and practice skills needed for the high-stakes tests they take in English language arts and mathematics in the fourth grade as well as the social studies test they take in the fifth grade. In this section, using the example of a unit on affirmative action, I suggest that the context of practicing skills can be interesting and challenging for all students.

About a month after studying the Montgomery bus boycott, Agosto wants to do something for Black History month. Together, we decide to have students examine one of the University of Michigan affirmative action cases, Gratz et. al. v. Bollinger (2003), being considered by the Supreme Court at the time. In order to get at the concept of the judicial system, we begin by discussing the question of what people do when they feel they have been wronged. We talk about the college admissions process and have students analyze the point system used by the University of Michigan for undergraduate admissions. To get at the underlying question of equity, we analyze President Johnson's 1965 speech about affirmative action and examine school funding and personal income data in Michigan and nationally. Finally, in order to help students answer the question of how they think the Supreme Court should decide the cases, we watch and examine transcripts of televised interviews with the plaintiffs and defendants. At the end of the 5-week unit, students explain their arguments in the form of a letter to the Supreme Court justices.

Although by the end of the unit Ms. Agosto and I decide that the question of affirmative action in college admissions is too abstract for the fourth graders, we feel that the students have learned from their experiences. Most students miss the complexities of the affirmative action debate in higher education, but several students understand and show interest in the general issue of equity. Significant for this research, all students learn about important concepts, players, and processes in the United States government and economics—knowledge they need for the social studies exam—in an authentic context. In addition, they all practice skills they need on the social studies exams, including reading for meaning, economics, critical thinking, vocabulary building, deciphering figurative language, making intertextual connections, and persisting when faced with difficult challenges. At the same time, they learn skills that evident on the math and ELA exams.

Reading for Meaning

As described in the section about the discussions of the Montgomery bus boycott notice, working with primary documents related to race and history allows students to practice reading for meaning, and understanding point of view and audience, key skills on both the social studies and ELA exams. Working with primary sources also engenders questions about historical cause and effect, allegiances, and choices, concepts evident on the social studies exam. Our activities help students identify and challenge assumptions about the past, another skill that, although not explicitly tested on the state test, is part of being an informed student of history.

On the social studies test, students have to make sense of multiple primary documents and synthesize them to answer an essay prompt. Constructing logical narratives out of disparate pieces of evidence is a sophisticated skill. Unlike a secondary document in which an author has already interpreted an event, students have to engage in higher-level analytical and critical thinking. Throughout the affirmative action unit, students weigh their conclusions from reading one document against the conclusions they draw from other documents as they construct their own answer to the question of whether Jennifer Gratz should have been admitted to the University of Michigan. When they first compare wage levels across race and gender, and per-pupil spending, several students think that the playing field is not level. However, when they see the point sheet that the University of Michigan admissions office used, students heatedly discuss the fairness of getting extra points for being Black or Latino. This constant comparison requires facilitation on the part of the adults in the room. It is difficult for most of the students to juggle all the factors presented. With a more appropriate question—and perhaps a more age-appropriate topic—the students might have a better chance of synthesizing the data they collect.

Whether the prompt is formulated by a teacher, a test writer, or the students themselves, it needs to encourage students to ask several questions of the documents: Who wrote this? Why did they write it? What does it mean? Who is the audience? How (for what purpose) was it used? Can we trust it? How does it compare with other sources? The documents in the affirmative action unit raise these questions. Students ask, for example, where I got the chart about wages. In another unit, when they study primary documents related to the Chinese Exclusion Act, students wonder how Blacks and Latinos were perceived. The discussions about the racial history of the United States become nuanced and lively when students raise these questions about the unstated subtexts of the documents (Wineburg, 2001). These kinds of questions, though not well-represented on the state test, are key to historical understanding (Grant, Gradwell, & Cimbricz, 2004). If students can grapple with these sorts of questions deftly, we hope that they will be better prepared to handle the DBQs on the statewide test.

Economics and Critical Thinking Skills

In conjunction with our exploration of the Supreme Court cases about affirmative action at the University of Michigan, the students learn about economics while practicing chart reading and critical thinking skills. They explore arguments about U.S. society having an unequal playing field—for Whites and people of color, and for wealthy and poor. "This is great!" Ms. Agosto exclaims when I introduce charts of census data so students can analyze wage differences across racial and gender groups. Students learn economics and critical thinking skills by hypothesizing and evaluating the causes and social significance of the income differences. Agosto appreciates this meaningful context in which students can apply social science skills, such as extracting data from a chart, one of many skills on the state exams. In addition, this lesson supports Agosto's preparation for the fourth grade math test where the skill of figuring out differences in wages earned using subtraction is tested.

Looking at charts of per-pupil revenue of various school districts in Michigan, students decipher how much various districts spend per student, what the differences are (both in terms of dollars and in terms of how services would differ), why the differences exist, and how to judge the situation. The exercise forces students to read and interpret a chart. The questions require that students use inferencing, hypothesizing, and evaluation skills. These are the higher level skills that Ms. Agosto believes her students most lack, and which are tested on all of the standardized exams. The activity also requires that students practice solving a mathematical word problem.

Although most students come to understand the idea of per-pupil spending, this is still a rather abstract exercise.[4] The fourth graders do not have a real grasp of what a $2,000 or $5,000 difference in per-pupil spending meant. Ms. Agosto asks students what costs money at school. Students guess that there might be more books and more computers in the districts that spend more money per student. Interestingly, some suggest that there might be less fighting at these schools because, they explain, the teachers are better. This leads to a discussion of equity, which we connect back to the Michigan affirmative action case that we were studying. Thus, working with one document allows us to address questions of social justice while covering a variety of basic and higher level economics, mathematics, and critical thinking skills.

Vocabulary

Having a good grasp of vocabulary and concepts is a critical aspect of all exams. On the 2003 social studies test, for example, 2/5 of the multiple choice questions were vocabulary questions such as "after a business pays its workers and its bills, the money it has left is called (A) interest, (B) debt, (C) tax, (D) profit." Encountering and learning new vocabulary happens throughout the affirmative action unit and whenever students deal with primary documents. In introducing the Gratz case, Ms. Agosto and I talk with students about due process and the federal court system. They see a picture of the Supreme Court justices and identify the judges as the people who ultimately decide if Jennifer Gratz should be allowed to go to the University of Michigan. A year later, at least some students remember the Supreme Court. When the class talks about women not being allowed to run track in the Olympics, students suggest that the women who wants to run could go to the Supreme Court. Even as I remind them that the Supreme Court deals with national rather than international affairs, I am pleased to see that students recall the Court as a powerful place to which people can turn with a legal battle. Students' understanding of the judicial system is important, and it is a concept that is often tested on the social studies exam.

Figurative Language

Students need to understand concepts in concrete terms and transfer them into another realm if they are to interpret political cartoons, a skill that is tested on the state social studies exam. In addition, students need to be able to interpret figurative language for both the social studies and the ELA exams. Reading primary documents reinforced these skills.

During the affirmative action unit, the students read an excerpt from President Johnson's 1965 speech that includes a metaphor about someone in shackles and being expected to run in a race. In order to understand Johnson's speech, students must figure out what the metaphor means and how it relates to the history of the United States.

Although students' test preparation activities typically provide them with decontextualized readings, this speech, in the context of a provocative question about affirmative action—Should Jennifer Gratz have been admitted to the University of Michigan?—gives students a reason to question and remember the metaphor's meaning. Indeed, students refer back to the metaphor, not an easy one to decipher, when they discuss the question of schools being on a level playing field.

Intertextual Connections

On the document-based portion of the social studies test as well as on the English language arts test, students have to make intertextual connections. When students discuss the primary documents in class, Ms. Agosto encourages them to make connections to other readings they have done and to other prior experiences. Many students ask questions and make hypotheses that link a document to something with which they are familiar. Some, for example, connect a story that Ms. Agosto told about the 1/8 rule—that if one's ancestry was 1/8 Black, one was considered Black—to explanations and questions that they have about the Montgomery bus boycott notice. After I describe the Women's Political Council to Devonte in an interview, he asks if the Council was made up of White people or Black people. In trying to figure it out, he incorporates into his response—albeit in a slightly muddled fashion—information Ms. Agosto has offered about the 1/8 rule and how some people who would legally be considered Black used to pass as White:

Devonte: Was it White people or Black people?

JB: That's a good question. What do you think?

Devonte: I think it was White people who had been treated the same way and that had a little bit of Black blood in them from their 8th ancestor who was Black. They would insist that they were Black. They knew they had to help people.... For a little while they was treated as White people. But then they found out and they would lose their jobs.

Devonte understands the emotional pain that Ms. Agosto described as experienced by the people who had been passing as White. He then connects this idea to a reason to protest the abusive treatment of Blacks.

Persistence

Another lesson that students can take from dealing with primary documents is persistence. Because most primary documents are inherently *not* neatly packaged for 9 year-olds, students often confront unfamiliar challenges when they look at these documents. For example, when they look at the 1779 legislation arguing that Margaret Corbin, a woman who fought in the Revolutionary War, should be paid for her services, students first have to decipher the handwriting and unfamiliar spellings. Helping students persist in such a decoding exercise is different from helping them figure out the meaning of a textbook. Reading the historical document is difficult for *all* of us, and it is more of a game to figure out the words than a matter of the teacher or quick students knowing the answers without even thinking.

Persistence is one of the skills that students need to take with them to a test setting where they have to tackle unfamiliar problems and passages. Even students who usually did not pay attention when they read from their social studies texts must grapple with the meaning of the strange-looking primary document. Their focus on this legislation and some of the other documents that I present to them may have been enhanced by the fact that I work with small groups. Yet my own interest in ferreting out meaning from a document that has not been predigested does a great deal to enhance the curiosity of the students; we are learning together, as opposed to the usual situation in which a teacher has both questions and answers about a topic or reading already prepared.

A CAVEAT

Ms. Agosto and I want the students to become critical thinkers and to see events from more than one point of view. Ironically, it may be that in some cases such thinking works at cross purposes with the standardized tests students had to take. The students in this study did not take the 2003 test, but had they done so, one of the multiple choice questions (#28, http://www.emsc.nysed.gov/osa/scostei/socstudeiarch/ss5bk1no03.pdf) may have given them pause. It showed a picture of the Statue of Liberty and asked:

What does the Statue of Liberty represent?
A.   a declaration of independence.
B.   a song of praise or dedication.
C.   a symbol of freedom for people coming to the United States.
D.   the importance of laws in the United States.

In class, the students had studied immigration. They had been told that the statue was a gift from France to celebrate liberty, and they read Emma Lazarus' *The New Colossus*: "Give me your tired, your poor, Your huddled masses yearning to breathe free" (Lazarus, n.d.). On that basis, they might have chosen C as the correct answer. Indeed, it is hard to claim any of the other answers as appropriate.

However, the students also studied the Chinese Exclusion Act. They read primary documents that gave them evidence of conflicted reactions to immigration policies. For example, they read and analyzed a pamphlet supporting the Exclusion Act written by the San Francisco Building Trades Organization (American Federation of Labor, 1902) and a letter to the editor of the *New York Sun* written in 1885. In the letter, Saum Song Bo argued that the statue was not a symbol of freedom for his Chinese countrymen:

That statue represents Liberty holding a torch which lights the passage of those of all nations who come into this country. But are the Chinese allowed to come?... Liberty, we Chinese do love and adore thee; but let not those who deny thee to us, make of thee a graven image and invite us to bow down to it. (Bo, 1885)

In the end, students debated whether or not the United States was a land of freedom and opportunity for all. Even those who argued that the United States was a land of freedom would have known that not everyone saw the Statue as an unambiguous symbol of freedom. Remembering the discussion, they may have hesitated before choosing C as the correct answer. I would argue that a moment's hesitation is a small price to pay for becoming a critical thinker, but there are those who may—understandably—disagree.

CONCLUSION

As a social studies educator, I seek to engage students in studying the rich history of the world, including the controversial history of race relations in the United States. By history I do not mean student encounters with textbooks. Rather, I want to offer students the primary stuff of history and enable them to judge the evidence themselves. I want students to develop life-long learning skills, see themselves in their studies, and be inspired to bring about egalitarian change in their classrooms, schools, and communities. I want them to study our multicultural history and problematize the history-as-progress paradigm commonly promoted and followed in schools. Students can accomplish these goals, in part, if they are allowed to construct their own racialized narratives of history.

In order to build these narratives, students need to demonstrate a range of thinking skills. These skills can be a struggle for students, though without them students' ability to access important ideas about their history is compromised. So, while I am not entirely comfortable with the fact that students must take standardized and high-stakes tests, and while I think the social studies test often invites an uncritical view of history, I do believe that the skills that it (and the ELA and math exams) purports to test are important for students to learn.

Skill development is critical, but not simply so that students will succeed on standardized tests. Whether confronting test questions, making meaning of new circumstances, or grappling with complex historical issues, students must tackle problems confidently, even—and perhaps particularly—when they are not sure of the answers. Using primary documents with students and encouraging them to create their own interpretations of past events provides meaningful challenges. Documents that address multicultural history are a natural place to begin helping students explore the past. Rather than being an add-on aspect of the curriculum, multiculturalism can be integrated into even the most test-conscious classrooms.

Nearly 20 years ago, Lisa Delpit (1988), argued that we must not ignore the need for all children to know basic skills in order to succeed in school, and that there may be times when we should be direct in our approach to teaching those skills. I argue here that meaningful social studies instruction using primary documents can help facilitate the learning of skills because the students see a reason to use the skills. Teachers can teach skills directly once they have established a context that has excited students' interest. Using primary documents and asking lively questions allows teachers to build that context.

Primary sources, moreover, can prepare children to participate in the historiographical revolution that has animated U.S. history for the past 50 years. In that time, African, Hispanic, Asian, and Native Americans along with women, gay men and lesbian groups, people with disabilities, and others have invoked history to narrate their struggles for equality and claim their rights. In the process of recovering artifacts of their pasts, these historically marginalized groups find a new sense of their individual and collective capacities to fight for justice. With their allies, they use the power of history in the process of dismantling the discriminatory legal, educational, cultural and social barriers that relegate individuals to secondary status or less throughout American history (Trouillot, 1995).

Unfortunately, students, particularly those in low-performing schools, face considerable pressure to do well on standardized tests. It does not follow, however, that teachers and students must respond by falling into decontextualized skills practice (Smith & Niemi, 2001). With the data reported here, I show how primary source materials can spark children's imaginations to interrogate the roots and branches of the country's racial history. I argue that using primary sources related to the United States' racial past enables teachers to open up conversations with children about our history while at the same time preparing for their state tests.

Taking standardized tests might be dreary, but preparing for them does not have to be. In the case of social studies, the inclusion of a Document-Based Question (albeit one that is only worth a small portion of the overall score) provides an opening for elementary teachers to go beyond the test. The fifth grade social studies test asks students to use the evidence they gather from careful analysis of primary sources to back up their arguments. Teachers can make this exercise even more meaningful to students by inviting debate about controversial questions.

We might not like the exams, but we can prepare students for them in lively and intellectually rigorous ways. Teachers can make use of the potential that primary sources, particularly of the racialized past, have for promoting basic and higher level skills. Contrary to my preservice students' fears that talking about race and racism would be harmful to students, students appreciate the chance to discuss these topics, and their engagement, particularly in a test-centered school culture, makes teaching all the more rewarding.

NOTES

1.   During the period of my research, the state-wide standardized science test scores were not reported by the city or state and were not used as criteria

for promotion. Since that time, however, they have begun to be reported and used as such.

2. Grant, Gradwell, and Cimbricz (2004) describe how the DBQ, while a step forward in terms of standardized testing, still does not provide students with an authentic history task.

3. The names of the teacher and students are pseudonyms.

4. When they started, many students do not know how to approach anything beyond the factual questions, and some even struggle with the subtraction. "Per person" is an important mathematical concept. Ms. Agosto and I scaffold. this activity by explaining what per-pupil spending meant.

REFERENCES

American Federation of Labor. (1902). *Some reasons for Chinese exclusion: Meat vs. rice*. Washington, DC: Government Printing Office. Retrieved from http://historymatters.gmu.edu/search.php?function=print&id=5036

Almarza, D. J., & Fehn, B. (1998). The construction of whiteness in an American history class: A case study of eighth grade Mexican American students. *Transformations, 9*(2), 196–211.

Anderson, J. D. (1994). How we learn race through history. In L. Kramer (Ed.), *Learning history in America: Schools, culture and politics* (pp. 87–106). Minneapolis: University of Minnesota Press.

Banks, J. A. (1996). Transformative knowledge, curriculum reform, and action. In J. A. Banks & C. A. M. Banks (Eds.), *Multicultural education, transformative knowledge, and action: Historical and contemporary perspectives* (pp. 335–348). New York: Teachers College Press.

Bo, S. S. (1885). *A Chinese view of the Statue of Liberty*. Retrieved from http://www.ftrain.com/AChineseViewoftheStatueofLiberty.html

Bolgatz, J. (2005). *Talking race in the classroom*. New York: Teachers College Press.

Chapman, T. (2003). *Stopping at the edge of the cliff: A White teacher's attempts at discussions of race, class and gender in an English class with a multi-ethnic, multi-racial student population*. Paper presented at the NCTE Assembly for Research Midwinter Conference: Teaching and researching across color lines, Minneapolis, MN.

Davis, N. J. (1992). Teaching about inequality: Student resistance, paralysis and rage. *Teaching Sociology, 20*, 232–238.

Delpit, L. (1988). The silenced dialogue: power and pedagogy in teaching other people's children. *Harvard Educational Review, 58*(3), 280–298.

Dipardo, A., & Fehn, B. (2000). Depoliticizing multicultural education: The return to normalcy in a predominantly white high school. *Theory and Research in Social Education, 28*(2), 170–192.

Ellsworth, E. (1989). Why doesn't this feel empowering? Working through the repressive myths of critical pedagogy. *Harvard Educational Review, 59*(3), 297–324.

Ellsworth, E. (1997). *Teaching positions: Difference, pedagogy, and the power of address*. New York: Teachers College Press.

Epstein, T. (1998). Deconstructing differences in African American and European-American adolescents' perspectives on U.S. history. *Curriculum Inquiry, 28*(4), 397–423.

Grant, S. G., Gradwell, J, M. & Cimbricz, S. K. (2004). A question of authenticity: The document-based question as an assessment of students' knowledge of history. *Journal of Curriculum and Supervision, 19*(4), 309–337.

Hatcher, R., & Troyna, B. (1993). Racialization and children. In C. McCarthy & W. Crichlow (Eds.), *Race, identity, and representation in education* (pp. 109–125). New York: Routledge.

Johnson, L. B. (1965, June 4). Commencement address at Howard University: "To fulfill these rights," *Public Papers of the Presidents of the United States: Lyndon B. Johnson, 1965* (Vol. II, pp. 635–640). Retrieved from http://www.lbjlib .utexas.edu/johnson/archives.hom/speeches.hom/650604.asp

Kuklin, S. (1993). *Speaking out: Teenagers take on sex, race, and identity.* New York: Putnam and Sons.

Ladson-Billings, G. (2003). *Still playing in the dark: Whiteness in the literary imagination of children's and young adult literature teaching.* Paper presented at the NCTE Assembly for Research Midwinter Conference, Minneapolis, MN.

Lazarus, E. (n.d.). *The new colossus.* Retrieved June 12, 2003, from http://www .libertystatepark.com/emma.htm

Levstik, L., & Barton, K. C. (1998). "It wasn't a good part of history": National identity and students' explanations of historical significance. *Teachers College Record, 99*(3), 478–513.

National Assessment of Educational Progress. (2001). *Nation's report card.* Retrieved from http://nces.ed.gov/nationsreportcard/pubs/main2001/ 2002483.asp#section5

New York State Department of Education (n.d.). *Instructional recommendations for elementary and intermediate instruction.* Retrieved from http://www.emsc.nysed .gov/ciai/mst/instructrec.htm

Noddings, N. (1997). Social studies and feminism. In E. W. Ross (Ed.), *The social studies curriculum: Purposes, problems, and possibilities* (pp. 59–70). Albany: State University of New York Press.

Poplin, M. (1999). The global classroom of the 21st century: Lessons from Mother Teresa and imperatives from Columbine. *Educational Horizons, 78*(1), 30–38.

Seixas, P. (1993). Historical understanding among adolescents in a multicultural setting. *Curriculum Inquiry, 23*(3), 301–327.

Smith, J., & Niemi, R. (2001). Learning history in schools: The impact of coursework and instructional practices on achievement. *Theory and Research in Social Education, 29*(1), 18–42.

Smith, M. L. (1991). Put to the test: The effects of external testing on teachers. *Educational Researcher, 20*(5), 8–11.

Stearns, P. N., Seixas, P., & Wineburg, S. (Eds.). (2000). *Knowing, teaching, and learning history: national and international perspectives.* New York: University Press.

Trouillot, M. (1995). *Silencing the past: Power and the production of history.* Boston: Beacon Press.

VanSledright, B. (2002). *In search of America's past: Learning to read history in elementary school*. New York: Teachers College Press.

West, C. (1994). Race and social justice in America. *Liberal Education, 80*(3), 32–39.

Wills, J. S. (1996). Who needs multicultural education? White students, U.S. history, and the construction of a usable past. *Anthropology and Education Quarterly, 27*(3), 365–389.

Wills, J., & Mehan, H. (1996). Recognizing diversity within a common historical narrative: The challenge to teaching history and social studies. *Multicultural Education, 4*(1), 4–11.

Wineburg, S. (2001). *Historical thinking and other unnatural acts: Charting the future of teaching the past*. Philadelphia: Temple University Press.

CHAPTER 8

TEACHING IN SPITE OF, RATHER THAN BECAUSE OF, THE TEST

A Case of Ambitious History Teaching in New York State

Jill M. Gradwell

I don't even think about the test to be honest…I really don't spend much of my instructional time devoted to the test. It doesn't even cross my mind.

– New York state global history and geography teacher, Fall 2001

In an earlier study, my colleagues and I interviewed 13 rural, urban, and suburban New York state (NYS) teachers about their perceptions of the recently-adopted 10th grade Global History and Geography state exam and the new test component, the Document-Based Question (DBQ) (Grant, Gradwell, Lauricella, Derme-Insinna, Pullano, & Tzetzo, 2002). From the interviews, we identified three themes with regards to their reactions to the test: The teachers were unsure if the new exam was an adequate measure of student learning, they questioned the exam being a

Measuring History: Cases of State-Level Testing Across the United States, 157–176
Copyright © 2006 by Information Age Publishing
All rights of reproduction in any form reserved.

move toward higher standards, and they did not believe the new exam or DBQ to be a strong influence on their teaching practice. The last theme intrigued me because representatives from the New York State Education Department (NYSED) have reported that, since the introduction of the DBQ on social studies exams, teachers' instructional programs have changed, largely for the better. However, as the above quotation suggests, teachers did not report significant changes to their teaching. I wondered, then, how are other teachers making sense of the changes in the NYS social studies exams, specifically the adoption of the DBQ? Do social studies teachers of other grade levels share these global history and geography teachers' views? Do tests influence teachers' instructional choices and, if so, to what extent?

In this chapter, I report on an interpretive case study I conducted in a middle school history teacher's classroom around the sense she is making of the state exam and the DBQ test component and her students' performance on it. I argue that, contrary to the current chatter about the negative impact of testing on teachers' practice, this is an ambitious teacher for she teaches in spite of the test rather than because of it. Ambitious teachers know their subject matter and students well and see in both the potential to create rich learning environments. In doing so, however, they recognize the need to negotiate a series of contextual factors like state standards, curriculum, and assessment (Grant, 2003, 2005). The teacher in this study is ambitious for although she is encouraging her students to think historically in her lessons and 98% of them are passing the state exam, she does not view the exam as a true measure of success. Rather, she pushes herself knowing there is yet another opportunity to make her teaching better and to improve upon what may appear to be a successful moment. This case study illuminates the possibilities for novice teachers working with a heterogeneously group of students in a high-stakes testing environment.

FACTORS INFLUENCING TEACHERS' INSTRUCTIONAL PROGRAMS

In recent research in history education, it has been suggested that several factors play a role in teachers' choices of instructional practices such as their subject matter knowledge (Wineburg & Wilson, 1991), pedagogical content knowledge (Grant, 2003; Shulman, 1987), a disciplinary lens (Wilson & Wineburg, 1988), epistemology (Slekar, 1998), notions of "best practice" (Hartzler-Miller, 2001), and conceptions of history (Evans, 1989, 1990). In other studies, key pedagogical influences include teachers' overarching purpose for teaching history such as "making students better people" (van Hover & Yeager, 2003) or "teaching history for the common good" (Barton & Levstik, 2004). However, as Grant (2003) points out, several forces are at work in most teachers' decision making around content, materials, and instructional strategies.

Recent attention has been directed at the relationship between testing and teachers' instructional practices. Some observers argue that tests drive instruction in less than thoughtful ways; teachers only teach the curricula that is expected to be on the test and use class time to engage students in test-prep activities (Stoskopf, 2001; Thompson, 2001). However, there has been a growing body of empirical research that suggests otherwise (Gerwin, 2004; Grant, 2003; Grant, et al., 2002; van Hover, 2004).

In Gerwin's (2004) study of 21 NYS preservice social studies teachers, he argues that, despite all the talk about the effects of high-stakes testing, "not much has had a widespread effect on classroom instruction in social studies" (p. 72). From discussions with teachers in a mentoring program, he notes that even the addition of the new testing component, the DBQ, has had little impact on teachers' practice: "The more things change the more they stay the same" (p. 72).

In Grant's (2003) study of two NYS 11th grade U.S. History and Government teachers, he observes that the "tests are an uncertain lever" (p. 114) and that there is "little direct, deep, and consistent influence of tests on these teachers' classroom teaching" (p. 128). Grant argues that the NYS Regents exam matters to the two teachers in his study, but what sense they make of the test and how it translates in their teaching is a different matter altogether. Although both teachers are aware of the state exam, the influence is "far from pure and direct" (p. 125) and other factors such as their views of subject matter and students matter more than the test.

A later study of NYS global history and geography teachers supports the claim that the impact of the state exams on teachers' teaching is complicated and uneven (Grant, et al., 2002). The global teachers make surface-level changes to their content, instruction, and assessment, but nothing deeper. They report altering the time spent on specific content, adding more test-like questions to their practice, and using more documents in ways modeling the DBQ test component. The teachers who do report making improvements to their teaching repertoire do so not because of the test, but because they are reflective practitioners.

An added layer to consider with respect to all the chatter about testing and teaching is the effects on beginning teachers. Stephanie van Hover (2004) investigated seven high school beginning teachers making sense of Virginia's History and Social Science Standards of Learning (SOLs) and associated high-stakes tests. The teachers in the study hold mixed views about the new accountability measures. Consistent with previous studies, the influences of the tests on planning, instruction, and assessment vary across the participants. The strongest lever of influence for this particular group of teachers is the unique set of challenges they face as novices. It is unclear, then, the extent to which high-stakes tests influence teachers' practices. This is not to say that tests are irrelevant, but instead to make the point that many influences compete for teachers' attention. Tests matter, but so too do a number of other factors.

The purpose of this case study is to understand a beginning teacher's perceptions of and responses to the NYS eighth grade exam. In particular, I focus on one component of the test, the Document-Based Question, asking what role it plays in her instruction. The teacher in this study does not let the test dictate her practice for she does not feel her students' performance on it reflects their true historical understanding. Therefore, this beginning teacher does not make her instructional decisions because of the state exam but rather in spite of it.

SOCIAL STUDIES TESTING IN NEW YORK STATE

New York state has a long history of testing and accountability. In recent years, policymakers have attempted to raise standards for all children through changes in curriculum such as the NYS *Social Studies Curriculum Resource Guide* (New York State Education Department, 1996) and revisions in the state testing program. Since June 2000, NYSED has revised the 10th grade level with the Global History and Geography exam and the 11th grade level with the U.S. History and Government exam and added two new exams at fifth grade and eighth grade. The stakes attached to these exams are higher than ever before because all students must pass the 10th and 11th grade exams to graduate.

One of the key changes on all the exams is the adoption of the Document-Based Question, loosely modeled after the DBQ component on the Advanced-Placement exams in history. On the first part of the DBQ, there are 6–8 primary source and secondary source documents (e.g., charts, maps, quotations, photographs, posters, political cartoons, and textbook passages). The students read the various texts and answer 1–2 short questions about each document (most questions call only for literal interpretations). Students then respond to an essay prompt for which they use the information available from the documents and their prior knowledge about the topic.

The NYS state curriculum calls for U.S. history to be taught for 2 years over Grades 7 and 8. Items on the eighth grade test, therefore, focus on people, places, and events central to U.S. history. Directions for the June 2003 DBQ asked students to read and respond to texts about the nineteenth century construction and effects of the Erie Canal and transcontinental railroad and to address the prompt: "Discuss how the Erie Canal and Transcontinental Railroad led to economic growth in the United States."[1] There were seven documents that included one textbook excerpt, one trade book excerpt, one government document excerpt, two maps, and two charts. For each document, there were one or two short answer questions that the students had to complete for one point each.

THE STUDY

This interpretive case study explores how a novice teacher makes sense of the Document-Based Question on the June 2003 New York state eighth grade test and her students' performance on it. This study is a slice of a larger study about how this teacher plans, implements, and uses primary sources to teach history in a high-stakes testing environment (Gradwell, 2005).

In this study, the selection of the participant was purposeful (Merriam, 1998). Because this study is an extension of my earlier work investigating a teacher's use of primary sources to teach history, my selection of Sara Cooper [2], a third-year middle school social studies teacher, was driven by the gaps in earlier research in this area. First, the existing studies detailing teachers' use of primary source documents typically focus on preservice teachers (e.g., Bohan & Davis, 1998; Fehn & Koeppen, 1998; Gillaspie & Davis, 1997-1998; Seixas, 1998; Wineburg & Fournier, 1994; Yeager & Davis, 1995; Yeager & Wilson 1997) or veteran teachers (e.g., Yeager & Davis, 1996). Choosing a novice teacher added a dimension to the growing body of research regarding teachers' use of primary sources to teach history to schoolchildren. Second, few teachers in the extant literature work in a high-stakes testing environment. The NYS state exam at the end of eighth grade, does not carry the same high stakes as the 10th and 11th grade exams, but Cooper is held accountable for her students' scores and they are made public.

The school district that Sara Cooper teaches in is a first-ring suburban school district outside of a large western New York city. Based on 2002–2003 New York State *School Report Card Comprehensive Information Report* (New York State Education Department, 2002–2003) the student ethnic make-up was as follows: American Indian, Alaskan, Asian, or Pacific Islander (1.3%), Black (Not Hispanic) (2.8%), Hispanic (1.3%), and White (Not Hispanic) (94.5%). Limited English language students in 2002–2003 were less than 1% of the enrollment. Also for the 2002–2003 school year, 11.6% of the students received free lunch, 9.6% received a reduced lunch, and less than 10% received public assistance. The school is a middle school with 597 students servicing Grades 6, 7, and 8.

My classroom observations were of one of Cooper's five eighth grade class sections. The class composition was 19 mainly white, lower and middle class students grouped heterogeneously by academic ability. Cooper selected this class for the study because she believed it to be representative of all of her other sections. Although most classrooms have a mix of student abilities, this section of Cooper's classes is an extreme: One third of the students were identified by the school as gifted, another third attended the resource room for extra academic assistance, and the remaining third of the class ranged across all academic levels.

This chapter draws on data collected over the 2003 spring semester. That data included a biographical questionnaire; six weeks of classroom observations during two units of study; five in-depth, semistructured interviews; a think-aloud session about the exam; and classroom artifacts (e.g., handouts, notes, assessments). Observations were recorded in a field notes journal. As soon as possible after each classroom stay, I revisited my field notes and added details not initially captured during the observation (Merriam, 1998). The interview questions focused on Cooper's sense of history, experiences as a history student, discipline knowledge, teaching experiences, goals for her students learning history, and view of state tests.

Much of the data for this study comes from the interview data in which Cooper discussed the state test and in the think-aloud session where Cooper interpreted her students' responses to the June 2003 DBQ. Think-alouds allow the participant to reason out loud making it possible for the researcher to understand the process of pedagogical reasoning (Afflerbach, 2000). To give context to her perceptions of their performance on the DBQ, I asked Cooper to select five students of varying ability levels from the eighth grade section I observed. Table 8.1 describes the students Cooper selected for the think aloud session. After explaining the basic ideas of how to approach the think-aloud session, I asked Cooper to talk through her impressions of the test documents, questions, and task. I asked her to think aloud about her sense of each student's responses to

Table 8.1

Gender	Ability Level (School Identifier)	DBQ Score (0-5 Rubric)
Male	Gifted and Talented	5
Female	Gifted and Talented	5
Male	Special Education	4.5
Male	Special Education	4
Male	Regular Education	4

the various test tasks. These tasks included both the short answer questions and the essay component. The think-aloud session was audiotaped and transcribed.

Data were analyzed using case study methodology (Stake, 1995). Case study methodology enables the researcher to evaluate thick data generated from one participant's teaching. Data analysis involved several general steps. First, interviews and the think-aloud session were taped and transcribed. Next, transcriptions were coded based on initial themes and patterns. Field notes of classroom observations were coded using similar procedures (Spradley, 1980). Finally, the initial themes emerging separately from the interviews, observations, and document-analysis of classroom artifacts were checked by triangulating across data sources and by probing for both confirming and disconfirming evidence (Bogdan & Biklin, 1982).

The themes that surfaced during data analysis fall into three categories. The first category deals with Cooper's perceptions of her students' performance on the DBQ. The second is Cooper's perceptions of DBQ task and accompanying documents. The last category relates to her views about the relationship between the DBQ and her practice.

TEACHING IN SPITE OF THE TEST RATHER THAN BECAUSE OF IT

I begin with a vignette of Cooper's teaching practice to show how she makes sense of the testing climate in which she works. I then explore Cooper's perceptions of her students' performance on their eighth grade state exam in general and on the DBQ in particular. I argue that, contrary to the current chatter about the negative impact of testing on teachers' practice, Cooper is a case of an ambitious teacher teaching in spite of the test rather than because of it.

A Vignette of Ambitious Teaching

As Sara Cooper's eighth graders enter the room on the second day of their 1920s unit, they see a large Venn diagram on the chalkboard with the heading, "Women," on the top and the headings "Early 1900s" and "1920s" on the sides. A large candle is depicted with lighted wicks on both ends and the phrase "my candle burns at both ends" written beside it. As students pass a desk in the front of the room, they pick up a reading packet before sitting down, a daily habit to which the students seem accustomed. With the students seated, Cooper asks the class to read silently the Edna St. Vincent Millay poem, "First Fig" and a short biography about her. After a few minutes, Cooper opens a class discussion about the poem and its author. Her questions begin with "Who is the author?" "What can you tell me about the author?" "Where did she live after college?" "Who did she live with that made her experience people with new and different ideas?" She then asks a student to read the poem aloud. When finished, Cooper asks, "what does the phrase 'candle burning at both ends' mean?" She continues with her questions about the poem, ending with, "what happens when you let a candle burn at both ends?" During the discussion, the students talk about the changing roles and identities of women during the 1920s. Cooper cautions them not to categorize all 1920s women as flappers, for women had multiple experiences during this era and should not be narrowly defined. With that advice, she directs the class to turn their reading over, to create a Venn diagram similar to the one on the chalkboard, and to use the collection of primary sources in their packets to record the various aspects of women during their respective time periods. The sources depict women from both eras doing various jobs and activities. As students work in small groups, Cooper plays a musical selection from Louis Armstrong noting that there were not as many female jazz artists as there were male artists at the time. Minutes later, Cooper asks the class to use the bottom of their papers to "define what a flapper is, not by the book, but *your interpretation*." A minute later, Cooper calls on volunteers to share their definitions. After several do so, Cooper shows several short clips from the Charlie Chaplin film, *City Lights*. As they watch the film, Cooper tells the class to think about "how are women viewed in the film and what attitudes about women are in the film?" As the class ends, Cooper solicits comments about the film and her questions. She concludes class by noting that women of this era can be perceived and depicted in various ways.

Teaching In Spite of the Test

I offer this vignette of Sara Cooper's teaching practice as a way to explore the ways in which she is making sense of the high-stakes testing environment in which she works and specifically her attention to the newest addition to the state social studies test, the Document-Based Question. Some observers argue that testing inevitably drives instruction in less than ambitious ways (e.g., McNeil, 2000). Presumably, a novice teacher with a wildly heterogeneous classroom would illustrate such an argument. If so, one might expect to observe a teacher focusing only the content most likely to appear on the state exam, giving up subject matter depth for breadth, doing "drill and kill" exercises for the sake of content coverage, and assessing students in ways mimicking the specific exam components.

The snapshot of Cooper's classroom contradicts these very notions. In short, she teaches the way she does in spite of rather than because of the state test.

Given Cooper's attention to the topic, one might expect the idea of women of the 1920s is prominent in the state curriculum or on the exam.[3] It is not. In the state curriculum unit entitled *The Roaring Twenties Reflected the Spirit of the Postwar Period*, the only mention of women is one phrase: "Women continued to increase their presence in the workforce" (Available at http://www.emsc.nysed.gov/ciai/socst/ssrg.html). Moreover, not one question on the 2001, 2002, and 2003 state exams asked about women during the 1920s. It appears that Cooper's selection of unit content is influenced neither by the state curriculum or the test. Cooper reports that she chooses content that matches her disciplinary lens ("I consider myself more of a social historian, like a lot of things I do is social history") and that resonates with her students ("I mean they seem to really get into it when we talk about ordinary people"). Rather than let her content selection be driven by the state curriculum or test, Cooper selects content based on her subject matter knowledge and the interests of her students.

If Cooper does not slavishly follow the state curriculum guide, neither does she sacrifice depth for breadth by marching her students through the content. New York teachers have their hands full trying to teach a swath of topics from "Global Heritage of the American People Prior to 1500" to "The Changing Nature of the American People from World War II to the Present" in two academic years. Cooper feels the curriculum coverage and time constraints that all teachers face, yet she provides students with a range of rich sources about women, offers them numerous opportunities to construct their own perspectives of women, and at no time lectures to them. The students are engaged from the moment they enter the classroom until the end of the period. Regardless of the seemingly daunting task of getting through the state curriculum Cooper chooses to spend time of topics that matter to her and to her students:

> There's so many topics that they want to debate and we've had about five debates this year and it takes about three days. But they love debates and they're really good at it…. It just takes so much time. But I like when they ask [to debate a particular issue] because that means that they really are interested in the topic. They usually want to debate topics that are interesting to them.

Like most history teachers, Cooper is well aware that there is never enough time to get through all the curriculum that the state test may target. She could choose to cover as much material as possible in the expectation that more is necessarily better. Cooper chooses otherwise, creating lessons that cover important content and entice her students into deep learning.

Cooper's choice of curriculum materials differs markedly from what one might expect of a teacher in a high-stakes testing environment. Although the inclusion of primary sources on the DBQs could be interpreted as promoting a change in the typical textbook-based curriculum, using new materials need not mean more ambitious instruction. Gerwin (2004) observed preservice teachers using primary sources in their teaching assignments, but they do so "in a cursory fashion, similar to the simplistic treatment they receive on the examination itself" (p. 72). Cooper bucks such an approach, using primary sources instead as opportunities for students to interpret and analyze texts. The tasks she assigns (e.g., "Define what a flapper is, not by the book, but your interpretation," and "How are women viewed in the film and what attitudes about women are in the film?") guide the students' inquiry, but they construct their own understandings about the past rather simply adopt their teacher's.

As an example, in Cooper's Great Depression unit, she selects numerous primary sources and creates activities such that her students can read and interpret various documents. In one lesson, Cooper selects two songs popular during the era "just so they had different material to work with and different examples, a variety. *Brother, Can You Spare Me a Dime* is a song that most social studies teachers use. I kind of wanted to give them a different perspective as well [like the song] *Somewhere Over the Rainbow*, just so they had a variety of different songs to listen to." Cooper uses more than one song from the era because "they were different, because one was more about being optimistic … and the other one was more about how hard times were so it just gave them both points of view, or two points of view." Cooper's decision to include the two songs stems from her desire to expose her students to multiple perspectives of the Great Depression, not to have them practice document-based skills needed for the state exam. In her daily instruction, Cooper's selection and use of source materials provides rich opportunities for students to deeply experience the past.

Given all that Sara Cooper does, one might assume that this is an Advanced-Placement class. It is not. All of Cooper's eighth grade classes are heterogeneously grouped and the class I observed featured a wide range of abilities. Her students are identified in equal thirds as gifted and talented, regular education, and special education. Asked if she varies her practice or course materials because of the diverse student population, Cooper replies, "not really, because there are so many kids at different levels in every class, which I really like. It's not like I have one group of special education [students] and one group of gifted [students]. With such a variety [of students] I don't vary the sources that I use." Cooper does not let the class make-up of students dictate her instructional materials or her strategies.

Although this is just one vignette of Cooper's classroom, the teaching represented here is consistent with her instruction from class to class and across both the 1920s and Great Depression units. Cooper never mentions the state exam explicitly during either unit nor are the final unit assessments modeled on the state exam: Students create skits based on modern day situation comedies that reflect the roaring 1920s era and they create a pictorial museum exhibit of the Great Depression. In the several interviews I did with Cooper, she never mentioned the test unless I specifically prompted her to do so. Sara Cooper teaches in ambitious ways (Smith & Niemi, 2001), but she does so in spite of the test, not because of it.

Cooper's Perception of the State Test, the DBQ, and her Students' Performance

Sara Cooper may not teach to the test or even talk much about it to her students, but she is well aware of it. She grew up in New York state and took Regents exams in high school. Cooper also meets regularly with other eighth grade teachers in the school district where discussions about the state test are frequent:

> They're very concerned about the exam. It's a big part of their teaching, and a big topic of conversation [at district meetings]. Where I'm just like, "Do we have to talk about the exam? Let's move on to other things." But, it's just a bigger part of what they teach; I can tell from just talking to them.

Cooper hears about the state test and the DBQ component from her colleagues regularly and she gets frustrated for she would rather discuss other topics related to improving teaching and learning.

So, what does Sara Cooper think about the test and what sense does she make of her students' performance on it? Despite liking the DBQ concept, believing in general that the documents composing the DBQ have some value and are generally age appropriate, Cooper is less than satisfied with the scope, rigor, and usefulness of the DBQ as a meaningful assessment of her students' understanding of history: "It was just limited, it was almost too easy I think, I was expecting more."

Cooper's Mixed Perceptions of the DBQ

Although Cooper has numerous reasons to feel good about her students' performance on the DBQ, she questions it as a reliable and valid assessment of her students' historical understanding. She believes that the DBQ task is too narrow in scope for it does not push her students' thinking and that the documents reflect limited perspectives and are too short in length to spark her students' prior knowledge. What stands out most for Cooper is that she believes the focus of the task and documents do not match her instructional practice. Cooper teaches in rich and meaningful ways and she perceives the DBQ as a far reach from her ambitious teaching style. As a result, Cooper does not teach to the test, she teaches past the test.

Cooper views the DBQ task, "Discuss how the Erie Canal and the transcontinental railroad led to economic growth in the United States," on the 2003 exam as narrow and "limiting." She is unhappy with the topic because it covers content from both the seventh and eighth grade years: "I was a little upset that they had a 7th grade topic, the Erie Canal in the DBQ, usually they just have an 8th grade topic, so that was a little annoying." Cooper assumes that, because in previous years the DBQ was usually composed of eighth grade material, it would likely be so again. On the June 2001 exam, the DBQ was about American life at home during World War II; on the June 2002 exam the topic was about the reformers of the late 1800s and early 1900s. Both topics are in the eighth grade state curriculum.

But what really seems to trouble Cooper is that the essay question prompt itself offer few opportunities for her students to display their knowledge of history: "I also was upset that it seemed kind of limited. It was about the railroads and the Erie Canal, and all the kids were just [giving answers] like faster, cheaper, easier." Cooper is unhappy with the DBQ task because it is narrow in scope, specifically because it focuses on the impact on economic growth. Cooper explains, "well, it was all about economics, which is fine. That is really important and the kids learned about that. But with my students, a lot of them [learned] about the transcontinental railroad [with respect to] the workers' [lives]." This quote hints at Cooper's preference for teaching social history and her dissatisfaction with the economic focus of the DBQ task.

If she views the DBQ task as limiting, Cooper expresses similar feelings about the documents available to students to construct their essays. Cooper dislikes the fact that all the documents focus on economics in similar ways: "Well, they were just all about obviously economic growth, but they were all the same types of benefits about economic growth. So one document talks about how much faster it was, and the other documents talk about how much faster it was. It was just hard for kids to pull other things out of it." Cooper's concern is real and important. She knows that for her students to earn a five, the highest score on the rubric, they have to include outside information in their essays:

[The students have to do] more than just the simple things that were in the documents, which is what you have to do to get a five. But there wasn't much about the economy that they could have added, which was my problem. Because [NYSED] says kids should be able to bring in this much outside information, and if you give them a DBQ that is that limited, it's hard for them to do.

With the documents all reflecting similar patterns and themes, Cooper believes her students may have been at a disadvantage for there is little in the way of prompts in the documents to include much outside information in their essays: "A lot of the kids, you could tell that they were just trying as hard as they could to find anything in the documents that they could write about."

Cooper also notes that, although having excerpted documents may help her students to complete the short accompanying questions, they limit the students' ability to cull enough information from them to complete their essays:

A lot of them were really short, which is good and bad when kids are writing essays. They usually get the right answer in the constructed response, but then they have less to pull from for their essay. It was a good variety of different types of sources, but they just said the same types of things.

Cooper sees some value in the documents in the DBQ because they are short, easy to read, respond to in short answer questions, and reflect some "variety." What she means by this last point is evidence of multiple types of documents: "I thought there was a pretty wide variety of documents that they gave the kids. It was pretty visual, and a good amount of reading for their age level … they had a couple charts, a few maps, they used a pretty good variety." Variety in this case meant variety of types not variety of perspectives, something Cooper took issue with.

What bothers Cooper most is that the DBQ focus and accompanying documents do not match her teaching practice. As noted, Cooper is bothered by the strict focus on economics, an area she teaches, but does not emphasize. In the vignette above, Cooper's students consider multiple interpretations of women of the 1920s. Unlike the emphasis on 1920s women in the workplace in the NYS core curriculum, Cooper focuses on the roles and activities of women at home and in the public as well as at work. Doing so reflects Cooper's preference for social history. As she points out, "[The DBQ topic] was different than the style that I usually do because it was economic." Asked what the DBQ task and the documents might be like in her hands, she explains, "[I would] probably have more photographs on the transcontinental railroad. I'd probably have more about the Native Americans and the buffalo." Cooper notes that all of the

DBQ documents are about how transportation became cheaper and faster because of the Erie Canal and the transcontinental railroad. None of the documents discusses the laborers who spurred the economic growth or the various group sacrifices that made these transportation systems prosper. These are the kinds of issues Cooper emphasizes in her practice and their absence explains much of Cooper's dissatisfaction with the DBQ.

Cooper's Perceptions of Students' Performance on the DBQ

Overall, Sara Cooper reports being satisfied with her students' performance on the DBQ and on the state exam. She believes their essays are more thoughtful than those of other district students. Her students' essays included far more outside information than did their peers' efforts and much of that information reflected material she presented. Yet Cooper's satisfaction with students' test performance is undercut by her dissatisfaction with the exam and the opportunities it provides students to show their historical understandings.

Although surprised by some individual students' performance, overall Cooper is pleased, especially with the scores her special education students earn: "I was really happy with their performance on the DBQ.... There were mostly fours and fives. A lot of the special education students had fours and fives, which was great." Of the class I observed, the lowest student score on the DBQ is a three on the five-point rubric. The exam scores range from 70 to 95, with eight of the 19 students at the mastery level (85% or higher). The overall passing rate on the state exam for Cooper's entire eighth grade classes is 98%,[4] higher than any other teacher's class in the district and well above the state average.

Cooper has cause to celebrate her students' DBQ and exam scores, but she is also pleased that her students could link their essay responses to what she is doing in the classroom. Moreover, Cooper believes that her students include much more outside information in their essays than their peers in other teachers' classrooms:

> My students' essays were definitely a lot longer, much longer [than other students' essays], like a couple pages. And my students brought in a lot more outside information. A lot of them quoted the Erie Canal songs, and things like that, and they talked about Chinese immigrants and working on the transcontinental railroad where the other teachers' kids used a lot of things from the documents.

Cooper observes that not only do her students write more in their essays and use more outside information, the information they use beyond the documents focuses on the social context of the era rather than on economic impacts. Pulling out Ken's essay, Cooper points to the information he included beyond the documents provided on the test:

He brings a lot of outside information about the laborers, with the railroad talking about the explosives that they used, things that weren't even in the documents. Like how [the laborers'] lives were at risk, how they weren't invited to the opening day celebration, which is outside information. And then he ties that into the buffalo hunting and the Native Americans. So he just chose to write a whole paragraph on a topic that wasn't in the documents.

Cooper then pulls Abby's essay and points to her ability to weave documents around the focus of her response rather than simply regurgitate the information in the provided documents:

I think that she didn't just use the documents to write the essay, that she had a strong background in what she was talking about. And yet the documents maybe reminded her of what she learned, but she didn't depend on them to write the essay. She probably could have written it without the documents, which is good. They were just kind of a guide.

Cooper and I find intriguing the wide range of information both students include. Asked to interpret Ken's use of outside information, Cooper explains,

well, he used it as an economic effect for the Native Americans. That they were losing their food source, and tied it in to how they were shooting the buffalo in the railway cars, which I think was a pretty interesting twist for him to throw in there.

She continues, "But a lot of [my] students, quite a few, did the same thing." Turning to Abby's paper, Cooper highlights the girl's skilled use of documents to support rather than constitute her response. Cooper smiles at this demonstration "because then you know that the kids know what they're talking about." Ken's essay demonstrates the importance of using outside information to expand on the documents provided; Abby's essay shows that students can use documents in thoughtful ways to build and support their ideas. A key pattern Cooper observes in most of her students' essays is that they can write their essays without the documents. This understanding reinforces her belief that they are learning and retaining information from the types and ways she uses primary sources in classes with them.

In addition to their use of the test documents, Cooper notices that students often refer to activities from her lessons in their essays. Returning to Ken's paper, Cooper pinpoints a lesson in which students debated to whom the transcontinental railroad might be dedicated:

It's something we spent a lot of time on. We debated the transcontinental railroad, whether it should be dedicated to the Chinese immigrants or the Native Americans. They lost their land, so it was a huge debate, and I think that's why they pulled in both for that.

As Cooper discusses other students' DBQ responses, I ask her why so many of the students comment on the opening of the transcontinental railroad. She links their decisions to another lesson in which students interpret primary sources about the event:

We looked at a lot of the photographs from the opening celebration and we talked about who's in the photographs and we talked about the Chinese not being invited…just to show that there weren't any Chinese immigrants in the photograph. Then they had to write a letter; I had them write one of two letters. One letter from someone who was at the celebration, explaining what happened, how it was, how great it was, and how it was going to have an economic impact on the United States. And then the other option was that they had to write a letter from someone who wasn't invited, from an immigrant who worked on the railroad. They had to draw a picture with the letter and then they traded letters. They responded back and forth, [to the questions of] "what would [it] have [been like for] the person who was there? How would they have reacted to the letter from the Chinese immigrant?" Then I sent them up in front of the room, we read them together and there was a final copy of them there in the display case with pictures. I had them take primary sources and create their own [letters] from the sources that we looked at, which they seem to remember a lot better when we do that.

Cooper believes that her students' retention of information about the opening of the transcontinental railroad stems from her primary source activity. Such activities, she believes help students recall information, wrestle with evidence, and construct their own interpretations.

Cooper is satisfied with her eighth graders' high passing rate, high mastery rate, and the fact that they outperformed other eighth graders in the district. She is also pleased that students use what they learned about document use and about ideas in their essay responses. With such a result, Cooper might have simply congratulated herself on her students' accomplishments. She does not, largely because she can see no direct relationship her teaching and the students' test scores. Cooper does not plan her lessons with the test in mind: "I honestly rarely even think about it … [for example] I don't just give them primary sources because they will see them on the state exam." Satisfaction with her students' scores, then, does not translate into self-satisfaction because she does not view the test as a faithful representation of either the students' efforts or her own. Cooper does not teach as she does because of the test, if anything, she teaches in spite of it.

Despite Cooper's happiness with her students' performance on the DBQ, she is discontented with the extent to which the test components assess her students' understanding of history. Cooper's students' DBQ essays are longer in length, include more outside information, and their overall test scores surpass other students in the district. However, Cooper does not believe the DBQ task is open-ended enough to warrant true historical investigation skills of her students. Cooper does not feel the need to change her teaching style because of the test because the opportunities she provides students throughout the school year to interrogate primary sources, to construct historical interpretations, and to publicly defend their judgments of the past far exceed any DBQ or test requirement. In a way, then, the test may drive Cooper's instruction, except that she steers not toward the exam, but beyond it.

IMPLICATIONS

Although not generalizable, Sara Cooper's case is instructive for it presents challenges for testing critics, for policymakers, and for teachers.

First, Cooper's experience confronts critical views of the testing and teaching. A novice teacher working in a high-stakes testing environment with students from an extreme range of abilities, many would expect Cooper to cave to the challenges and teach in pedantic ways. Yet, she allows the testing context to define neither her selection of content and materials nor her instructional strategies. Cooper's curricular choices reflect her notions of history and her concern for students' interest and learning rather than the state tests. In this light, Cooper's case flies in the face of widespread predictions of test-driven teaching and learning.

Second, Cooper's case defies the claims of policymakers that new tests will inspire ambitious teaching. New test items like the DBQ might be a step up from multiple-choice, but Cooper is not satisfied. The DBQ task, she believes, is not open-ended enough and the documents provided are too short and represent too few perspectives. Ambitious teachers may disregard the more pedantic messages the test sends and continue to use documents in rich, creative ways. Others, however, may feel constrained by the test parameters and tailor their teaching practices to those parameters. Ironically, then, policymakers may be most pleased with those teachers who least follow the dictates of the state test.

Finally, Cooper's case challenges teachers, novice and veteran, who argue they are hamstrung by tests. An untenured, third-year teacher, teaching a heterogeneous group of middle-schoolers, Cooper does not shy away from using multiple texts or taking time during lessons to deeply explore topics. She depends on neither the textbook nor the test to drive her instruction. Instead she blends the content with students' interests and creates opportunities where students can develop their own historical interpretations of the past, and she does so in a climate of testing accountability. Cooper's students emerge from her class with a strong sense of history and with passing grades on the state exam. Teachers who give over large parts of their classroom practice to test preparation may also get positive test scores. Cooper's experience suggests that they may not need to.

CONCLUSION

Clearly Sara Cooper is not a typical history teacher (Goodlad, 1984). Although pleased with her students' performance, Cooper is dissatisfied with the rigor of the test component and with its usefulness for assessing students' historical understanding. So Cooper teaches in spite of the test, and because she is an ambitious teacher who does not let the testing context constrain her instructional choices (Grant, 2003, 2005).

In Cooper's case, policymakers err in their belief that they can leverage big changes in teachers' practice by changing only one part of teaching, the context. Ambitious teachers like Cooper clearly show that subject matter, learners, and context all interact and do so in complicated ways. If policymakers want to make substantive change in the ways teachers teach, then focusing on tests may not be the answer. And until more is understood about the nature of how subject matter, learners, and context interact to create ambitious learning environments, it is unlikely that significant change will occur.

NOTES

1. The entire June 2003 exam and DBQ is available at: http://emsc33.nysed .gov/osa/elintsocst.html.
2. All names are pseudonyms.
3. In addition to this one lesson, Cooper spent parts of three other lessons on the role of women during the 1920s.
4. Per New York State Education Department instructions, teachers do not grade their own exams. In Cooper's school district, her students' tests were graded by two other teachers and her role was to act as monitor and third grader for any grade disputes.

REFERENCES

Afflerbach, P. (2000). Verbal reports and protocol analysis. In P. D. Pearson, R. Barr, P. Mosenthal, & M. Kamil (Eds.), *Handbook of reading research* (3rd ed., pp. 163–179). New York: Longman.

Barton, K. C. & Levstik, L. S. (2004). *Teaching history for the common good*. Mahwah, NJ: Erlbaum.

Bogdan, R. C., & Biklen, S. K. (1982). *Qualitative research for education: An introduction to theory and methods*. Boston: Allyn & Bacon.

Bohan, C. H., & Davis, O. L., Jr. (1998). Historical constructions: How social studies student teachers' historical thinking is reflected in their writing of history. *Theory and Research in Social Education, 26*(2), 173–197.

Evans, R. W. (1989). Teacher conceptions of history. *Theory and Research in Social Education, 17*(3), 210–240.

Evans, R. W. (1990). Teacher conceptions of history revisited: Ideology, curriculum, and student belief. *Theory and Research in Social Education, 28*, 101–138.

Fehn, B., & Koeppen, K. E. (1998). Intensive document-based instruction in a social studies methods course and student teachers' attitudes and practice in subsequent field experiences. *Theory and Research in Social Education, 26*(4), 461–484.

Gerwin, D. (2004). Preservice teachers report the impact of high-stakes testing. *The Social Studies, 95*(2), 71–74.

Gillaspie, M. K., & Davis, O. L., Jr. (1997–1998). Historical constructions: How elementary student teachers' historical thinking is reflected in their writing of history. *International Journal of Social Education, 12*(2), 35–45.

Goodlad, J. I. (1984). *A place called school: Prospects for the future*. New York: McGraw-Hill.

Gradwell, J. M. (2005). *Practicing the past: Primary sources and pedagogy*. Unpublished doctoral dissertation, University at Buffalo, New York.

Grant, S. G. (2003). *History lessons: Teaching, learning, and testing in U.S. high school classrooms*. Mahwah, NJ: Erlbaum.

Grant, S. G. (2005). More journey than end: A case study of ambitious teaching. In O. L. Davis, Jr. & E. Yeager (Eds.), *Wise practice in teaching social studies in the age of high stakes testing* (pp. 117–130). Greenwich, CT: Information Age.

Grant, S. G., Gradwell, J. M., Lauricella, A. M., Derme-Insinna, A., Pullano, L., & Tzetzo, K. (2002). When increasing the stakes need not mean increasing standards: The case of the New York state global history and geography exam. *Theory and Research in Social Education, 30*(4), 488–515.

Hartzler-Miller, C. (2001). Making sense of "best practice" in teaching history. *Theory and Research in Social Education, 29*(4), 672–695.

McNeil, L. (2000). *Contradictions of school reform: Educational cost of standardized testing*. New York: Routledge.

Merriam, S. B. (1998). *Qualitative research in case study applications in education*. San Francisco: Jossey-Bass.

New York State Education Department. (1996). *Social studies resource guide*. Albany, NY: Author. Retrieved from http://www.emsc.nysed.gov/ciai/socst/ssrg.html

New York State Education Department. (2002–2003). *School report card comprehensive information report*. Retrieved from http://www.emsc.nysed.gov/repcrdfall2003/schools/142601030003.html

Seixas, P. (1998). Student teachers thinking historically. *Theory and Research in Social Education, 26*(3), 310–341.

Shulman, L. (1987). Knowledge and teaching: Foundations of the new reform. *Harvard Educational Review, 57*(1), 1–21.

Slekar, T. D. (1998). Epistemological entanglements: Preservice elementary school teachers' "apprenticeship of observation" and the teaching of history. *Theory and Research in Social Education, 26*(4), 485–507.

Smith, J., & Niemi, R. (2001). Learning history in school: The impact of course work and instructional practices on achievement. *Theory and Research in Social Education, 29*(1), 18-42.

Spradley, J. P. (1980). *Participant observation*. New York: Holt.

Stake, R. E. (1995). *The art of case study research*. Thousand Oaks, CA: Sage.

Stoskopf, A. (2001). Reviving Clio: Inspired history teaching and learning (without high-stakes tests). *Phi Delta Kappan, 82*(6), 468–473.

Thompson, S. (2001). The authentic standards movement and its evil twin. *Phi Delta Kappan, 82*(5), 358–362.

van Hover, S. D. (2004, November). *Teaching history in the Old Dominion: The impact of Virginia's accountability reform on seven secondary beginning history teachers*. Paper presented at the annual meeting of the College and University Faculty Assembly of the National Council for the Social Studies, Baltimore.

van Hover, S. D., & Yeager, E. A. (2003). "'Making' students better people?" A case study of a beginning history teacher. *International Social Studies Forum, 3*(1), 219–232.

Wilson, S., & Wineburg, S. S. (1988). Peering at history through different lenses: The role of disciplinary perspectives in teaching history. *Teachers College Record, 89*, 525–539.

Wineburg, S. S., & Fournier, J. (1994). Contextualized thinking in history. In M. Carretero & J. F. Voss (Eds.), *Cognitive and instructional processes in history and the social sciences* (pp. 285–308). Hillsdale, NJ: Erlbaum.

Wineburg, S., & Wilson, S. (1991). Subject-matter knowledge in the teaching of history. In J. Brophy (Ed.), *Advances in research on teaching* (Vol. 2, pp. 305–347). Greenwich, CT: JAI Press.

Yeager, E. A., & Davis, O. L., Jr. (1995). Between campus and classroom: Secondary student-teachers' thinking about historical texts. *Journal of Research and Development in Education, 29*, 1–8.

Yeager, E. A., & Davis, O. L., Jr. (1996). Classroom teachers' thinking about historical texts: An exploratory study. *Theory and Research in Social Education, 24*(2), 146–166.

Yeager, E. A., & Wilson, E. K. (1997). Teaching historical thinking in the social studies methods course: A case study. *The Social Studies, 88*, 121–126.

CHAPTER 9

TEACHING IN A HIGH-STAKES TESTING SETTING

What Becomes of Teacher Knowledge?

Cinthia Salinas

The nationwide instantiation of the Texas accountability blueprint into No Child Left Behind elevated the state's educational system to near mythical/miracle status (Haney, 2000). New curricula and new tests created tensions and debates regarding reading, writing, and mathematics and the use of high-stakes exams to measure both student and teacher performance. However, only recently did Texas state legislators decide to add social studies to the testing landscape. For nearly 2 decades, social studies educators remained outside the policymakers' interests. In the spring of 2004, however, an 11th grade Social Studies Exit Level Texas Assessment of Knowledge and Skills (TAKS) assumed its place alongside the other high-stakes tests in Texas public schools.

Several scholars note a pernicious influence of high-stakes testing upon teaching, curriculum, and learning. Teachers in high-stakes testing states appear to be increasing instruction in tested subject areas and may be more likely to shift instruction towards test preparation strategies

Measuring History: Cases of State-Level Testing Across the United States, 177–193
Copyright © 2006 by Information Age Publishing
All rights of reproduction in any form reserved.

(Lynn, 2002; Paris & Urdan, 2000). Haertel (1999) explains, "when rewards and sanctions are attached to these tests, getting high scores became an end in itself, and distortion of classroom instruction inevitably followed" (p. 663). Moreover, some researchers question the increase in student scores, the manipulation of passing standards, and the rigor of test content (Linn, 2003; Pahl, 2003; Paris & Urdan, 2000; Savage, 2003; Stake, 1991). Shepard (2000) concludes, "yes, end-of-year tests can be used to evaluate instruction and even tell us something about individual students," but we must "understand the limits to what can be accomplished with accountability tests" (p. 13).

Other scholars argue that, although tests matter, they may not be the commanding lever on instructional change that policymakers estimate (Darling-Hammond, 1991; Segall, 2003). Grant (2000) explains that teachers enact their own ambitious teaching in a high-stakes testing context within the confines of their own understanding of teaching, the content, and their students. Segall (2003) adds that teachers in high-stakes contexts cite changes to curriculum and content more than changes to pedagogy. Indeed it is plausible that implementation of high-stakes tests in social studies may not result in a significant change in curriculum, instruction, and assessment (Cimbricz, 2002). Darling-Hammond (1991) argues that, even if tests do exert some influence over teachers' practices, "tests that are externally designed and imposed can never play an important role in school improvement, since they deny teachers and students the opportunity to be part of the process of developing and wrestling with standards" (p. 224).

In this chapter, I examine the roles teachers can and do assume in a high-stakes setting. The American history teachers described in this qualitative case study accepted the responsibility of aligning curriculum standards to test objectives, developing and/or administering benchmark exams, employing pedagogical choices, and evaluating and reflecting upon student performance. There is little doubt that these Texas teachers' knowledge and subsequent actions were instrumental in preparing for a new high-stakes test in the social studies. However, while McNeil (2000) and others (McNeil & Valenzuela, 2001; Segal, 2003; Shepard, 2000) ask what reforms can do to teachers, in this chapter, I explore what teachers can do to reforms. At the center of the discussion is Shulman's (1987) notion of teacher knowledge, "a codified or codifiable aggregation of knowledge, skills, understanding, and technology, of ethics and disposition, of collective responsibility—as well as a means for representing and communication it" (p. 4). What becomes of teacher knowledge in a high-stakes testing context? What facets of teacher knowledge are revealed or concealed in conversations about curriculum, teaching, and assessment?

SOCIAL STUDIES CURRICULUM AND TESTING IN TEXAS

The Texas legislature began mandating content and performance standards known as the Texas Essential Knowledge and Skills (TEKS)[1] in 1997 and in 2003 high school "exit level exams" under the title of the Texas Assessment of Knowledge and Skills (TAKS) program. Together, these reforms aim at creating what Hamilton and Stecher (2004) have described as a "test-based accountability system." School districts and campuses are consigned highly-publicized ratings and consequences or rewards,[2] and students' performance in designated grade levels is used to determine their promotion and graduation.[3] For close to 20 years, however, high-stakes testing bypassed the social studies largely because, as Segal (2003) notes, the social studies was "a second rate subject area not regarded as worthy enough to be included" (p. 321). By 2004, however, the 11th grade Social Studies Exit Level TAKS exam became a full member of the Texas accountability blueprint.[4]

The 55 question multiple-choice exam includes five overall objectives that cover the traditional range of social studies concepts: issues and events in U.S. history, geographic influences on historical issues and events, economic and social influences on historical issues and events, political influences on historical issues and events, and critical-thinking skills to analyze social studies information (Social Studies Center, 2001). The explicit and governing focus of the 11th grade exam is the post-reconstruction American History Studies curriculum covered in 11th grade, yet questions covering material from the 8th grade American History Studies, 9th grade World Geography, 10th grade World History Study, and the 12th grade American Government and Economics curricula are included as well. In sum, the social studies TAKS represents a daunting mass of social studies content.

DESIGN OF THE STUDY

Several questions drive the larger study which this chapter represents: What facets of teacher knowledge are demanded, neglected, and/or ignored in a high-stakes testing setting? What notions of teacher knowledge are teachers sharing, withholding, and fostering in a high-stakes testing setting? What are the implications for outcomes of high-stakes testing preparation in the social studies?

I located the study in five predominately Latina/o (Mexican American) South Texas and Lower Rio Grande Valley high schools of varying student enrollments (300 to 2,300 students). The two smaller schools represent rural communities and feature social studies departments with only one American history teacher. The third high school, located in a more affluent suburb, and the last two high schools, located in more heavily populated communities, have much larger student enrollments and social studies departments. This collection of schools offers opportunities to explore the relationships among school size, community, and preparation in light of the new high-stakes social studies exam.

Although the social studies TAKS covers more than one grade level curricula, American History Studies teachers were purposefully selected for this study because of their direct involvement with the 11th grade exam (see Table 9.1). Using several open-ended protocols attentive to curriculum, pedagogy, assessment, and staff development, I interviewed 11 (five women and six men; five White and six Mexican American Latina/o) teachers about their understandings of and ensuing roles and responsibilities in the introduction of a high-stakes social studies test. Their years of teaching experience varied from 2 to 24 years and all but one had been teaching American History Studies for 5 years or more.

For context-building purposes, I added seven interviews with local decision makers—social studies department heads, curriculum directors, high school principals, and superintendents—about the choices they

Table 9.1.   Informants

Pseudonym	Years of Experience	Position	School
1. John Francis	30	Principal	Queens
2. Sylvia White	15	American History Teacher	Queens
3. Cynthia Martinez	20	Principal/Sup of Curriculum	Peñaville
4. David Mario	20	Principal	Peñaville
5. Sylvia Hinojosa	2	American History Teacher	Peñaville
6. Christy Pedro	15	Curriculum director	Cat
7. Martha Smith	10	American History Teacher/AP	Cat
8. Richard Nelson	11	American History Teacher/coach	Cat
9. Will Dizdar	15	American History Teacher/coach	Cat
10. John Henry	20	American History Teacher/coach	Cat
11. Richard Franquiz	30	Assistant Sup of Curriculum	Texas Valley
12. Amanda Rios	25	Assistant Sup of Curriculum	Texas Valley
13. Bryan Rodriguez	5	American History/Dept head/AP	Texas Valley
14. Jeanna Alanis	20	American History Teacher	Texas Valley
15. Carlos Yzaguirre	15	American History Teacher	Texas Valley
16. Ramon Dante	25	Assistant Principal	Brown
17. Rosa Lydia Gomez	11	American History/Dept head/AP	Brown
18. Melissa Sanchez	24	American History/Dept head/AP	Brown

made in preparing the social studies teachers for the 2003 benchmark and 2004 Social Studies Exit Level TAKS. I also reviewed state, district, and teacher-generated documents (e.g., overviews by the Texas Social Studies Center, TEA "Letters to the Administrator Addressed," and scope and sequence documents) to build detailed descriptions of the testing background and to triangulate data from the teacher interviews.

I manually coded the transcripts of informant interviews and the documents collected in order to generate meaning for analysis. Following Huberman and Miles's (1984) suggestion, my data analysis proceeded from noting patterns and themes to arriving at comparisons and contrasts to determining conceptual explanations of the case studies. For example, because American history teachers identified knowledge of content and curriculum as prerequisite to their participation in the high-stakes testing context, teacher knowledge became a useful framework to apply when analyzing the interview data for patterns and themes.

A CALL FOR TEACHERS' KNOWLEDGE

Cognitive psychologists like Borko and Putnam (1996), assert a relationship among multiple teacher cognitions, knowledge, and action. They conclude that "teachers' thinking is directly influenced by their knowledge. Their thinking, in turn, determines their actions in the classroom" (p. 37). Two studies highlight the importance of teacher thinking and knowledge in response to teacher participation in high-stakes testing settings. Grant's (2003) seminal work about two history teachers in the New York Regents exam context explores the teachers' personal and professional choices to be knowledge givers and/or knowledge facilitators and content and/or pedagogy specialists. Grant emphasizes three facets of ambitious teaching, arguing that teacher knowledge of content, of students, and of context are crucial to understanding the ways in which teachers teach—even in a high-stakes setting. In an equally compelling study, Segal (2003) describes a complex teaching dynamics around the Michigan Educational Assessment Program (MEAP): "How teachers teach encompasses—not only what teachers do in the classrooms, but also the stances, dispositions, commitments, and investments they bring to that 'doing'" (p. 291). Grant and Segal fuse teacher knowledge, perceptions, judgments, and decision making into an intricate and, at times, contradictory portrayal of what happens in high-stakes testing contexts.

The introduction of the Social Studies Exit Level TAKS challenged Texas teachers' knowledge as they gathered for professional development opportunities, created and/or purchased curricular and assessment materials, and prepared themselves and their students. American history teachers, not building administrators or curriculum directors/specialists, were charged with tremendous responsibilities. Teachers became well aware of the importance of their knowledge and the upcoming roles they would play in preparations for the Social Studies Exit Level TAKS. Rosa Lydia Gomez, an American history teacher and department chair at Brown High Schools, highlights the new context in which Texas teachers found themselves:

> We're all new to this testing thing, but we have a pretty good idea of what we need to do. I mean we've been watching everybody else for sometime now (laughs). The district has been very generous giving us lots of in-service time and also paying for some Saturday writing time too. For the most part the principal is just letting us do what we need to do. We worked on aligning the TEKS and the test objectives with what we usually teach. I know we should have done it a while back, but we didn't have the pressure of the test.

Continuing, she describes the content choices she and her peers face as they attempt to rebuild the content of their curriculum:

> To be frank, I most worry about the breadth of the exam—too much material in too little time. I mean we barely make it to the Civil Rights Movement, but now they want us to cover 8th grade American History, and World History and Geography, and some Government and Economics concepts, and get to the 1970s. It's not totally a bad thing since we do tend to all have our favorite period of history and that ends up shortchanging other topics or periods. But I think we are all trying to figure out how to squeeze it all in…. We (she and her six American History colleagues) sat down the other day and figured out that we had to include a review of 8th grade American History as well as the other TEKS from the other courses that are on the exam. The scope and sequence we wrote is packed!

The complexity of the work Ms. Gomez and other Texas teachers face might be analyzed through a number of lenses. Because it has gone relatively unexamined in the research on high-stakes testing, I use this chapter as an opportunity to examine teachers' knowledge and its role in a context of high-stakes. To guide my analysis, I draw on Shulman's (1987) portrayal of teacher knowledge:

> The key to distinguishing the knowledge base of teaching lies at the intersection of content and pedagogy, in the capacity of a teacher to transform the content knowledge he or she possesses into forms that are pedagogically powerful and yet adaptive to variations in ability and background presented by the student. (p. 15)

Underscoring the inherent connection between teachers' knowledge and the pedagogical decisions they make, Shulman enumerates several domains of teachers' professional knowledge, including content knowledge, curriculum knowledge, and knowledge of educational contexts. In the sections that follow, I employ these domains as I explore the roles of teachers play in a high-stakes testing milieu.

Knowing the Content

The five testing objectives of the Social Studies Exit Level TAKS reflect numerous content standards (TEKS) which cover an incredibly wide curriculum scope—American history, world history, world geography, government, and economics—taught over five grades. Not surprisingly, then, the teachers in this study viewed content knowledge as paramount in the test preparation process. Annoyed but undaunted, they made adjustments to their taught curriculum. At the same time, they preserved those pedagogical elements important to them regardless of whether they were part of the testing parameters,

Although students took the Social Studies TAKS in 11th grade, the material covered on the test covers a wide swath of the social studies curriculum. Eleventh grade teachers, then, expanded the American History Studies course content to accommodate the tested curriculum. Richard Nelson from Cat HS, like several other informants, taught both American and World History or World Geography and discussed the overlap between the two courses:

> I think you can't isolate the U.S. and so I always put history in a larger picture. We talk about our relationship to the rest of the world and the relationship of the world to our own history. But this new exam is explicit about what connections I'm supposed to make.

Texas teachers traditionally have made cross-course links when teaching and learning moments presented themselves. As Mr. Nelson notes, the Social Studies TAKS places a premium on those connections. Schwab (1964) argues that the content of any school subject can be organized in numerous ways. The challenge to Texas teachers comes when they try to respond to a set of externally-constructed substantive structures. The challenge, however, is even greater for students who are now responsible for content taught as much as three grades earlier. Carlos Yzaguirre from Texas Valley HS describes the struggle teachers and their students face:

> The new test covers TEKS from every social studies course. That's going to be quite a challenge for our students and for us too. Since our students take

> early American History in 8th grade, there is no way they remember much and to connect what they do remember to 11th American History.... You need to be realistic about what they remembered from last year's World History or World Geography course. You have to make those connections for them—a review or some kind of activity that ties it all together. I think what is difficult is that you used to make those ties when it came up or when you thought it was best or relevant or appropriate. Now you kind of have to build in all that stuff whether you want to or your students want to or not.

Although teachers typically made their own choices about how and when to connect the social studies, the advent of state-level testing creates a different dynamic for teachers. As a result, teachers lament the expansiveness of a new American History Studies curriculum and the constraint of making mandated rather than opportunistic connections across social studies ideas.

Disappointed but resolute, the teachers in this study refuse to turn over all content decisions to the state test. The teachers hold on to the "basic concepts and principles of the discipline" (Shulman, 1986, p. 9) that they feel are fundamental in teaching their American history content. Teachers at Texas Valley and Brown High School, for example, cite the importance of local histories and explain how they merge this content into the curricula. "We have a rich history," explains Bryan Rodriguez, a teacher and department chair at Brown High School, "but you are not going to find it in those textbooks or in the TEKS or certainly not the new exam. So we put it in. We don't do 'Remember the Alamo.' We do 'Forget the Alamo.'" Rodriguez and his colleagues are not alone: Each teacher distinguishes between pieces of American history they will surrender and those they will safeguard regardless of the new exam. Will Dizdar, for example, stakes a claim to the importance of the period around World War I:

> I know that only a part of the new test includes World War I, but I think you can't really understand much of the 20th century without an in-depth understanding of the events and issues that remained unresolved. I will find a way to get it in.

Ms. Sanchez is equally invested in teaching several social movements that she feels "[are] imperative in helping students become active citizens and critical thinkers about modern day issues. I can't imagine not including the material—regardless of what the state thinks we should include or exclude." These teachers clearly understand the parameters of the state test, but they refuse to let those parameters dictate the entire content of their courses.

As the teachers in this study rebuild their American History course, they feel forced to adopt some changes that seem unnatural. Making connections between and across social studies concepts is normal; having to make those connections explicit and to make them across a wide expanse of content is frustrating. Although the teachers seem open to some change, they will not surrender numerous concepts and ideas that have long defined their domain of content knowledge. Willing to make some changes that fit within their knowledge frameworks and unwilling to make other changes that were contrary to their knowledge frameworks, the teachers negotiate between their own content knowledge and the demands of the state-level test.

Knowing the Curriculum

In the previous section, I talk about how teachers, as individuals, negotiate the relationship between their content knowledge and the expectations of the new state tests. Even the strictest content controls, however, still leave teachers with considerable room to navigate within the waters of their own classrooms (Cornbleth, 2002). That said, teachers also work within curriculum contexts that can influence their practices. With the new high-stakes test on the horizon, administrators asked American history teachers to translate the state curriculum and tests into specific local curricula. School districts offered generous weekly release time and/or financial compensation for Saturday curriculum writing sessions so that teachers could share their "particular grasp of the materials and programs that serve as 'tools of the trade' for teachers" (Shulman, 1987, p. 8). Although a range of curriculum specialists were available, administrators at all five campuses emphasized the importance of their American history teachers as curriculum writers, creators, and experts. As the teachers engaged the task of creating local curricula, however, they drew on their accumulated curriculum knowledge in ways similar to the ways they used their content knowledge: They accepted the assignment and made some changes, but resisted others. The resultant negotiation underscores the complexity of the teachers' responses.

Although one might have expected state policymakers to do this, the burden of aligning the state curriculum standards with the state test strictures falls on Texas teachers. Obvious to all is the disconnect between the 11th grade state social studies standards for and the 11th grade state social studies test. Teachers who typically follow the textbook, the AP curricula, and/or their own understandings of American history in determining what would be taught and when, now realize that the materials released by the Social Studies Center require a curriculum revision as the 11th grade test covered pre-Reconstruction American History Studies (8th grade), World Geography (9th grade), World History (10th grade), post-Reconstruction American History Studies (11th grade), and Economics and Government (12th grade). "When we sat to write we realized, 'Geez, have you seen how much we are supposed to add to the course?'" declares Mr. Dizdar an American History teacher at Cat HS, "It became very worrisome when we started to add all those TEKS from all those other courses. Frankly, it's material I don't usually include." His colleagues at Cat HS as well as the other informants are equally troubled by the substantial amendment to the American History Studies course.

Not only are broad curriculum strokes necessary, but teachers find it necessary to tweak even small elements of the 11th grade American History Studies course. For example, state education agency documents make clear that the history of the early 1970s needs to be reached for the late April testing date. Most of the American history teachers report that they do not customarily reach that era before mid to late May. Some teachers, like Ms. Sanchez, accept this modification:

> I guess it's not a bad thing. We should be getting through modern American History, but we often don't. We may just need to move faster through the material or leave out stuff we used to prioritize that the exam doesn't. That's going to be a big decision for me to make.

Other teachers balk at this compromise. Ms. White comments, "I have no idea how we are going to get through all this material. It was hard enough to go back and review the first part of American History and include some of the World Geography and World History material, but now we have to add stuff and get through it faster. It's kind of crazy." While many American history teachers explain that they typically included some early American history and/or other social studies content in their coursework, the new test parameters prompt a major curriculum revision. The teacher discussions and writing of the scope and sequence document heighten their awareness of the monumental undertaking of a comprehensive high-stakes exam within the span of a single course.

The teachers in this study admit to giving the state standards little attention until the Social Studies TAKS emerged. Asked now to create an alignment guide, the teachers begin by creating elaborate tables and charts showing an integration of the content and testing parameters.

Documents created, however, need not be documents used. In some cases, the teachers use the alignment tables and charts, but just as many find the effort to create them unnecessary. Sylvia White, the American history teacher at Queens HS, believes the tables are helpful:

> I asked my department chair for her help. We took several Saturdays and created a chart with all the TEKS that are on the exam--similar to the other departments (Language Arts and Mathematics). I call it my cheat sheet

when I'm writing my lesson plans or getting ready for one of the benchmarks. It's rather handy.

Jeanna Alanis from Texas Valley HS adds, "You have to become so much more conscious of the TEKS in all the grade levels and courses and which ones are going to be included in the exam. That was new to us." In contrast, Ms. Sanchez disregards the new curriculum guide:

> Though I'm the only one teaching American history this year, I did get lots of help from my colleagues in writing the TEKS to test connections. However, I must say I don't really use the table. I figure that I'm covering all I need to cover—maybe I should pay a little more attention to it.

Mr. Nelson also acknowledges that he rarely "looked at the materials we worked on. They're just not that useful since I pretty much cover all the stuff already." Although every campus produced curriculum alignment resources, many teachers rely on their own understanding of the relationships between the standards and content to decide whether or not to actually use curriculum alignment guides.

Regardless of the American history teachers' apprehensions regarding alignment, course content, and an expanding and fast-paced scope and sequence, they use their accumulated knowledge to develop new curriculum materials. Teachers comply with the task assigned. But when asked how they will use the ensuing documents, teachers simultaneously appear to be consigned and opposed to the impending changes. Willing to understand the demands of a new test while hesitant to commit to implementing the very curriculum materials they developed, American history teachers reveal a complex reaction to the new high-stakes test.

Knowing the Context

One last category helps us explore teachers' knowledge in response to high-stakes tests. Although American history teachers once enjoyed an extraordinary degree of immunity from the high-stakes testing frenzy, they well knew the ways in which tests penetrated their schools. They watched and learned from their language arts and mathematics colleagues and from an accountability-laden discourse that dominated the educational context. Now, social studies educators find they have to learn the elements of test formats and passing rates, testing and retesting dates, curriculum alignment, testing strategies and materials, and acts of overt/covert resistance. Although he makes no specific reference to teacher's knowledge in the educational context of high-stakes testing, Shulman (1987) cites the importance of teachers' knowledge of educational contexts that can range from "workings of the group or classroom, the governance and financing of school districts, to the character of communities and culture" (p. 8). As noted above, the teachers in this study comply with administrators' requests to develop curriculum alignment guides. The teachers make a point, however, of only specifying the content to be taught: They do not share their pedagogical knowledge. This act of resistance grows as teachers administer the benchmark exams districts purchase or develop, for although they give the exams to their students, they do not allow the outcomes to alter their own assessment practices. Guarding their knowledge, teachers treat the test preparation process in a segmented, if not fragmented, way demonstrating a sensitivity to those facets of the high-stakes testing context they must abide by as well as those with which they can take liberties.

The American history teachers included in this study understand the potential value of connecting the content of social studies within specific instructional practices, but they do not include the latter in the development of district curriculum materials. Teachers narrowly follow their administrators' requests by identifying content in an isolated manner. Mr. Dizdar describes how his colleagues define their task:

> They [district and campus administrators] asked us to come in and decide what content would be included, but we did not need to write lessons or decide how it could best be taught or how what connections we would need to alter. All they asked for was to line up the standards with the testing objectives. It was a simple and painless experience.

A Texas Valley HS teacher offers a similar account about "making sure we were covering the required material and giving the benchmark exams, but we were not asked to change our teaching or share our lessons, or debate the loss or addition of material." In effect, teachers narrow the development of curriculum products to the inclusion or exclusion of content and/or assignments and the challenges of an expanded and rushed curriculum. Including neither lessons nor activities, the resultant curriculum documents merely lists topics, dates, historical figures, and events. Mr. Rodriguez smiles and explains, "never give 'em more than what they ask for." These teachers hold rich teacher knowledge about instruction, but they read the context to require only their selective offering of curriculum products.

Another instance of teacher compliance and resistance emerges around the benchmark exams that district administrators view as formative assessments. Teachers administer the exams and receive item analyses of their students' performance on each question. Presumably, they will use this information to make changes in their content and/or instruction. The teachers in this study, however, report feeling baffled by the analyses.

"After we give those [benchmark] exams, I get these sheets from time to time, but I have no idea what they want me to do with them," explains Ms. Sanchez, "I can tell what the students know and don't know but, hey, if the district wants to spend the big bucks." Administrators provide training on the benchmark software, but there is little indication that teachers utilize the benchmarks and accompanying analyses to alter their planning, teaching or assessment strategies. Ms. Gomez explains, "I know we should pay attention to those item charts, but I usually don't have the time to prepare for class, do my own testing, and pay attention to the stuff our curriculum director hands us."

The pattern of giving benchmark tests, but ignoring the results emerges in all but one of the schools we studied. Queens HS stands in singular contrast largely because Ms. White and her department chair developed their own benchmark exams. "We wrote the benchmarks and then we sat and figured out how the students are doing," explains Ms. White, "Once I learned how to write the questions like the test format, I started doing some of the same with my own tests." Ms. White's experience understood, the teachers in this study pointedly do not transform their own assessment strategies to resemble those of the Social Studies Exit Level TAKS. Teachers are aware of the importance of the benchmark and ensuing high-stakes tests in the state and local context, but they rebuff those tests when they impinge on their classroom practices.

In many ways, the American history teachers in this study acquiesce by publicly partaking in the test preparation process. Aware of a changing content, curriculum, and context that create new boundaries, teachers respond to several high-stakes testing demands, but remain faithful to their professional understandings of the ways in which American history should be designed, taught, and assessed. The knowledge crafted over years of teaching enables the teachers to modify the content taught and the way that content is represented in curriculum documents. But that knowledge also empowers them to draw a line at modifying their instructional and assessment practices in any substantive way. Instead of being mutually reinforcing then, content, curriculum, and context become operationalized as independent variables in each teacher's practice. Teachers participate in the tasks demanded of them, but the extent of their participation and the impact of that participation on their pedagogies is keenly managed. "Teachers," Shulman (1986) observes, "must learn to use their knowledge base to provide the grounds for choice and action. The knowledge base must therefore deal with the purposes of education as well as the methods and strategies of educating" (p. 13).

THE POSSIBILITIES OF TEACHER KNOWLEDGE IN
A HIGH-STAKES TESTING CONTEXT

The data reported on in this chapter underscore the ways in which teachers chose to use portions of a complex and entwined knowledge base to create a parcel of curriculum materials that satisfy the letter of their tasks, but that yield minimal impact upon teachers' conceived ideas and approaches to the social studies. The teachers comply with mandated demands while at the same time they enact their own set of beliefs and practices about the teaching of history (Grant, 2000). In effect, then, how those high-stakes tests manifest in curriculum, teaching, and assessment depends on teachers' knowledge and the subsequent deliberate choices they make. Three points exemplify the possibilities of teacher knowledge in a high-stakes testing context.

First, teachers' subject matter knowledge of American history figures prominently in the test preparation process and in determining the ways in which teachers respond. In short, these American history teachers use their knowledge to negotiate within the new terrain of high-stakes testing. Although most of the teachers do not have the opportunity to "employ the cognitive tools necessary to effectively investigate the past and think historically" (Borko & Putnam, 1996, p. 5), they readily recognize its importance to a deeper understanding of the subject matter. They do not, however, concede entirely to the state-enacted testing frameworks that would reorganize the 11th grade American History Studies course. The Social Studies Exit Level TAKS have the potential to change the relationships teachers recognize within the discipline and the declarative or procedural knowledge they use to teach their courses (Chamot & O'Malley, 1994). Accepting or rejecting changes to the content is dependent upon individual teacher's knowledge.

Second, the teachers' complex and nuanced reactions also surface in the curriculum writing tasks and implementation of benchmark exams. In each case, complying with administrators' expectations still leaves plenty of room for teachers to construct their own pedagogical and assessment practices. In the end, these teachers' understandings of and interaction with content, curriculum, and assessment is a combination of acceptance and circumvention of the consequences related to the new Social Studies Exit Level TAKS.

Third, well versed in the high-stakes testing policies and rules that directly influence their planning, teaching, and assessment practices, the teachers' knowledge of the high-stakes testing context leverages their ability to negotiate within the demands of testing preparations. Consider one last example of how teachers apply their knowledge and experience: Teachers learn that 11th grade students only need to answer 22 of the 55 test items correctly in order to meet the state's passing standard. Every teacher interviewed notes the low standard and then dismisses any concerns about students' performance on the high stakes social studies exam. Apparently they are right in doing so: The first year passing rate on the Social Studies Exit Level TAKS is 98% state-wide.

With each passing mandate and moment, then, American history teachers develop an intricate understanding of the demands in a high-stakes testing context. The paradoxical portrayals reveal the complexity of and the need to view a continuum of possibilities regarding teachers' responses to high-stakes exams in the social studies. Ranging from defensive (McNeil, 2000) to ambitious (Grant, 2003), teachers' participation is influenced by multiple factors and circumstances and the many facets of teacher knowledge.

CONCLUSION

Before asserting any definite claims, it is important to note that data for this study were gathered at the onset of the Texas social studies exam in the fall of 2002. Initial responses were gathered and analyzed, yet the prospects of additional and changing responses are possible as the Social Studies Exit Level TAKS become cemented into the everyday lives of teachers and students. The chapter provides a snapshot of teacher knowledge and the permeability of the many domains that guide teachers' actions.

Caveats aside, examining teacher knowledge is instrumental in distinguishing ways in which teachers respond to high-stakes testing. Borko and Putnam (1996) note that "teachers' knowledge and beliefs affect how they perceive and act on various messages about changing their teaching" (p. 59). Although content, pedagogy, and assessment are frequently separated in high-stakes testing settings (Grant 2003; Segal, 2003), what is learned and how it is to be taught deserves a comprehensive view of teacher knowledge domains (Shulman, 1987). The focal point remains on teacher knowledge and how and when domains are used in response to high-stakes testing. The acknowledgement of the many domains of teacher knowledge provides a useful lens through which to understand the complex interactions between state policies and teachers' classroom practices.

NOTES

1. The first adoption of state curriculum standards, the Essential Elements, were in place in 1983.
2. Although several performance indicators are included, the TAKS, along with the disaggregating of data by ethnic/class and economically disadvantaged subgroups, drive the assignment of consequences and rewards. Rat-

ings at the district level include Exemplary, Recognized, Academically Acceptable, and Academically Unacceptable. Ratings at the campus level include Exemplary, Recognized, Acceptable, Low Performing (Texas Education Agency, 2003).

3. Within the comprehensive testing program for Grades 3–11 (reading, writing, English language arts, mathematics, science, and social studies), it is the TAKS scores in reading, writing, and mathematics that determine students' promotion in Grades 3, 5, and 8. Students' performance on four 11th grade Exit Level TAKS (English III, Algebra I, Biology, and Social Studies) determine high school graduation.

4. There are currently three social studies TAKS exams: the 8th grade Social Studies, the 10th grade Social Studies, and the 11th grade Exit Level Social Studies TAKS. Only the 11th grade exam is considered high stakes.

REFERENCES

Borko, H., & Putnam, R. T. (1996). Expanding a teacher's knowledge base: A cognitive psychological perspective on professional development. In T. Guskey & M. Huberman. (Eds.), *Professional development in education* (pp. 35–65). New York: Teachers College Press.

Chamot, A. U., & O'Malley, J. M. (1994). *The CALLA Handbook: Implementing the cognitive academic language learning approach*. New York: Addison-Wesley.

Cimbricz, S. (2002, January 9). State testing and teachers' thinking and practice: A synthesis of research. *Educational Policy Analysis Archives, 10*(2). Retrieved from http://epaa.asu.edu/epaa/v10n2.html

Cornbleth, C. (2002). What constrains meaningful social studies teaching. *Social Education, 63*(3), 186–190.

Darling-Hammond, L. (1991). The implications of testing policy for quality and equality. *Phi Delta Kappan, 81*(3), 220–225.

Grant, S. G. (2000, February 24) Teachers and tests: Exploring teachers' perceptions of changes in a new state-mandated testing program. *Education Policy Analysis Archives, 8*(14). Retrieved from http://epaa.asu.edu/epaa/v8n14.html

Grant, S. G. (2003). *History lessons: Teaching, learning, and testing in U.S. high school classrooms*. Mahwah, NJ: Erlbaum.

Haertel, E. (1999). Performance assessment and education reform. *Phi Delta Kappan, 80*(9), 662–666.

Hamilton, L., & Stecher, B. (2004). Responding effectively to test-based accountability. *Phi Delta Kappan, 88*(8), 578–583.

Haney, W. (2000). The myth of the Texas miracle in education. *Education Policy Analysis Archives, 8*(41). Retrieved from http://epaa.asu.edu/epaa/v8n41.html

Huberman, M. A., & Miles, M. B. (1984). *Qualitative data analysis: A sourcebook of new methods*. Thousand Oaks, CA: Sage.

Linn, R., (2003). Accountability: Responsibility and reasonable expectations, *Educational Researcher, 32*(7), 3–13.

Lynn, O. (2002). Survey shows state testing alters instructional practices, *Education Week, 21*(32), 14–15.

McNeil, L. (2000). *Contradictions of school reform: Educational cost of standardized testing*. New York: Routledge.

McNeil, L., & Valenzuela, A. (2001). The harmful impact of the TAAS system of testing in Texas: Beneath the accountability rhetoric. In M. Kornhaber & G. Orfield (Eds.), *Raising standards or raising barriers? Inequality and high-stakes testing in public education* (pp. 127–150), New York: Century Foundation.

Pahl, R. H. (2003). Assessment traps in K–12 social studies. *The Social Studies*, *94*(5), 212–215.

Paris, S. G., & Urdan, T. (2000). Policies and practices of high-stakes testing that influence teachers and schools. *Issues in Education*, *6*(1/2), 83–108.

Savage, T. V. (2003). Assessment and quality social studies. *The Social Studies*, *94*(5), 201–206.

Schwab, J. J. (1964). The structures of the disciplines: Meanings and significances. In G. Ford & L. Pugno (Eds.), *The structure of knowledge and the curriculum* (pp. 1–30). Chicago: Rand McNally.

Segall, A. (2003), The impact of state-mandated testing according to social studies teachers: The Michigan Educational Assessment Program (MEAP) as a case study of consequences. *Theory and Research in Social Education*, *31*(3), 287–325.

Shepard, L., (2000). The role of assessment in a learning culture. *Educational Researcher*, *29*(7), 4–14.

Shulman, L. (1986). Those who understand: Knowledge growth in teaching. *Educational Researcher*, *15*(2), 4–14.

Shulman, L. (1987). Knowledge and teaching: Foundations of the new reform. *Harvard Educational Review*, *57*(1), 1–22.

Stake, R. E. (1991). The teacher, standardized testing, and prospects of revolution. *Phi Delta Kappan*, *73*(3), 243–247.

Social Studies Center. (2004). *Texas social studies frameworks*. Retrieved March 15, 2004, from http://socialstudies.tea.state.tx.us/ssc/ssc

Texas Education Agency. (2003). *2003 accountability plan*. Austin: Author.

CHAPTER 10

TEACHING HISTORY IN THE OLD DOMINION

The Impact of Virginia's Accountability Reform on Seven Secondary Beginning History Teachers

Stephanie D. van Hover

My first two years of teaching have definitely been a roller coaster. I have to admit I've definitely questioned if I want to be a teacher.... Sometimes I feel like it's my calling, and sometimes I'm like, well, maybe not.... I know that I love my students, I love history and I have a passion for the subject.... [My greatest success] the past year and a half is surviving. I spent some afternoons crying ... but for now, I think [teaching] is where I want to be.

The picture that Valerie, a second-year history teacher, paints in this quote reflects the experiences of many secondary beginning teachers in their first years of teaching. Researchers well document the myriad challenges facing beginning teachers, including heavy teaching loads, multiple preparations, little collegial or administrative support, unfamiliarity with the content, extracurricular duties, discipline and management issues, and disjuncture between their expectations of teaching and the

Measuring History: Cases of State-Level Testing Across the United States, 195–219
Copyright © 2006 by Information Age Publishing
All rights of reproduction in any form reserved.

realities of the classroom (Darling-Hammond, 1998; Lawson, 1992; Rust, 1994). And, in Virginia, as in many states, beginning teachers must now add to this list the pressures imposed by state-mandated Standards of Learning (SOLs) and high-stakes accountability measures (SOL tests). As Virginia's beginning history teachers work through the complex process of learning to teach, they do so within a context that includes content-specific standards and a fact-recall, multiple-choice, end-of-course examination that directly affects school accreditation and students' opportunities to graduate from high school.

Although research on Virginia's reform efforts has included attention to the role of Virginia superintendents and principals in the implementation of these reforms (Grogan & Sherman, 2003; Tucker, 2003), characteristics of classroom instruction of math, language arts, and biology teachers with high SOL scores (Grogan & Roland, 2003), the impact of the SOLs on classroom instructional and assessment practices before and after implementation of the testing program (McMillan, Myran, & Workman, 1999), attitudes of new and veteran teachers towards the SOLs, (Winkler, 2002a), teacher beliefs and perceptions about state educational accountability systems in Virginia versus Vermont (Winkler, 2002b), and the effects of the history SOLs and SOL tests on the "wise practice" of secondary history teachers (van Hover & Heinecke, 2005), no in-depth empirical research has focused on beginning history teachers' perceptions of this high-stakes testing environment.

Beginning teachers (1–4 years of experience) in Virginia are developing their teaching craft within a high-stakes environment; they know and have known no other context. What are their perceptions of the influence of standards and accountability on their emerging teaching practices? This question is important because, as Avner Segall (2003) notes in his study of Michigan's mandated testing program, what a high-stakes tests entails "for teachers and how they respond to it are, to a large extent, dependent on [teachers'] perceptions" of that assessment (p. 288). How beginning history teachers perceive and respond to the Virginia SOL tests will, in a large part, influence how new history teachers conceptualize and develop their instructional practice and, possibly their decisions about staying in the teaching profession. In the literature on the teaching and learning of history, there exists a notion of "effective practice" or what S. G. Grant (2003) terms "ambitious teaching," teaching that defies the "typical, conventional" notion of history teaching (Shulman, 1987). Do beginning teachers' perceptions of state standards and tests allow for the possibility of ambitious teaching, or do they interpret the pressures of the test as reason to employ conventional reliance on textbook, drill, and recitation?

This study investigates beginning teachers' perceptions of the influence of the SOLs and SOL tests on their planning, instruction and assessment. I open with a description of the context of accountability surrounding history teaching in Virginia and briefly review the existing literature on beginning teachers and the teaching of history. Then, I explain the research design and methods utilized and provide an in-depth discussion of the findings that emerged from analysis of data. Finally, I conclude with a discussion of these findings and analysis of implications for the teaching and learning of history in Virginia.

THE ACCOUNTABILITY SYSTEM IN THE COMMONWEALTH OF VIRGINIA

In the late 1990s, the Commonwealth of Virginia implemented a massive standards-based reform effort that incorporated three components common to accountability systems across the nation: (1) aligning standards and assessments, (2) rating schools and reporting school and/or district performance, and (3) creating consequences for schools that fail to perform adequately (Heinecke, Curry-Cocoran, & Moon, 2003). Virginia established general guidelines and standards for virtually all aspects of education, referred to as the Standards of Quality (SOQ). Additionally, the Department of Education established Standards of Accreditation (SOA) that provide benchmarks for school accreditation and create school performance report cards that include the school's accreditation rating, comparison of school-wide and state-wide SOL scores, graduation rates, enrollments in advanced academic programs, and information on teacher training, drop-out rates, school attendance rates, and school safety records (Duke & Reck, 2003). Virginia's content-based standards, the Standards of Learning (SOLs) set expectations for teaching and learning in all subject areas and list knowledge and skills that every child is expected to learn.

The History and Social Science Standards of Learning at the high school (Grades 9–12) include United States and Virginia History, World History I and II, World Geography, and Virginia and United States Government (for an example of an SOL, see Table 10.1). The history standards are arranged, for the most part, chronologically and can be characterized as "traditional history" (Fordham Foundation, 2003; Fore, 1995). The accompanying SOL tests are 70-item multiple-choice exams that emphasize the recall of factual content (for sample test items, see Table 10.2). At the high school level, students take the SOL tests at the end of each course and, in order to graduate, they must pass each test. The tests are scored on a scale from 0–600. A student must earn a score of

Table 10.1.   Example of Virginia and U.S. History Standard

History and Social Science Standards of Learning: Virginia and United States History
Civil War and Reconstruction: 1860–1877 VUS.7—The student will demonstrate knowledge of the Civil War and Reconstruction Era and its importance as a major turning point in American history by identifying the major events and the roles of key leaders of the Civil War Era, with emphasis on Abraham Lincoln, Ulysses S. Grant, Robert E. Lee, and Frederick Douglass; analyzing the significance of the Emancipation Proclamation and the principles outlined in Lincoln's Gettysburg Address; examining the political, economic, and social impact of the war and Reconstruction, including the adoption of the 13th, 14th, and 15th Amendments to the Constitution of the United States.

Table 10.2.   Sample Questions from End-of Course SOL Tests (1998)

End-of-Course United States History	*End of Course World History I*
Which of the following was written specifically to encourage ratification of the Constitution?	Which of the following philosophers was the teacher of Alexander the Great?
Federalist Papers Declaration of Independence Articles of Confederation *Common Sense*	Socrates Plato Agamemnon Aristotle

400 or higher in order to pass the test, and 70% of students who take the SOL test must pass in order for a school to be considered for accreditation (Virginia Department of Education, 2003). A growing body of research has examined the enactment of these reforms and their effects on teaching and learning in Virginia (Grogan & Roland, 2003; van Hover & Heinecke, 2005; Winkler, 2002b). MacMillan et al. (1999), for example, conducted a study that investigated the impact of the Virginia statewide SOL testing on classroom instructional and assessment practices. Using a longitudinal design, the researchers collected survey data from 570 secondary school teachers and 152 elementary school teachers pre- and postimplementation of the reform across school subjects. They found that 47% of the secondary teachers indicated that the SOLs "somewhat" or "extensively" impacted their instruction or assessment. Written comments fell under one of three categories—changes in the content taught, changes in how the content is taught, and changes in classroom assessments. This study, however, took place in 1998 during the field-testing phase of the SOL tests; the "high-stakes" component of the tests was not fully implemented until a year later. Additionally, the study did not provide insight into how beginning teachers within a specific discipline per-

ceive the influence of the SOLs. Winkler (2002a) did focus her attention on beginning teachers. Comparing experienced and beginning teachers' perceptions of the SOL tests, she asserted that experienced teachers viewed the SOLs in terms of losses, while inexperienced teachers saw the test in terms of gains. Specifically, the experienced teachers emphasized the loss of autonomy, power, and professionalism while beginning teachers commented on the increased collaboration and the pedagogical freedom permitted within the reforms. Winkler's study, however, did not focus on beginning secondary history teachers nor did it delve into discipline-specific issues. Instead, she focused on general perceptions of the accountability policy. This chapter extends Winkler's study through a specific focus on beginning history teachers.

BEGINNING TEACHERS

Beginning teachers experience a sudden and dramatic transition during their first year(s) of teaching and are forced to confront profound changes in their personal and professional lives (Bullough, 1987, 1989; Gold & Roth, 1993). Many beginning teachers are placed in demanding assignments and left to sink or swim (Darling-Hammond, 1998). Attrition rates for beginning teachers are high as approximately 20% leave the profession after their first year and 30% within the first 3 years (Education Week, 2000). Gold (1996) notes that "the greatest problems encountered by beginning teachers were overwhelming feelings of disillusionment and believing that they were unable to cope with the multitude of pressures encountered each day" (p. 556). As beginning teachers confront these daily challenges and slowly achieve an understanding of the complexities of teaching, many researchers argue that they experience a natural, personal process of teacher development (Burden, 1979; Cornett, 1990; Fuller, 1969; Fuller & Brown, 1975; Huberman, 1989; Rust, 1994; Ryan, 1986). Although researchers continue to debate the nature and process of this development, researchers show that learning to teach effectively is a difficult and complex process.

What, then, does effective or ambitious teaching look like for beginning teachers? Many research-based frameworks exist. The Interstate New Teacher Assessment and Support Consortium (INTASC), for example, offers an outline of what beginning teachers should know and be able to do. These generic criteria include an understanding of content pedagogy, student development, diverse learners, multiple instructional strategies, motivation and management, communication and technology, planning, assessment, reflective practice and professional growth and school and community involvement (Council of Chief State Officers, 1987).

THE TEACHING OF HISTORY

Although generic descriptions can be useful, researchers increasingly point to discipline-specific notions of effective practice (Grant, 2003; Shulman, 1987; Yeager, 2000). The National Research Council (2000), for example, describes "expert history teachers" as being sensitive to the key issues and practices in the field:

> For expert history teachers, their knowledge of the discipline and belief about its structure interacts with their teaching strategies. Rather than simply introduce students to sets of facts to be learned, these teachers help people to understand the problematic nature of historical interpretation and analysis and to appreciate the relevance of history for their everyday lives. (p. 159)

The assumption in the National Research Council definition that expert teachers should help students to "understand the problematic nature of historical interpretation and analysis" (p. 159) is consistent with the ideas articulated in the *National Standards for History* (National Center for History in the Schools, 1996). The authors of the *Standards* assert that teachers should teach both historical understanding and historical thinking. Historical understandings are the content, or what students should "know" about history. Historical thinking skills emphasize ways of thinking about history. As such, they "enable children to differentiate past, present, and future time; raise questions; seek and evaluate evidence; compare and analyze historical stories, illustrations, and records from the past; interpret the historical record; and construct historical narratives of their own" (p. 4). In addition, historical thinking includes historical decision-making, historical issues-analysis, historical research, historical analysis and interpretation, historical comprehension, and chronological thinking.

Lee Shulman (1987) and S. G. Grant (2003) also highlight the importance of teachers' subject matter knowledge, but do so by tying that knowledge to other elements of schooling. Shulman's notion of pedagogical content knowledge emphasizes the connection between content knowledge and learners. Pedagogical content knowledge is "the blending of content and pedagogy into an understanding of how particular topics, problems, or issues are organized, represented and adapted to the diverse interests and abilities of learners, and presented for instruction"

(p. 8). Grant's conception of ambitious teaching takes the relationship between content and learning one step further by locating it within a schooling context. Ambitious teaching develops when:

> Teachers know well their subject matter and see within it the potential to enrich their students' lives;
>
> When teachers know their students well, which includes understanding the kinds of lives they lead, how they think about and perceive the world, and that they are capable of far more than they and most others believe; and
>
> When teachers know how to create the necessary space for themselves and their students in environments that may not appreciate the efforts of either (p. xi).

Teachers' knowledge of subject matter, learning, and contexts also surfaces in the broader literature on history teaching (Hartzler-Miller, 2001; Pajares, 1992; Slekar, 1998; Thornton, 1991; VanSledright, 1996; Wineburg, 1991, 2001; Yeager & Davis, 1996) and the struggle to realize these knowledges in practice is only compounded in the inexperienced hands of beginning teachers (Slekar, 1998; van Hover & Yeager, 2003, 2004; Yeager & Davis, 1994, 1996).

In this light, how does the added layer of state-mandated standards and high-stakes assessment influence beginning history teachers' development as teachers? Do beginning teachers in Virginia's high-stakes testing context have the opportunity to develop into expert teachers who engage in effective or ambitious teaching? Or will the felt need to survive and the pressures of the test lead these teachers to choose conventional approaches to teaching history? As Grant (2003) notes, these are open questions:

> Ambitious teaching and learning develop when smart teachers, curious students, and powerful ideas come together. Policymakers may assume that standards-based reforms support the efforts of ambitious teachers, but until we better understand how these teachers, and the students in their classes, think and act, that assumption is hollow at best. (p. 198)

This purpose of this study is to gain a deeper understanding of how beginning teachers think and act within the context of the SOLs. Specifically, this exploratory study examines how beginning history teachers make sense of the influence of the SOLs and SOL test on their planning, instruction, and assessment.

METHODOLOGY

As this study focused on the sense-making and meaning perspectives of teachers, I employed a qualitative research design to examine the following question: What are beginning (1–4 years of experience) secondary history teachers' perceptions of the influence of Virginia's standards-based reform on their planning, instruction, and assessment?

Participants and Setting

The participants included seven high school (Grades 9–12) beginning history teachers: three European American males (Vincent, Matthew, Fred), two European American females (Valerie, Patricia), one Asian American female (Kathleen), and one African American male (Richard) (See Table 10.3; All participants were assigned pseudonyms). Five of the seven teachers (Vincent, Matthew, Valerie, Patricia, and Fred) graduated from the Masters of Teaching (MT) social studies teacher education program at the local public university. Kathleen graduated from the undergraduate social studies teacher education program of another state university. Richard did not attend a teacher education program; he became certified to teach social studies through an alternative licensure program.

I chose to focus on these seven teachers on the basis of several criteria. First, all of the teachers had between one and 4 years of teaching experience and taught history at the high school level. Second, the participants taught in public school systems close to the university. Finally, these teachers were willing to participate in the study. The department head of each of the four local high schools provided me with a list of faculty members with one to four years experience teaching history. Of the 12 names provided, seven beginning teachers agreed to participate in this study. The others declined due to time constraints or discomfort with the prospect of being interviewed and observed.

These sample teachers taught at three different high schools within two school districts located in central Virginia. Blue Ridge High School (Valerie and Patricia) and Piedmont High School (Fred and Richard) are located in rural areas in a fairly affluent county. Both schools are fully accredited with high SOL pass rates. Jefferson High School (Vincent, Matthew, Kathleen) is located in a city district; the school has exceeded the required 70% pass rate for history, but has not met the cut-off score in mathematics and science. Therefore, this school is labeled by the state as "provisionally accredited/needs improvement."

Table 10.3.   Study Participants

High School	Pseu- donym	Demo- graphics	Years Teaching	Classes Taught	Educational Background
Jefferson	Vincent	White Male	>1	World History 2 World Geography	BA: History MT: Social Studies Education
Jefferson	Matthew	White Male	>1	World History 1 World Geography	BA: History MT: Social Studies Education
Jefferson	Kathleen	Asian Female	>1	World History 2	BA: Social Studies and Secondary Education
Piedmont	Valerie	White Female	1 1/2	American History	BA: History MT: Social Studies Education
Piedmont	Patricia	White Female	1 1/2	World History 1 AP Psychology	BA: History MT: Social Studies Education
BlueRidge	Fred	White Male	3	World History 1 Newspaper	BA: Politics MT: Social Studies Education
BlueRidge	Richard	African American Male	4	World History 1	BA: History Alternative Licensure

Data Collection

The data sources for this study included interviews, observations, e-mail communications, and classroom documents. I conducted a semi-structured interview with the teachers, using a protocol that addressed the teachers' educational and personal background; their approaches to planning, instruction, and assessment; their experiences during their first year(s) of teaching; their conceptions of history and historical thinking; their definitions of effective history teaching; and their perceptions of the impact of SOLs and SOL testing on the teaching and learning of history. The interviews lasted approximately 2 hours and were audiotaped and transcribed.

Participants were observed for one to five class periods. During the observations, I took field notes documenting instructional strategies utilized by the teacher, the content covered, references to SOLs and the SOL tests, and other pertinent information. These field notes were later transcribed and annotated. I also collected a variety of classroom materials including assessments, hand-outs, and graphic organizers. I had served as advisor and professor to two of the beginning teachers (Vincent and Matthew); therefore, in an attempt to encourage more candid responses from these two participants, a social studies doctoral student with no previous relationship with the teachers conducted the interviews and the observations.

Data Analysis

Data analysis included several stages. First, I read through the interviews and observation transcripts in order to conduct a systematic content analysis, searching for patterns, themes, similarities, differences, and general categories of responses (Stake, 1995). Second, I generated an extensive list of codes, categories, and labels, and then I coded the interview and observation transcripts by hand, line by line (Miles & Huberman, 1994). Finally, I generated an outline of the major themes emerging from the data and triangulated these themes through a rigorous search for confirming and disconfirming evidence and alternative explanations.

SURVIVAL VERSUS STANDARDS AND ACCOUNTABILITY

How do these seven secondary beginning history teachers, who have never known a context without standards and accountability, interpret the influence of content standards and a high-stakes, fact-recall, multiple-choice end-of-year exam on their teaching practice? What are their perceptions of these state-mandated reform efforts? A range of interesting issues emerge as the teachers' views are less consistent than one might suppose. First, these beginning teachers hold mixed feelings about the standard and accountability measures implemented by Virginia. Second, the teachers' perceptions of the influence of the SOLs and SOL tests on planning, instruction, and assessment vary across function and across the seven participants. Rather than define their practices, most of the teachers feel that the SOLs represent simply another layer of challenges to be dealt with during their first years of teaching. In fact, anxiety about day-to-day survival often trumps concern over the state-mandated tests.

Mixed Views Towards the SOLs and SOL Tests

Overall, the seven beginning teachers hold mixed views towards the SOLs and SOL tests. Many appreciate the standards as a curricular guide, and express a need for some form of accountability, but disagree with the nature of and possible effects of the year-end high-stakes test. Patricia, for example, cites both positive and negative aspects of the reform. She notes that the SOLs help her by creating a context that encourages teachers to collaborate and by providing her with a structure, with the "basics of what I need to teach and knowing that my students will be assessed at the end of the year on what I've taught them." At the same time, she laments the time crunch created by the tests, and that the tests "try to cover so much and teach breadth and not depth—lots of little details." Fred also expresses mixed feelings about the SOLs and SOL tests. On the one hand, he sees the curricular guidance offered as valuable:

> In some ways, SOLs are considered a good thing, or good for teachers because they tell you what to teach. I think a lot of new teachers don't know what's important so it's good, someone is telling me what's important.... The SOLs have improved education because when you hold teachers accountable and kids accountable I think things tend to get better.

At the same time, Fred worries about the negative effects of a high-stakes exam: "I don't like the punitive aspects of the SOLs, about the kids not graduating. I think there will be a huge drop out rate, starting soon."

Other teachers express stronger, more negative views about the SOLs and accompanying tests. Richard raises the conventional problems of a one-shot test measuring a year's study and the possible negative effects of children's lived experiences. But he also suggests that the new curriculum and exams provide cover for state politicians:

> I don't think a 71 multiple-choice question test given at the end of May can assess how much a kid learns in a year for a variety of reasons. What happens if the kid is sick that day, or the kid's mother died in a car wreck the week before? There are too many variables and there's too much pressure— whether or not they can graduate depending on a one-shot test. Personally, I feel like the SOLs are for politicians to say that they are doing something about education. Here are the standards, here are the tests, we're holding schools accountable. But they haven't thought the process all the way through.

Matthew worries that the SOLs and SOL tests have a dampening effect on teachers and students:

[The SOLs] have moved us from a well-balanced student to a bunch of clones who know exactly the same amount of information about exactly what the government tells them they should know about and I don't agree with that. But I think that as a professional, I pay great lip service to the SOLs. In essence, it's a good idea to have a framework. It's the assessment that I view as the problem. They are trying to assess everybody on the same level.... In my opinion [the SOL tests] have stifled social studies because it has stifled thinking and stifled creativity in too many people. And I am the first person to agree that it doesn't have to do that, but even though you can still have a great classroom with the SOLs, many people don't.

As these quotations illustrate, the teachers' views toward Virginia's standards-based reform reflect a range of opinions. The SOLs provoke feelings ranging from appreciation to ambivalence to cynicism. Perceptions of the state tests are more consistent, but still vary from general frustration to obvious concern about the nature of and stakes attached to the end-of-year tests. That said, the seven beginning teachers, who have known no other teaching context, admit that they have no conception of what it would be like to teach in a world without standards and high-stakes accountability. Asked to reflect on how their instruction, planning, and assessment might change in a world without SOLs, most pause and reply, "I don't think I'd change much." Then, after a moment's thought, they list changes including the opportunity to go into more depth with topics, to assign long-term projects, and to not use multiple-choice tests.

Just One More Thing: The Influence of the SOLs on Teachers' Practices

The SOLs and SOL tests do influence these beginning teachers' practices. But those influences vary by function and by teacher. In general, the teachers cite the strongest influence on their content decisions, a modest influence on their assessment decisions, and virtually no influence on their instructional decisions. That said, considerable variation develops across these patterns as each teacher constructs his or her own perceptions of the state politics. Of particular note, however, is the finding that, in some instances, the beginning teachers interpret the typical challenges faced by new teachers as exerting a greater influence on their decision-making than the state reforms. Concern, anxiety, and apprehension about behavior management, respect from colleagues, dealing with diverse learners, learning the content, time to grade, block scheduling, multiple preparations, pressure from the school culture, and other day-to-day survival issues emerge as equal or greater influences on planning, instruction, and assessment than the existence of the SOLs and SOL tests.

Table 10.4.   Example of Scope and Sequence Guides

Organizing Topic	Essential Understandings, Knowledge, and Skills	Related SOL	Classroom Assessment Methods	Resources
U.S. Constitution	Explain that during the Constitutional Era, the Americans made two attempts to establish a workable government based on republican principles.	VUS5a	Projects Quizzes Student reports Unit tests Writing assignments Class Discussion	A Commonwealth of Knowledge Audiovisual materials Center for Civic Education Library of Congress Smithsonian Institute Textbook

Table 10.5.   Blueprint

Reporting Category	Number of Items	World History to 1500 A.D. Standards of Learning
Human Origins and Early Civilizations	6	WH1.2b-d WHI.3b-e
Classical Civilizations and the Rise of Religious Traditions	14	WHI.4a-f WHI.5b, d-g WHI.6b, d-k
Postclassical Civilizations	13	WHI.10c-d WHI.11b WHI.12b-d WHI.12c-d

Influences on Teachers' Content Planning

The SOLs and SOL tests exert the strongest influence on teachers' content planning. Teachers' planning includes curricular, unit, and lesson development. In terms of long-range curricular planning, the teachers note that they work collaboratively to develop curriculum with other teachers who teach the same subject, use curriculum guides already created by their department, or follow curriculum outlines inherited from predecessors. These curriculum guides include attention to material covered on the SOL tests and provide pacing recommendations—the amount of time designated to cover a topic generally correlated with the number of items on the test dedicated to that topic (see Tables 10.3 and 10.4). The SOL tests, implemented in May, serve as the endpoint for the curriculum.

All of the teachers loosely follow these curricular guides in their content planning. Several teachers note that they tweak these curriculum guidelines, while others do not. For example, Patricia states that "basically, when I came in last year there was a rough outline of how they went about sequencing things.... I kind of followed what the other World History 1 teachers were doing last year, and then this year have made a couple of changes on the placements of things."

Asked to describe their lesson planning process, Richard, Valerie, and Kathleen explicitly mention the SOLs. Richard explains that when planning his curriculum and his individual lessons, he thinks about what chapter they are studying, "how much time I have, how much time each activity is going to take, which SOLs I need to make sure I cover." Valerie notes that she tries to determine essential questions and objectives for her units and lessons, she thinks about how to relate the material to her students, and then she considers "the main points on the SOLs that they have to know and then what skills that I need to go over." Richard and Valerie both comment that the longer they teach and the more comfortable they grow with the content, the less they refer to the SOLs, glancing at them only occasionally in order to double-check that they are meeting the mandates of the state.

Kathleen, still in her first few months of teaching, describes her planning process as beginning with the SOLs:

> First [I] look at the SOL guidelines, and then I write down what they have to have. And then I read the chapter and then I read the outside materials, and then I look at what other teachers have done in the past, I have notebooks and stuff. I borrow stuff that would be good and I try to plan lessons about what they need to know about the SOLs.

In contrast, the other four beginning teachers do not mention the SOLs initially as part of their lesson planning process; their descriptions focus on unit and lesson objectives, instructional strategies they might use, and time allotted per topic and activity. They mention SOLs only when asked directly. For example, in her lesson planning, Patricia reviews her unit outline, reads through the relevant textbook chapter, and searches for primary sources and other materials on the Internet. "I try to type one [lesson plan] up every day" she said, "I have to write stuff down. I have three objectives [understand, know, and be able to do] for each day...and then materials...and then procedures and then assessment." Her notebook of lesson plans matches this description, but it includes no explicit mention of the SOLs. Asked to comment on the influence of SOLs on her lesson plans, Patricia explains they are part of the overall fabric of her planning:

> Yes, I do check that stuff [the SOLs] off, especially what is important. But we do so much beyond the SOLs … [and] actually, [the SOLs] are already built into my curriculum now … so I don't necessarily have to reference the SOLs that much.

Other teachers also observe that the SOLs are built into the curriculum or into lesson plans inherited from other teachers. Matthew comments that "the way the [World History 1] team set [the curriculum] up was due to the weighting of the SOLs. So I know I'm aligning with what I should be doing in terms of SOLs." In terms of his day-to-day planning, he states that he never looks at the SOLs. Fred's description of his lesson planning echoes Matthew's. He notes that the department provides him with curriculum guides that break the SOLs down by topic and address the specific content matter to be covered. He notes that occasionally he looks "at that stuff [the pacing guide] and see, did I cover that, cover that, cover, that."

According to the teachers, the most salient influence of SOLs and SOL tests on their curricular planning is the issue of time. All of the teachers express concern about SOL-imposed time pressures—specifically, the rush to cover "everything" before the SOL tests in May. Additionally, the teachers note that this time crunch precludes them from covering topics in depth. Rapid coverage of topics and a focus on breadth of content comprise a central component of their teaching lives. Patricia describes the frantic pace of her teaching:

> The biggest influence of the SOLs is the pressure to cover everything…. I've had to cover stuff in a day. We do Africa, the Americas, and I do Japan in about 20 minutes. Because literally, last year I didn't do it all. It's not something they have to have a lot of knowledge about and it wasn't a player in early history. The way it works out, I'll probably spend three class periods on civilizations in Africa and Americas after Egypt. And it's eight or nine civilizations—like Ghana and Mali and Aztecs and Incas and Mayans. It's crazy. It's my least favorite thing to teach because it's always so rushed and the nature of how much stuff has to be covered around the world from the beginning of time to 1500. The decision [to spend so little time on this topic] is based on SOL [tests]. The number of questions, it's so random. You have to know this one little thing about Ghana, and one little thing about Mali, and that the Mayans created the calendar and the Aztecs did this and it's so choppy.

Richard echoes this sentiment, commenting that, "if there are only two questions on Africa and Asia, I can't spend much time on that, which ties my hands … time is crazy, the hurricane took up time and then snow … and this year I feel like I'm more and more behind and trying to catch up." Valerie reflects that, "given my time [limitations], I find it's really hard to go in depth given the amount that they are required to know." Fred sums up the time frustrations of most teachers:

> All teachers feel [time pressures]. I compensate by trying to stay ahead and
> to keep us moving…. You do feel the pressure all the time of those tests,
> particularly when it comes down to you and you haven't covered 200 years
> of material. [That's why you observed] the Enlightenment in a day. That's
> all they're getting. Then we're done.

Interestingly, the teachers who have taught at least a year and have experienced the SOL tests emphasize the time issue more than the teachers in
their first months of teaching. Although all teachers everywhere struggle
with managing time, the seven beginning teachers perceive the time pressures imposed by the SOL tests as extreme.

The teachers' curriculum planning guides incorporate the standards,
provide a structure for teaching, establish pacing guidelines, and appear
to mitigate the teachers' concerns about including SOL content in their
instruction. Asked to discuss their planning process, most of the teachers
mention issues other than the SOLs and SOL tests and only address the
influence of SOLs when prodded. In the interviews, all of the teachers
emphasize more pressing influences on their planning, namely, the struggle to learn the content, their attempts to plan for varying student
achievement levels, and concerns about planning for a block schedule.
For example, Patricia observes that, in her first year, "I definitely put in
the hours and everything. When I first began teaching, I was teaching
three subjects that I did not know … so for me, [the major challenge] was
content." She recalls that, when meeting with a teacher to collaboratively
plan a unit, "he'd ask, so how many days are you spending on each of
these groups of people? And I looked at the list and I didn't even know
when those [civilizations] were, chronologically, or what they did."

Still in his first few months of teaching, Matthew cites a range of concerns, but stresses that the major influence on his planning is the need to
learn content: "I have no content background in this area, well I've taken
one class in college. I was prepared, but how can you ever really be prepared, starting out from scratch. It's a lot of work." He notes that when he
plans for class, he thinks about "how long the class is, what I want them to
learn, what are we going to do, and what I have to learn." He also mentions experiencing frustrations planning for the six classes he teaches
(one more class than the typical load at High School A), and that he
teaches two groups of students at opposite ends of the school's tracking
system. He expresses the opinion that if he had a firmer grasp of World
History 1 content, had one less class to plan for, and only taught one
achievement level, he might have more time to meaningfully plan for
instruction and feel less overwhelmed. Day-to-day survival rather than the
SOLs seems to be his priority.

It appears that, in many instances, these teachers interpret issues like learning the content, organizing their planning process, finding outside materials, figuring out approaches to relate information to students, and developing instruction that can fill a block period as larger influences on their planning than attention to SOL content and SOL tests. However, due to the curriculum guides, the SOLs seem to comprise an essential component of their planning, whether or not the teachers recognize this pervasive influence. This tacit influence manifests itself in many ways, including the topics teachers choose to cover, the pace at which they plan to cover these topics, and the key facts or essential understandings they expect to emphasize.

Influences on Teachers' Instruction

Although critics typically cite the deadening influence of high-stakes tests on teachers' instruction, such is not the case with the teachers in this study. Interview and observation data reveal that the seven teachers describe and use a variety of instructional methods in their day-to-day teaching. As with their content choices, the teachers' instructional decision-making appears to be influenced by a number of confluent factors: the block schedule of the three high schools, the achievement level of the students in their classes, the level of comfort with the content, their aims for their classes, and issues related to student behavior. So far as day-to-day choices involving instructional methods, the teachers seem to view the influence of the SOLs and SOL tests as minimal.

Teachers do not perceive a strong causal link between the instructional methods that they use in class and the SOL tests. The reduction of teaching to lecture and recitation, drill and practice that many critics of high-stakes testing posit is not evident in these teachers' classrooms. Like most of his peers, Matthew portrays his teaching as a mix of practices:

> I use quite a bit of group work. I use lots of jigsaw type stuff. In [the] applied [level class] they do basic reading comprehension in their book then we'll talk about it and see what they know. For [the] honors [class], mostly group work and discussion. Very little lecture. [Every day] in [both] classes, we do a do-now at the beginning, we discuss it, some type of group work, some guided practice. Honors, the do-now is more in depth and then we'll do some kind of activity and a PEV check [a reading quiz].

In an observation of his applied level class, Matthew asks students to answer an introductory question written on the board, designed to settle the students down as they entered the classroom—in other words, an activity that the students "do-now." They briefly discuss their answers, and then open the textbook in order to read sections of the book out loud. Matthew stops them after each paragraph in order to explain difficult vocabulary words or complex geographic terms. Then, he asks students to copy the boldface words and to define them using the glossary. After collecting this work, Matthew explains the idea of human versus physical geography. He distributes a chart and asks students to take 10 minutes to walk around the school building and to list the physical and human aspects of geography in their school. He identifies this lesson as one of his better lessons, observing that the task of day-to-day planning is overwhelming him. At no time during his lesson does Matthew refer to the SOLs; his mix of practice seems uninfluenced by the SOLs and SOL tests.

Second-year teacher Patricia also describes her instructional approaches as a mixture of approaches uninfluenced by the state reforms:

> I have them do a lot of reading and questions and thinking about something.... With block periods you cannot do a content lecture for 90 minutes, especially with ninth graders. It just does not work. I do use a lot of lecture and guided discussion, but for a small percentage of each class. I try to give them information that's not in the textbook.... I use PowerPoint, I do group work, jigsaw, graffiti. I do interactive stories and drama, I have them act a lot. Read alouds. We have story time sometimes.... I use a lot of manipulatives.

Like Matthew, Patricia's classroom practices appear of her own choosing and independent of the state's SOLs. For example, in a lesson that introduces the upcoming unit on Greece, Patricia organizes students into groups of Greek city-states. She plays a song and students have to guess how this piece of music relates to the unit. She quizzes students on their nightly reading assignment, engages them in an interactive read aloud about pre-Greek civilization, lectures on Greece, and shows pictures from a trip she took to Greece. She then provides an overview of the next few lessons, exuding enthusiasm and excitement for the topic. On the board, she writes an agenda, objectives for the day, and responses to her interactive read aloud. There are no direct references to the SOLs or SOL tests anywhere in her room, or anywhere in her instruction. Patricia's teaching appears to reflect her explanation that block scheduling requires multiple activities and her desire to cover content not presented in the textbook.

These two examples highlight the fact that these seven beginning teachers utilize a mix of instructional approaches that appear uninfluenced by the SOLs and SOL tests. As teachers discuss their instructional approaches, they assert that the challenges facing them as beginning teachers exert a more powerful influence on their teaching than do the SOLs or the SOL tests. That is, although teachers perceive the issue of time as a major influence of the SOL tests on the pace of their instruction, they cite the greater impact of other factors like the block schedule, new content to learn, beliefs about student achievement, and years of experience.

Influences on Teachers' Assessment

Different from both their content and instructional decision-making, all of the participants state that the SOL tests exert a strong influence on certain aspects of their assessment planning. Each of the seven teachers describes a variety of assessment formats used to measure student learning; however, they acknowledge that their unit tests resemble the fact-recall, multiple-choice format of the end-of-year SOL tests. End-of-unit tests collected as archival evidence support this interview data; these tests have 50 multiple-choice items that emphasize recall of factual content. All of the teachers note that the nature of the end-of-year exam, combined with the time pressures created by this exam, leads them to utilize this multiple-choice, fact-recall format on a regular basis.

Valerie uses a variety of formats to assess student learning throughout her units. She describes using group projects and presentations, debates, graph interpretation exercises, essay writing, exit passes (questions students answered before leaving class), and analysis of primary sources. During a lesson on life in the United States immediately before the Civil War, Valerie asks students to complete an exit pass that addresses the essential question of the day: "Did the geography or people of the North and South contribute to the tension leading to the Civil War?" Students hand in their written responses at the end of the class period. In addition to daily and weekly assessments, Valerie develops SOL-like tests at the end of each 6-week grading period. These tests include 25–50 fact-recall, multiple-choice questions. To prepare the students to take this test, she explains that "I try to have a quiz at least once a week with fill-in-the-blank and multiple-choice because they need smaller chunks." She also mentions that as part of her weekly quiz, she includes minilessons on test-taking skills.

Vincent and Fred also combine more ambitious classroom assessments with SOL-like tests. Vincent explains that, for each unit, students complete a project or performance-based assessment as well as take a test with questions framed in a manner similar to the SOL tests. He observes that "kids learn differently and tests are boring and can only do so much. I want kids to grapple with the material in a way that is engaging for them." Fred assigns several essays, projects and graded discussions throughout the year; for tests, however, he follows the SOL format. He explains, "[when I write a test] I think multiple-choice—we just need practice with that. So I try to include a multiple-choice component for all tests."

By contrast, Patricia assigns an essay for each unit and gives students daily fact-recall reading quizzes and end-of-unit tests composed of multiple-choice and fill-in-the-blank questions. During one observation, students take a five-question reading quiz. Patricia claims her assessment reflects her sense of the need to prepare students for future multiple-choice tests:

> [My tests emphasize] recall—if they can't spit it back out to me, they're not going to know it later on. I choose multiple-choice because most of these kids are on the track to be taking [Advanced Placement] … and those test formats are multiple-choice.

She notes that her tests are cumulative and include fill-in-the blank items in which anything they study "is fair game." (The students refer to this section of the test as "old enemies.") Patricia also justifies her testing decisions on increasing students' performance on the SOL test:

> The SOLs … it's important [for my students] to recall stuff we studied previously. If they are going to have a cumulative test on the year, it makes sense that I keep bringing stuff in. I try to bring up information that we studied in the past, just constantly.

Many of the teachers describe other modes of assessment that measure the skills they value (e.g., writing, debating, presenting). Overall, the teachers view the SOL tests as an influence on their assessments through their choice to use multiple-choice tests structured like those on the end-of-year exam. Also, the teachers observe that they tend to ask questions that emphasize recall of factual content, and avoid questions that encouraged critical or historical thinking.

DISCUSSION AND IMPLICATIONS

This chapter examines the question of beginning secondary history teachers' perceptions of the influence of Virginia's standards-based reform on their planning, instruction, and assessment. Although a small sample, these teachers' experiences raise several interesting issues that can add to and enrich the conversation about standards and testing in the Commonwealth of Virginia. The state-mandated reforms clearly exert an influence on the teachers. The seven teachers do not cite the SOLs as a large influence on their content planning. Yet, one day I visited three different World History I teachers in three different schools—all three were beginning their unit on early Greece and Rome. And while these teachers used very different instructional methods and outside sources, the core content covered was identical. Whether the seven beginning teachers recognize the direct link between their planning, instruction, and assessment or not, the curricula is created by the tests, not by the teachers. Yet, because these teachers are so focused on surviving day-to-day, and because they know no other teaching context, they interpret the major influences of the SOL tests in terms of time available to cover certain topics and of how they chose to structure their unit tests. It seems as though a culture shift has taken place in Virginia's schools—these beginning teachers are so used to the existence of the SOL tests, the influence has become as undetectable as it is pervasive.

And yet, despite the pervasive and tacit influence of the SOLs on these teachers' content planning, their instruction and assessment practices do not fit neatly into the existing literature on high-stakes testing. Rather than emphasizing drill and recitation, or favoring lecture of SOL-related facts to students, these teachers employ a variety of instructional approaches and assessment approaches in their classrooms. This variation remains constant across contexts—from Vincent, Matthew, and Kathleen, who teach in a school fighting to raise their SOL scores, to Fred and Richard, who work in a school with the highest SOL scores in central Virginia—and across experience levels.

It appears that the beginning teachers are left to make sense of the standards and tests on their own: None of the participants mentioned any type of induction or meaningful professional development focused on instruction or assessment. Thus, the teachers' perceptions of the standards tend to reflect their beliefs about standards and testing, their experiences as beginning teachers, the context and culture of their school, their beliefs about history instruction, and their beliefs about the achievement level of their students. All of the teachers appear to believe that block scheduling requires multiple instructional methods; that lower-achievement level students can not perform well on the test; that honors students can teach themselves; that standards help them plan; and that the one-shot multiple-choice high-stakes test is problematic. Yet there appears to be no mechanism to help them make sense of this bewildering array of influences.

Additionally, meaningful attention to student learning seems largely absent from the beginning teachers' discussion of their planning, instruction, and assessment. These teachers focus on their own survival—they discuss what they do to plan, teach, and assess, but these discussions center around their role as teacher and whether students appear to enjoy or like the class. In very few instances do the teachers discuss student learning in any depth. In terms of assessment of student learning, teachers mention the different approaches they use, they mention "preparing students for the test," and "preparing them to recall facts," but they do not mention how these approaches measure what students learn about history in their class or how they use this data to make instructional decisions.

This condition fits with existing research on beginning teachers (e.g., Rust, 1994). Rather than focusing on student learning, novice teachers tend to worry about managing student behavior, learning the content, and figuring out how to fill a block period. Ambitious or expert teachers use data derived from assessment to determine how much students have learned and use this information to inform their instructional decision-making. In a context of high-stakes testing, the issue of student learning plays a central role: Although widespread debate surrounds the issue of whether memorization of facts constitutes meaningful learning, students must learn historical content in order to pass the end-of-year exam. This notion of student learning remains largely absent from teachers' discussion of their teaching. Meaningful induction could have assisted teachers in shifting some attention to what students were actually learning in their classes.

These and other issues raise interesting questions for the teaching and learning of history in Virginia and the induction of beginning teachers in Virginia. How can we continue to encourage beginning teachers to consider and think about ambitious history teaching within a high-stakes context in which the standards and end-of-year tests pervade all aspects of teaching? In observations, the teachers use a variety of relevant and appropriate instructional approaches. They appear to be using a variety of primary and secondary materials. They emphasize critical thinking and reading and writing activities. They cite their teacher education program as the source of these ideas, and the nature of block scheduling as their reason for implementing these approaches. They do not rely exclusively on conventional methods. Yet, as noted earlier, rich discussion about student learning is absent from the interview and observation data. And none of the teachers mentions any meaningful induction from mentor teachers or by school and district programs. This all points to the need for quality induction and the difficulties in providing it—a call raised in most of the literature on beginning teachers (Bullough, 1987; Gold, 1996).

Induction within the age of accountability, however, needs to focus on the tricky issue of how to foster ambitious teaching and student learning within a context that promotes uniformity and fact-recall. How much can we expect from beginning teachers early in their teaching careers? What structures will assist beginning teachers in grappling with the day-to-day challenges as well as the larger challenge of ambitious teaching? How can we prevent beginning teachers from developing beliefs that assessment-driven reform and ambitious teaching are mutually exclusive? As Grant (2003) notes, there is a need for thoughtful mentors who possess rich conceptions of ambitious teaching. These teachers all hold the potential to become expert teachers who engage in effective or ambitious teaching—

however, we need to prepare teachers to handle the dissonance between the world of effective practice, professionally defined, and practice, politically defined.

REFERENCES

Bullough, R. V. (1987). Planning and the first year of teaching. *Journal of Education for Teaching, 13,* 231–250.

Bullough, R. V. (1989). *First-year teacher: A case study.* New York: Teachers College Press.

Burden, P. R. (1979). *Teacher's perceptions of the characteristics and influences on their personal and professional development.* Columbus: Ohio State University Press.

Cornett, J. W. (1990). Teacher thinking about curriculum and instruction: A case study of a secondary social studies teacher. *Theory and Research in Social Education, 18,* 248–273.

Council of Chief State School Officers. (1987). *Interstate New Teacher Assessment and Support Consortium (INTASC) Standards.* Retrieved from http:/www.ccsso.org/projects/Interstate_New_Teacher_Assessment_and_Support_Consortium

Darling-Hammond, L. (1998). Teacher learning that supports student learning. *Educational Leadership, 55*(5), 6–11.

Duke, D. L., & Reck, B. L. (2003). The evolution of educational accountability in the Old Dominion. In D. L. Duke, M. Grogan, P. D. Tucker, & W. F. Heinecke (Eds.), *Educational leadership in an age of accountability: The Virginia experience* (pp. 36–68). Albany, NY: SUNY Press.

Education Week. (2000). *Quality Counts 2000.* Retrieved January 12, 2006, from http://www.edweek.org/ew/toc/2006/01/05

Fore, L. C. (1995). *A case study of curriculum controversy: The Virginia standards of learning for history and the social sciences.* Unpublished doctoral dissertation, Virginia Polytechnic Institute and State University, Blacksburg, VA.

Fordham Foundation. (2003). *Effective state standards for U.S. history: A 2003 report card.* Retrieved January 12, 2006, from http://www.edexcellence.net/foundation/publication/publication.cfm?id=320

Fuller, F. (1969). Concerns of teachers: A developmental conceptualization. *American Educational Research Journal, 6*(4), 207–226.

Fuller, F., & Brown, O. H. (1975). Becoming a teacher. In K. Ryan (Ed.), *Teacher education* (pp. 25–52). Chicago: University of Chicago Press.

Gold, Y. (1996). Beginning teacher support: Attrition, mentoring, and induction. In J. Sikula, T. G. Buttery, & E. Guyten (Eds.), *Handbook of research on teacher education* (pp. 548–593). New York: MacMillan.

Gold, Y., & Roth, R. A. (1993). *Teachers managing stress and preventing burnout: The professional health solution.* London: Falmer Press.

Grant, S. G. (2003). *History lessons: Teaching, learning, and testing in U.S. high school classrooms.* Mahwah, NJ: Erlbaum.

Grogan, M., & Roland, P. B. (2003). How superintendents in Virginia deal with issues surrounding the black-white test score gap. In D. L. Duke, M. Grogan,

P. D. Tucker, & W. F. Heinecke (Eds.), *Educational leadership in an age of accountability: The Virginia experience* (pp. 155–180). Albany, NY: SUNY Press.

Grogan, M., & Sherman, W. H. (2003). A study of successful teachers preparing high school students for the standards of learning tests in Virginia. In D. L. Duke, M. Grogan, P. D. Tucker, & W. F. Heinecke (Eds.), *Educational leadership in an age of accountability: The Virginia experience* (pp. 114–134). Albany, NY: SUNY Press.

Hartzler-Miller, C. (2001). Making sense of "best practice" in teaching history. *Theory and Research in Social Education, 29,* 672–695.

Heinecke, W. F., Curry-Cocoran, D. E., & Moon, T. R. (2003). U.S. schools and the new standards and accountability initiative. In D. L. Duke, M. Grogan, P. D. Tucker, & W. F. Heinecke (Eds.), *Educational leadership in an age of accountability: The Virginia experience* (pp. 7–35). Albany, NY: SUNY Press.

Huberman, A. M. (1989). The professional life cycle of teachers. *Teachers College Record, 91*(1), 31–56.

Lawson, H. (1992). Beyond the new conception of teacher induction. *Journal of Teacher Education, 43*(3), 163–172.

McMillan, J., Myran, S., & Workman, D. (1999, April). *The impact of mandated state-wide testing on teachers' classroom assessment and instructional practices.* Paper presented at the American Educational Research Association. Quebec, Canada.

Miles, M. B., & Huberman, A. M. (1994). *Qualitative data analysis.* Thousand Oaks, CA: Sage.

National Center for History in the Schools. (1996). *National history standards.* Los Angeles: National Center for History in the Schools.

National Research Council. (2000). *How people learn: Brain, mind, experience, and school.* Washington, DC: National Academy Press.

Pajares, M. (1992). Teachers' beliefs and educational research: Cleaning up a messy construct. *Review of Educational Research, 62,* 907–922.

Rust, F. (1994). The first year of teaching: It's not what they expected. *Teaching & Teacher Education, 10*(2), 205–217.

Ryan, K. (1986). *The induction of new teachers.* Bloomington, IN: Phi Delta Kappa Educational Foundation.

Segall, A. (2003). The impact of state-mandated testing according to social studies teachers: The Michigan Educational Assessment Program (Meap) as a case study of consequences.*Theory and Research in Social Education, 31*(5), 287–325.

Shulman, L. (1987). Knowledge and teaching: Foundations of the new reform. *Harvard Educational Review, 57*(1), 1–22.

Slekar, T. D. (1998). Epistemological entanglements: Preservice elementary school teachers' "apprenticeship of observation" and the teaching of history. *Theory and Research in Social Education, 26*(4), 485–508.

Stake, R. E. (1995). *The art of case study research.* Thousand Oaks, CA: Sage.

Thornton, S. J. (1991). Teacher as curricular-instructional gatekeeper in social studies. In J. P. Shaver (Ed.), *Handbook of research on social studies teaching and learning* (pp. 237–249). New York: Macmillan.

Tucker, P. D. (2003). The principalship: Renewed call for instructional leadership. In D. L. Duke, M. Grogan, P. D. Tucker, & W. F. Heinecke (Eds.), *Edu-*

cational leadership in an age of accountability: The Virginia experience (pp. 97–113). Albany, NY: SUNY Press.

van Hover, S. D., & Heinecke, W. (2005). The impact of accountability reform on the "wise practice" of secondary history teachers: The Virginia experience. In E. Yeager & O. L. Davis, Jr. (Eds.), *Wise social studies teaching in an era of high stakes testing* (pp. 89–116). Greenwich, CT: Information Age.

van Hover, S. D. & Yeager, E. A. (2003). "'Making' students better people?" A case study of a beginning history teacher. *International Social Studies Forum, 3*(1), 219–232.

van Hover, S. D., & Yeager, E. A. (2004). Challenges facing beginning history teachers: An exploratory study. *International Journal of Social Education, 19*(1), 8–26.

VanSledright, B. (1996). Closing the gap between school and disciplinary history? Historian as high school teacher. In J. Brophy (Ed.), *Advances in research on teaching: Teaching and learning history* (pp. 257–289). Greenwich, CT: JAI Press.

Virginia Department of Education. (2003). *Information on the Virginia Standards of Learning.* Retrieved from http://www.pen.k12.va.us/VDOE/Instruction/sol.html#history

Wineburg, S. (1991). On the reading of historical texts: Notes on the breach between school and academy. *American Educational Research Journal, 28*(3), 495-519.

Wineburg, S. (2001). *Historical thinking and other unnatural acts: Charting the future of teaching the past.* Philadelphia: Temple University Press.

Winkler, A. M. (2002a). Division in the ranks: Standardized testing draws lines between new and veteran teachers. *Phi Delta Kappan, 84*(3), 219–225.

Winkler, A. M. (2002b). *Factors that affect teacher beliefs about state educational accountability systems: A comparison of Virginia and Vermont.* Unpublished dissertation, University of Virginia, Charlottesville, VA.

Yeager, E. A. (2000). Thoughts on wise practice in the teaching of social studies. *Social Education, 64*(6), 352-353.

Yeager, E. A., & Davis, O. L., Jr. (1994). Understanding the "knowing how" of history: Elementary student teachers' thinking about historical texts. *Journal of Social Studies Research, 18*(2), 2–9.

Yeager, E., & Davis, O. L., Jr. (1996). Classroom teachers thinking about historical texts: An exploratory study. *Theory and Research in Social Education, 24,* 144-166.

CHAPTER 11

NEGOTIATING CONTROL AND PROTECTING THE PRIVATE

History Teachers and the Virginia Standards Of Learning

Ann Marie Smith

Policymakers in the state of Virginia responded to the national call for school accountability by implementing the Virginia Standards of Learning (SOL) in the late 1990s. What began as a program designed to raise the standards of student performance in public schools escalated into a public outcry over high stakes tests (Hsu, 1995a). The social studies curricula, the last set of SOL documents to be completed, received the most public criticism for its emphasis on Western European history and fact-based content. Off center stage were the social studies teachers at Northwest High School, poised to prepare students for these new standardized tests.

In the current political climate, high-stakes tests and mandated curricula have become the norm. Although some scholars document benefits from such mandates, most researchers argue that high-stakes tests drive teachers to reduce their teaching methods to test preparation (Darling-

Measuring History: Cases of State-Level Testing Across the United States, 221–247

Hammond, 1997; Duke & Reck, 2003; Grant, 2000; Lipton, 2004). Of more concern is the disconnect between how policymakers define knowledge and what educators know about learning and meaning making. Scholars emphasize inquiry, process, and problem solving. Policymakers often refer to knowledge as static, using such terms as outcomes, essential knowledge, and accountability (Wells, 2001). Scholars have only begun to study how teachers respond to systems of accountability. As Mathison and Freeman (2003) observe, teachers do not simply accept or reject top-down standards or assessments. Even for experienced teachers, negotiations between satisfying mandated requirements and teaching every student to become a critical reader, writer and thinker is a complex process. Further, public and political arenas complicate how teachers think about their work in the classroom even when teachers are comfortable with their own educational philosophies and convictions about how to best help students learn.

The purpose of this study was to investigate how Virginia high school social studies teachers think about and respond to the new SOL mandates. Informed by theories on the teaching of social studies and historical text, I became interested in how social studies teachers at Northwest High School[1] responded both privately and publicly to conflicts between their teaching philosophies and the SOL curricular and test requirements. This ethnographic investigation focuses on these Northwest High School social studies teachers as they work with students and colleagues to negotiate control over curriculum and classroom methods and how they worked with other social studies teachers in their department to align county curricular objectives with the SOL curriculum and tests.

In the next section, I review the Virginia SOLs, placing them in the context of recent scholarship on trends in statewide curricula, high-stakes assessments, and other accountability policies. I also address implications of educational policies for the teaching of history, along with the ways in which SOL controversies call attention to theories on social studies education. Then, I present data from my study on social studies teachers at Northwest High School in Virginia. In a discussion of my findings, I focus on two themes: The first theme, *Heritage History: Transmission and Critique*, captures the teachers' processes of negotiating the parameters of the SOLs in their selection of texts, teaching methods and content choices. The second theme, *Public Policies and Private Classrooms*, illustrates how I interpret Northwest teachers' ongoing negotiations between public involvement and private work in classrooms as they respond to the ideological and educational constraints of the SOL curriculum and tests. Finally, I apply the results of my study to an analysis of the problems and possibilities of social studies pedagogy as these teachers continuously negotiate within public and private arenas.

THE VIRGINIA STANDARDS OF LEARNING IN CONTEXT

The Virginia social studies curriculum became a public and political issue during the initial writing process (Fore, 1998). Initiated by Virginia state governor George Allen, the central purpose of the Virginia SOLs was to develop "tough" academic content standards and statewide tests. Beginning in 1994, Governor Allen created the Champion Schools Commission. One objective of the commission was to design higher learning standards while developing a system of accountability through testing (Duke & Reck, 2003). Before the Champion Schools Commission began work, the Virginia State Department of Education chose four large school districts to participate in revising the existing standards of learning. Each district solicited input from parents, teachers, and other community leaders. Writing teams from each school district submitted drafts to the Governor's Commission. Meanwhile, members of the Commission wrote their own standards by receiving suggestions directly from their own school leaders (Duke & Reck, 2003). Next, Commission members chose to redesign the school districts' standards to match the Commission's own version of the Virginia Standards of Learning. This action created a controversy when educators learned that their SOL drafts had essentially been dismissed. The educators who submitted these drafts publicly criticized the narrow view of history education evident in the Commission's standards. Further, educators claimed that the standards reflected the governor and commissioner's own political ideologies (Farmer, 1995). Some educators and politicians believed that Allen's primary goal was to create support for charter schools and vouchers by placing blame on public schools who, as Allen suggested, were responsible for a "crisis" in education (Berliner & Biddle, 1995; Fore, 1998). Members of the Governor's Commission claimed that they revised the standards to reflect both the school districts' and the commission's drafts. According to the Commission's report, there was no way to communicate the revisions to the committee of educators before the standards became public. This failure to communicate appeared to be the Commission's method of anticipating objections by educators. If the educators did not know about the Commission's revisions, they could not object, and the Commission could maintain control over this final draft, which is exactly what occurred. In fact, according to one teacher, the Commission's revisions "made the educators' drafts unrecognizable" (Farmer, 1995, p. A8).

Once the social studies standards were publicized, educators and parents appeared at public hearings to voice their opposition to the standards (Farmer, 1995; Fore, 1998; Holland, 1995; Stallsmith, 2000). The social studies SOL curriculum was criticized because it did not address the importance of teaching students to critically read and evaluate historical texts (Farmer, 1995; Hsu, 1995b). Further, the standards, which reflected a "conservative political bent" (Farmer, 1995, p. A8) and a narrow pedagogical view of culture and history, did not reflect social studies educational practice and research (Farmer, 1995; Holland, 1995; Hsu, 1995a; *Position paper,* 1999). In fact, the original curriculum was modeled after E. D. Hirsch's (1987) *Cultural Literacy.* As such, the members of the Governor's Commission insisted that historical knowledge be treated as authoritative and static while social studies educators viewed historical knowledge as evolving and open to critique (Farmer, 1995; Fore 1995). The Virginia State Board of Education, fearing outright rejection of the standards by the Virginia Education, agreed that revisions to the social studies curricula were necessary. The question then became "whose revisions?"

State social studies education association leaders drafted a "compromise" between the drafts created by an original committee of educators and the Governor's Commission. The State Board of Education, dominated by Governor Allen appointees, refused to consider the draft, claiming that the educators had "no authority from the State Board to work on an alternative version" (Fore, 1998, p. 571). Subsequently, members of the State Board of Education created their own subcommittee. Although social studies educators attended the subcommittee meetings, their revisions were excluded from the final drafts by a private editing committee comprised of three State Board members (Fore, 1998).

By 1996, the Standards of Learning curricula for other subjects were nearly complete. At the same time, educators and parents continued to openly criticize drafts of the social studies curricula, which would subsequently go through several more revisions before the first SOL tests were administered. The Virginia Board of Education purchased test questions from Harcourt Brace, and educators received notification of test content by late spring 1996 (Duke & Reck, 2003). Virginia policymakers also informed the public about the high stakes attached to SOL scores. Beginning with the graduating class of 2004, students must pass at least 6 of the 11 SOL exams in order to graduate. High school students must pass two of the following three social studies tests: World History, Geography and American History. By 2007, schools could lose their accreditation if their students were unable to produce the required test scores (Duke & Reck, 2003). Ignored were criticisms by teachers and school administrators, who reminded the SOL design team that previous standardized test results showed that students in poorer districts generally scored lower than did their more advantaged peers (Fore, 1998). Students and teachers of low-income school districts worried about unfair penalization by future SOL tests as there were no solutions offered for students who did not perform well on the tests.

By spring 2000, the social studies teachers at Northwest High School began preparing their students for the SOL tests. Produced by Harcourt Educational Measurement, the tests presumably matched the SOL curriculum objectives (Werner, 2001). As of 2004, the multiple-choice social studies SOL tests were still considered problematic due to discrepancies between students' social studies scores and their scores on SOL tests other subjects.

HERITAGE HISTORY AND OBJECTIVE TESTS

Social studies scholars have criticized standardized assessments for their emphasis on rote memorization at the expense of higher-level critical reading and writing. Further, objective assessments that test "official knowledge" (Apple, 1990) often reflect a *heritage* approach to teaching history where history is presented as truth, and sources of information are not interrogated. History and social studies educators recommend that students learn how to read, evaluate and make comparisons across multiple sources (Afflerbach & VanSledright, 2001; Apple, 1990, 1992; Brophy & VanSledright, 1997; Darling-Hammond, 1997; Grant, 2001, 2003; McNeil, 2000; Nash, Crabtree, & Dunn, 1997; Popkewitz, 1984; Seixas, 1999; Stahl, Hynd, Britton, McNish, & Bosquet, 1996; VanSledright, 1996, 2002; Wineburg, 1991, 2001). Although Virginia educators alluded to similar pedagogical concerns, the Governor's Commission essentially dismissed them. For example, one of the Grade 11 objectives of U.S. History states: "The student will analyze and explain events and ideas of the Revolutionary period" (*Virginia Standards Test Blueprints*, 2001). After this statement are listed several key events and acts that teachers must cover. The one positive word in this statement is "analyze," but how much or what kind of analysis each teacher should actually work toward is unclear. Some researchers have concluded that when teachers rush to prepare students for standardized tests, they may decide that test preparation takes precedence over in-depth analysis (See, for example, Duke & Tucker, 2003; McNeil, 2000; Wraga, 1999).

Revisionist historians who suggest that historical truth is a social construction call into question the notion of teaching history as a process of presenting facts for students to memorize. Further, feminist scholars have interrogated a heritage history curriculum that focuses on public and political arenas, including female historical figures only when they have contributed to the political and economic progress deemed historically important by men (Arendt, 1968; Coulter, 2002; Elshtain, 1995; Wineburg, 2001). Feminist and political historians theorize that these exclusions reflect the devaluation of the private realm where women and ethnic minorities in the United States served supportive roles within home and family, arenas which were not readily visible nor important to public politics (Elshtain, 1995; Jones, 1988; Morris, 2000; Pateman, 1989; Saxonhouse, 1992; Wineburg, 2001). According to Fore (1998), women's issues were purposely edited out of the Virginia SOLs by the State Board of Education subcommittee. Women's rights were labeled as a "red flag issue ... controversial issues [had] no place in the standards" (p. 567). Although these curricular omissions have not prohibited the teachers in my study from discussing women's lived histories, the public realm of the white male remained the center of historical study at Northwest High School.

An SOL curriculum statement on "cultural diversity" received a fate similar to the women's rights objectives. This "cultural diversity" statement was removed because it was criticized as "ideological instruction" (Fore, 1998, p. 570). One African American educator, present during the SOL subcommittee revision meetings, expressed concerns about the treatment of the Civil Rights movement and challenged the SOLs during the revision process. In the end, Civil Rights was represented in the SOL curricula, but the White, Western European emphasis remained (Fore, 1998). Researchers find that African American students are aware of attempts to cover over contributions of African Americans (Price, 2000; VanSledright, 2002). Students have also noted that African Americans' histories were not included in class lessons unless these experiences were related to White people's experiences (Epstein, 2001).

SOCIAL STUDIES EDUCATION AND THE "PUBLIC SPHERE"

Although largely missing from the education literature, public sphere theories are relevant to school contexts where politics pervade both private and public arenas. Public and private boundaries become blurred within schools as teachers perform multiple roles characteristic of public and private spheres (Coulter, 2002; Felski, 2000). Teachers are trusted to prepare students for success as public citizens, yet their parental role mirrors the private sphere historically associated with women (Grumet, 1988). Coulter (2002), who analyzed the workings of public and private arenas in Canadian public schools, theorizes that teachers have the daunting responsibility of instructing students to excel as private individuals as they develop their own identities and interests. At the same time, teachers prepare students for active participation in public settings outside of school, such as community, family, and state. Each school is a unique place, affected by the ideologies and politics underlying community and state (Coulter, 2002; Grunewald, 2003; Kincheloe, 1991).

Typically, teachers' relationships with students and the classroom activities they design are private in the sense that other adults (the public) are not present in the classroom. Unless a teacher publishes an article or presents at a conference, his or her teaching methods remain essentially private. The isolation of classroom teaching can create a private haven, however, when the "public" requirements of policies like the SOLs prove contradictory to teachers' goals and philosophies. The political contexts that informed the SOLs came to symbolize the public realm into which teachers may be invited, but may choose not to participate.

THE STUDY

As a former high school English teacher who experienced the high-stakes nature of standardized tests, I want to focus my analysis on the voices of social studies teachers. Concerned that Virginia policymakers ignored educators' recommendations and criticisms, my desire is to encourage teachers to voice their perspectives on the Virginia SOL social studies curriculum and tests (Strauss & Corbin, 1998). Guiding my study are these questions:

- What is the nature of these teachers' instructional methods and what are their underlying beliefs about how social studies should be taught? How are these methods and beliefs shaped by the SOLs?
- What is the nature of these high school teachers' responses to the SOLs in private and public arenas?

As these teachers invited me into their classrooms and professional lives, I learned about the layers of politics embedded within social studies education. Recognizing that their perspectives have often been eclipsed by the voices of those who hold more public power, I encouraged them to talk about any aspect of the social studies SOLs they deemed important (DeVault, 1999).

Methodology

This study can best be described as an interpretive ethnography, drawing from feminist (Clandinin & Connelly, 1998; DeVault, 1999) and critical (Lareau & Schultz, 1996; Van Manen, 1994; Wolcott, 1990) ethnographic traditions. Feminist ethnographers are often concerned with applying methods that "excavate" or bring women into the research dialogue (DeVault, 1999, p. 30). Research is conducted *with* instead of *on* participants. The researcher is reflexive, recording and describing thoughts, feelings and experiences affecting interpretations of data (Clandinin & Connelly, 1998; DeVault, 1999; Edwards & Ribbens, 1998; Lareau & Schultz, 1996 ; Lather, 1991; Wolcott, 1990).

Methods and Data

To enhance research validity, I collected data from a variety of sources. I interviewed five teachers, attended social studies department meetings and observed classes over a period of 1 school year. I also collected teacher handouts, official SOL curriculum guidelines and state newspaper articles. Table 11.1 includes the number of hours I spent interviewing and observing each teacher.

Participants

I interviewed and observed Mr. Anderson, Mrs. Lawrence, Mrs. Hanson and Mrs. Thompson. Although I was unable to observe Mrs. Jones's classes, we spent time talking about social studies teaching and the SOLs. In what follows, I provide background information and a brief profile of each teacher. The interviews and observations were conducted primarily during the 1999–2000 school year. I returned to interview the teachers again in fall, 2000.

Mrs. Jones had been teaching at Northwest High school for over 25 years, and was the social studies department chair from the beginning of her employment until June 2000. She held a master's degree in history. As with all of the Northwest teachers, Mrs. Jones criticized the test design and was displeased with the amount of content she felt she was forced to cover for the tests. During the 1999–2000 school year, Mrs. Jones was

Table 11.1.   Study Participants

Teachers	Classroom Observations in # of Hours	Class Subject	Grade Level	Interviews in Hrs.
Mrs. Jones, dept. chair, 1999–2000	did not observe	American History	11	4
Mr. Anderson, dept chair, 2000–2001 year.	6	American History	11	3
Mrs. Lawrence	6	World History	9	2.5
Mrs. Hanson	6	Humanities	9	3
Mrs. Thompson	6	American History	11	2

responsible for writing and documentation tasks as required by the school district.

Mr. Anderson became the social studies chair during the 2000–2001 school year. After teaching at Northwest for about 10 years, Mr. Anderson volunteered for this position, demonstrating enthusiasm for leading the department. Mr. Anderson held a master of arts in history and was working toward a PhD. Although Mr. Anderson supported the idea of "standards," he criticized the SOL curricula and tests, claiming that they were too "fact-based" and did not teach kids to think and write critically. Higher-level readers comprised most of Mr. Anderson's American History classes. Mr. Anderson required frequent writing assignments both in and out of class. His primary concern was that students learn to think, read and write critically; SOL preparation came second. The class atmosphere was usually relaxed, with students interrupting to ask questions or to express opinions about historical issues or events. Students were often involved in class discussions or small group activities. Occasionally, Mr. Anderson would lecture or present historical information.

Mrs. Lawrence taught ninth grade World History. Mrs. Lawrence had worked as a technology specialist for the school district before choosing to return to the classroom. She had been teaching at Northwest High School for about 5 years. Perhaps because most of her students were below average to average readers, Mrs. Lawrence taught reading and study strategies more frequently than the other teachers. Mrs. Lawrence explained that one of her goals was to help her ninth grade students learn to read and remember historical texts. She echoed the complaints of other teachers that the SOL test questions were written at too high a reading level for most of her students. Sensitive to students' reading and learning problems, Mrs. Lawrence thought it was important to teach students how to use graphic organizers while reading and studying. Mrs. Lawrence designed many of the graphic organizers and notetaking outlines herself; she also taught students how to design their own graphic text representations using a software program called *Inspiration*. Similar to Mr. Anderson, Mrs. Lawrence used small group activities and whole class discussions. However, she also spent considerable time reviewing content and teaching students how to use graphic organizers and other study methods.

Mrs. Hanson taught ninth grade humanities classes. Unlike Mrs. Lawrence's students, Mrs. Hanson's students were above average readers. Humanities classes were taught by both English and social studies teachers, so these classes were interdisciplinary in the sense that the content was an amalgam of history, art, literature, politics, philosophy, economics and geography. Students learned to analyze historical documents in depth, well beyond the historical events and ideas that Mrs. Lawrence taught in her World History classes. Mrs. Hanson held a master's degree in history, and she had taught at Northwest for over 25 years. She was quite frustrated with the SOLs, and openly criticized the social studies curricula for being too "Western European and white." Similar to Mr. Anderson's Advanced Placement American History classes, Mrs. Hanson's Humanities classes were student-centered. Students took responsibility for learning as they worked on small group activities and individual projects; presentations and critical writing were also primary activities. Mrs. Hanson also required students to write in a journal during class. Journal questions required students to apply historical content to their own lives.

Mrs. Thompson arrived at Northwest High School with 15 years of experience working in both education and business. Mrs. Thompson had been teaching at Northwest for about 5 years. Mrs. Thompson expressed dissatisfaction with the SOLs and indicated that if the SOL tests and curriculum were strictly enforced, she was prepared to resign. "I'm doing this job because I want to," she said, "I don't have to be here." Mrs. Thompson taught American history to sophomores who were below average to average readers. She felt, however, that it was important to push students to read and write critically, and she believed lowering her standards would not benefit the students. Mrs. Thompson used a variety of teaching methods including lecture, discussion, and small group activities. Mrs. Thompson also taught students to critique visual media; for example, in one class students critiqued war propaganda posters. During another class, students compared a movie to a documentary. Unfortunately, Mrs. Thompson chose to resign after the 2001–2002 school year.

Generally, Northwest teachers claim that the SOL social studies curriculum guides their choices of content. Each, however, asserts that the guidelines are too expansive, requiring teachers to prepare students for more material than time allows. This increased amount of content encourages some of the teachers to alter their teaching methods slightly by spending more time lecturing and teaching test-taking skills. Modifying one's pedagogy rather than engaging wholesale change coincides with other studies on teachers' responses to state-level tests (Grant, 2000; McNeil, 2000). The central criticism of all Northwest social studies teachers is that the SOL tests undermine their professionalism as educators, forcing them to take time away from teaching students to think, read, and write critically (Darling-Hammond, 1997; McNeil, 2000).

Research Setting

Essential to this study is the sense that schools are situated within communities and states permeated by underlying political ideologies. At the same time, each school is unique as a "place" within society, a place that informs teachers' work and language (Coulter, 2002; Grunewald, 2003; Kincheloe, 1991). Northwest High School, a suburban high school in Northern Virginia, is comprised of approximately 2,200 students from middle and working class families. The student population is multicultural: Approximately 39% of the students are African American, 38% Caucasian, 11% Hispanic, 8% Middle Eastern, and 4% Asian. Most of the teachers in the social studies department are white.[2]

Data Collection

Interviews were audiotaped, and I wrote detailed notes during classroom observations. I noted if teachers or students mentioned the SOLs, or if an SOL objective was written on the board or in a class handout. I also watched for consistencies and contradictions between teacher's actual classroom methods and their descriptions of their own methods. As I observed classroom activities, I wrote down the exact language of teachers and students especially when teachers and students criticized official knowledge or texts. Most of the teachers did not lecture constantly, but I noted days when the teachers either lectured or mentioned that they needed to "cover" more material quickly.

In interviews, teachers explained their goals for the students and how the classroom activities met these goals. My role during these interviews was "listener" in order to capture the teachers' words (DeVault, 1999). The teachers knew that I was studying their reactions and opinions of the SOLs, so I encouraged them to direct our conversations, following an open-ended interview format (Bogdan & Biklen, 1998; Clandinin & Connelly, 1998). I used two questions to open the conversation during each interview: (1) What are your opinions on the SOL tests and curriculum? (2) How have your teaching methods changed (or not changed) since the implementation of the SOLs? I also asked each teacher to describe any new reporting or writing required for the SOLs.

I also collected classroom artifacts such as teacher-created handouts and quizzes. I obtained the social studies SOL documents along with documents that teachers designed for the county.

Data Analysis

First, I transcribed interview tapes and reviewed observation notes. While reviewing transcripts and observation notes, I wrote down words and phrases in the margins after every couple of sentences, using the language of the participants (both teachers and students). For example, in an interview with Mrs. Lawrence, I wrote the word "connections" and the phrase "conceptual standpoint" because these are words Mrs. Lawrence used to describe how she grouped the individual SOL facts into larger ideas to teach to students. Next, I looked for repeated words and phrases in both my codes and in the interview transcripts and notes. For example, all of the teachers mentioned their concern for their students' reading problems. I observed two of the teachers working on reading and study skills strategies during class, so these observation notes were coded for "reading problems." Finally, I refined these "patterned regularities" (Creswell, 1998, p. 152) into theme statements (Bogdan & Biklen, 1998; Lather, 1991; Wolcott, 1994). Although I describe this process as a series of steps, my construction of codes and themes was a recursive process; I wrote frequent informal notes and memos describing the themes and my interpretations of the themes (Wolcott, 1994). Originally, I began my draft with four themes. As I became more familiar with the teachers' classroom methods and beliefs about social studies education, I talked to the teachers informally about the transcripts, rechecking my themes with the teachers' feedback on the transcripts (Bogdan & Biklen, 1998). Subsequent reflection led me to collapse my four themes into two.

FINDINGS

None of the social studies teachers interviewed believes that their teaching strategies have changed because of the SOLs. However, Mr. Anderson, Mrs. Jones and Mrs. Thompson indicate that they have less class time for inquiry learning and critical analyses because they feel rushed to include all the SOL content. Perhaps because they are all experienced teachers, I observed ambitious, critical teaching in all of these teachers' classes. Criticisms of the Western heritage inherent in history textbooks has not been eliminated from classroom discussions. Mrs. Jones expresses the most concern about the future of teaching at Northwest High; she predicts the rise of a structured bureaucracy with all teachers on the same page at the same time, and all employing a mechanized system of presenting data for students to memorize.

Hints of Northwest teachers giving in to the SOL requirements surface, but in the end, these periods of compliance appear to be part of the teachers' strategies for coping with public SOL documentation requirements. As long as Northwest teachers provide written proof to the state that they are following the curriculum, they can maintain more ambitious instructional goals for their students within their private classrooms. Two themes capture the essence of their dilemma: (1) Heritage History: Transmission and Critique and (2) Public Policies and Private Classrooms.

Heritage History: Transmission and Critique

Heritage history is both transmitted and critiqued in Northwest High. The social studies teachers believe that students need to learn the traditional content. But at the same time, they believe that students need to reconstruct history by analyzing and evaluating multiple sources. Conflicts emerge when teachers feel the need to transmit knowledge quickly and efficiently in order to prepare students for the SOL tests. Northwest teachers do not advocate a transmission model of teaching social studies nor do they frequently lecture to their students. Across all my observations, at least one example surfaces where each teacher interrogates the notion of heritage history by noting exclusions in their class textbooks or by criticizing the content of the SOLs.

The department chair, Mrs. Jones, describes changes in her practice since the SOLs:

> We would read other historians' perspectives, then we would have discussions. We don't have time for that anymore. Basically they get the straight facts, as the state wants them to know...there is not much time for analysis and connections. It's facts—names, dates, places. I used to be a good teacher—now I'm cramming this stuff down their throats.

Mrs. Jones, like her colleagues, emphasizes SOL preparation because each student's diploma is contingent on SOL scores. But Northwest teachers also want students to learn the essence of history, culture, ideas, and problems. Each of these teachers values multiple approaches to teaching history. "I use reading strategies ... I believe in a variety of strategies," Mrs. Lawrence explains, "With this class, we'll spend a day or so with questions, then I'll have them create things—travel brochures, maps, for example." For Northwest teachers, learning history is more than reciting facts. However, transmission through lectures occurs most when teachers believe they are behind in the curriculum or they need to prepare students for upcoming SOL tests.

With experience comes knowledge, not only about the teaching of social studies, but also about how to teach under time constraints, overcrowded classroom conditions and political mandates, such as the Virginia SOLs. However, the SOLs creates political and personal conflicts for these experienced teachers whose goals for their students include intellectual challenges as well as high test scores. The social studies teachers at Northwest High School experience value conflicts—they must make complex choices about how to improve students' understanding of history while helping them remember content for the SOL tests.

Complex Choices Around Texts

One example of the teachers' choices can be seen in their selections of classroom texts. As Mrs. Jones indicates, primary source use declines as class textbooks are perceived to be the most efficient way to teach to the SOL tests. However, primary sources do not disappear. Northwest teachers use primary sources to help students learn about the interpretive nature of history and to evaluate the authors, contexts, and purposes of historical documents. They also use sources to teach students about non-official histories. As with many school history textbooks, these students' history books reflect heritage history, only occasionally spotlighting the contributions of women and minorities. SOL test questions downplay primary documents and historical information on minorities and women, but Northwest teachers resist this condition. For example, Mr. Anderson asks students to write critical evaluations of primary source narratives by explaining how the authors' experiences reflect the circumstances of the Civil War.

Mrs. Thompson uses both visual media and written texts to demonstrate how U.S. history is interpreted and reinterpreted. For example, she directs students to explain the rhetorical purposes behind World War II propaganda posters during one class discussion. During a Civil War unit, Mrs. Thompson shows a documentary on African American soldiers. The film presents information and analyses on racial and cultural issues affecting the soldiers. Later, the students write about the videotape and compare the events to the Hollywood movie *Glory*. They question events and criticize *Glory* as "Hollywood history" while analyzing racial issues presented in both movie and documentary (Afflerbach & VanSledright, 2001).

Mrs. Lawrence, by contrast, appears less interested than other Northwest teachers in teaching her students to critique heritage history. However, in one class, she asks her World History students what they learned about Africa in previous years. "We never studied Africa in school," one African American boy says sarcastically. Mrs. Lawrence does not appear surprised; she tells the class they will read an article about Africa because their textbook skirts the topic. Mrs. Lawrence does not discuss reasons for these exclusions; instead, she seems more focused on students understanding and remembering historical events and ideas. Still, Mrs. Lawrence wants students to go beyond the rote memorization of facts required by the SOL tests. "Students need connections and background knowledge in order to remember facts for the SOLs," she explains.

Complex Choices Around Instruction

A second instance of the complex choices teachers make involves instruction. In spite of Mr. Anderson's insistence that he emphasizes critical thinking and writing, he occasionally reverts to a transmission model. After one rapid lecture, he explains, "we were behind on the SOLs, so I had to get the students caught up." Fast-paced activity is typical for his classroom, but students usually direct class discussions or present information they gather. Mr. Anderson teaches students to cite quotes from both primary sources and textbooks to defend their oral and written analyses. Yet, on this day, SOL preparation appears to force Mr. Anderson to deliver the necessary information by lecturing.

To enhance learning and reading comprehension, Mrs. Lawrence teaches students to use graphic organizers while they read the textbook and primary sources. Mrs. Lawrence explains that teaching study and reading strategies is necessary for students to understand and remember historical facts and ideas for the SOL tests. And yet, Mrs. Lawrence resists teaching such strategies in rote and pedantic fashion. For example, during one class, students work on a "story board" project, a visual reading chart on the Protestant Reformation. After class, Mrs. Lawrence describes the purpose of the assignment: "I want to help these ninth graders remember and analyze the teachings, effects, and beliefs of the leaders who were instrumental in the Protestant Reformation, specifically Martin Luther, John Calvin, King Henry VIII." Students reference the class textbook and other primary sources to create a bibliography for the storyboard, and they draw pictures or symbols on the storyboard to visually aid their memories. Mrs. Lawrence hopes the visual organizers will enhance students' comprehension and learning as they reread and write down key ideas and facts from texts.

Mrs. Thompson agrees that reading comprehension is an obstacle for many high school history students and that the awkward language of the SOL questions skews test results. She explains that the wide variety of reading levels also complicates the process of teaching students to read critically: "A lot of them are nonreaders or they may be able to decode the word so they can say it, but they have absolutely no idea what it means when they look at the whole sentence. They can't even decode a question." Mrs. Thompson worries that even if students learn content, their poor reading skills may prevent them from performing well on the SOL tests: "When trying to teach this much material, we *cover* it rather than *teach* it, and I think that's a mistake. Also, its very difficult to know which [information] you drill into your children to remember." Mrs. Thompson describes an activity from her advanced-level history class that she continues to use despite the fact that it takes more class time than lecturing on the material:

> Yesterday we were in multiple groups representing a different country, an allied country, in Europe prior to WWII. They had to solve eight crises in

terms of how their country would respond starting with the taking of the
Sudan land.... So they start to see the pattern each time of U.S. isolationism
with power, of Swiss isolationism without power, of Russian Survivalist—
"make a deal with the devil that protects me"—and Britain and France—
"please, please, please, I'll let you have whatever you want as long as you
don't bother me again." That's something you can say in five minutes, but
its something that imprints when you do this exercise that takes an hour.

Students actively experience history through this problem-solving activity. Mrs. Thompson explains that the students move beyond the U.S. perspective by imagining what people in other countries thought and
experienced during World War II.

Although Northwest teachers know the limitations and prejudices of
the SOL heritage curriculum, one teacher in particular, Mrs. Hanson,
interprets the complexities of instructional choice differently than her
peers as she spends more time interrogating exclusions with her students
than do her peers. Most of the teachers assert the importance of critical
thinking and reasoning. However, their versions of critical thinking do
not often involve interrogating exclusions in history textbooks or questioning the Western emphasis inherent in the SOLs. By contrast, Mrs.
Hanson, the most experienced teacher in the department, emphasizes
critical literacy in her text selections, teaching methods or class content.
She encourages questions and criticisms in her Humanities classes, but
cultural criticism is most evident in her upper-level elective *Minority Cultures* class. Mrs. Hanson's enthusiasm during this class is contagious; students participate actively and comfortably in class discussions. Near the
end of one class on China, a student asks about a documentary they just
watched about the cultural differences between Europe and Asia. "Why
are they saying that Chinese schools are bad?" the student asked. Mrs.
Hanson replies, "sometimes a videotape is biased. This one seems to be
centered toward European thinking." The narrator of the documentary
implied that China's education system is inferior to Europe's. Class discussion came to a close with the end of the class period, but Mrs. Hanson's comments on the documentary reinforce the idea that there are
various ways of interpreting history and culture, some of which are
informed primarily by Western European ideologies.

Complex Choices Around Content

One last set of complexities concerns the broad range of content
Northwest teachers must cover for the SOL tests. Although the teachers
view the SOL objectives as guides, simplifying the complex process of
choosing which historical content to teach at which grade level, that sim-
plification is not without problems.

Mrs. Lawrence explains the most evident contradiction: "The idea of standards is good because it defines parameters. The problem is that it's too much—the parameters are too large." Mrs. Lawrence criticizes the "entire millennium of world history" she must teach during one school year in ninth grade World History. However, she capitalizes on her teaching experiences to negotiate the SOL curriculum:

> A lot of people get caught up in the amount of content that's in the SOLs. Basically, its the concept of "chunking" and relating content—you can get through or present effectively most of it ... even though the curriculum is too big for this course.

Mrs. Lawrence adapts to SOL demands by grouping related content and choosing logical quantities of objectives to teach. Along with other Northwest teachers, she views the SOLs as just another political trend written in a language teachers have to translate into classroom practice. As with politicians who employ rhetoric to inform and persuade the public, teachers transform the discourse of their field into activities and language their students will understand. Yet, the professional and personal conversations between teachers and students can clash with underlying messages of quick fix political discourse.

To complicate the matter of teaching content, the SOLs, designed to test an entire school year, are administered in April. Teachers acknowledge that they need May and June to teach all of the required content for the tests. Mr. Anderson adds, "we've also received a mandate from the county asking us to develop critical thinking skills. While this is important, the state and county keep expanding the curriculum without expanding our time." Although the county's educational objectives appear to more closely reflect those of Mr. Anderson and the other Northwest teachers, the SOL tests, with their list of required names, dates, and places, reinforce the "fact as truth" theory of teaching history. Eventually, the county's objectives were replaced by the SOL essential questions.

Some researchers on teachers' reactions to mandated curricula and tests have found that teachers set aside their beliefs about effective teaching to focus on test preparation (Darling-Hammond, 1997; Lipman, 2004) In fact, McNeil (2000) argues that more frequent skill and drill occur as teachers give in to testing requirements. These curriculum and test requirements produce a spiraling effect, encouraging teachers to spend less time on creative teaching and problem solving activities and more time on test preparation. However, Grant (2003) finds little or no change in teachers' choices of content and methods following the implementation of standardized tests. At Northwest, the SOL curriculum guide teachers' choice of what to teach but not *how* to teach. However, the downward spiral that McNeil (2000) describes seems possible at Northwest if test scores begin to slide or if Northwest's accreditation comes under siege.

Public Policies and Private Classrooms

The SOLs have not created entirely new conditions for teachers; any new educational policy intrudes into the private sphere of the classroom. As Mathison and Freeman (2003) suggest, teachers continually negotiate their responses to state tests as they prepare students for tests and teach creatively and intellectually. However, teachers' individual and private classroom decisions and negotiations in reaction to state mandates are infrequently documented. Classrooms offer a private sphere for teachers to critique state mandates with their students.

In order to negotiate control over their teaching methods, teachers move in and out of public arenas dominated by discourses of accountability and state standards, but this is not always a smooth process for Northwest teachers.

Public controversy over the SOL social studies curriculum and high stakes assessments offers teachers opportunities to enter public conversations with politicians and community members. For example, teachers were invited to submit SOL curriculum and test revision suggestions online to the Virginia Board of Education web site. Teachers could also post lesson plans and class activities for professional development credits (Virginia Standards, 1998). Northwest teachers choose not to submit lesson plans online or to participate in political forums. Instead, they choose to fight their own battles by both accommodating and resisting state SOL requirements largely within the protective walls of their classrooms. Rarely does public criticism of the SOLs go beyond social studies department meetings at Northwest. Although these teachers choose the path of least resistance in response to the county request for SOL documentation, these teachers respond actively in other ways with colleagues and students.

Northwest teachers collaborated with their colleagues to write public documents that the county required. The state sent the SOL tests and objectives to the county, who, in turn, asked curriculum supervisors to advise teachers as they wrote lesson plans and assessments to match the SOL objectives. These plans and assessments are intended to help social studies teachers prepare students for the SOL tests. Upon completion, these teacher-created documents are also submitted to the county office where, Northwest teachers are told, they "remained on file" for the state. Faced with writing these documents that they assume will enter public arenas, the Northwest teachers move between the public discourse of behavioral objectives and their private work with students. These teachers translate their teaching methods into "public" SOL language by writing lesson plans and essential questions that match the SOL objectives. "We also have to meet to do mapping for the SOL assessments," explains Mrs. Jones, "We've already written the essential questions ... now we have to map teaching strategies." Mrs. Jones holds up the thick, three-ring binder containing all of the SOL objectives for the high school social studies classes along with instructions on aligning essential questions and quizzes with the SOLs. Writing the SOL essential questions demands that teachers break their teaching methods into observable, measurable skills. For example, an objective for the Revolutionary War reads, "students should be able to explain the rationale of the Stamp Act." An example of the questions that teachers write is: "What is stated in the Stamp Act and why was it issued?" The teachers appear to resign themselves to writing in behaviorist discourse, accepting these SOL objectives and essential questions as typical of educational curricula, translating their complex work with students into specific questions about content. Eventually, these questions are collected from every school within the county. The county combines and revises them and distributes the product to all schools. In this way, Northwest teachers contribute to public documents at the county level.

On the surface, Virginia teachers appear to have local control over their unit assessments. However, these teacher-created tests must cover the content governed by the SOL curricula, and teachers perform this formative test-writing labor so the county can monitor processes and final outcomes. However, the teachers do not view such documentation as county surveillance. Mrs. Jones suggests that this task is an outcome of the county's attempt to help teachers help themselves prepare for the SOL tests. Teachers seem to view the county administrators as mediators between schools and the state even though one-on-one support is minimal. It appears that Northwest teachers choose to follow directions because it is the easiest path. Yet, with compliance comes criticism. For example, Mrs. Thompson expresses her frustrations with the county's dictates:

> First, the social studies department had to align instructional methods with SOL objectives. Then Mrs. Jones and I sat down and came up with a list of about twenty-five assessments we use during the course of the year for these students—anywhere from outlining to graphic organizers.... So I guess I have a problem with having to sit here and write in these little squares— they are manufacturing work for me to do.

The word "manufacturing" in her description closely reflects a factory model of education, a term used by some researchers to describe schools where teachers transmit knowledge to passive students in order to efficiently produce effective citizens (Apple, 1992; Darling-Hammond, 1997; Freire, 1993). A structure of control is evident in the SOL design, with its emphasis on rote memorization, official Western curriculum, and multiple-choice standardized tests. To guarantee productivity, teachers need to document their classroom assessment methods even though other assessments have already been designed without these teachers' input. Except for excess paperwork, Northwest teachers are not forced to change their classroom assessments; they only have to produce the appropriate discourse necessary for public approval or what Mrs. Jones referred to as "administrivia." The intrusion, for Northwest teachers, is the "busy work" that infringes on teaching and preparation time.

Some of the work required by the state and county never enters public arenas beyond the county administration office even though the teachers assume it would. For example, Northwest teachers are asked to design classroom quizzes to reflect the SOL objectives and prepare students for the SOL tests. Mrs. Thompson and Mrs. Jones collaborate in creating these quizzes. However, the quizzes are never mentioned again by the county or state. "Well, we put them in the department notebook," Mrs. Jones explains, "Mrs. Thompson and I have used some of them in our classes, and they are available for any social studies teacher who wants to use them." In the end, the quizzes become resources for teachers who want ideas for classroom assessments, but the teachers are not formally recognized by the county for their assessment ideas.

Further complicating the relationship between private and public realms are the potential high stakes associated with the SOLs. Northwest teachers contemplate the ramifications should their students perform poorly on the SOL tests. The teachers hope that policy reforms will benefit all students. However, in the case of the SOLs, Northwest teachers brace themselves for a bleak future where the blame for low test scores will be placed squarely on the shoulders of teachers and administrators. Mrs. Hanson provides one example:

> The SOLs make the teacher responsible for the learning these kids have not had over the years. This not learning is a product of what has happened over a number of years in school. The problem is that the SOLs have been put together in a very haphazard way. There is one teacher in our school who teaches history classes of low readers. Test scores were horrendous, and she was called on the carpet ... no one to support her. And she's a strong teacher, and she knows her material well. You have politicians and people who have not been in a classroom for twenty or thirty years. The world has changed. They don't understand the problems.

Mrs. Hanson is certain that the SOLs alone will not solve the educational problems that the politicians claim exist. She believes that Virginia policymakers have covered over school problems such as overcrowded classrooms and poor student support services with the rhetoric of teacher accountability. Teachers are blamed publicly for conditions they did not produce, and teachers who create small miracles with students every day are rarely recognized in public arenas. Northwest teachers seem to have accepted criticism as a natural consequence of working for the public, and choose to focus their energies on their students.

The SOL curriculum is broad enough to allow history teachers to interpret the content as they wish. The problem Northwest teachers face is predicting the specific information that the tests cover. Although all of the history teachers add historical content about women and minorities, Mrs. Hanson is the only teacher who seems to create a "counter-public sphere" within the privacy of her classroom (Fraser, 1997; Morris, 2000). She attempts to initiate her students into critical analyses of heritage history in a variety of ways. By viewing the classroom as a sanctuary away from public scrutiny, Mrs. Hanson, encourages students to question SOL-sanctioned truths. Journal questions such as "why do you think we have not had an African-American president?" and "why would you vote or not vote for an African-American candidate?" are used to instigate class discussions. Mrs. Hanson implies that the SOLs are a form of hegemony, as a predominantly white middle class controls people of other races and classes:

> Well, I have very little in the way of respect for the SOLs, to tell you the truth. I feel that the SOLs were developed and provided by a bunch of people who are white, middle class, and came out of the school of the fifties. And I think they purposely tried to bring all of that time period back because it enhances one group's power, I suppose.

Mrs. Hanson has experienced the effects of previous educational policies, and she has learned to adapt to oppressive mandates by teaching cultural criticism in her classroom.

Mrs. Hanson privately subverts the notion of heritage history by ensuring the existence of her senior-level elective social studies course, *Minority Cultures*. "Every year I have to fight to keep this class," she said, "The administrators don't see this as an important class, but these students work well together in here—they make a lot of friends in this class that they normally wouldn't." This class serves as its own counter-culture—interrogating the Western European focus in textbooks while highlighting the histories of non-European people. Unfortunately, the last time I spoke with Mrs. Hanson, her *Minority Cultures* class had been canceled for the following semester because she needed to teach another ninth grade class due to increased enrollment. However, Mrs. Hanson thinks that the tightly-structured SOL curriculum is an underlying cause. "It's the SOLs," she said, "No room for this kind of class."

In contrast to most of his colleagues, Mr. Anderson embraces a more active role in the public sphere. When Mr. Anderson became the social studies department chair near the end of my study, he moved further into the public arena than other Northwest teacher. Mr. Anderson is able to reconcile the publicness of the SOLs with his private teaching goals by producing proof of effective instruction. One of his assignments is to continue the department's work in creating curriculum documents that match the SOL essential questions and learning objectives. Mr. Anderson moves beyond his duties by developing graphic representations in the form of maps and charts to illustrate historical events. With input from other department members, he creates a booklet with concept maps that can be used by other teachers to help students remember historical facts and understand connections among events, people, and the like in preparation for the SOL tests. These graphic organizers reflect the reading comprehension techniques Mrs. Lawrence uses in her World History classes. The county administrators seem impressed with this booklet. "They offered to buy it from me," Mr. Anderson reports. In this situation, he takes control by designing content reading strategies that reflects the social studies department's teaching strategies while satisfying the requirements of SOL discourse. In the end, these documents showcase the department's efforts to improve students' reading comprehension in preparation for the SOL tests.

In departments where the teaching culture is collaborative, teachers typically feel more comfortable bringing their private teaching methods into public arenas (Little, 1990). Yet this claim can be complex in the reality of state policies and teacher practices. For example, as the other social teachers learn about some of Mrs. Lawrence's mapping strategies during a department meeting, Mr. Anderson borrows some of them for his SOL study guides for American History. Although Northwest social studies teachers generally are comfortable working with each other and borrowing each other's ideas, this comfort only goes so far. When the state of Virginia mandates the documentation of unit quizzes, Mrs. Jones and Mrs. Thompson resent this sharing of ideas only for the sake of providing information to the state. Mr. Anderson is comfortable showing his booklet to the county perhaps because it is not a requirement—he designed it to help other teachers prepare students for the SOL tests. Teachers who are pushed into mandated collaboration may move further into the private realm, viewing future collaborations as a violation of their individuality, creativity, and professionalism. Little (1990) suggests that teachers are willing to collaborate if they share decision-making on matters of curriculum, instruction, and testing. As a result of the SOLs, Northwest teachers' collaborations reflect top-down requirements instead of a desire to learn from each other as professionals.

CONCLUSIONS AND IMPLICATIONS

Northwest teachers have not completely given over their teaching to the structure of the SOL tests. I observed teachers covering required SOL content, but most place facts in meaningful contexts even during review lectures. Those who teach students with poor reading skills emphasize comprehension strategies, so that students learn main points and perhaps improve their reading skills enough to understand the SOL test questions. In spite of the SOL tests, teachers are able to maintain private professional goals for their students, such as teaching them to question historical facts while critically evaluating texts.

The conflicts and tensions these teachers experience may be unique to social studies; however, teachers of other academic subjects who must teach to the SOLs or other curricular mandates likely grapple with similar contradictions. Although all of the Northwest teachers insist that they have not changed their teaching methods—only added more content—I observed occasional rapid-transmission lecture sessions. After such sessions, the Northwest teachers usually comment that they need to complete a unit quickly to catch up with the SOLs. I did not interview students, but I observed that these lecture classes transform students into passive versions of earlier selves. Otherwise actively engaged in reading, writing and discussion, students passively take notes while the teachers lecture on required SOL content. Future research at Northwest High School may determine that teachers are able to exercise more or less control over the curriculum design. From previous experiences, these teachers seem to be able to read political trends, thinking that the Virginia Standards of Learning are another temporary mandate that will eventually run its course.

As mentioned earlier, parent organizations publicly oppose the SOLs. At least one parent group emerged as a result of the mandates (*Parents Across Virginia United to Reform SOLs, 2003*). However, Northwest teachers generally prefer to fight SOL battles privately in classrooms and with colleagues in department meetings. At Northwest, teachers make assessment and instructional decisions and are able to work with and circumvent the SOLs when deemed necessary. Outside support from the county or from university professors was not evident as I conducted this study. Action research and partnerships between schools and universities seem to be the best mode of empowering teachers, however, university professors need to go further to help teachers self-advocate and anticipate possible outcomes of unfair systems of accountability. Especially where political agendas overshadow teachers' voices, professional organizations and researchers must support teachers and administrators as they negotiate the public and political nature of their profession.

Preservice teachers need to be prepared for the social and political pressures they will encounter, so they can read the contexts of their schools and communities. In the case of the SOLs, the Virginia Board of Education did not consider changes until parents and community members spoke out against the tests. Preservice teachers should consider the extent to which they are willing to influence and collaborate with administrators and parents under circumstances such as those created by the SOLs. University faculty must also be prepared to assist public school teachers who are placed in the position of defending their professionalism.

Finally, future educational scholarship should continue to move the privacy of the classroom into the public realm in ways that benefit teachers and students. Qualitative research with its thick descriptions of people and settings is one way of portraying the private realities of public schools. No concise formula exists for effective teacher-student relationships or effective instructional strategies. Although each school and classroom is obviously unique, our next step as educational scholars should be to convince policymakers that it is this uniqueness that is worthy of examination.

ACKNOWLEGMENT

I would like to acknowledge the invaluable advice I received during the process of writing this chapter from Peter Afflerbach, Patti Emmons, Keith Johnson, Linda Kinch, and Jeremy Price.

NOTES

1. All proper names are pseudonyms
2. There are 14 social studies teachers in the department. Out of these 14, I interviewed five and observed four. Mrs. Jones, the department chair, recommended the four teachers I observed.

REFERENCES

Afflerbach, P., & VanSledright, B. (2001). Hath! Doth! What? Middle graders reading innovative history text. *Journal of Adolescent and Adult Literacy, 44*, 696–707.

Apple, M. (1990). *Ideology and curriculum.* New York: Routledge.

Apple, M. (1992). The text and cultural politics. *Educational Researcher, 21,* 4–11.

Arendt, H. (1968). *Between past and future: Eight exercises in political thought.* New York: Viking Press.

Berliner, D., & Biddle, B. (1995). *The manufactured crisis: Myths, fraud, and the attack on America's public schools.* Reading, MA: Addison Wesley.

Bogdan, R., & Biklen, S. (1998). *Qualitative research for education* (3rd ed.). Boston: Allyn and Bacon.

Brophy, J., & VanSledright, B. (1997). *Teaching and learning history in elementary schools.* New York: Teacher's College Press.

Clandinin, D., & Connelly, M. (1998). Personal experience methods. In N. Denzin & Y. Lincoln (Eds.), *Collecting and interpreting qualitative materials* (pp. 150–178). Thousand Oaks, CA: Sage.

Coulter, D. (2002). Creating common and uncommon worlds: Using discourse ethics to decide public and private in classrooms. *Journal of Curriculum Studies, 33,* 25–42.

Creswell, J. (1998). *Qualitative inquiry and research design.* Thousand Oaks, CA: Sage.

Darling-Hammond, L. (1997). *The right to learn: A blueprint for creating schools that work.* San Francisco: Jossey-Bass.

DeVault, M. (1999). *Liberating methods: Feminism and social research.* Philadelphia: Temple University Press.

Duke, D., & Reck, B. (2003). The evolution of educational accountability in the Old Dominion. In D. Duke, M. Grogan, P. Tucker, & W. Heinecke (Eds.), *Educational leadership in an age of accountability* (pp. 36–68). New York: State University of New York Press.

Duke, D., & Tucker, P. (2003). Initial responses of Virginia high schools to the accountability plan. In D. Duke, M. Grogan, P. Tucker, & W. Heinecke (Eds.), *Educational leadership in an age of accountability* (pp. 69-92). New York: State University of New York Press.

Edwards, R., & Ribbens, J. (1998). Living on the edges: Public knowledge, private lives, personal experience. In J. Ribbens & R. Edwards (Eds.), *Feminist dilemmas in qualitative research* (pp 1–23). London: Sage.

Elshtain, J. (1995). *Democracy on trial.* New York: Basic Books.

Epstein, T. (2001). Racial identity and young people's perspectives on social education. *Theory and Practice, 40,* 42-47.

Farmer, R. (1995, June 18). Revision battle lines are formed: Language skills, social studies focus of conflict. *Richmond-Times Dispatch.* Retrieved from http://archivesva.com

Felski, R. (2000). *Doing time: Feminist theory and postmodern culture.* New York: New York University Press.

Fore, L. (1998). Curriculum control: Using discourse and structure to image educational reform. *Journal of Curriculum Studies, 30,* 577–592.

Fraser, N. (1997) *Justice interruptus: Critical reflections on the "post-socialist" condition.* New York: Routledge.

Freire, P. (1993) *Pedagogy of the oppressed.* New York: Continuum.

Grant, S. G. (2000). Teachers and tests: Exploring teachers' perceptions of changes in the New York state testing program. *Education Policy Analysis Archives, 8*(14). Retrieved from http://epaa.asu.edu/epaa/v9n39.html

Grant, S. G. (2001, October 3). When an "A" is not enough: Analyzing the New York state global history and geography exam. *Educational Policy Analysis Archives, 9*(39). Retrieved from http://epaa.asu.edu/epaa/v9n39.html

Grant, S. G. (2003). *History lessons: Teaching, learning and testing in U.S. high school classrooms.* Mahwah, NJ: Erlbaum.

Gruenewald, D. (2003). The best of both worlds. A critical pedagogy of place. *Educational Researcher, 32,* 3-12.

Grumet, M. (1988). *Bitter milk: Women and teaching.* Amherst: University of Massachusetts Press.

Hirsch, E. D. (1987). *Cultural literacy: What every American needs to know.* Boston: Houghton-Mifflin.

Holland, R. (1995, April 12). VEA/NEA confirms corollary to education reform law. *Richmond-Times Dispatch.* Retrieved from http://archivesva.com

Hsu, S. (1995a, March 30). Allen school plan praised, panned at hearing. *Washington Post,* p. B6.

Hsu, S. (1995b, April 26). Allen's education plan causes division in GOP. *Washington Post,* p. B1.

Jones, K. (1988). Towards the revision of politics. In K. Jones & A. Jonasdottir (Eds.), *The political interests of gender* (pp. 11–32). London: Sage.

Kincheloe, J. (1991). *Teachers as researchers: Qualitative inquiry as a path to empowerment.* New York: Falmer Press.

Lareau, A., & Schultz, J. (1996). Introduction. In A. Lareau & J. Schultz (Eds.), *Journeys through ethnography* (pp. 1–7). Boulder, CO: Westview Press.

Lather, P. (1991). *Getting smart: Feminist research and pedagogy with/in the postmodern.* New York: Routledge.

Lipman, P. (2004). *High stakes education: Inequality, globalization and urban school reform.* New York: Routledge.

Little, J. (1990). The persistence of privacy: Autonomy and initiative in teachers' professional relations. *Teachers College Record, 91*(4), 509-536.

Mathison, S., & Freeman, M. (2003). Constraining elementary teachers' work: Dilemmas and paradoxes created by state mandated testing. *Education Policy Analysis Archives, 11*(34). Retrieved from http://epaa.asu.edu/epaa/v11n34/

McNeil, L. (2000). *Contradictions of school reform: Educational costs of standardized testing.* New York: Routledge.

Morris, D. (2000). Privacy, privation, perversity: Toward new representations of the personal. *Signs: Journal of Women in Culture and Society, 25,* 323–351.

Nash, G., Crabtree, C., & Dunn, R. (1997). *History on trial: Culture wars and the teaching of the past.* New York: Knopf.

Parents Across Virginia United to Reform SOLs. (2003). Retrieved from http://solreform.com

Pateman, C. (1989). *The disorder of women: Democracy, feminism and political theory.* Stanford, CA: Stanford University Press.

Popkewitz, T. (1984). *Paradigm and ideology in educational research.* New York: Falmer Press.

Position paper on the standards of learning prepared by the faculty of the graduate school of education. (1999). George Mason University. Retrieved from http://gse.gmu.edu

Price, J. (2000). *Against the odds: The meaning of school and relationships in the lives of six young African-American men.* Stamford, CT: Ablex.

Saxonhouse, A. (1992). Public and private: The paradigm's power. In B. Garlick, S. Dixon, & P. Allen (Eds.) *Stereotypes of women in power: Historical perspectives and revisionist views* (pp. 1–9). New York: Greenwood.

Seixas, P. (1999). Beyond "content" and "pedagogy": In search of a way to talk about history education. *Journal of Curriculum Studies 31,* 317–337.

Stahl, S., Hynd, C., Britton, B., McNish, M., & Bosquet, D. (1996). What happens when students read multiple source documents in history? *Reading Research Quarterly, 31,* 430–456.

Stallsmith, P. (2000, March 22). Critic says state tests crowd out creativity. *Richmond Times Dispatch.* Retrieved from http://timesdispatch.com

Strauss, A., & Corbin, J. (1998). *Basics of qualitative research.* Thousand, Oaks, CA: Sage.

Van Manen, M. (1990). Researching lived experience. London, Ontario, Canada: The University of Western Ontario.

VanSledright, B. (1996). Closing the gap between school an disciplinary history? Historian as high school history teacher. *Advances in Research on Teaching, 6,* 257–289.

VanSledright, B. (2002). *In search of America's past: Learning to read history in elementary school.* New York: Teachers College Press.

Virginia Standards of Learning Assessments Test Blueprints. (2001). Retrieved from http://www.pen.k12.va.us/VDOE/Assessment/soltests

Wells, G. (2001). The case for dialogic inquiry. In G. Wells (Ed.), *Action, talk & text* (pp. 171–200). New York: Teachers College Press.

Werner, J. (2001, October 18). SOL tests added: History examinations to be on new schedule. *Richmond-Times Dispatch.* Retrieved from http://timesdispatch.com

Wineburg, S. (1991). On the reading of historical texts: Notes on the breach between school and academy. *American Educational Research Journal, 28,* 495–519

Wineburg, S. (2001). *Historical thinking and other unnatural acts.* Philadelphia: Temple University Press.

Wolcott, H. (1990). On seeking—and rejecting—validity in qualitative research. In E. Eisner & A. Peshkin (Eds.), *Qualitative inquiry in education* (pp. 121–152). New York: Teachers College Press.

Wolcott, H. (1994). *Transforming qualitative data: Description, analysis and interpretation.*Thousand Oaks, CA: Sage.

Wraga, W. (1999). The educational and political implications of curriculum alignment and standards-based reform. *Journal of Curriculum and Supervision, 15,* 4–25.

CHAPTER 12

"DOES ANYBODY REALLY UNDERSTAND THIS TEST?"

Florida High School Social Studies Teachers' Efforts to Make Sense of the FCAT

Elizabeth Anne Yeager and Matthew Pinder

As S. G. Grant states in his introduction, "lost in much of the shouting [about high-stakes testing] is the empirical study of what happens in classrooms as history teachers and students read and respond to new or revised state-level, and increasingly high-stakes, social studies tests. If tests drive teaching, as so many policymakers seem to believe, then what does that relationship look like, and more importantly, do new tests ensure more ambitious teaching and learning?" This question takes on a unique dimension in Florida, where social studies is *not* an explicit part of the Florida Comprehensive Assessment Test (FCAT). And yet this test has implications for teachers' classroom practices as they try, to various degrees, to find time and reason to teach history when their attention is continuously drawn to the subjects covered on the state exam.

It has long been understood that major trends in the larger educational environment (e.g., high-stakes testing and stringent state stan-

Measuring History: Cases of State-Level Testing Across the United States, 249–272
Copyright © 2006 by Information Age Publishing
All rights of reproduction in any form reserved.

dards) create an impetus for social studies curricular change (Lippitt, 1969); that these changes are aimed at student-specific improvement (Iozzi & Cheu, 1978); and that they are designed to facilitate students' capacity to make socially effective choices by enhancing their academic ability (Cherryholmes, 1971). With the recognition that for more than a decade social studies has been a field measured and remeasured by standards (Thornton, 1999), today's social studies educators bear the responsibility of integrating the press for heightened accountability (Thornton, 2000) with their best pedagogical intentions.

In the recent era of high-stakes testing and stringent, often poorly constructed, mandatory state standards, social studies teachers face ever-expanding levels of accountability. The result is that by means of "coercion and exhortation ... teachers are expected to implement a curriculum [while] having played no part in the formulation of its aims" (Thornton, 2000, p. 3). This increasingly aggressive environment leaves many social studies teachers wondering exactly what path their chosen profession will take. Indeed, with recent literature showing the complexities arising at the intersection of high-stakes testing, teaching, and learning (McNeil, 2000), combined with the decidedly nonstandardized professional preparation experiences of teachers in the key areas of historical inquiry (Yeager & Davis, 1994, 1995), use of primary documents (Fehn & Koeppen, 1998; Seixas, 1998a, 1998b; Yeager & Wilson, 1997), and understanding of wise classroom practice (Adler 1993; Davis, 1997; Purkey & Stanley, 1991; Shulman, 1987; Yeager & Wilson, 1997), many history teachers face a sort of identity crisis. Certainly, one hears teachers asking, am I a history teacher or a reading teacher? Am I a facilitator of learning or a purveyor of test-related content? Must I abandon the reasons I became a teacher in order to prepare students for this test?

In Florida, we hear such questions among both preservice and practicing teachers. Confounding the Florida situation is the fact that, although policymakers have specified state social studies standards (the Sunshine State Standards) at all levels of schooling, social studies content is not tested on the Florida Comprehensive Assessment Test. The FCAT, administered to students in Grades 3–11, is the latest version of Florida's statewide assessment program and contains two basic components: criterion-referenced tests, measuring selected benchmarks in mathematics, reading, science, and writing from the Sunshine State Standards; and norm-referenced tests in reading and mathematics, measuring individual student performance against national norms. The Florida Commission on Education Reform and Accountability began conceptualizing the FCAT well before the first test was administered in 1998. In 1995, the Commission recommended procedures for assessing student learning in Florida that would "raise educational expectations for students and help them compete for jobs in the global marketplace" (Florida Department of Education, 2005). The State Board of Education adopted the recommendations, called the Comprehensive Assessment Design, in June 1995. The Design specified the development of new statewide assessments to address four broad areas described in the first four standards of Goal 3 of Blueprint 2000. These four areas highlighted reading, writing, mathematics, and creative and critical thinking. In addition, the Design required that educational content standards be developed and adopted. Subsequently, the Florida Sunshine State Standards were developed and adopted by the State Board. The frameworks and standards established guidelines for a statewide system that incorporated assessment, accountability, and in-service training components.

According to the Florida Department of Education, the FCAT was designed to meet both the requirements of the Comprehensive Assessment Design and the rigorous content defined by the Sunshine State Standards. The FCAT measures the content specified within the strands, standards, and benchmarks of the Sunshine State Standards and does so in the context of real-world applications. (Florida Department of Education, 2005). Initially, the FCAT was designed to assess reading, writing, and mathematics at four grade levels so that each subject was assessed at all levels of schooling. With legislative approval of Governor Jeb Bush's A+ Plan in 1999, the FCAT was expanded to include Grades 3–10. In 2001, achievement for all grade levels was reported for the first time.

At the high school level, the testing situation impacts teachers and students in diverse, often unsystematic ways, as teachers struggle to figure out what their roles are supposed to be within the overall goals of their school. In our experience of observing and working with dozens of Florida high school history teachers over the past 10 years, it strikes us that teachers are all over the map when it comes to how they perceive their responsibilities with regard to FCAT preparation in particular and student achievement in general, and certainly schools are all over the map with regard to the in-service training component specified by the state.

For a history teacher, especially one new to the profession, to move beyond a fragmented (Thornton, 2000) and frantic identity to a wiser or more ambitious practice (Brighton, 2002; Davis, 1997; Feldman, 1997; Foster & Hoge, 2000; Grant, 2003, Grant & VanSledright 2005; Hoge, 2000; Purkey & Stanley, 1991; Riley, Wilson, & Fogg, 2000; Shulman, 1987; Stone, 2002; White, 1987; Work, 2002; Yeager, 2000; Yeager & Davis, 2005; Yeager & Wilson, 1997) that both engages students and prepares them for a standardized test is a tall order. Such a mandate seems especially frustrating and confining when one's content is not even on the test. Not surprisingly, then, we hear teachers ask if they should scale back their content to do test preparation activities, if their subject will be eliminated or tested, and if and how they are supposed to contribute to student achievement on the test.

One way in which we have thought about ambitious history teaching in Florida is the inclusion of more and better content-specific reading and writing strategies in history classes. Dobbs (2003) asserts that "there is a high failure rate in the content area because children [with regard to reading] have problems understanding text material, poor study skills, and lack of motivation" (p. 3). She suggests a variety of methods to monitor and improve reading skills and behaviors that will "help the student think about what they are reading, create mental pictures, and ask questions" (p. 3), which eventually can reduce drop-out rates and behavior problems as well as improve academic achievement. Kameenui and Carnine (1998) argue that improved reading and writing skills in the social studies classroom directly benefit diverse learners both in and out of the classroom. Additionally, the focus on content-specific reading and writing skills provides for the inclusion of historically ignored groups (McElroy & Downey, 1982) and for academic stabilization or improvement in high-poverty and high minority-populated schools as a whole (Education Trust, 2002) and for member students specifically (Dodge & Price, 1994). Other researchers (Irvin, Lunstrum, Lynch-Brown, & Shephard, 1995; Patrick & Leming, 2001; Sandman, 2004; Wright, 2002) support the conclusion that tailored use of reading and writing strategies in social studies classrooms can "deepen students' understanding of the social sciences" and motivate them to engage in the dialogue of "reading and writing in the social studies class" (Irvin et al., 1995, p. 1). If true, such an approach could constitute evidence of the truly "powerful teaching" (National Council for the Social Studies, 1994) that has been described and desired for more than a decade.

PURPOSE OF THIS CHAPTER

As we know from Stephanie van Hover's chapter in this volume and from an abundance of additional research, beginning teachers face unique issues and challenges related to workload, support and mentoring, and classroom management, not to mention the fact that they are still learning the content they are expected to teach (Darling-Hammond, 1998; Lawson, 1992; Rust, 1994). van Hover's chapter focuses on teachers who deal with the high-pressure environment of the Virginia SOLs test, which mandates the teaching and testing of an extensive, detailed list of historical facts and skills. The teachers in her study have known no other teaching environment, thus their perceptions of the test and of their own teaching practices with regard to the test are of special significance, a conclusion reminiscent of Segall's (2003) study of Michigan teachers.

In a sense, the new standards and testing mandates may make many teachers feel like rookies in an entirely new ball game. In Florida, these policies take on a unique cast insofar as the absence of a state-mandated history test leaves teachers struggling to understand where they fit into their school's FCAT mission. Our experiences with Florida high school history teachers at all levels of experience suggest that these teachers believe that, on some level, they are expected to help raise scores, but how they do so appears largely idiosyncratic.

In this chapter, we juxtapose two stories that typify some of the issues and challenges of the Florida testing context. We present a snapshot of two history teachers, in very different school settings, trying to make sense of the FCAT and their roles in preparing students for it. Although one has more experience, both teachers can claim the FCAT environment as the only one they have known. We discuss their perceptions of the FCAT's impact on their teaching, and on what they consider to be ambitious practices as they use various reading and writing strategies to "deepen students' understanding of the social sciences" and motivate students to engage in the dialogue of "reading and writing in the social studies class" (Irvin et al., 1995, p. 1)

METHODS

We used a case study methodology (Miles & Huberman, 1994; Stake, 1995) to study two secondary history teachers, Suzanne and Isabel (pseudonyms), completing their first and seventh years of teaching, respectively. The case study approach allowed us to investigate the classroom lives of these teachers as "bounded systems" (Stake, 1995). Our research examined the following question: How do these two history teachers make sense of their role in preparing students for a test from which their content area is excluded?

Participants and Setting

We selected the two teachers on the basis of several criteria. First, they were full-time history teachers in the Florida public school system. Second, they were at different points in their teaching careers—one in her first year, the other in her seventh—but both were within the "FCAT generation" of classroom teachers. Third, the teachers worked in schools reflecting substantial differences in student population composition, geographic setting, and school-wide approach to preparation for the FCAT. Finally, both teachers articulated a commitment to professional excellence and independently sought out what they considered to be new and/or better teaching practices to implement in their history classrooms.

Suzanne, a White female in her early 20s, taught 11th grade U.S. history at 105-year-old University High School, a large, diverse school of 1,700 students in a small North Central Florida city where, in addition to a mix of African Americans and Whites, the school draws Asian and Hispanic students because it houses the district's main ESOL program. The school's FCAT scores declined in recent years, going from a B in 2001 to a D in 2005 via the state's school accountability grading system. Suzanne was in her 1st year as a full-time teacher, after having earned a bachelor's degree in sociology and a master's/certification degree in social studies education at the large public university in the same city as University High.

Isabel, a Hispanic female in her late 20s, with 7 years of full-time classroom experience, taught ninth grade world history at Jose Marti High School, a large urban school with an enrollment of 3,200 students. Isabel earned her bachelor's degree in criminal justice and her social studies certification from a large public university in the same city and recently began work on a master's degree in education. The South Florida high school is over 100 years old and is the fourth largest school district in the nation. The school's enrollments are approximately 92% Hispanic students, 6% African American students, and 2% from other groups. When we began this study, 83% of the 10th grade students had failed the FCAT. The school received a grade of D for 2 years in a row via the state's school accountability ratings. As of this year, however, perhaps due to a systematic school-wide reading and writing skills program, test scores have risen significantly and the school earned a C grade for the second year in a row.

Data Sources

The data sources for this study included 10 interviews and 10 classroom observations per teacher. We audiotaped and transcribed each of the interviews, which were semistructured because our primary interest was to accept the validity of the responses and to learn more about the participants' perspectives. We took only field notes during observations. We designed the interview protocol to elicit the teachers' views on the issues described above, as well as the relevant personal background information that provided the basis for their responses. The first author observed Suzanne's classroom once a week during the fall 2004 semester and observed Isabel's classroom a total of 10 times between 2003 and

2005, in order to gain a sense of each teacher's lesson planning, instructional methods, and classroom dynamics. The observations lasted for one class period each. Because the first author also had an open invitation from both participants to visit their classrooms at any time, she also visited the teachers' classrooms on an informal basis. During the observations, she took extensive free-form field notes, and then completed reflective notes afterward.

Data Analysis

We analyzed the data in several phases. First, we each conducted independent, systematic content analyses of the interview transcripts and field notes, looking for similarities, differences, patterns, themes, and general categories of responses (Stake, 1995; Miles & Huberman, 1994). Second, we each prepared our own tables for categorization of responses, as well as research memos detailing our analysis. Then we met to compare our analyses and generate an outline of the major themes and issues emerging from the data. We adhered to Kvale's (1994) discussion of the social construction of validity and the conception of "moderate postmodernism," which accepts the possibility of specific local, personal, and community forms of truth, with a focus on daily life and local narrative" (p. 231). We also employed "experiential" and "consequential" types of analysis (Kvale, 1994). "Experiential" questions attempt to clarify what the interviewees have said about a particular subject—the content. "Consequential" questions ask about the implications of the interviewees' statements. Furthermore, our analysis of the interview text followed what Kvale (1994) has called "meaning categorization" and "meaning interpretation." For the former, we read the interview transcripts and identified and coded prominent themes into categories. These were listed as main points in our internal research memoranda. We employed the latter for particular statements that we thought were both representative and meaningful.

AMBITIOUS TEACHING: PRESERVING CONTENT, INTEGRATING LITERACY

As with van Hover's study, we wondered how these two high school history teachers, who have worked only within a context of standards and accountability, interpret the influence of a high-stakes test on their teaching practice—but with the added dimension of a test that did not include their disciplinary content. We found the two teachers, Suzanne and Isabel, had highly divergent experiences, yet reached some of the same conclusions. We explore some of the essential differences in their experiences and perceptions, focusing on the nature of their students, their school culture, their professional development/training with regard to the FCAT, and their instructional and assessment decisions in the classroom. After discussing the teachers' situations separately, we analyze their views on ambitious teaching, how they feel the FCAT has impacted their ambitions, and how they respond to what they perceive to be the message from the "powers that be": Generic skills matter, social studies content does not.

ISABEL: "YOU CAN'T AVOID IT ... BUT GOOD TEACHING IS GOOD TEACHING"

A veteran teacher working in a school identified as underachieving, Isabel sees as important both her history content and helping students develop the literacy skills necessary to pass the FCAT. Her school context supports Isabel more explicitly with the latter than the former and it is clear that she forefronts test-based literacy in her planning, instruction, and assessment. Still, Isabel believes that history is a vehicle for helping her students become "better people."

Snapshots from Isabel's Classroom

A typical day in Isabel's classroom begins with literacy. The first 10 minutes of the 100-minute block period feature mandatory, school-wide silent reading. One day, the literacy focus continues when Isabel directs the class to take out paper and turn to an article in entitled "What's At Stake: The 2004 Election" in a *New York Times Upfront* magazine for students. The Sum It Up activity begins with students taking turns reading aloud individually, a paragraph or so at a time. After four paragraphs, Isabel pauses, asks students to "sum it up" in three sentences, then calls on several students to read their responses. Three students volunteer, though all seem off the mark. After the class reads the next three paragraphs, Isabel pauses and assigns another summary task, this time advising students that the main idea "has to do with the war in Iraq." Predictably, the students' responses this time seem more focused.

Halfway through the article, Isabel tells the class to write down words that "you have no clue about the meaning." After a few minutes, they offer *rhetoric, exclusion, referendum, myopic,* and *irresolute.* The students seem to enjoy talking through the words as they discuss sentences such as "Kerry accuses Bush of being myopic in his view on Iraq, to the exclusion of things that are in fact necessary to make the world safer," and "Bush accuses Kerry of being a flip flopper, casting his opponent as irresolute." As Isabel and the students decipher these passages, she asks additional questions such as, "who is speaking in this sentence? What is he saying?" The class occasionally follows tangents around issues like undecided voters and the issue of being forced to vote versus doing it because one should. On the latter, Isabel displays outrage that anyone would not bother to vote, announcing to the class, "if you don't want to vote, then maybe you should just go back to Cuba. And you girls had better vote when you turn 18!"

On another day, Isabel uses a Reciprocal Teaching (RT) activity to examine an article the class reads about the end of apartheid in South Africa, post-apartheid elections, and current issues the country is facing with regard to AIDS, crime, and unemployment. She modifies the RT strategy, preferring to do it with the entire class instead of in small groups as she originally learned the strategy. Isabel begins by going leading a recitation of the RT process:

> Isabel: What is the first thing you do?
> Students: (in unison) Predict!
> Isabel: OK, predict what the article is about from the title, "South Africa's Decade of Freedom."

A few students respond to this request, reading a few paragraphs aloud.

> Isabel: Now what is the second thing you do?
> Students: (in unison) Visualize!
> Isabel: OK, visualize what you've read.... Make a picture in your head and write about what you see.

The students briefly take time to write down their thoughts, and then share them.

> Student 1: I see a lot of black people treated like nothing.
> Student 2: I see blacks with no freedom and their lives changing.

Acknowledging these responses, Isabel asks students to continue reading.

> Isabel: What is the third thing you do?
> Students: (in unison) Clarify!

Isabel directs the class to write down words they do not know, and then they discuss words such as *segregation* and *throngs*.

> Isabel: What is the fourth step?
> Students: (in unison) Write a teacher-like question.

Isabel tells students to do this, they write their ideas down on paper, and then she notes that time is running short so they finish reading the article.

> Isabel: And what is the last step?
> Students: Summarize.

At this point, Isabel asks students to write a summary of this article. She collects these papers as class ends.

Understanding the Balance of History and Literacy in Isabel's Practice

As these descriptions illustrate, Isabel's focus on the FCAT-inspired literacy concepts of summarizing and finding the main idea appear central to her planning and teaching. While early in the school year, and even with the multiple challenges of teaching students new to the high school setting (many of whom are non-native English speakers), Isabel is already familiarizing her students with the routines and strategies she considers essential for the FCAT, and she clearly intends to have the students continue practicing every day.

Although literacy seems to dominate Isabel's teaching, her impulse to become a social studies teacher had everything to do with the content: "I like world events, issues, the idea of civic and personal responsibility. Social studies has to do with what you believe and your moral perspective. I ask students, what does society mean to you?" She still believes that social studies content, issues, and questions drive her instruction:

> [My purpose is to] make better people. Use history as a tool to achieve this goal. For example, when it comes to talking about religion in history, I don't tell them what to believe, but I talk about why it has been important to so many people. Everything I teach has a moral lesson. Why do people make the choices they do? Why do we now? Why do we think the way we do? Why do we have the leaders we have? We need to examine how people have thought about things and have made decisions about things over history.

Content matters to Isabel, but she recognizes that her students face real literacy challenges. Teaching mostly ninth grade World History students, she finds that all of her students are "low level," with many students reading on a third or fourth grade level. The connection between learning content and learning to read, she believes, is also tied into students' behavior:

> Reading ability is connected to behavior.... And I also talk to the kids a lot about what's going on with them. Some of them say they don't have anyone at home who cares about their education. I have a 17-year-old student who can't read, but he'll sit next to me at my desk and do his work with help.

When Isabel plans for instruction and assessment, she juggles attention to content, literacy, and students' behavior. Yet, ever-present is her question, "what will get my students' brains working for FCAT practice?" In other words, regardless of the kind of lesson she is teaching, Isabel incorporates a measure of FCAT practice:

> I make up my own questions for a lesson, not the ones from the book. I try not to use the book much. I know I will give notes, and I know I will do some of the FCAT strategies on maps, charts, tables, etc. I give them chances to practice these skills. I also think of some whole-class activities. I like these better than small groups, because I can monitor what they are doing better. I always try to do one or two FCAT things in each lesson. We do a lot of Sum It Ups and Reciprocal Teaching because they are poor writers and need practice summarizing the main idea.... Like I gave them a practice question on Homer's *Odyssey* where they describe their adventures as if they were Odysseus.

That Isabel's written lesson plans seem to privilege literacy practice over content knowledge, may reflect the school requirement that teachers use an FCAT-based lesson plan format and submit their lessons for weekly checks. The lesson plan format does require a list of the content to be taught, the methods and assessments to be used, and the correlation of the lesson with the state standards, but it also demands that teachers list the FCAT skills addressed in each lesson. As the vignettes above indicate, however, Isabel's actual teaching reflects more of a content focus than her written plans seem to imply, as well as her desire to "make students better people" through social studies topics (Homer's *Odyssey*) and issues (voting, racism, AIDS).

So how does Isabel judge the influence of the Sunshine State Standards and the FCAT test on her planning? Not only does she see the state polices as a major factor, but she would do little different if those policies were to disappear:

It's a big influence. It takes time away from the history material. But yes, I feel like I need to do an FCAT thing every day. You know what, though? If there were no FCAT, I wouldn't do anything differently. My kids need this practice with reading, critical thinking. They are so behind grade level. It's helping them, helping me teach them. I do feel more like an English teacher than a history teacher sometimes. If you do everything you're supposed to do for FCAT, you are an English teacher. But I would do a lot of things the same.

Not surprisingly, then, the FCAT largely defines Isabel's thinking about assessment as well: Her test items stem directly from classroom lectures and activities, including items that require students to summarize information from a short reading passage. She asserts that this approach "holds them accountable for participating in class, reading in class, listening and taking notes in class. I value participation. If you study my notes and all we talked about in class, you do OK." As to the influence of the standards and the FCAT on her assessment strategies, and what she would do if there were no FCAT, again Isabel feels that she would make no significant changes:

The same as with my planning. Maybe not to the extreme I do it now, but I still think there are benefits [from the FCAT practice] for the students I teach. They need this stuff because they don't get it anywhere else, not at home for sure. The kids I have this year ... wow. But it's great when I see them still in school and when they come back and show me what they've done.

Finally, when we asked Isabel how she understood the influence of the Sunshine State Standards and the FCAT on the teaching and learning of history at her school and in her classroom, she argues that, although the FCAT does not inspire good teaching, it is a dynamic presence in her classroom practice:

Well, as far as the FCAT goes—definitely yes, in every way. You can't avoid it. Every two weeks we focus on a new strategy. Has it influenced the way I teach? Totally.... But the main thing is—good teaching is good teaching. I don't think the FCAT itself has had much to with improving teaching. The thing is, it's exhausting for teachers ... the pressure is intense. But the pressure is also on the kids to do more to pass the test.

Isabel's case illustrates the pervasive form that state-level testing can take. Social studies is not part of the state exam and yet Isabel and her content-area teaching colleagues are drawn in into the its wake through both implicit and explicit means. Her actual teaching practice suggests that she is developing significant content connections with her students, but the overall effect of the FCAT can not be missed.

SUZANNE: "THIS FEELS SO UNPROFESSIONAL ... I WANT TO DEVELOP MY OWN MATERIALS"

Suzanne takes a much different approach to balancing history content and literacy skills than does Isabel. A rookie teacher, Suzanne nevertheless feels sufficiently capable and empowered to forefront the historical ideas she chooses to teach, working the necessary literacy skills into the content-based activities she designs. Complicating Suzanne's approach is the fact that she works within a school context that offers no particular support for her ambitious practices.

Snapshots from Suzanne's Classroom

In contrast to Isabel, Suzanne teaches in traditional 50 minute periods. The two vignettes presented below capture something of the activities Suzanne leads on her "FCAT practice" days.

Suzanne begins by directing the class to write down a definition of the term "Emancipation Proclamation," using the glossary from their textbook, and to explain the statement: "The Emancipation Proclamation had far more symbolic than real impact." Asked to recite their answers to these questions, most students do so accurately. Next, Suzanne tells students that they will read a secondary source related to U.S. history, "The Emancipation Proclamation: An Act of Justice," by John Hope Franklin (1993), an article on the context and significance of the act. The four-page document is relatively long, with some high-level vocabulary (e.g., trenchant, deliberation, enfranchisement) that is not discussed. Suzanne instructs the class to respond in writing to several questions: What is the significance of the correction Lincoln made to the Proclamation before signing it? Describe the scene in which he formally signed it. Where is the original document today? List and describe two differences between preliminary and final drafts of the Proclamation. How did people around the country react to it? If the Proclamation did not actually free slaves in many areas, what did occur because of it? Why does the author say it is more common to celebrate the Emancipation Proclamation than the 13th Amendment? How did President Kennedy reference the Proclamation as a defense for equal rights for blacks? What is the author's opinion of Lincoln's position as compared to U.S. leaders today? The students work on this assignment for the rest of the period and turn in their papers when the bell rings.

In a subsequent class period, Suzanne reviews the major problems the students had with the assignment, focusing on vocabulary issues and the perspectives described in the document. A content lesson, in part, she focuses specifically on the literacy skills of vocabulary development and identifying point of view. Suzanne tells the class that they are going to do an exercise on opposing viewpoints on the question, "should black soldiers fight for the Union?" She explains that she will give them either one "pro" or one "con" reading on this topic. This time, the readings are short (less than two pages each). Before the students start reading, Suzanne provides some scaffolding by telling them,

> as you read, write down all the facts to support your argument, write down the underlined words on your handout, and match each one to the word(s) in the list at the end of your reading. Then after you read, I'm going to ask you to defend your argument, listen to the other side, and decide who has the best argument on the basis of the facts.

Suzanne closely monitors their work, making sure they are on the right track.

After a brief period, she calls time, tells them to turn to the person next to them with the opposing viewpoint, and explain their viewpoints to each other. At the conclusion of the conversation, students decide who has the better argument and engage the activity productively. Before the bell, Suzanne calls time again, says "all eyes on me," and directs the students to write a one-paragraph reflection on which argument is best and why, supporting their stand with facts from their reading. Some of the students grumble about the paragraph, but she tells them it is "writing practice you need."

Understanding the Balance of Content and Literacy in Suzanne's Practice

Evident in her interviews and in these classroom illustrations, Suzanne finds ways to justify her preferred content-heavy instructional practices, believing that they provide the best route both to engage her students' thinking and to help them practice for the FCAT. The Emancipation Proclamation activity is typical of her "big idea" content focus that demands far more of her students than the FCAT writing test. Yet, when she tries content-based writing without taking into consideration her students' lack of basic literacy skills, she realizes that her lessons have to include these skills if students are to understand the content. Although the FCAT is not the daily focus that it is for Isabel, Suzanne believes there are certain reading and writing skills that her students need to practice, whether or not the FCAT exists.

Having come from a sociology background, Suzanne jokes that the reason she teaches history is because "it's the job I was offered." Continuing, she notes the importance of history as an "application to today ... how does this affect us? What can we learn now from the past.... Relevance is the key to the meaning of history. Instead of giving students dates and time lines, I want them to remember perspectives, viewpoints, stories—not just events but overall themes."

In her first year, Suzanne teaches five classes of U.S. history to a diverse group of mostly 11th graders (25% African American, 70% White, and 5% Hispanic and Asian; about 20 of her students were in the school's ESOL program). The students are diverse academically and ethnically, but many exhibit ability and behavior issues that are "very challenging ... the application is the problem. They have the ability, but the motivation is not there. A lot of them think it's not cool to achieve." Many of her students read below grade level and demonstrate "a lot of comprehension problems." Thirteen of Suzanne's students failed the FCAT reading test when they took it in 10th grade; and three students have with 504 Exceptional Student Education accommodation plans for reading problems. Twenty-five students are assigned to the "strategies" class for "at-risk" learners; thus, she regularly attends scheduled meetings with the teacher of the strategies class.

The school context in which Suzanne teaches is also challenging. She believes that the school is "not as strict as it needs to be to improve achievement.... Extracurricular stuff seems more important and it always disrupts the class schedule." She credits the principal with his plan to bring new energy and ideas into the school by hiring 30 new teachers. But she characterizes the veteran teachers as "very negative and cynical.... When new teachers act enthusiastic or suggest new ideas, the older teachers put them down." Suzanne seeks out colleagues for advice, including the media specialist and the ESOL teacher, and her colleagues have become friendlier to her. Still, most of them continue to disparage the more ambitious ideas she tries in her classes. Interestingly enough, the FCAT seems discounted by most of Suzanne's colleagues. The principal led some in-service activities in which he instructed the teachers to begin their classes by writing a Sunshine State Standard objective on the board each day. Suzanne reports that few teachers took the principal or the state test seriously:

A lot of the teachers in my department make fun of this behind his back and don't do it. And the FCAT is not taken seriously at all, especially compared to [the school where she did her internship]. Some kids didn't even know they had to do the FCAT retake this year and were totally surprised when they came to school that day!... So since the FCAT is not on the test, the teachers just don't care. The honors and AP teachers could care less. A few new teachers have tried to work with some of the English teachers to plan for the practice days, but most teachers say that they are just going to drag their feet about the whole thing.

Perhaps sensing his staff's resistance, the principal issued a directive to faculty with students taking the FCAT that they must teach FCAT-based reading skills every Tuesday and Wednesday with a prescribed, but generic literacy skills workbook. A few weeks later, the principal conducted a workshop that Suzanne found "silly and demeaning":

> I think some of the older teachers are using it, just copying stuff out of the FCAT book. I guess some are taking the path of least resistance. They just hand out the stuff and it's like a day off from lesson planning. But I can't stand the time away from my content. The new teachers feel the same way. It feels unprofessional, like not what I was taught to do. I want to come up with my own readings and questions. Yet if someone came in and observed me doing the generic stuff, which I've been told will happen, it would be considered perfectly acceptable.

Suzanne explains that she attempted to follow the guidelines and implement some of the practice activities from the workshop, but she quickly concluded that the students "saw through them, and I knew I was wasting my time and theirs." Reflecting on this sequences of experiences, Suzanne decided to locate content-oriented reading and writing activities directly tied to her U.S. history curriculum. She rejects the lack of ambition in some of the test-related measures her school is promoting, and resolves to resist this "laziness."

Unlike Isabel, Suzanne seems determined to make the policy fit her practice. For example, when she plans for instruction and assessment, she initially focuses on "the outcome.... What do I want them to learn/achieve? Then I decide how much in depth I want them to go. Only then do I decide how to apply the [Sunshine State] standards. I can apply the standard to any lesson I want. I don't try to fit into the standards." She uses the Internet as a resource for primary sources and documents and the textbook as her main secondary source. Lesson plans are not required or checked in her school, but she finds the lesson planning format she learned in her master's program to be practical and she continues to use it. Her preferred teaching methods include cooperative learning activities and lecture with question-and-answer sessions. When she received the FCAT practice directive, Suzanne feared that these preferred methods, and most of her content, would have to be abandoned. But just as she rejects the negativism of her colleagues toward "new" ideas, so too does she reject the notion of boilerplate FCAT practice, and she resolves to use her own judgment about what will and will not work for her students.

But when asked about the influence of the FCAT on her practice, Suzanne's response reveals the complex feelings the test generates. First, she clearly feels pressure to help her students perform well on the test:

> Now I'm concerned because I feel the weight of getting the kids to pass the test. I have to do this practice every Tuesday and Wednesday, but it's hard because the ones who need it the most are the ones who are absent all the time.

At the same time, Suzanne seems a bit overwhelmed trying to figure out how to do what she wants to do:

> My concern is how to incorporate more reading, but I'm concerned the students won't do it if there is too much reading involved in an activity. They just will not read anything for too long. They just give up. It's a big task for them to read. What do I do?... I just am not sure what to do.... Right now it's not clear how to connect the content I want to cover with the FCAT strategies.

And yet, Suzanne seems determined not to let the test and the mindless drill-and-practice suggestions from her principal define her practice:

> I've been given a workbook, but I think I have more flexibility than that. I've talked to others, and I feel like I can take historical fiction, primary sources, and so forth, that are relevant to U.S. history and just model my activities for these after the workbook. The workbook is not relevant at all.

Although the FCAT is not the daily priority that it is for Isabel, Suzanne finds that the historical document and primary source reading and writing activities she prefers happen to be beneficial with regard to FCAT practice. She also finds that her preference for including a writing section on each of her tests is consistent with helping students prepare for the FCAT. She thinks she may be asked to do more explicit FCAT activities in the future, but for now she believes she is helping her students gain expertise in tested skills without sacrificing the content she thinks is so important.

Suzanne's case stands in some contrast to Isabel's for while both teachers attend to their content and to the state test, how they do so differs considerably. Where Isabel shapes the content around the literacy skills she teaches, Suzanne chooses the content she wants to teach and then determines which literacy skills she can teach within it. In some ways, this distinction may seem minor, but it appears that, despite her novice teacher doubts, Suzanne is far more in control of her teaching than is Isabel.

DISCUSSION

This chapter examines the question of how two high school history teachers in Florida struggle to understand their role in the high-stakes environment of state standards and testing. In the cases of Isabel and Suzanne, we find that the idea of ambitious teaching takes on some new meanings for us. Certainly, these teachers confirm the widely accepted notion that ambitious teaching is focused on student success, as well as on the preservation of the social studies as a distinct and necessary discipline. Yet, as Grant (2003) and Grant and VanSledright (2005) and others in this volume have demonstrated, ambitious teaching cannot be defined simply on the basis of a set of external criteria, although such criteria can be quite useful. What struck us about these two teachers, however, is the *personal* and *contextual* nature of ambitious teaching. Here the teachers' similarities emerge clearly.

First, both teachers seem to possess an intense personal drive to find ways to make the FCAT work for them and to not allow the test to completely dictate the nature of their work. In short, they refuse to let the FCAT diminish their enjoyment of the art of teaching. At Isabel's school, daily FCAT practice becomes mandated following the shock of getting a D from the state. However, FCAT preparation has become such an ingrained priority among the entire faculty and student body that they simply accept the test as a fact of life and get on with their tasks. At Suzanne's school, the faculty and students seem either complacent about or hostile to the FCAT. But Suzanne, after a brief period of FCAT "culture shock," rebels against the competing pressures from her colleagues to succumb to the easy path of mindless test preparation activities or to ignore the test altogether, both of which paths she believes are detrimental to her students.

Second, both teachers demonstrate an ambition that is geared toward the particular contexts in which they work. Clearly, Isabel's and Suzanne's school settings and student populations differ such that what may seem ambitious to Isabel may make no sense to Suzanne, and the reverse. Yet they both work hard to understand their students' needs and abilities, to set realistic goals for what they can accomplish, and to push their students to become engaged in the history content rather than "just sit there" filling out worksheets. Nor does either teacher want to "just sit there" grading test-based worksheets; taking the path of least resistance is inconceivable.

These similarities notwithstanding, the two teachers demonstrate some key differences of a personal and contextual nature.

Isabel, the more experienced of the two teachers, works in a much more collegial environment than does Suzanne, and she reports having numerous, in-depth professional development opportunities related to reading and writing strategies. Her school administrators have articulated—in fact, demanded—clear achievement goals for the teachers and the students. FCAT rhetoric is a daily part of school lesson plans, assemblies, the Reading Rocks program, and even announcements on the school television broadcasts. Consequently, Isabel is able to articulate a strong, clearly elucidated purpose for her social studies teaching. At her school, there is no doubt that the FCAT comes first and the content second. In our conversations with her, Isabel implies that her personal feelings about the FCAT are beside the point. The test is here to stay, she and her students must deal with it, and she is intent upon making it work for them both.

Suzanne, on the other hand, struggles with the challenges typical of a beginning teacher whose assignment involves content with which she is relatively unfamiliar. In the absence of strong administrative leadership and/or directives at her school, and in the midst of an FCAT-hostile school culture that leaves her feeling isolated, she adopts a strategy of mastering the content first, the reading and writing skills second. At the same time, she tries to tie these two elements together instead of treating them as discrete goals. Her articulated instructional purposes focus on "relevance" and "perspectives" in the history curriculum. Clearly, she is still grappling with the implications and the influence of the test, and she certainly lacks the professional development opportunities afforded to Isabel that might provide more subject-specific reading/writing strategies. And yet it is this uncertain, rookie teacher who embraces the opportunity to remake the state policies to be more in line with her purposes.

And so it seems that one of the most striking differences between these two teachers is their expressed purpose or aim (Barton & Levstik, 2004). While Isabel expresses a definite moral bent exemplified in her inclusion of certain topics, Suzanne is more discipline-oriented. It seems reasonable to assume that their respective aims influence how the teachers interpret the role of the test in their practices. Thus, we see Isabel's focus on "making better people" driving her to compensate for what she knows her students are not getting outside of school and to ensure that her students will be functional, productive members of society through improvement in their literacy skills. And we see Suzanne's focus on "perspectives" driving her to infuse these into her curriculum via primary sources, which she believes will help her students better understand the world and which can be used as a vehicle for developing students' reading and writing skills.

CONCLUSIONS

Although in different ways, both of these teachers are ambitious in their efforts to find ways to make the FCAT work. But their different purposes, contexts, and levels of experience lead us to ask: How do we recruit and retain new teachers in the FCAT environment? In light of the fact that social studies is not currently on the state test, how can we show them that they do not have to give up on the idea of teaching their content even while practicing FCAT skills? How can we make meaningful social studies reading and writing activities a part of their daily instructional routines, instead of reinforcing the notion that practicing such skills constitutes a discrete mandate that must take over their lives and render their content useless? How do we encourage these teachers to be defenders of their discipline as well as facilitators of achievement on standards and tests, regardless of the idiosyncrasies of their individual school environments? In other words, how do we help teachers remake the policy to fit what we know are wise practices?

We believe that both of these teachers provide useful models of how to discuss these questions with preservice teachers in terms of the personal and contextual issues involved in any attempt to accommodate a standardized test, as well as the specific coping strategies each teacher uses to facilitate student achievement. Despite their differences, both Isabel's and Suzanne's approaches describe realistic FCAT experiences. The integration of their experiences into a social studies teacher education program could provide preservice teachers with the highly explicit, content-based reading strategies that Isabel embraces, while also pushing them towards Suzanne's more perspective-driven approach that requires students to activate their reading and writing skills to engage in historical inquiry. Thus, we now believe more deeply in the importance of developing reading/writing skills with primary and secondary sources, and learning to ask historical questions, in the methods course, infusing and modeling the strategies that Isabel uses, but also with the attention to content that Suzanne emphasizes.

As teacher educators, we need to spend time reflecting on our own practice with regard to the issue of teaching skills versus maintaining content integrity. In other words, our task has become more difficult. Although it is fascinating, for example, to have students read a wide variety of perspectives on the dropping of the atomic bomb and to frame important questions as a means of understanding this event, we also have to keep in mind that such an activity will be useless and frustrating to beginning teachers if they are not equipped with methods to scaffold these readings for their students.

The larger question that we need to deal with in social studies teacher education is how these tests influence our work. Without a doubt, accountability related to high-stakes testing and mandatory state standards is on the rise in Florida and shows no sign of going away. These accountability measures exert a definite influence upon Isabel's and Suzanne's classrooms. Moreover, it seems clear that truly ambitious teaching takes on a significant level of difficulty and complexity in the potentially schizophrenic environment of high-stakes accountability in Florida. The two teachers described in this chapter, as well as a great many others, hold the potential to be powerful advocates of ambitious, effective, and challenging social studies teaching in an uncertain, frustrating time. Certainly, the simple fact that these two teachers have chosen to work in challenging settings, and that they do so gladly and energetically, reflects a form of ambitiousness in itself. Working with Isabel and Suzanne has planted the questions above firmly in our consciousness and causes us to rethink how we structure our teacher education programs. Most important, they show us that the concept of ambitious teaching includes both personal and contextual dimensions, and that we must take these dimensions into consideration in order to ensure that our preservice teachers are afforded the opportunities and support they need to fulfill their potential as effective social studies educators with strong professional identities.

REFERENCES

Adler, S. A. (1993). Teacher education: Research as reflective practice. *Teaching and Teacher Education, 9,* 159–167.

Barton, K. C., & Levstik, L. S. (2004). *Teaching history for the common good.* Mahwah, NJ: Erlbaum.

Brighton, C. M. (2002). Straddling the fence: Implementing best practices in an age of accountability. *Gifted Child Today Magazine, 25*(3), 30–33.

Cherryholmes, C. H. (1971). *Toward a theory of social education.* Publication of the Office of Education (DHEW), Washington, DC. (Eric Document Reproduction Service No. ED065373). Retrieved from http://newfirstsearch.altip.oclc.org.lp.hscl.ufl.edu/WebZ/FSFETCH?fetchtype=fullrecord:sessionid=sp03sw05-62258-eae4g17r-jdsffd:entitypagenum=8:0:recno=2:resultset=2:format=FI:next=html/record.html:bad=error/badfetch.html:entitytoprecno=2:entitycurrecno=2:numrecs=1

Darling-Hammond, L. (1998). Teacher learning that supports student learning. *Educational Leadership, 55*(5), 6–11.

Davis, O. L., Jr. (1997). Beyond "best practices" toward "wise practices." *Journal of Curriculum and Supervision, 13*, 1–5.

Dobbs, O. (2003). *Using reading strategies to reduce the failure rate in the content area. Subject: Social studies. Grade level: 6–7–8*. Publication of the Georgia State Department of Education. Retrieved from http://newfirstsearch.altip .oclc.org.lp.hscl.ufl.edu/WebZ/FSQUERY?format=BI:next=html/records .html:bad=html/records.html:numrecs=10:sessionid= sp03sw05-33702-eae1yy85-u19njz:entitypagenum=2:0:searchtype=basic

Dodge, K. A., & Price, J. M. (1994). On the relation between social information processing and socially competent behavior in early school-aged children. *Child Development, 65*(5), 1385–1397.

Education Trust. (2002, August 8). *The funding gap: Students who need the most get the least. New school finance data analysis shows deep inequities, but gaps in some states decreasing*. Retrieved from http://www2.edtrust.org/EdTrust/ Press+Room/funding+gap.htm

Fehn, B., & Koeppen, K. (1998). Intensive document-based instruction in a social studies methods course and student teachers' attitudes and practice in subsequent field experiences. *Theory and Research in Social Education, 26*(4), 461–484.

Feldman, S. (1997). Passing on failure. *American Educator, 21*(3), 4–10.

Florida Department of Education. (2005). *History of statewide assessment program (HSAP)*. Retrieved from http://www.firn.edu/doe/sas/hsap/hsap9000 .htm#1995

Foster, S. T., & Hoge, J. D. (2000). Dismantling the wall, one brick at a time: Overcoming barriers to parochialism in social studies classrooms. *Social Education, 64*(6), 368–370.

Franklin, J. H. (1993). The Emancipation Proclamation: An act of justice. *Prologue, Quarterly of the National Archives, 25*(2), 149-154.

Grant, S. G. (2003). *History lessons: Teaching, learning, and testing in U.S. high school classrooms*. Mahwah, NJ: Erlbaum.

Grant, S. G., & VanSledright, B. A. (2005). *Elementary social studies: Constructing a powerful approach to teaching and learning*. (2nd ed.). Boston: Houghton Mifflin.

Hoge, J. D. (2000, November). *Best practices in elementary social studies*. Paper presented at the annual meeting of the National Council for the Social Studies, San Antonio, TX.

Iozzi, L. A., & Cheu, J. (1978, October). *Preparing for tomorrow's world: An alternative curriculum model for the secondary schools*. Paper presented at first annual conference of the Education Section of the World Future Society, Clear Lake City, TX.

Irvin, J., Lunstrum, J., Lynch-Brown, C., & Shepard, M. (1995). *Enhancing social studies through literacy strategies* (Bulletin 91). National Council for the Social Studies Bulletin. Retrieved from http://newfirstsearch.altip.oclc.org.lp.hscl .ufl.edu/WebZ/FSFETCH?fetchtype=fullrecord:sessionid =sp03sw05-33702-eae1yy85-u19njz:entitypagenum=

98:0:recno=1:resultset=24:format=FI:next=html/record.html:bad=error/
badfetch.html:entitytoprecno=1:entitycurrecno=1:numrecs=1

Kameenui, E., & Carnine, D. (1998). *Effective teaching strategies that accommodate diverse learners*. Des Moines, IA: Prentice Hall.

Kvale, S. (1994, April). *Validation as communication and action: On the social construction of validity*. Paper presented at the Annual Meeting of the American Educational Research Association, New Orleans, LA.

Lawson, H. (1992). Beyond the new conception of teacher induction. *Journal of Teacher Education, 43*(3), 163–172.

Lippitt, R. O. (1969). *The socialization community: Resources in education*. Ann Arbor: University of Michigan.

McElroy, J. C., & Downey, H. K.. (1982). Observation in organizational research: Panacea to the performance-attribution effect? *The Academy of Management Journal, 25*(4), 822–835.

McNeil, L. M. (2000). *Contradictions of school reform: Educational costs of standardized testing*. New York: Routledge.

Miles, M. B., & Huberman, A. M. (1994). *Qualitative data analysis*. Thousand Oaks, CA: Sage.

National Council for the Social Studies. (1994). *Expectations of excellence: Curriculum standards for social studies*. Washington, DC: Author.

Patrick, J., & Leming, R. S. (Eds.). (2001). *Principles and practices of democracy in the education of social studies teachers: Civic learning in teacher education*. Bloomington, IN: ERIC Clearinghouse for Social Studies/Social Science Education.

Purkey, W., & Stanley, P. (1991). *Invitational teaching, learning, and living: Analysis and action series*. West Haven, CT: NEA Professional Library.

Riley, K., Wilson, E., & Fogg, T. (2000). Transforming the spirit of teaching through wise practice: Observations of two Alabama social studies teachers. *Social Education 64*(6), 361–363.

Rust, F. (1994). The first year of teaching: It's not what they expected. *Teaching & Teacher Education, 10*(2), 205–217.

Sandman, J. (1994, March). *"What can we reasonably expect at the end of freshman composition?"* Paper presented at the annual meeting of the Conference on College Composition and Communication, Nashville, TN.

Segall, A. (2003). The impact of state-mandated testing according to social studies teachers: The Michigan Educational Assessment Program (MEAP) as a case study of consequences. *Theory and Research in Social Education, 31*(3), 287–325.

Seixas, P. (1998a). Forces for change in the teaching and learning of history. *Canadian Social Studies, 32*(2), 44–68.

Seixas, P. (1998b). Student teachers thinking historically. *Theory and Research in Social Education, 26(3),* 310–341.

Shulman, L. (1987). Knowledge and teaching: Foundations of the new reform. *Harvard Educational Review, 57*(1), 1–22.

Stake, R. E. (1995). *The art of case study research*. Thousand Oaks, CA: Sage.

Stone, R. (2002). *Best practices for high school classrooms: What award-winning secondary teachers do*. Thousand Oaks, CA: Corwin Press.

Thornton, S. J. (1999, November). *Method in an age of national standards.* Paper presented at the annual meeting of the College and University Faculty Assembly of the National Council for the Social Studies, Orlando, FL.

Thornton, S. J. (2000, November). *The pedagogical demands of subject matter: Implications for teacher education.* Paper presented at the annual meeting of the College and University Faculty Assembly of te National Council for the Social Studies, Alexandria, VA.

White, J. J. (1987). The teacher as broker of scholarly knowledge. *Journal of Teacher Education, 38*, 19–24.

Work, B. (Ed.). (2002). *Learning through the eyes of a child: A guide to best teaching practices in early education.* Publication of North Carolina State Dept. of Public Instruction, Raleigh. Early Childhood Section. (Eric Document Reproduction Service No. ED472193).

Wright, W. E. (2002, June 5). The effects of high stakes testing in an inner-city elementary school: The curriculum, the teachers, and the English language learners. *Current Issues in Education, 5*(5). Retrieved from http://cie.ed.asu.edu/volume5/number5

Yeager, E. A. (2000). Thoughts on wise practice in the teaching of social studies. *Social Education, 64*, 352–353.

Yeager, E. A., & Davis, O. L. (1994, April). *Understanding the "knowing how" of history: Elementary student teachers' thinking about historical texts.* Paper presented at the Annual Meeting of the American Educational Research Association, New Orleans, LA.

Yeager, E. A., & Davis, O. L.. (1995). Between campus and classroom: Secondary student-teachers' thinking about historical texts. *Journal of Research and Development in Education, 29*(1), 1–8.

Yeager, E. A., & Davis, O. L.. (Eds.). (2005). *Wise social studies teaching in an age of high stakes testing: Essays on classroom practices and possibilities.* Greenwich, CT: Information Age.

Yeager, E. A., & E. Wilson. (1997). Teaching historical thinking in the social studies methods course: A case study. *Social Studies, 88*(3), 121–126.

CHAPTER 13

THE IMPACT OF A HIGH SCHOOL GRADUATION EXAMINATION ON MISSISSIPPI SOCIAL STUDIES TEACHERS' INSTRUCTIONAL PRACTICES

Kenneth Vogler

I use the entire academic year preparing my students for the United States history subject area exam. My choice of instructional delivery and materials is completely dependent on preparation for this test. Therefore, I do not use current events, long-term projects, or creative group/corporate work because this is not tested and the delivery format is not used. All my tests reflect the testing format of the subject area tests- multiple-choice and open ended questions. This delivery and curriculum format is not used in my other classes (United State Government and Economics). In these non-tested classes, I do use a variety of instructional methods and curriculum resources. While I agree with the principle of student/teacher/administrator accountability, but by making the goal of my United States history course the ability to pass the state test, I'm afraid that all meaningfulness and relevancy to history is being lost on my students. As a result, they have a better factual base but a worse conceptual understanding of the subject and what it is good for.

—*A Mississippi High School United States History Teacher*

Measuring History: Cases of State-Level Testing Across the United States, 273–302
Copyright © 2006 by Information Age Publishing
All rights of reproduction in any form reserved.

The high school history teacher's comments above echo a frustration felt by many Mississippi U.S. History teachers. On the one hand, these teachers want to use instructional practices that make their classes interesting, develop students' higher-level thinking skills, and at least spark students' interest in the subject. On the other hand, these teachers have the immense responsibility to prepare their students for the examination. Failure to do so may put in jeopardy their students' ability to earn a high school diploma and their regard as effective teachers.

The impact of a high-stakes high school graduation examination on teachers' instructional practices is a relevant concern, with, as of yet, no clear consensus as to what the impact is. Although researchers such as Barksdale-Ladd and Thomas (2000), Jones and Johnston (2002), McNeil (2000), Vogler (2002), and Yarbrough (1999) have found that teachers change their instructional practices in response to high-stakes testing, there is still considerable ambiguity about the nature and intensity of this relationship (Firestone, Monfils, Camilli, Schorr, Hicks, & Mayrowetz, 2002; Grant, 2001). Factors such as subject and grade level taught, personal beliefs, type of high-stakes assessment, and professional development all have the potential to impact this relationship in varying degrees (Cimbricz, 2002; Jones, Jones, & Hargrove, 2003).

The purpose of this chapter is to explore further the impact of high-stakes tests on teachers' instructional practices. This study focuses on the instructional practices used and factors influencing their use by Mississippi social studies teachers who teach under their state's high school graduation examination. Employing a state-wide teacher survey, I designed the study to answer the following questions:

Central question:

> In what manner does a high school graduation examination influence instructional practices?

Additional questions include the following:

1. What instructional practices do teachers use?
2. How often do teachers use these instructional practices?
3. What factors have influenced their use?

I begin with a brief review of testing policies and accountability systems and the history of Mississippi's high school graduation examination. Then I describe the research method and examine the results of the study's central question and three additional questions.

TESTING POLICIES AND ACCOUNTABILITY SYSTEMS

Accountability, high standards, and curriculum alignment are just a few of the terms used in conjunction with the newest method to reform public schools—state-level testing. The reauthorization of the Elementary and Secondary Education Act (1965) and its instantiation in No Child Left Behind (2001) is an example of the tremendous confidence policymakers such as the President of the United States and members of Congress have in testing and assessment systems to improve public education.

According to Natriello and Pallas (1999), there are three very compelling reasons for policymakers to justify the use of statewide testing and accountability systems. First, testing has the potential to influence the behavior of students, teachers, and administrators. For students, individual test results can help pinpoint areas in which they need additional instruction. For teachers and administrators, test results allow the public to scrutinize and compare the achievement of students under their charge with student achievement in other public schools. Second, attaching stakes such as high school graduation to the results of testing and accountability systems assures the public of a basic level of competency for high school graduates. Finally, testing has an inherent efficiency and scientific legitimacy as a performance monitoring process. The ratio of information gathered to expenses incurred as well as the ability to assess the validity and reliability of scores generated by standardized measures seem to make testing and accountability systems a very inexpensive investment.

Besides the inherent benefits as seen by policymakers, proponents of testing and accountability systems generally fall into two camps (Firestone et al., 2002). The first group focuses on the accountability of testing programs. This group believes that the way to improve education is to test and use the results to hold teachers and students accountable for their actions. The form of the assessment is not as important as the rewards or sanctions attached to the test results (National Alliance of Business, 2000).

The second camp also believes that the use of testing and accountability systems is a sure way to improve education. But for this group, the key to improving education is not the rewards or sanctions attached to the test results, but the tests themselves. They contend that tests can serve as "powerful curricular magnets" (Popham, 1987, p. 680), and that standardized assessments can guide the educational system to be more productive and effective (Popham, 1987). This group believes that the use of assessment systems such as portfolios, performance assessments, and other forms of authentic tasks will spur teachers to focus on more than just facts and procedures and help students construct knowledge and developing higher level thinking skills (Baron & Wolf, 1996; Bracey,

1987a, 1987b; Newmann & Associates, 1996; Resnick & Resnick, 1992; Rothman, 1995).

Opponents of testing and assessment systems believe that contrary to the idea of promoting constructivist teaching and high level thinking, state-level assessments force teachers to focus on facts and procedures without meaning or context (Firestone et al., 2002; McNeil, 2000). They argue that these high-stakes assessments create negative side effects such as narrowing the curriculum, de-skilling teachers, pushing students out of school, and inciting fear and anxiety among students and teachers (Darling-Hammond & Wise, 1985; Gilman & Reynolds, 1991; Jones & Whitford, 1997; Madaus, 1988a, 1988b; McNeil, 2000; Shepard, 1989). These observers argue that the side effects outweigh any possible benefits of measurement-driven reform.

Between the proponents and opponents of testing and accountability systems lies a third, more moderate group. These researchers assert that the effects of testing depend not on the tests themselves but on factors relating to their implementation (Firestone et al., 2002; Grant, 2003). These factors include how tests are interpreted by teachers and administrators, the content knowledge assessed, and the opportunities teachers have to learn about and try out instructional practices in preparation for the exams (Borko & Putnam, 1995; Cohen & Hill, 1998; McLaughlin, 1990; Saxe, Franke, Gearhart, Howard, & Michele, 1997; Supovitz, Mayer, & Kahle, 2000).

The presumed linchpin of testing and accountability systems are the stakes attached to test scores. These stakes include incentives such as cash awards to schools or individual teachers who demonstrate high levels of student performance. They may also mean consequences for schools, individual teachers, and students such as publishing test results, delaying grade-to-grade promotion, taking over schools that continue to demonstrate low levels of student performance, and putting off high school graduation. Currently, 20 states require students to pass a statewide exit or end of course examination to receive a high school diploma. But of these 20 states, only Georgia, Louisiana, Mississippi, New Mexico, and New York include passing an examination on social studies as a high school graduation requirement (Skinner & Staresina, 2004).

HISTORY OF THE MISSISSIPPI HIGH SCHOOL GRADUATION EXAMINATION

In response to the minimum competency movement in the late 1970s and early 1980s, the Mississippi Department of Education created the Mississippi Curriculum Content Assessment System (MCCAS) under the state's

1982 Educational Reform Act (Marchette, 2003). The MCCAS was designed to: (a) compare the performance of Mississippi school districts and schools to national normative data, (b) evaluate the performance of Mississippi schools and districts in teaching the Mississippi Curriculum Framework (see Appendix A), (c) improve instructional practices in schools and districts, (d) provide an important part of the accountability system for schools and districts, (e) evaluate the strengths, weaknesses and proficiency levels of individual students, and (f) create benchmarks for student performance (Marchette, 2003). By 1989, students were required to pass the Functional Literacy Examination (FLE) for high school graduation (Jacob, 2001). The FLE used multiple-choice questions in reading, mathematics, and written communications and a writing prompt (Mississippi Department of Education, 2004a).

In 2000, under State Board of Education Policy IHF-1, the Subject Area Testing Program (SATP) was designated to replace the FLE as a requirement for high school graduation (Mississippi Department of Education, 2004b). The SATP consists of end-of-course, criterion-referenced tests in Algebra I, Biology I, United States History from 1877–present, and English (Mississippi Department of Education, 2004c). In August 2001, the Mississippi Board of Education approved the results of the SATP standard setting, and thus began the phase-in process (Mississippi Department of Education, 2004d). In 2002, the social studies portion of the SATP was implemented (see Appendix B) (Mississippi Department of Education, 2004d). Students now must pass the United States History from 1877–present SATP examination in order to graduate from high school.

METHODOLOGY

A survey instrument (Appendix C) was used to answer the research questions. As discussed above, factors such as subject and grade level taught, personal beliefs, type of high-stakes assessment, and professional development can have an impact on the relationship between high-stakes testing and teachers' instructional practices. The survey instrument was designed to provide data clarifying these relationships.

The survey instrument includes three broad categories: Part I asks about teachers' instructional practices and the extent to which they are used; Part II asks about factors influencing instructional practices used; and Part III asks for demographic information. Also, included is a section asking if and how much instructional time is spent preparing students for the high school graduation examination. Finally, there is a section called "Comments" which offers respondents an opportunity to talk at greater length about the instructional practices they use to prepare students for the high school graduation examination.

Survey Instrument's Validity and Reliability

I took two approaches to ascertain the validity and reliability of the survey instrument. First, I sought evidence for the content validity of the 54 items on the initial draft of the survey instrument. Because this chapter is part of a larger study about the impact of a graduation examination on English, science, mathematics, and social studies teachers' instructional practices, 36 high school teachers (nine English, nine science, nine mathematics, and nine social studies) reviewed the items on the survey instrument for clarity and completeness in coverage of the instructional practices used and possible influences. Using their recommendations, the number of items on the survey instrument was reduced to 48.

Second, 34 different high school teachers (nine English, seven science, nine mathematics, and nine social studies) completed the revised 48-item survey instrument. These same 34 teachers completed the revised survey again following a 3-week interval. Reliability was assessed by comparing each teacher's responses. Sixty-four percent of the teachers had exact matches for all items; 88% of the matches were within one point on the six point scale, and 92% of the matches were within one point on the five point scale.

Sample Selection

The study sample features a stratified random sample of high school social studies teachers using geographic region and past student success on the SATP. First, school systems were grouped according to geographic region: East, Middle, and West Mississippi. Second, the school systems in each region were ranked according to student success on the latest (2002–2003) SATP. Quartiles were generated using this ranking. At least four, but no more than six school systems from each quartile participated in the study.

A total of 55 school systems agreed to participate in the study. All high school social studies teachers teaching United States History 1877–present from each participating school system were given the survey instrument by their principals. The content covered in this course, according to the Mississippi State Framework, is the basis for the SATP. One hundred and seven teachers, or 63.7% of the total population surveyed, completed and returned the survey.

**Table 13.1.   Comparison of Survey Response Sample and
Mississippi High School United States History
Teacher Population for Gender**

Gender	Survey Response Sample %	State Population %
Female	47.751	47.1192
Male	52.356	52.9216

**Table 13.2.   Comparison of Survey Response Sample and
Mississippi High School United States History
Teacher Population for Teaching Experience**

Teaching Expereience	Survey Response Sample %	State Population %
0–6 years	26.228	39.6162
7–14 years	28.030	20.2081
15–24 years	22.424	16.6068
25+ years	23.425	23.6097

**Table 13.3.   Comparison of Survey Response Sample and
Mississippi High School United States History
Teacher Population for Education**

Education	Survey Response Sample	State Population
Bachelor's	58.963	62.5255
Master's	37.440	35.8146
Specialist's	02.803	01.5006
Doctorate	00.901	00.2001

I compared survey respondents with the state's teaching population using data obtained from Part III of the survey instrument and the Mississippi Department of Education. Table 13.1 is a comparison of the frequency distribution showing the survey response sample and the Mississippi high school United States history teacher population for gender. The demographic variable teaching experience is compared in Table 13.2. Table 13.3 presents the frequency distribution between the survey sample and the Mississippi high school United States history teacher population for highest education level obtained. With the exception of a slightly lower percentage of teachers with 0–6 years of experience, Tables 13.1–13.3 show that participants in this study represent the Mississippi high school United States history teaching population in terms of gender, teaching experience, and highest level of education attained.

Data Analysis

My analysis of the data began by computing frequency and means on questions in Parts I and II of the survey instrument, followed by a frequency analysis on questions in Part III of the instrument. For Part I, instructional practices, data analysis determined the instructional practices teachers used and the extent to which those practices were used. For Part II, factors influencing instructional practices, data analysis determined which factors have the greatest influence on teachers' instructional practices. For Part III, demographic information, a frequency analysis determined a profile of the respondents.

Chi-square analysis is a useful means of uncovering relationships among variables. My first chi-square analysis looked at the relationship between the teachers' demographic information (Part III) and their instructional practices (Part I). I followed this task with another chi-square analysis between the demographic information (Part III) and the factors influencing teachers' instructional practices (Part II). The third chi-square analysis explored the relationship between respondents who acknowledged spending instructional time preparing students for the high school graduation examination and the instructional practices they reported using. Finally, I conducted a chi-square analysis between respondents acknowledging spending instructional time preparing students for the high school graduation examination and the factors they believe influence their instructional practices. For each calculation, categories were collapsed, if necessary, to meet requirements for a chi-square analysis.

Finally, I analyzed and grouped responses in the "Comments" section according to content expressed. The groupings included timing of the test, teacher frustration, and clarifying instructional practices used.

RESULTS

I begin this section with a preview of the study's most interesting results. First, in what I call the persistence of traditional, teacher-centered practices, teachers report that they most often use textbooks, multiple-choice questions, open-response questions, visual aids, lecturing, and textbook-based assignments, while they least use instructional practices such as role playing, project-based assignments, interdisciplinary instruction, and problem-solving activities. Second, in what I conclude as the correlation between teacher-centered practices and test preparation, 89 teachers (83.2%) acknowledge spending class time preparing students for the high school graduation examination. Teachers spending over 2 months preparing students for the graduation examination are more likely to use more textbooks, multiple-choice questions, visual aids, textbook-based assignments, rubrics or scoring guides, and worksheets and are less likely to use creative/critical thinking questions, project-based assignments, group projects, true-false questions, and role playing than teachers spending 1 day to 2 months preparing students for the examination. Teachers spending 1 day to 2 months preparing students for the graduation examination typically use more open-response questions and creative/critical thinking questions, and fewer lessons-based on current events, cooperative learning/group work, newspaper and magazines, computers/internet and education software, and interdisciplinary instruction than the other group. Third, in what I describe as the powerful influence of high-stakes testing, teachers overwhelmingly feel that their instructional practices are more influenced by sanctions attached to the high-stakes test scores than by factors such as personal beliefs. An "interest in helping my students attain test scores that will allow them to graduate high school" and an "interest in helping my school improve high school graduation scores" were the most commonly reported influences.

The Persistence of Traditional, Teacher-Centered Practices

Before I discussing Part I of the survey, the instructional practices used, I think it best to first have an understanding of the teaching methods most understood to be most effective for student learning. Researchers have identified two general methods or approaches to teaching—student-centered and teacher-centered (Airasian & Walsh, 1997; Eggen & Kauchak, 2001).

Student-centered teaching can be thought of as an application of a constructivist theory of student learning. Constructivists believe that students actively construct their knowledge through interacting with their physical and social environments (Piaget, 1973; Vygotsky, 1978), rather than act as empty vessels into which knowledge is poured. The other approach to teaching is called teacher-centered. This approach places the teacher at the center of all activities during instruction (Jones, Jones, & Hargrove, 2003). Typically, this method of instruction includes a preponderance of practices such as lecture, lecture and discussion, and direct instruction (Eggen & Kauchak, 2001). The survey data support the finding that respondents are using more teacher-centered instructional practices than student-centered instruction.

A Preference for Teacher-Centered Practices.

Tables 13.4 and 13.5 present a picture of the instructional practices and tools being used and not being used by the survey respondents.

Table 13.4 represents those practices respondents reported using regularly or often. Table 13.5 represents those practices that teachers reported using less often or not at all.2

By implication, the data in Tables 13.4 and 13.5 provide a glimpse into which teaching approach, student-centered or teacher-centered, is more often used by Mississippi history teachers.[3] An analysis of the data supports the conclusion that the survey respondents largely favor more traditional, teacher-centered approaches over student-centered prac-

Table 13.4.   Regularly and Mostly Use Instructional Practice or Tool

Instructional Practice or Tool	Mean	SE	SD	% Reg. Use	% Mostly Use	Total % Reg. and Mostly Use
Textbooks	4.38	.06	0.68	47.7	46.7	94.4
Multiple-choice questions	4.28	.06	0.71	47.7	41.1	88.8
Open-response questions	4.11	.07	0.75	53.3	30.8	84.1
Visual aids	4.07	.07	0.78	54.2	29.0	83.2
Lecturing	4.03	.08	0.85	54.2	28.0	82.2
Textbook-based assignments	4.00	.08	0.90	47.7	30.8	78.5
Supplementary materials	3.97	.06	0.67	65.4	17.8	83.2
Audiovisual materials	3.86	.07	0.79	46.7	21.5	68.2
Charts/webs/outlines	3.83	.09	0.94	39.6	26.4	66.0
Writing assignments	3.79	.05	0.59	66.4	07.5	73.9
Creative/critical thinking quest	3.75	.07	0.76	54.2	13.1	67.3
Rubrics or scoring guides	3.64	.10	1.09	42.1	21.5	63.6
Worksheets	3.32	.10	1.05	39.0	10.5	49.5

**Table 13.5.   Occasionally, Rarely and
Don't Use Instructional Practice or Tool**

Instructional Practice or Tool	Mean	SE	SD	% Occas. Use	% Rarely Use	% Don't Use	Total % Occas., Rarely, and Don't Use
Lessons-based on current events	3.25	.08	0.84	47.7	15.9	09.9	64.5
Coop. learning/ group work	3.24	.08	0.83	50.0	07.5	04.7	62.7
Discussion groups	3.23	.09	0.94	44.9	13.1	04.7	62.7
Modeling	3.18	.08	0.86	40.0	14.3	04.8	59.1
Inquiry/investigation	3.09	.08	0.91	44.3	17.9	03.8	66.0
Newspaper/magazines	3.07	.07	0.80	45.8	22.4	00.9	69.1
Computers/Internets	3.03	.09	0.92	44.9	19.6	04.7	69.2
Problem-solving activities	2.96	.10	1.03	37.1	25.7	05.7	68.5
Interdisciplinary instruction	3.83	.09	0.95	41.1	21.5	07.5	70.1
Computers/educational software	2.94	.09	1.00	39.6	26.4	06.6	72.6
Project-based assignments	2.93	.09	0.97	42.1	25.2	06.5	73.8
Group projects	2.83	.08	0.89	54.2	20.6	08.4	83.2
True-false questions	2.32	.10	1.11	23.4	37.4	25.2	86.0
Role playing	2.15	.10	1.08	18.9	36.8	32.1	87.8
Response journal	2.00	.10	1.08	21.7	25.5	43.4	90.6

tices. First, teachers (94.4%) report that textbooks are, by far, the most commonly used instructional practice. This finding is followed by instructional practices or tools such as multiple-choice questions (88.8%), visual aids (83.2%), supplementary materials (83.2%), lecturing (82.3%), and textbook–based assignments (78.5%). These practices and tools are typical of a teacher-centered approach. In fact, of the first seven instructional practices or tools respondents report using most, only open-response questions (84.1%) can be considered instruction in line with a student-centered approach. Second, respondents report spending the least amount of instructional time using response journals (90.6%), role playing (87.8%), true-false question (86%), group projects (83.2%), project-based assignments (73.8%), computers/educational software (72.6%), interdisciplinary instruction (70.1%), and problem-solving activities (68.5%). With the exception of true-false questions, the instructional practices used least are student-centered approaches.

Minimal Demographic Differences in Instructional Preferences

I conducted a number of cross-tabulations and chi-square analyses to determine if any significant differences arose between the instructional practices used or not used and the demographic categories. Table 13.6 represents statistically significant instructional preferences divided along gender lines. Table 13.7 represents statistically significant practices broken down by years of experience. Categories were "collapsed"[4] to meet the statistical requirements for a chi square analysis. As evident in these analyses, although there are some statistically significant differences such as a greater percentage of females regularly or mostly use project-based assignments, charts/webs/outlines, and computers/internet than males and a greater percentage of teachers with 7-14 years of experience regularly or mostly use open-response questions than teachers with 15-24 years of experience, the effect is minimal. These exceptions aside, there are no glaring dissimilarities between the instructional practices or tools

**Table 13.6.   Percent of Regularly and
Mostly Use Instructional Practice or Tool by Gender**

Instructional Practice or Tool	Female	Male	Sig.	Effect
Project-based assignments	71.4%	28.6%	.003	.27
Charts/web/outlines	55.7%	44.3%	.004	.32
Computers/Internet	69.7%	30.3%	.002	.31

**Table 13.7.   Percent of Regularly and
Mostly Use Instructional Practice or Tool by Gender**

Instructional Practice or Tool	0–6 Years	7–14 Years	15–24 Years	25 Years	Sig.	Effect
Writng assignments	67.%	76.7%	58.3%	92.0%	.048	.27
Open-resource Questions	82.1%	100.0%	66.7%	84.0%	.011	.32
Computers/Internet	28.6%	16.7%	25.0%	56.0%	.013	.31

used or not used by any demographic group or by the response population as a whole.

An analysis of Part I of the survey instrument has shown two things. First, teachers are using instructional practices and tools more in line with a teacher-centered rather than a student-centered learning approach. Second, there are no real differences in the use of instructional practices across any demographic category. Mississippi teachers, then, consistently favor traditional over more ambitious instructional practices.

The Correlation Between Teacher-Centered Practices and Test Preparation

Questions #31 and #32 in the survey instrument ask about preparing students for the high school graduation examination. Eighty-nine respondents acknowledge spending instructional time preparing students for the high school graduation examination.[5] Table 13.8 compares the instructional practices and tools most used by respondents with the instructional time spent preparing students for the high school graduation examination.

**Table 13.8.   Comparison of Regularly and
Mostly Use Instructional Practice or Tool by Survey Respondents
Spending Instructional Time Preparing Students for Exam**

Instructional Practice or Tool	Total % Regularly and Mostly Use Time Preparing Students for Exam	
	1 Day to 2 Months	Over 2 Months
Textbooks	95.5	95.7
Multiple-choice questions	91.3	92.4
Open-resource questions	87.0	84.8
Visual aids	78.3	84.8
Lecturing	78.3	84.8
Textbook-based assignments	82.6	83.3
Supplementary materials	73.9	89.4
Audiovisual materials	65.2	71.2
Charts/webs/outlines	60.9	70.8
Writing assignments	60.9	78.8
Creative/critical thinking quest	78.3	59.1
Rubrics or scoring guides	56.5	65.2
Worksheets	48.4	56.5

**Table 13.9. Comparison of Occasionally, Rarely and
Don't Use Instructional Practice or Tool by Survey Respondents
Spending Instructional Time Preparing Students for Exam**

	Total % Occassionally, Rarely, and Don't Use Time Preparing Students for Exam	
Instructional Practice or Tool	*1 Day to 2 Months*	*Over 2 Months*
Response journal	91.3	87.9
Role playing	77.3	89.4
True-false questions	73.9	87.9
Group projects	78.3	83.3
Project-based assignments	65.2	80.3
Computers/educational software	78.3	70.8
Interdisciplinary instruction	73.9	69.7
Problem-solving activities	63.6	67.7
Computer/Internet	73.9	65.2
Newspaper/magazines	69.6	68.2
Inquiry/investigation	63.6	65.2
Modeling	54.6	58.2
Discussion groups	60.9	68.2
Coop. learning/group work	65.2	57.6
Lessons-based on current events	69.6	62.1

Table 13.9 compares the instructional practices and tools least used by survey respondents with the instructional time spent preparing students for the graduation exam.

Table 13.8 shows that teachers preparing their students for the high school graduation examination are using instructional practices and tools more in line with a teacher-centered learning approach rather than a student-centered approach. In fact, of the six instructional practices used most often, five are teacher-centered. And, as evidenced in Table 13.9, all 15 of the instructional practices and tools used the least by both groups of teachers are in line with a student-centered learning approach.

Looking more closely, it appears teachers who spend the most time preparing students for a high-stakes test are using a greater percentage of teacher-centered learning approaches. Table 13.8 shows that teachers spending over 2 months preparing their students for the high school graduation examination use a far greater percentage of teacher-centered instructional practices and tools such as textbooks (95.7%), multiple-choice question (92.4%), lecturing (84.8%), textbook-based assignments (83.3%), and worksheets (56.5%) than teachers spending 1 day to 2 months in test preparation. Moreover, student-centered instructional practices such as open-response questions, audiovisual materials, and charts/webs/outlines are being used the least by teachers spending over 2 months preparing their students for the high school graduation examination when compared to teachers spending 1 day to 2 months preparing students for the high-school graduation examination. In fact, teachers spending over 2 months preparing their students for the high-school examination report using creative/critical thinking questions (a student-centered instructional practice) almost 20% less than their peers. So, teachers spending the most amount of instructional time preparing their students for the high-school graduation examination are using a greater percentage of teacher-centered approaches.

I wondered what instructional practices were being used by teachers who did not use any instructional time preparing their students for the high school exam. Because only 18 respondents reported offering no test-preparation time, I included those who used the least amount of instructional time preparing their student for the high school graduation examination (1 day to 1 week) in these calculations. Combining these respondents brought the total to 30 teachers or 28% of the sample. Unfortunately, no clear pattern emerged. These teachers are using all the instructional strategies and tools listed in the survey instrument in varying degrees.

The Powerful Influence of High-Stakes Testing

Are Mississippi high school United States history teachers using more teacher-centered and less student-centered instructional practices and tools because of the graduation test, or are there other reasons? The research evidence is mixed with few studies looking directly at the relationship between teachers' practices and the influence of state-level tests on those practices.

Table 13.10 shows an analysis of Part II of the survey instrument, the factors influencing the instructional practices and tools respondents report using.[6]

A cursory examination of Table 13.10 reveals that 96.3% of respondents cite an "interest in helping my students attain test scores that will allow them to graduate high school" and 94.4% cite an "interest in helping my school improve high school graduation examination scores" as influences on the instructional practices they use. Following these factors are the "format of the high school graduation examination" (83.1%), "personal desire" (83.1%), and "belief these are the best instructional practices" (80.3%). The factors least influencing teachers' use of instruc-

Table 13.10.   Influence Factors

Item	Mean	SE	SD	% Agree	% Strongly Agree	Total % Agree
37. Interest in helping my students attain test scores that will allow them to graduate high school	4.60	.05	0.56	32.7	63.6	96.3
36. Interest in helping my school improve high school graduation examination scores	4.45	.06	0.63	43.0	51.4	96.4
35. Format of the high school graduation examination	4.11	.08	0.89	46.7	36.4	83.1
33. Personal desire	3.94	.09	0.99	55.7	27.4	83.1
34. Belief these are the best instructional practices	3.90	.08	0.92	57.9	22.4	80.3
41. Interactions with colleagues	3.75	.09	1.00	52.3	19.6	71.9
38. Interest in avaiding sanctions at my school	3.71	.12	1.25	39.3	29.9	69.2
42. Staff development in which I have participated	3.47	.11	1.18	50.5	14.0	64.5
40. Interactions with school principal(s)	3.45	.11	1.23	40.2	18.7	58.9
43. Interactions with parents	2.92	.12	1.25	31.8	08.4	40.2
39. Interest in obtaining a monetary award for my school	2.03	.11	1.17	12.3	02.8	15.1

tional practices are "interactions with parents" (40.2%) and an "interest in obtaining a monetary award for my school" (15.1%).

Note that the three test-related factors, "interest in helping my students attain test scores that will allow them to graduate high school," "interest in helping my school improve high school graduation examination scores," and the "format of the high school graduation examination" are reported as more influential than factors such as "personal desire" and "belief these are the best instructional practices" suggesting that the stakes attached (i.e., high school graduation) to the test have a greater influence on these teachers' instructional practices than do their own beliefs.

Table 13.11. Comparison of Influence Factors for Survey Respondents Spending Instructional Time Preparing Students for Exam

	Total % Agree Time Preparing Students for Exam	
Item	1 Day to 2 Months	Over 2 Months
37. Interest in helping my students attain test scores that will allow them to graduate high school	93.9	100.0
36. Interest in helping my school improve high school graduation examination scores	92.4	100.0
35. Format of the high school graduation examination	78.3	89.4
33. Personal desire	77.3	86.4
34. Belief these are the best instructional practices	73.3	83.3
41. Interactions with colleagues	69.6	69.7
38. Interest in avoiding sanctions at my school	78.3	68.2
42. Staff development in which I have participated	47.8	66.7
43. Interaction with parents	30.4	37.9
39. Interest in obtaining a monetary award for my school	08.7	16.7

I also compared the influence factors with respondents spending over 2 months and respondents spending 1 day to 2 months of instructional time in test preparation.

In Table 13.11, we see the impact that attaching stakes has on teachers who spend the most instructional time preparing their students for the state test. One hundred percent of respondents spending over 2 months preparing students for the graduation examination say that an "interest in helping my students attain test scores that will allow them to graduate high school" and an "interest in helping my school improve high school graduation scores" factor into their instructional practices. These two factors also appear to influence respondents spending far less time in test preparation. And, for all but one factor, "interest in avoiding sanctions at my school," the agreement is greater for respondents spending over 2 months of instructional time preparing their students for the high school graduation examination than for their peers.

Finally, I compared the various influences on teachers and respondents who either do not use or use relatively little instructional time (1 day to 1 week) preparing their students for the history test. The result shows little difference from the previous analysis: The influence these factors have on these teachers is remarkable similar to those teachers who spend a lot more instructional time in test preparation. One hundred percent of respondents who either do not use or use relatively little instructional time in test preparation state that an "interest in helping my students attain test scores that will allow them to graduate high school," and 96.6% agree that an "interest in helping my school improve high school graduation examination scores" influences their instructional practices. These influences are followed by "interaction with colleagues (76.6%),"personal desire" (73%), "belief these are the best instructional practices" (73%), "interest in avoiding sanctions at my school (70%), and "format of the high school graduation examination" (66%). The factors least influencing these teachers' use of instructional practices are "interactions with parents," (46.6%) and an "interest in obtaining a monetary award for my school" (13.3%).

Although Mississippi teachers indicate a heavy influence of state testing on their instructional choices, many are uncomfortable with this relationship. A male with a bachelor's degree and 0–6 years of experience notes, "unfortunately I must teach the test. We as teachers no longer have the freedom to do otherwise. It's all about test scores." A female with a master's degree and 0-6 years of experience declares:

> I despise the emphasis on testing and insistence we teach to the test. That is not teaching! That is spoon feeding! I am probably going to leave teaching because they don't allow time for creative, in-depth, critical thinking teaching.

A male with a bachelor's degree and 7–14 years of experience asserts:

> We have reverted to "drill and kill" which guarantees a minimum level of proficiency on the test. In order to pass a state examination, I must teach to the lowest common denominator, yet my principal and district superintendent pressure all schools in our district to have the highest test scores in the state. We no longer group students according to documented historical ability. Instead of a "smart" class and an "average" class, we are forced to use the same methods and techniques across the board. I'm afraid we stifle some of our students because of this.

Only one teacher offers a positive comment about the influence of state testing. A male with a master's degree and over 30 years of experience explains:

> I teach the content of the subject thoroughly, enthusiastically, daily. For 33 years I've completed every textbook, and there were many, every year at the rate of five pages per day. They [students] see everything. No, I don't specifically teach the test, but I do use the guide and sample tests they sent. The result, 94% passed last year, first try.

DISCUSSION

The purpose of this chapter is to explore the impact of high-stakes tests on teachers' instructional practices. This study focuses on the instructional practices used and factors influencing their use by Mississippi social studies teachers who teach under their state's high school graduation examination. From my analysis, three themes emerge: (1) the persistence of traditional, teacher-centered practices; (2) the correlation between teacher-centered practices and test preparation; (3) the powerful influence of high-stakes testing.

Mississippi teachers are far more likely to use traditional, teacher-centered practices than more ambitious, student-centered practices. But, what does this mean? If the question is which of these approaches, student-centered or teacher-centered, is most effective, the answer is both. Student-centered methods typically are more effective for teaching complex objectives and developing higher level thinking skills, and teacher-centered methods presumably are more effective for teaching procedural skills and organizing knowledge to review facts and identify relationships (Good & Brophy, 2000). Effective teachers use both methods, depending upon the needs of their students and objectives of each lesson (Airasian & Walsh, 1997; Pressley, Rankin, & Yokor, 1996; Zemelman, Daniels, & Hyde, 1998).

Although it is impossible to describe the perfect balance between student-centered and teacher-centered instruction due to factors such as subject, grade level, and lesson objectives (Jones, Jones, & Hargrove, 2003), research on best practices (Zemelman, Daniels, & Hyde, 1998; Wenglinsky, 2000) and position papers of professional teaching organization (e.g., National Council of Teachers of Mathematics and National Council of Social Studies) advocate instructional practices more connected to constructivist theory and student-centered methods. For example, according to the *National Standards for Social Studies Teachers: Volume 1* prepared by the National Council for the Social Studies:

> The primary teaching tasks of schools and teachers are (1) to provide constructivist-rich learning experiences, (2) to stimulate and guide learner constructivist thinking, and (3) to remember continuously that all members of the community—students, teachers, staff members, administrators, and parents—are learning all the time in their unique ways. (p. 11)

So, while educators recognize that both teacher-centered and student-centered approaches are effective for student learning, student-centered approaches encourage students to connect new ideas to their previous knowledge and experience, to think critically and creatively, and thereby develop higher-level thinking skills. Teacher-centered approaches, by contrast, may be most useful for developing lower-level skills such as identifying, memorizing, and listing information.

According to the data, Mississippi teachers use instructional practices and tools such as textbooks, multiple-choice questions, lecturing, and textbook-based assignments far more than role playing, project-based assignments, interdisciplinary instruction, and problem-solving activities. These results imply that respondents favor instructional approaches more in line with a teacher-centered learning approach. This persistence of traditional, teacher-centered practices rather than student-centered instruction flies in the face of ideas advanced by professional teaching organizations such as the National Council for the Social Studies and represents a style of instruction more suitable for developing lower-level learning. Teachers may perceive this type of instruction as useful for state-level tests, but it reduces history to merely a list of people, places, and dates rather than as an opportunity for students to experience history and use it as a bridge to connect all academic areas.

State-level tests in Mississippi matter considerably to teachers. Over 80% of the total sample acknowledge spending class time preparing students for the state exam. Comparisons between teachers spending 1 day to 2 months in test preparation and teachers spending over 2 months lead to the second theme—the correlation between teacher-centered practices and test preparation.

Teachers spending the most instructional time preparing their students for the graduation examination are far more likely to use teacher-centered approach than their peers. Presumably, these teachers feel that using teacher-centered instructional practices is the best way to prepare students for the test. According to the SATP test "blueprint" (Appendix B), this is probably an accurate assessment. The SATP United States history high school graduation examination asks 70 multiple-choice questions and one open response question. This type of test format can be read as requiring less of what Grant (2003) calls "ambitious teaching," and more teacher-centered instruction to achieve higher student test scores (Segall, 2003; Smith & Niemi, 2001).

I now focus on the issue of what factors influence teachers' instructional decisions. Well over 90% of respondents believe the state test influences the instructional practices they use. Comparisons between respondents reporting more and less attention to test preparation yield predictable results: Teachers who spend more than 2 months on test preparation are far more likely to use teacher-centers practices than those who spend less time on test preparation.

For respondents, the amount of instructional time they spent preparing their students for the high school graduation examination matters little. Their message is clear and can be summed up in a comment expressed by a female with a bachelor's degree and 25–29 years of experience: "Regardless of how I feel about them, tests and the high stakes attached to test results matter the most. They affect not only the curriculum taught but the instructional practices used to teach it."

Segall (2003) suggests that state-mandated tests and the high-stakes attached may have become a convenient excuse for teachers to engage in less ambitious teaching by focusing more on breath rather than depth and on more teacher-centered rather than student-centered instruction. It may be that teachers use the preparation for state-mandated testing to justify their use of the instructional practices with which they feel most comfortable.

CONCLUSION

The blueprint to achieve educational accountability is seemingly quite simple. First, design a state-wide curriculum for each content area—a "framework" that includes standards and benchmarks for each grade level. Then, to make sure teachers teach to this curriculum, mandate a statewide test to assess students' knowledge of the curriculum and attach high-stakes to the test for all those involved (e.g., administrators, teachers, and students).

What is not so simple is the impact that educational accountability has had on all those involved. There is still considerable ambiguity about the impact state testing has on instructional practices (Firestone et al., 2002). This study provides an insight into the instructional practices teachers use and factors influencing their decisions. In the end, however, it leaves a number of questions open to further exploration.

NOTES

1. Analysis of Part I of the survey instrument begins with an examination of frequency tables and the mean response for each item. The larger the mean of an item, the more respondents used the particular instructional practice or tool.

2. Instructional practices or tools used regularly and often means respondents either circled "4" for RU (regularly) or "5" for M (mostly) on Part I of the survey instrument. Instructional practices or tools used less often or not at all means respondents either circled "1" for D (don't use), "2" for R (rarely), or "3" for O (occasionally) on Part I of the survey instrument.

3. Because this study is part of a larger study about the impact of a graduation examination on English, science, mathematics, and social studies teachers' instructional practices, two instructional tools not known to be frequently used by social studies teachers, lab equipment and calculators,

were listed in Part I of the survey instrument. A frequency analysis showed that respondents either said "don't use" or "not applicable" for both items. Because of this finding, the two instructional tools were removed from any further calculations and not discussed.

4. Some response categories listed in the survey instrument were "collapsed" in order to ensure cell numbers sufficient to meet minimum requirements for a chi-square analysis.

5. After collapsing the preparation time categories into "1 day to 2 months" and "over 2 months," crosstabulations and chi-square analyses were conducted to determine if there were any significant differences between the instructional practices used or not used and the "collapsed" preparation time categories.

6. Frequency tables provide the mean, standard deviation, and standard error for each item. Any mean over 3.00 indicates some perceived amount of influence.

APPENDIX A: MISSISSIPPI SOCIAL STUDIES FRAMEWORK UNITED STATES HISTORY 1877 TO THE PRESENT

Example of Social Studies Framework (United States History: 1877 to the Present)

Content Strands

Civics (C)
History (H)
Geography (G)
Economics (E)

Compentencies

1. Explain how geography, economics, and politics have influenced the historical development of the United States in the global community (H, G, E).

   a. Apply economic concepts and reasoning when evaluating historical and contemporary social developments and issues (e.g., gold standard, free coinage of silver, tariff issue, laissez faire, deficit spending, etc.).

   b. Explain the emergence of modern America from a domestic perspective (e.g., frontier experience, Industrial Revolution and organized labor, reform movements of Populism and Progressivism, Women's Movement, Civil Rights Movement, the New Deal, etc.).

c. Explain the changing role of the United States in world affairs since 1877 through wars, conflicts, and foreign policy (e.g., Spanish American War, Korean conflict, containment policy, etc.)

d. Trace the expansion of the United States and its acquisition of territory from 1877 (e.g., expansionism and imperialism).

Appendix B: Subject Area Testing Program (SATP) U.S. History from 1877 Test Blueprint

Assessment Strand	Multiple-Choice	Open-Ended
International Relations	16	
Domestic Affairs	28	
Geography	13	
Economics	6	
Civics	7	
Total	70 Items	1 Item*

*Only one open-ended item is included. It may appear in any strand.

APPENDIX C: THE SURVEY INSTRUMENT

Part 1

Please circle the number indicating the extent to which you use each of the following:

Use the following scale:

D = Don't Use
R = Rarely (Average 1 day per week)
O = Occasionally (Average 2 to 3 days per week)
RU = Regularly (Average 2 to 3 days per week)
M = Mostly (Average 4 to 5 days per week
NA = Not Applicable (Not used in your hight school academic program)

Instructional Stratgies	D	R	O	RU	M	NA
1. Writing assignments	1	2	3	4	5	6
2. Group projects	1	2	3	4	5	6
3. Textbooks based assignments	1	2	3	4	5	6
4. Discussion groups	1	2	3	4	5	6
5. Multiple-choice questions	1	2	3	4	5	6
6. Open-resource questions	1	2	3	4	5	6
7. True-false questions	1	2	3	4	5	6
8. Inquiry/investigation	1	2	3	4	5	6
9. Problem-solving activities	1	2	3	4	5	6
10. Worksheets	1	2	3	4	5	6
11. Lessons based on current events	1	2	3	4	5	6
12. Project-based assignments	1	2	3	4	5	6
13. Worksheets	1	2	3	4	5	6
14. Lessons based on current events	1	2	3	4	5	6
15. Use of charts, webs and or outlines	1	2	3	4	5	6
16. Use of response journals	1	2	3	4	5	6
17. Use of rubrics or scoring	1	2	3	4	5	6

Teaching Techniques	D	R	O	RU	M	NA
18. Interdisciplinary instruction	1	2	3	4	5	6
19. Lecturing	1	2	3	4	5	6
20. Modeling	1	2	3	4	5	6
21. Cooperative learning/ group work	1	2	3	4	5	6

Instructional Materials and Tools	D	R	O	RU	M	NA
22. Textbooks	1	2	3	4	5	6
23. Supplementary materials	1	2	3	4	5	6
24. Newspaper/magazine	1	2	3	4	5	6
25. Audiovisual materials	1	2	3	4	5	6
26. Lab equipment	1	2	3	4	5	6
27. Calculators	1	2	3	4	5	6
28. Computers/educational software	1	2	3	4	5	6
29. Computers/Internet and/ or on-line research service	1	2	3	4	5	6
30. Visual aids (i.e., posters, graphs	1	2	3	4	5	6

31. Do you prepare students for the high school graduation examination?

— Yes (Please answer question 32

— No (Please skip questions 32. Go to question 33).

32. Preparation Time (Amount of instructional time you spend preparing students for the high school graduation exam.)

— No more than 1 day
— 2 to 4 days
— 1 week
— Over 1 to 3 weeks
— 1 to 2 months
— Over 2 to 3 months
— Over 3 to 6 months
— Over 6 months

Part II

Please circle the number indicating your responses to the statements below, using the following scale:

SD = Strongly Disagree
D = Disagree
U = Undecided
A = Agree
SA = Stongly Agree

Th Instructional Practices I use Have Been Influenced by the Following	SD	D	U	A	SA
33. Personal desire	1	2	3	4	5
34. Belief these are the best instructional practices	1	2	3	4	5
35. Format of the high school graduation examination	1	2	3	4	5
36. Interest in helping my school improve high school graduation examination scores	1	2	3	4	5
37. Interest in helping my students attain test scores that will allow them to graduate high school	1	2	3	4	5
38. Interest in avoiding sanctions at my school	1	2	3	4	5
39. Interest in obtaining a monetary award for my school	1	2	3	4	5
40. Interaction with school principal(s)	1	2	3	4	5
41. Interaction with colleagues	1	2	3	4	5
42. Staff development in which I have participated	1	2	3	4	5
43. Interactions with parents	1	2	3	4	5

Part III

Please mark the responses that describe you:

44.   — Male
      — Female

45.   Teaching Experience

      — First year
      — 2–6 years
      — 7–9 years
      — 10–14 years
      — 15–19 years
      — 20–24 years
      — 25–29 years
      — 30 years or more

46.   Education (Highest level attained)

      — Bachelor's Degree
      — Master's
      — Master's + 15
      — Master's + 30
      — Master's + 45
      — Master's + 60
      — C.A.G.S or Specialist's
      — Doctorate

47.   Teaching Assignment (Primary teaching assignment)

      — English
      — Science
      — Mathematics
      — Social Studies

48.   State (State you teach in)

      — Mississippi
      — Tennessee

Thank you very much for your time. Comments regarding instructional practices you use to prepare students for the high school graduation examination:

REFERENCES

Airasian, P., & Walsh, M. (1997). Constructivist cautions. *Phi Delta Kappan, 78*(6), 444-449.

Barksdale-Ladd, M. A., & Thomas, K. F. (2000). What's at stake in high-stakes testing: Teachers and parents speak out. *Journal of Teacher Education, 51*(3), 384–397.

Baron, J. B., & Wolf, D. P. (1996). *Performance-based student assessment: Challenges and possibilities.* Chicago: University of Chicago.

Borko, H., & Putnam, R. T. (1995). Expanding a teacher's knowledge base: A cognitive psychological perspective on professional development. In T. R. Guskey & M. Huberman (Eds.), *Professional development in education* (pp. 35–65). New York: MacMillan.

Bracey, G. W. (1987a). Measurement-driven instruction: Catchy phrase, dangerous practice. *Phi Delta Kappan, 68*(9), 683–686.

Bracey, G. W. (1987b). The muddles of measurement-driven instruction. *Phi Delta Kappan, 68*(9), 688–689.

Cimbricz, S. (2002). State-mandated testing and teachers' beliefs and practice. *Educational Policy Analysis Archives, 10*(2), Retrieved August 20, 2004, from http://epaa.asu/epaa.v10n2.html

Cohen, D. K., & Hill, H. C. (1998). Instructional policy and classroom performance: The mathematics reform in California. *Teachers College Record, 102*(2), 294–343.

Darling-Hammond, L., & Wise A. E. (1985). Beyond standardization: State standards and school improvement. *The Elementary School Journal, 85*(3), 315–336.

Eggen, P., & Kauchak, D. (2001). *Educational psychology: Windows on classrooms.* Upper Saddle River, NJ: Merrill Prentice Hall.

Elementary and Secondary Education Act of 1965, Pub. L. 89–110 (1965).

Firestone, W. A., Monfils, L., Camilli, G., Schorr, R., Hicks, J., & Mayrowetz, D. (2002). The ambiguity of test preparation: A muiltmethod analysis in one state. *Teachers College Record, 104*(7), 1485–1523.

Gilman, D. A., & Reynolds, L. A. (1991). The side effects of statewide testing. *Contemporary Education, 62*(4), 272–278.

Good, T. L., & Brophy, J. E. (2000). *Looking in classrooms* (8th ed.). New York: Longman.

Grant, S. G. (2001). An uncertain lever: Exploring the influence of state-level testing in New York station teaching social studies. *Teachers College Record, 103*(3), 398–426.

Grant, S. G. (2003). *History lessons: Teaching, learning, and testing in United States high school classrooms.* Mahwah, NJ: Erlbaum.

Jacob, B. A. (2001). Getting tough? The impact of high school graduation exams. *Educational Evaluation and Policy Analysis, 23*(2), 99–121.

Jones, B. D., & Johnson, A. F. (2002, April). *The effects of high-stakes testing on instructional practices.* Paper presented at the annual meeting of the American Educational Research Association. New Orleans, LA.

Jones, M. G., Jones, B. D., & Hargrove, T. Y. (2003). *The unintended consequences of high-stakes testing.* New York: Rowman and Littlefield.

Jones, K., & Whitford, B. L. (1997). Kentucky's conflicting reform principles: High-stakes school accountability and student performance assessment. *Phi Delta Kappan, 79*(4), 276–281.

Madaus, G. F. (1988a). The distortion of teaching and testing: High-stakes testing and instruction. *Peabody Journal of Education, 65*(3), 29–46.

Madaus, G. F. (1988b). The influences of testing on the curriculum. In L.N. Tanner (Ed.), *Critical issues in curriculum: Eighty-seventh yearbook of the national society for the study of education* (pp. 83–121). Chicago: University of Chicago Press.

Marchette, F. (2003). *Impacts of scheduling configurations on Mississippi biology subject area testing.* (ERIC Document Reproduction Service No. ED482467).

McLaughlin, M. W. (1990). The Rand Change Agent study revisited: Macro perspectives and micro realities. *Educational Researcher, 19*(9), 11–16.

McNeil, L. (2000). *Contradictions of school reform: Educational costs of standardized testing.* New York: Routledge.

Mississippi Department of Education. (2004a). *Functional literacy examination.* Retrieved August 24, 2004, from http://www.mde.k12.ms/acad/osa/fle.html

Mississippi Department of Education. (2004b). *Graduation requirements.* Retrieved from http://www.mde.k12.ms.us/acad/osa/newgrad.html

Mississippi Department of Education. (2004c). *Subject area testing program.* Retrieved from http://www.mde.k12.ms.us/acad/osa/satp.html

Mississippi Department of Education. (2004d). *Subject area and FLE graduation requirements.* Retrieved from http://www.mde.k12.ms.us/acad/osa/grad.pdf

National Alliance of Business. (2000). *Improving performance: Competition in American public education.* Washington, DC: Author.

Natriello, G., & Pallas, A. M. (1999). *The development and impact of high-stakes testing.* (ERIC Document Reproduction Service No. ED443871).

Newmann, F. M., & Associates. (Eds.). (1996). *Authentic achievement: Restructuring schools for intellectual quality.* San Francisco: Jossey-Bass.

No Child Left Behind Act of 2001, Pub. L. No. 107-110, 115 Stat. 1425 (2002).

Piaget, J. (1973). *To understand is to invent.* New York: Grossman.

Popham, W. J. (1987). The merits of measurement driven instruction. *Phi Delta Kappan, 68*(9), 679–682.

Resnick, L. B., & Resnick, D. P. (1992). Assessing the thinking curriculum: New tools for educational reform. In B. R. Gifford & M. C. O'Connor (Eds.), *Changing assessments: Alternative views of aptitude, achievement, and instruction* (pp. 37–75). Boston: Kluwer Academic.

Rothman, R. (1995). *Measuring up: Standards, assessment, and school reform.* San Francisco: Jossey-Bass.

Saxe, G. B., Franke, M. L., Gearhart, M., Howard, S., & Michele, C. (1997). *Teachers'shifting assessment practices in the context of education reform in mathematics* (CSE Technical Report 471). Los Angeles: CRESST.

Segall, A. (2003). The impact of state-mandated testing according to social studies teachers: The Michigan Educational Assessment Program (MEAP) as a case study of consequences. *Theory and Research in Social Education, 31*(5), 287–325.

Shepard, L. A. (1989). *Inflated test score gains: Is it old norms or teaching the test? Effects of testing project.* Washington, DC: Office of Educational Research and Improvement. (ERIC Document Reproduction Service No. ED334204)

Skinner, R. A., & Staresina, L. N. (2004, January 8). State of the states. *Education Week, 23*(17), 97–153.

Smith, J., & Niemi, R. G. (2001). Learning history in school: The impact of course work and instructional practices on achievement. *Theory & Research in Social Education, 29*(1), 18–42.

Supovitz, J. A., Mayer, D. P., & Kahle, J. B. (2000). Promoting inquiry-based instructional practice: The longitudinal impact of professional development in the context of systemic reform. *Educational Policy, 14*(3), 357–384.

Vogler, K. E. (2002). The impact of high-stakes, state-mandated student performance assessment on teachers' instructional practices. *Education, 123*(1), 39–55.

Vygotsky, L. (1978). *Mind in society. The development of higher psychological processes.* Cambridge, MA: Harvard University Press.

Wenglinsky, H. (2000). *How teaching matters: Bringing the classroom back into discussions of teacher quality.* Princeton, NJ. Educational Testing Service.

Yarbrough, T. L. (1999). *Teacher perceptions on the North Carolina ABC program and the relationship to classroom practice.* Unpublished doctoral dissertation, University of North Carolina at Chapel Hill.

Zemelman, S., Daniels, H.. & Hyde, A. (1998). *Best practices: New standards for teaching and learning in American's public schools* (2nd ed.). Portsmouth, NH: Heinemann.

CHAPTER 14

MEASURING HISTORY THROUGH STATE-LEVEL TESTS

Patterns and Themes

S. G. Grant

> Ironically, then, policymakers may be most pleased with those teachers who least follow the dictates of the state test.

> —Jill Gradwell (Chapter 8)

Although one of the first volumes to deeply explore the effects of state-level history testing, the chapter authors and I can make no grand claims. Standardized tests of all stripes have gotten considerable attention in both the academic and popular presses, yet relatively little of that attention has taken the form of empirical work. What people *think* could or should or may happen is interesting. But what does happen, as the quote above suggests, though more difficult to describe, ultimately may be more revealing. For in and around teachers' responses to history tests is evidence that confirms *and* challenges both policymakers' hopes and critics' fears.

The principal benefit of this book is the collective inquiry into the classroom lives of nearly 150 history teachers who face state-level exams.

Measuring History: Cases of State-Level Testing Across the United States, 303–320

Through various research methods—interview, field study, survey, and action research—the chapter authors portray teachers' complex, layered, and nuanced reactions to a range of state testing contexts. Although students' reactions to the new tests await another volume, this book takes us one step closer to understanding how a potentially powerful influence on history teaching and learning is playing out.

In this chapter, I examine the findings presented. The ability to peer inside teachers' responses to their respective state tests is useful, but so too is the ability to look across their responses. Given differing teacher backgrounds, different school contexts, and different state curriculum and testing policies, it makes sense that some interesting distinctions would arise. But equally interesting are the similarities which, while not statistically significant, may be useful to teachers, teacher educators, and policymakers.

STAKES AND STATE-LEVEL HISTORY TESTS

In chapter 1, Catherine Horn and I review of the number, kind, and range of state history tests across the United States. That overview highlights aspects of state-level testing such as the quick rise of and subsequent stabilization in the number of tests, the various content areas assessed, and the different grades at which tests are administered. We also note the number of states that attach a consequence to students' test performance. That number proves problematic, however, as one reads the ensuing chapters for, in reality, attaching consequences to tests tells us little about what those consequences mean in teachers' classrooms. Who would have predicted, for example, the reactions of the Florida teachers Elizabeth Yeager and Matthew Pinder (chapter 12) profile who do not even face a state-level history test? So it makes some sense to begin this chapter with a brief review of the different testing contexts teachers encounter.

As the editor, I considered adding the phrase "high stakes" to the book title as a way to excite reader interest and to promote sales. But as the various chapters indicate, not all state history tests have explicit and direct consequences for teachers and/or their students. *High stakes* is vaguely defined at best (Amrein & Berliner, 2002; Kornhaber, Orfield, & Kurlaender, 2001), but as Firestone and Mayrowetz (2000) point out, how teachers perceive test-related consequences or stakes may be as important as how policymakers intend them.

Consider the array of student consequences linked with the tests described in this book. At the high end are the exams administered in

Texas, Virginia, Mississippi, and New York. In these states, high school students' scores can have an immediate and potentially dramatic effect on their graduation. By contrast, the test scores of high school students in Michigan and Kentucky hold no particular meaning for them: In both states, students' social studies test scores count toward the assessment of their schools, but in neither state do students' scores carry any explicit consequences and, in Michigan, social studies scores are expressly *not* considered as part of the formula for awarding student scholarships. Complicating the stakes issue further are the elementary and middle school students in New York and other high-stakes states who take state exams, but whose scores have relatively little direct impact on their lives.

Things get really complicated, however, as teachers come into the stakes picture. Teachers in no state need fear immediate dismissal for low student test performance. So test performance in high-stakes states has far greater implications for students than for their teachers. And yet the potential impact of state tests on teachers may be just as real regardless of the consequences attached. For evidence of this claim, one need look no further than the fact that teachers who face *no* state social studies test may feel just as pressed to change their teaching (or not!) as teachers who do. Consider these two sets of quotes:

Has it influenced the way I teach? Totally.

I use the entire academic year preparing my students for the United States history subject area exam. My choice of instructional delivery and materials is completely dependent on preparation for this test.

* * *

[First, I decide] what do I want them to learn/achieve. Then I decide how much in depth I want them to go. Only then do I decide how to apply the [Sunshine State] standards. I can apply the standard to any lesson I want. I don't try to fit into the standards.

A lot of people get caught up in the amount of content that's in the SOLs. Basically, its the concept of "chunking" and relating content—you can get through or present effectively most of it ... even though the curriculum is too big for this course.

Expressing the view that state tests heavily influence their practice, the first two quotes are from Isabel, a teacher from Florida which has no state history test, and a teacher from Mississippi which has a very prescriptive and high-stakes exam. The second two quotes downplay the importance of state tests, yet come from teachers who teach in radically different contexts: Suzanne, another Florida teacher, and a Virginia teacher who works with the very rigid state Standards of Learning (SOLs). Any set of data can be manipulated, but the similarities within each set of teacher responses and the differences between the two sets hint at a conclusion that the stakes attached to state-level tests may matter less than the mere existence of a test. In other words, it may be as much the *test* part of the phrase "high-stakes test" that teachers are reacting to as the consequences.

The notion of *measuring* history is complicated by a host of factors described in the chapter authors—the blurry distinction between *history* and *social studies*, the potential for mixed messages between states' curriculum and testing policies, the different consequences attached to tests in some subject areas than in others. But the fact that teachers are responding in similar ways to fundamentally different testing conditions suggests something else is going on beyond a strict, "if we test it, they will teach it" phenomena.

THE RELATIONSHIPS BETWEEN STATE TESTS AND TEACHERS' PRACTICES

Although the teachers described in this book represent no scientifically-drawn sample, they do reflect a fair portion of the population of history teachers in terms of experience (novice, experienced, and veteran teachers), school context (rural, suburban, and urban), location (northern, southern, midwestern, and western parts of the United States), gender (male and female), and students taught (high, middle, and low socioeconomic status; high, middle, and low ability levels). In many areas of schooling and life, such characteristics matter considerably. They do not here. There are patterns in teachers' reactions to state tests, but those patterns offer no predictable lines. Novice teachers are no more likely to be cowed by state tests than their veteran peers; blue state teachers are as likely as their red state colleagues to carve out their own pedagogical paths. There are many ways to interpret the chapters in this book, but one can not escape the conclusion that, as policy lever, state-level tests produce a crazy quilt of responses.

In this section, I summarize the chapter authors' findings regarding the relationships between state-level testing and teachers' content decisions, their assessment practices, their instructional strategies, and their understandings of local and state contexts. In doing so, I point both to the similarities in their responses and to the exceptions.

The Relationship Between Tests and Teachers' Content Decisions

Although untangling the relative influence of state curricula from state exams can be difficult, the principal pedagogical effect of state history tests seems to be on teachers' content decisions. Most of the teachers profiled in these chapters report making a range of small to large changes in the subject matter ideas they teach.

Two examples highlight the influence of state tests on the content teachers choose to teach:

> We have to start with the Constitution, because there are a lot of constitutional principles on the MEAP. We're afraid that if we do it in order, by the time we get to the Constitution, it's going to be so close to the MEAP that we may not focus as much on that as we should. So we start with that at the beginning and then go backwards: Do the Constitution, the Core Democratic Values, then backtrack to the colonial times and work our way forward from there. (Chapter 5/Michigan)

> First [I] look at the SOL guidelines, and then I write down what they have to have. And then I read the chapter and then I read the outside materials, and then I look at what other teachers have done in the past, I have notebooks and stuff. I borrow stuff that would be good and I try to plan lessons about what they need to know about the SOLs. (Chapter 10/Virginia)

That these teachers and most of their peers modify their taught curriculum in response to state tests makes considerable sense given that it is the content which is most explicit. State tests do not tell teachers how to teach (Grant, 1997; Grant, Gradwell, Lauricella, Derme-Insinna, Pullano, & Tzetzo, 2002) so if teachers are going to "teach to the test," then changing their taught curriculum would seem the easiest response.

Many teachers may find themselves in a predicament though. State curricula typically present far more content than even the longest test can cover. Over time, teachers can become fairly adept at predicting the topics most tested, but newly-designed tests present them with a challenge in terms of knowing what content may be tested. Teachers in Virginia, Michigan, Kentucky, and Texas seem particularly frustrated by perceived inconsistencies between state standards and the attendant state tests.

Predictably, the novice teachers profiled (chapter 10/Virginia and chapter 6/Michigan) struggle to make content choices that will most advantage their test-taking students. Surprisingly, veteran teachers (chapter 5/Kentucky, chapter 9/Texas, and chapter 11/Virginia) struggle as well. As described in the Kentucky and Virginia chapters, departmental discussions lead even seasoned teachers to question the content they teach. For example, George and his Kentucky colleagues decide "we are not doing thematic stuff. We made a decision that for now we were going to go on the old fashioned march through time thing."

At the same time, other teachers resist the temptation to tailor their curriculum to either state standards or state exams. Sara Cooper (chapter 8/New York) develops a unit on the women of the 1920s knowing that the topic is barely mentioned in the New York history curriculum and is ignored altogether on the state test. Jane Bolgatz (chapter 7/New York) works with a fourth-grade teacher willing to teach about racism. The Kentucky teachers at Wilson County High (chapter 5) create a new, required course for freshmen that represents a set of ambitious content goals. And in a different way, Suzanne (chapter 12/Florida) resists pressure to follow a state test when she balks at using the school-wide literacy workbook: "I can't stand the time away from my content…. It feels unprofessional, like not what I was taught to do. I want to come up with my own readings and questions." So while many teachers translate testing pressures into new content choices, others hold to their own perspectives on what ought to be taught.

An interesting aspect to the ambitious actions of Sara Cooper, Suzanne, and others is that they occur in required courses. Many of the teachers described in this book teach rich and engaging content, but they do so in elective rather than required courses (see chapter 5/Kentucky and chapter 11/Virginia). Resolving content dilemmas in this fashion makes some sense in high-stakes testing situations. Still, it is noteworthy when teachers demonstrate the possibilities for more ambitious teaching in classes that enroll students of all levels.

The Relationship Between State Tests and Teachers' Assessment Practices

If both testing proponents and critics are surprised to learn that teachers are not using state exams as the default curriculum in their classrooms, they may be even more surprised to see teachers using a variety of assessment methods.

Few teachers are making wholesale changes in their student assessments. That finding is less remarkable perhaps than the reason why: Most teachers already use test questions that mirror those on state history exams—multiple choice, short answer, and essays. Further complicating an understanding of teachers' assessment practices is the idea that most teachers do not give test-based exams exclusively. Instead, they employ these exams as part of larger assessment plans. For example, the beginning teachers in Virginia (chapter 12) use test-inspired, fact-based multiple-choice items on their end-of-unit tests. But each also incorporates other assessment practices—debates, individual and group projects, graded discussions—reflecting the conclusion that one teacher offers: "Kids learn differently and tests are boring and can only do so much."

The teachers described in these chapters are not sanguine about the state tests they administer. They dislike the additional pressure on their practices and on their students, the ways that scores are used, the kinds of test items employed, and the mix of messages that tests send about what is important. Yet, few dismiss outright the *idea* of a state-level test. Protesting a feature of test construction or how a score is interpreted is one thing; protesting against the existence of a test is quite another. The chapter authors record plenty of the former, but little of the latter. There are lots of possible reasons for this omission—coercion by school and district administrators, pressure from parents, an unwillingness to buck what seems like an overwhelming trend. These explanations and more may account for the lack of teacher resistance to the concept of testing, but one other looms large: Testing is a long-accepted means of judging student performance. Acknowledging this point helps explain why teachers are making relatively few changes in their classroom assessments: They accept the premise that tests are useful and that multiple-choice questions and essay prompts represent reasonable ways of knowing what students know.

But just as testing seems rooted in U.S. school cultures, so, too, is the idea that tests measure only some kinds of knowledge and ability. So it is not too surprising that a large number of Mississippi teachers (chapter 13) report spending considerable time in test preparation. Tests efficiently screen those who know from those who do not, but they are a screen with wide mesh: Americans know well the case of the student who tests poorly, but accomplishes much.[1] So a kind of schizophrenia exists: Faith in tests, but doubts as to their import.

The Relationship Between State Tests and Teachers' Instructional Strategies

The big surprise in this book is the generally minimal influence state tests seem to have on teachers' instructional decisions. Some teachers say they do more test preparation than they would like and some may no longer do activities that they have in the past. The dismayed assertion by a Virginia teacher that "it's facts—names, dates, places. I used to be a good teacher—now I'm cramming this stuff down their throats" (chapter 11) echoes loudly in the survey of Mississippi teachers' instructional practices (chapter 13). And yet many teachers continue to teach in ways they think are appropriate for students to learn.

Consider the comments of two beginning teachers who work in the high-stakes context of Virginia's Standards of Learning (Chapter 10):

> I have them do a lot of reading and questions and thinking about something.... With block periods you cannot do a content lecture for 90 minutes, especially with ninth graders. It just does not work. I do use a lot of lecture and guided discussion, but for a small percentage of each class. I try to give them information that's not in the textbook.... I use PowerPoint, I do group work, jigsaw, graffiti. I do interactive stories and drama, I have them act a lot. Read alouds. We have story time sometimes.

> I use quite a bit of group work. I use lots of jigsaw type stuff. In [the] applied [level class] they do basic reading comprehension in their book then we'll talk about it and see what they know. For [the] honors [class], mostly group work and discussion. Very little lecture.

What is going on here? If any teachers' practices are going to be heavily influenced by state tests, one would imagine them to be novices in an explicitly high-stakes environment. How come these teachers and several others profiled in this book do not follow the conventional thinking that low-level tests demand low-level teaching? Make no mistake: There are teachers who apparently have ceded control over their practices to state tests as the survey of Mississippi teachers suggests. Still, as with most things related to schooling, layers of complexity confound simple understandings: Even within the seeming dominance of traditional practices are hints of teachers whose practices buck this trend. In short, even in the states with the most explicit and most extensive consequences, teachers continue to demonstrate variation in their classroom instruction. Tests may well be influencing teachers at the margins of their teaching, but little evidence exists to show wholesale change.

On the surface, this claim may cause testing critics to cheer and proponents to cringe. Both groups, however, would be wise to reflect first. Although critics like to imagine that all teachers plan and deliver rich and engaging lessons and that tests stifle this creativity, researchers (Cusick, 1983; Goodlad, 1984; Lynd & Lynd, 1929) have long described a good portion of history teaching as pedantic at best. If so, then state history tests are as unlikely to induce large-scale instructional change as any other innovation. Dull teachers, presumably the target of many test proponents' aim, may be no more likely to invoke test-based practices than their more ambitious peers, but that does not mean that their students are any better off.

If critics and proponents both miss their predictions with the bulk of American teachers, so too do they misunderstand the best teachers in the system. Excellent teachers may always be in short supply, but they exist (Barton, 2005; Grant, 2005; Hartzler-Miller, 2001). And the shame of the testing movement may well be the way these teachers perceive the new exams. Rather than embrace the tests and the attendant results as confirmation of their good work, most ambitious teachers view the tests as annoying at best. True, some educators like Jane Bolgatz (chapter 7/New York) see the test as a vehicle for more engaging instruction, but most feel undercut by exams that feel more pedagogically confining than liberating. For example, a Michigan teacher (chapter 6) notes,

> [The MEAP] really makes me mad—there is like nothing! Oh, my gosh! It's like our whole year is not necessary at all. That just blows me away.... It's almost as if we don't even need to teach the curriculum if we can teach them how to read a graph or look at a map. It almost makes you feel like, why bother, they don't have to know this stuff anyway.

and a Virginia teacher (chapter 10) observes,

> In my opinion [the SOL tests] have stifled social studies because it has stifled thinking and stifled creativity in too many people. And I am the first person to agree that it doesn't have to do that, but even though you can still have a great classroom with the SOLs, many people don't.

Ambitious teachers will continue to negotiate the relationship between the tests and their teaching, though not always to their satisfaction (Grant, 2005). It is too early to know if new history tests will drive the best teachers into other professions, but that outcome seems possible as the psychic rewards of teaching (Lortie, 1975) become less obvious.

The Relationship Between Tests and Teachers' Perceptions of Local and State Contexts

Context is the ultimate bugaboo for policymakers. Because education remains largely a state function, policymakers are right in thinking that their efforts at state-level change ought to influence teachers' practices. Their efforts do have some effect, but the state context defines only one part of a teacher's world. Community, school, department, and even individual classroom contexts can matter as much or more than that created at the state level. The long-noted decentralized nature of American schools (Cohen & Spillane, 1992) may diminish in response to the No Child Left Behind testing agenda, but it has not yet.

So the teachers in these chapters and their peers in classrooms around the United States face the continuing challenge of negotiating their classroom teaching, learning, and assessment in the context of state-level tests. That context produces no uniform result, however, as even teachers in the same school setting read and respond to history tests in different ways. That said, it is the similarities in teachers' reactions across very different contexts that may be the biggest challenge to understanding the effects of testing.

That similarities and differences in teachers' practices emerge across contexts is, in some ways, well-documented in the extant literature (Evans, 1990; Grant, 2003). Apparent in these chapters, however, is the fact that state-level testing, especially that with high stakes attached, seems to leave untouched the variation in teachers' classroom practices. If context matters much, then a reasonable prediction would be that, although teachers in low-stakes states react variously to their exams, surely there should be more conformity across teachers' practices in states with high-stakes exams. Reason need not reflect realities, though, and in the experiences of the teachers represented in this book, there are many realities and they overlap in interesting if unpredictable ways. Patterns emerge, but the value of those patterns is in post-hoc analysis rather than in prediction. Tests and the contexts into which they are introduced influence teachers' pedagogical ideas and actions. That they do so in no inevitable and foreseeable ways may tell us more about the nature of teaching than it does about the nature of testing.

HISTORY TESTING AND TEACHING: MEASURING THE UNMEASURABLE?

This book offers some surprises, but it also offers points of convergence between the findings advanced by the chapter authors and those described by researchers in the extant literature. That state policymakers and critics of testing have acted as though there is no research on history testing can be understood, in part, because this area has been so little studied. Along with the recent volumes by McNeil (2000) and Yeager and Davis (2005), this book goes some distance toward building a research-based understanding of how teachers interact with tests. In doing so, however, it also undercuts the idea that history teaching and learning are easily and satisfactorily measured.

The Nature of Teachers' Responses to State History Tests

One of the surprises that runs through the chapters is the difficulty in determining what constitutes a *response* to state-level history tests. As the authors make clear, teachers' reactions can occur in any number of settings (e.g., individual classrooms, department meetings, school-level inservices, district-sponsored work sessions, state-invited forums) and take any number of forms (e.g., changing content, assessment, and/or instructional practices, revising old courses and creating new ones, giving over part of one's practice to test preparation while retaining other parts, teaching ambitiously in spite of the tests). Administering a new history test may seem like a straight-forward move, but any move within a complex social institution like schools is bound to create a complex ripple of reactions.

Complicating the issue of teacher response to state tests is the question of to which policy teachers are responding. In each state case, new history tests have accompanied new history curricula. Policymakers may see these as seamless policies; teachers don't. Even a single policy can send mixed messages (Grant, 1997) so when states issue multiple policies, the potential for mayhem increases as teachers perceive different, and even competing messages. The teachers in all the states represented in this book talk about conflicts between the ideas expressed in their state curriculum and those evident on the state tests. For example, the Kentucky teachers (chapter 5) see their state history standards as in sync with the department's ambitious pedagogical goals. They perceive the state test, however, as advancing more pedantic goals. Similarly, the teacher in Jill Gradwell's study (chapter 8) feels supported by the New York social studies curriculum, but undercut by the state exam. So charting teachers' responses to state-level tests presents an immediate challenge as it is not always clear whether teachers are reacting to the test itself, the associated curriculum, or both.

A second complication involves the *timing* of an observation. Teaching is an incredibly complex activity (Cohen, 1988; Jackson, 1968), one that demands continual attention both to broad strokes and minute details. A single glimpse at a teacher's practice, then, can yield a distorted understanding. Consider this example described by Ann Marie Smith (chapter 11/Virginia):

> In spite of Mr. Anderson's insistence that critical thinking and writing are emphasized in his social studies classes, he occasionally reverts to a transmission model. After one rapid lecture, he explains, "We were behind on the SOLs, so I had to get the students caught up." Fast-paced activity is typical for his classroom, and students usually direct class discussions or present information they had written. Mr. Anderson also teaches students

to cite quotes from both primary sources and textbooks to defend their oral and written analyses; however, on this day, preparation for the SOLs appears to force Mr. Anderson to quickly deliver the necessary information by lecturing.

Judged by one observation and a single quote, Mr. Anderson might be lumped with teachers who have given over their teaching to extended test preparation. Looking longer and deeper, as is often the case, reveals new realities: In Mr. Anderson's case, what might be standard practice in some teachers' classrooms, is an aberration. A similar misreading of Suzanne's practice described by Elizabeth Yeager and Matthew Pinder (chapter 12/ Florida) could also occur if one were to happen past her room on a Tuesday or Wednesday as she conducts the requisite practice for the FCAT rather on any other day when she teaches history in ways she thinks more appropriate.

One last complication to the issue of teachers' test-based responses is what counts as a *significant* change. Corbett and Wilson (1991) remind us that observing a change does not necessarily tell us what the change means. Here, Cinthia Salinas's description of the veteran Texas teachers (chapter 9) is most instructive: Teachers can appear to be cooperating with a policy directive and yet hold in abeyance the dimensions of their teaching practice that matter most to them. Kirst and Walker (1971) offer a key insight here when they observe that ultimately teachers hold a "pocket veto" over the policies that are stuffed into their school mailboxes. That the changes they make in response to those policies radically shift the direction of their classroom practices is a possibility, but no certainty.

The Influence of State Tests on Teachers' Classroom Practices

If the question of what constitutes a teacher's response to state history tests is something of a surprise, few observers will be similarly surprised to learn that tests constitute but one *influence on teachers' practices.*

Several studies point to the lengthy list of factors that go into teachers' pedagogical decisions (Grant, 1996, 2003; Romanowski, 1996; Sturtevant, 1996). Tests make it on to that list, but as an influence, tests are tempered by personal considerations (e.g., subject matter knowledge), organizational constraints (e.g., time to teach), and policy issues (e.g., coherence across curriculum and assessment policies). Beginning teachers face these influences no more or less than do veterans and negotiating among them is an on-going dilemma (Grant, 2005).

Two points, however, add considerably to our understanding of the influences on teachers' practices and the place of state history testing in that mix. One is the tension between the public and private lives teachers lead in the face of state testing. The other is the relationship between tests and the stakes that are attached to them.

Ann Marie Smith (chapter 11/Virginia) and Avner Segall (chapter 6/ Michigan) offer slightly different takes on the definitions of teachers' public and private roles. Segall includes teachers' classroom actions as part of their public role while Smith limits that role to teachers' actions outside their classrooms. That distinction aside, the notion that teachers must continually negotiate their ideas and actions in both visible and invisible settings hints at the range of factors that press on their decision making. As Cinthia Salinas (chapter 9/Texas) reminds us, any appearance of seamlessness in teachers' thinking and actions is an artifact of our post hoc observation rather than an apparent quality of teachers' in-the-moment practice. So whether is it balancing a sudden student concern about the possibilities of global terrorism with the curricular need to discuss the American Revolution or balancing the bureaucratic demands of a district administrator with a sense of professionalism, researchers and policymakers alike need to appreciate the complex worlds in which teachers live and work.

Locating state history tests in the wider context of influences on teachers is important, but so too is understanding the relationship between tests and the consequences assigned to them. I make this point above, but it bears recalling: The presence or absence of stakes attached to a state history test may make less difference to teachers than the mere existence of a test. And as the case of the Florida teachers (chapter 12) suggests, the *test* in question need not even be in history. Consider this quote from a Michigan teacher (chapter 6) about the state exam:

> Every time we step into the classroom to start the school year one of the end results needs to be: Are these kids going to be ready to take the MEAP? And are they going to do well?... You always teach with the pressure of the MEAP hovering over you.

This teacher's lament must be read against the context of the relatively low-stakes Michigan Educational Assessment of Progress. But after reading the cases in this book, one can imagine virtually the same words being uttered by any of the teachers. The state history test each teacher faces is likely to figure somehow into her or his practice. But how the test matters, to what degree, and in what combination with other influences varies widely.

The Quality of Teachers' Responses to State Tests

By now it ought to be clear that the range of teachers' responses to state history tests covers considerable ground. Charting the ways teachers' respond is not the same thing as exploring the *quality of their responses* however. Just as there are no generic "wise" teaching practices (Yeager & Davis, 2005), nor are there any generic "wise" responses to state-level tests. Instead, policymakers, critics, and researchers alike would be better served if they looked deeply into the contextualized reasoning and practices of teachers.

One common way of understanding the quality of teachers' responses to state tests is to see them as *defensive*. Based on a construct first developed and elaborated by Linda McNeil (1988, 2000), the notion of defensive teaching suggests that teachers exist primarily in a reactive mode: State policymakers enact new curricula and new tests and then teachers react. This explanation holds considerable surface-level power and numerous examples percolate through the chapters in this book. Yet on continued reflection, the notion that teachers are merely reacting defensively leaves the outcome of their response unexamined. One way to read Ken Vogler's survey of Mississippi teachers (chapter 13) is as a simple cause and effect situation: A new high-stakes test is created and most teachers, when asked, say that they now teach in ways they believe consistent with that test. But that formula fails on two counts. First, it does not account for those teachers who continue to use more open-ended practices (or use them in concert with traditional practices). And second, it does not enable us to look deeply into the ways that teachers are responding. Here, the benefit of qualitative research shines as the depth of study evident in the case studies highlights the autonomy and creativity teachers can exhibit.

Consider three brief examples. First, recall the instances where teachers either individually or in departmental action appear to cooperate with the dictates associated with a new state test (e.g., chapter 9/Texas and chapter 11/Virginia) and yet do so with neither inspiration nor with any particular plans to use the test-based material once it is produced. Second, recall the way that some teachers (e.g., chapter 5/Kentucky and chapter 7/New York) turn the dictates associated with a new test into an opportunity to create new courses and to explore new content. And finally, recall the numerous instances where teachers acknowledge the presence of a new test, but hold firmly to practices that they firmly believe best serve the students they teach.

Yes, these teachers are, in some sense, *reacting* to state history tests, but in doing so, they are *acting* in ways that are more than defensive. They recognize that the tests constitute a potential constraint (Cornbleth, 2002) on their teaching. They also recognize, however, that there are many potential constraints and that *potential* constraints need not apply to them. No teacher teaches in a vacuum; the possibility of external influences is ever-present. Those influences rarely line up to promote a single direction, however, so teachers are always faced with the prospect of competing influences (Grant, 2003). This situation, Thornton (1991) observes, puts teachers in the role of "gatekeeper." This role does not mean that teachers operate in complete autonomy, but it does mean that teachers continually make decisions that shape their classrooms.

Avner Segall (chapter 6/Michigan) argues that the teachers he studied are "learning to live with [the test] but not by it." This distinction seems subtle, but it turns out to be profound. Teachers may choose to live with a state history test by orienting their entire practices around it, but they may also choose differently. The latter group's choices may be no less reactive than the former's and it would be a mistake to conclude that the difference between the choices made are always clear-cut and immutable. The dynamic quality of most teachers' pedagogies means that simplistic portraits of teachers' responses to tests are of little value.

It is with these ideas in mind that I offer an alternative to the notion of defensive teaching, one that allows for a range of teachers' responses, but also captures the negotiations among competing factors that teachers typically face. The construct I employ, *ambitious teaching*, is rooted in the notion that teaching is nuanced, complex, and contextualized regardless of the presence of state tests and the consequences they may hold. Borrowing liberally from the ideas of Dewey (1902/1969), Schwab (1978), Hawkins (1974), and Shulman (1987), I argue that ambitious teaching develops a) when teachers know their subject matter well and see within it the potential to enrich their students' lives; (b) when teachers know their students well, which includes understanding the kinds of lives their students lead, how these youngsters think about and perceive the world, and that they are far more capable than they and most others believe them to be; and (c) when teachers know how to create the necessary space for themselves and their students in environments in which others (e.g., administrators, other teachers) may not appreciate either of their efforts. In other words, ambitious teachers understand deeply both their subject matter and their students, and they are willing to push hard to create opportunities for powerful teaching and learning despite contextual factors (e.g., state curriculum, state tests, unsupportive administrators and colleagues) that may be pushing them in different directions (Grant, 2003, 2005).

In some ways, the notion of ambitious teaching is best illustrated in Jill Gradwell's case of Sara Cooper (chapter 8/New York) who teaches *in spite of* rather than *because of* the state history test. Cooper, a novice teacher with a challenging class composition (equal parts gifted, "regular," and special education students), is fully cognizant of the state exam. She takes some actions (e.g., after-school review sessions) that she believes will advantage students. But the test figures in as only one of several factors behind Cooper's pedagogical decisions. Equally important are her ideas about the subject matter in question and her ideas about the particular students she teaches. It is a complex situation, to be sure, but it is one that every teacher faces in one form or another. And it is the facing up to that situation that distinguishes an ambitious teacher. Cooper and other ambitious teachers know that they must make difficult choices and do so with uncertain results and with uncertain support from colleagues and administrators. Like other ambitious teachers (Grant, 2005), Cooper is not always satisfied with the choices she makes, but she realizes that she can choose differently in the future.

CONCLUSION

In some ways, state-level history tests are changing teaching in fundamental ways. Until recently, few history teachers have had to deal with standardized tests, particularly those with important consequences attached. That teachers factor the emergent exams into their classroom practices should surprise no one. *How* they do so, however, has been more a matter of speculation than evidence to this point. This book and others (McNeil, 2000; Yeager & Davis, 2005) provide real-world illustrations of teachers' responses to state tests. This recent scholarship leaves some questions open, but by enriching our understanding of teacher action, it offers the possibility of encouraging more ambitious teaching.

NOTES

1. That the current president, whose C average at Yale was presumably based on test scores, pushes tests as the panacea for American education is ironic at best.

REFERENCES

Amrein, A., & Berliner, D. (2002). High-stakes testing, uncertainty, and student learning. *Educational Policy Analysis Archives, 10*(18). Retrieved from http://epaa.asu.edu/epaa/V10n18

Barton, K. (2005). "I'm not saying these are going to be easy": Wise practice in an urban elementary school. In E. A. Yeager & J. O. L. Davis (Eds.), *Wise social studies teaching in an age of high-stakes testing* (pp. 11–32). Greenwich, CT: Information Age.

Cohen, D. (1988). Teaching practice: Plus que ca change. In P. Jackson (Ed.), *Contributing to educational change: Perspectives on research and practice* (pp. 27–84). Berkeley, CA: McCutchan.

Cohen, D., & Spillane, J. (1992). Policy and practice: The relations between governance and instruction. In G. Grant (Ed.), *Review of research in education* (Vol. 18, pp. 3–49). Washington, DC: American Educational Research Association.

Corbett, H. D., & Wilson, B. (1991). *Testing, reform, and rebellion.* Norwood, NJ: Ablex.

Cornbleth, C. (2002). What constrains meaningful social studies teaching. *Social Education, 63*(3), 186–190.

Cusick, P. A. (1983). *The egalitarian ideal and the American high school.* New York: Longman.

Dewey, J. (1969). *The child and the curriculum.* Chicago: University of Chicago Press. (Original work published 1902)

Evans, R. (1990). Teacher conceptions of history revisited: Ideology, curriculum, and student belief. *Theory and Research in Social Education, 28*(2), 101–138.

Firestone, W., & Mayrowetz, D. (2000). Rethinking "high stakes": Lessons from the United States and England and Wales. *Teachers College Record, 102*(4), 724–749.

Goodlad, J. (1984). *A place called school.* New York: McGraw-Hill.

Grant, S. G. (1996). Locating authority over content and pedagogy: Cross-current influences on teachers' thinking and practice. *Theory and Research in Social Education, 24*(3), 237–272.

Grant, S. G. (1997). A policy at odds with itself: The tension between constructivist and traditional views in the New York state social studies framework. *Journal of Curriculum and Supervision, 13*(1), 92–113.

Grant, S. G. (2003). *History lessons: Teaching, learning, and testing in U.S. high school classrooms.* Mahwah, NJ: Erlbaum.

Grant, S. G. (2005). More journey than end: A case of ambitious teaching. In E. A. Yeager & J. O.L. Davis (Eds.), *Wise social studies teaching in an age of high-stakes testing* (pp. 117–130). Greenwich, CT: Information Age.

Grant, S. G., Gradwell, J. M., Lauricella, A. M., Derme-Insinna, A., Pullano, L., & Tzetzo, K. (2002). When increasing stakes need not mean increasing standards: The case of the New York state global history and geography exam. *Theory and Research in Social Education, 30*(4), 488–515.

Hartzler-Miller, C. (2001). Making sense of "best practice" in teaching history. *Theory and Research in Social Education, 29*(4), 672–695.

Hawkins, D. (1974). I, thou, and it. In *The informed vision: Essays on learning and human nature* (pp. 48–62). New York: Agathon Press.

Jackson, P. (1968). *Life in classrooms.* New York: Holt, Rinehart, & Winston.

Kirst, M., & Walker, D. (1971). An analysis of curriculum policy-making. *Review of Educational Research, 41*(5), 479–508.

Kornhaber, M., Orfield, G., & Kurlaender, M. (2001). *Raising standards or raising barriers? Inequality and high-stakes testing in public education.* New York: Century Foundation Press.

Lortie, D. (1975). *Schoolteacher*. Chicago: University of Chicago Press.

Lynd, R., & Lynd, H. (1929). *Middletown: A study in American culture*. New York: Harcourt, Brace and World.

McNeil, L. (1988). *Contradictions of control*. New York: Routledge.

McNeil, L. (2000). *Contradictions of school reform: Educational cost of standardized testing*. New York: Routledge.

Romanowski, M. (1996). Issues and influences that shape the teaching of U.S. history. In J. Brophy (Ed.), *Advances in research on teaching* (Vol. 6, pp. 291–312). Greenwich, CT: JAI Press.

Schwab, J. J. (1978). Education and the structure of the disciplines. In I. Westbury & N. Wilkof (Eds.), *Science, curriculum, and liberal education* (pp. 229–272). Chicago: University of Chicago Press.

Shulman, L. (1987). Knowledge and teaching: Foundations of the new reform. *Harvard Educational Review, 57*(1), 1–22.

Sturtevant, E. (1996). Lifetime influences on the literacy-related instructional beliefs of experienced high school history teachers: Two comparative case studies. *Journal of Literacy Research, 28*(2), 227–257.

Thornton, S. (1991). Teacher as curricular-instructional gatekeeper in the social studies. In J. Shaver (Ed.), *Handbook of research on social studies teaching and learning* (pp. 237–248). New York: Macmillan.

Yeager, E. A., & Davis Jr., O. L. (Eds.). (2005). *Wise social studies teaching in an age of high-stakes testing*. Greenwich, CT: Information Age.

CHAPTER 15

THE FUTURE OF HIGH-STAKES HISTORY ASSESSMENT

Possible Scenarios, Potential Outcomes

William Gaudelli

> The future is an opaque mirror. Anyone who tries to look into it sees nothing but the dim outlines of an old and worried face.
>
> —Jim Bishop (1959)

High-stakes assessment has been the most significant policy change in education during the past decade. Accountability measures shape most considerations related to public education, as resource allocation, curriculum, staffing, and perceptions of success increasingly depend on high-stakes tests. In social studies curriculum history specifically, the implementation of high-stakes assessment has been uneven, and generally, unexamined (Grant, 2003). While there has been some debate within the field as to whether social studies should be included in high-stakes assessments, many argue that a failure to include social studies may cause the withering of history teaching (Savage, 2003). This volume provides ample evidence that such tests do matter. The heuristic that *what gets tested is what gets taught* is problematized and enriched, however, as illustrated by

Measuring History: Cases of State-Level Testing Across the United States, 321–333
Copyright © 2006 by Information Age Publishing

321

Jill Gradwell's study in New York and Stephanie van Hover's work in Virginia.

Given what is known about high-stakes testing in history, what might the future hold for the field on this weighty policy matter? The nature of state-level testing in the history curriculum is thoughtfully articulated through the case studies presented in this volume. Rather than review that has been said, my aim is to broadly survey what has been documented in order to speculate about what might happen next. Borrowing loosely on a trend extrapolation methodology of future studies, I outline three possible scenarios for high-stakes assessment in history, detailing the contours and lineage of each while examining the short and long-term plausibility of all. I develop these scenarios by projecting current trends and by examining the interactions of these phenomena in a broader social context. The questions that frame this speculation include: (1) How might these trends interact given the general policy direction outlined in the scenario? (2) What effects might these interactions cause in the short and long term? (3) To what extent is the emergent policy of high-stakes history testing congruent with larger social trends?

CURRENT TRENDS

High-stakes assessment is so closely tied to macrolevel policy directives that frequently vacillate, predicting what might happen is at least as difficult as predicting the next round of elections. Although heightened uncertainty remains, a remarkable consensus about the need for curriculum standards and high-stakes accountability has emerged. Bipartisan support for this version of educational accountability is evident among policymakers in Washington and most legislatures and statehouses throughout the country. The No Child Left Behind Act (NCLB) of 2001 illustrates this consensus. The bill passed the House (384–41) and Senate (87–10) just over a week after it was reported out of committee (Manna, 2004). NCLB received unanimous support from the National Governors Association and was embraced by conservatives like Orrin Hatch and Thomas DeLay and shepherded through the U.S. Senate by the otherwise liberal stalwart Ted Kennedy. What little dissent exists typically emerges from educational researchers, professional organizations, and teacher unions, whose motivations and conclusions are viewed skeptically by policymakers.

What has resulted from bipartisan support for high-stakes assessment? As one might suspect, every state in the nation has adopted some form of minimum competency exit examination in the past decade (Savage, 2003). The sporadic inclusion of history (and other social studies related curricula) however, suggests somewhat less agreement about the need to assess this curriculum area. Ten states currently have some form of history *exit* exam (Georgia, Louisiana, Maryland, Massachusetts, Mississippi, New Mexico, New York, North Carolina, Texas and Virginia) with two others (Alabama and Ohio) planning high-stakes testing in the next 5 years. Education Week's *Quality Counts* (2001) survey found that 31 states had *some* form of history/social studies assessment in a secondary grade, the difference being that the former looked only at exit exams and the latter at any history testing.

Of the 12 states that require some form of exit examination in history, only five had such high-stakes exams prior to 2000, representing a 260% increase in 10 years (Savage, 2003). Many of the states cited in this report indicate movement toward a high-stakes test in history or a related field (i.e., civics/government, geography) in the near future, so it is difficult to precisely ascertain the state of testing. Florida, for example, despite its aggressive stance with respect to high-stakes assessment and school-wide accountability measures (i.e., school funding formulas fixed to school grades that are based almost entirely on aggregate high-stakes test scores), has indefinitely postponed adding a social studies component to its graduation test, leaving many social studies teachers grasping for a role in this new environ (see Yeager & Pinder, in this volume; Gaudelli, 2002a). Alfie Kohn (2002) suggests that teachers in marginalized fields like history have fallen into the *test us too* trap, as they are dually aware of the dangers of standardization and high-stakes assessment as well as the rewards of being attended to and funded because of such measures (see also Stanley, 2001). The trend toward more testing related to history curriculum, although unevenly represented, seems inexorable.

The national picture is more unclear with respect to high-stakes assessment in history. NCLB requires that national assessments which are *valid and reliable* will be conducted in history, which is later identified as a *core academic subject*. The act goes on to differentiate history from social studies, suggesting that the former merits assessment and professional development funding while the latter does not. The mandate to assess historical knowledge is tempered, however, by the following legalese: "to the extent time and resources allow." Though significant money has been dedicated to the professional development of teachers in teaching *traditional* U.S. history from the federal government, as evidenced by the serial professional development grants initiated in 2001, there have been no meaningful signs that a national assessment plan for history is on the horizon. Moreover, as NCLB has never come close to receiving full appropriation, a federal stalemate on the inclusion of a high-stakes history assessment seems possible.

The format of extant high-stakes tests in history has a clear trajectory, mirroring question types that are used in other subject areas. State-level assessments largely consist of multiple-choice tests that are relatively inexpensive to evaluate, providing apparently objective data about student achievement. Although evidence suggests that history assessments vary somewhat (compare the state tests as described by Avner Segall and Ann Marie Smith in this volume), didactically-oriented, multiple-choice questions predominate on high-stakes history tests nationally. By contrast, high-stakes assessment based on alternative models (i.e., portfolio and performance) are, to the best of my knowledge, unrepresented at a policy level in the United States. Hill (2000) suggests that alternative forms of assessment that are textured, complex, and closely aligned to meaningful curricula should be considered for high-stakes assessment policy. Such assessments where students find information, synthesize ideas, organize a presentation, and communicate it to a wider audience are viewed, however, as unwieldy by policymakers who either do not understand or fail to appreciate the intricacies of pedagogy.

The effect high-stakes assessment is having on those who matter most, students and teachers, is the last trend considered and indeed the most significant one. Linda McNeil (2000) documents the profoundly negative effects tests have had on Texas public education. She finds that the *one size fits all* quick fix implemented in Texas ignores the guidance and aid of teachers and students. She documents both those teachers who driven out of the profession as well as those who remain, but are forced to jettison meaningful curriculum in order to teach to the test. McNeil's study provides ample evidence that high-stakes assessment contributes to the deprofessionalization of teaching, encourages moribund curricula, deadens classrooms, and stultifies students in the nation's laboratory for standards and high-stakes assessment, Texas. Cinthia Salinas's chapter in this volume problematizes these findings, however, as she explores the complex and nuanced ways that Texas history teachers leverage their knowledge of the larger high-stakes environment to guide their pedagogical choices. Letitia Fickel's chapter further complicates the deprofessionalization argument as she finds that teachers account for state content through collegial planning and cooperative curriculum-making. To summarize the current situation with respect to high-stakes assessment in history, then, the five characteristics depict the situation generally, though not comprehensively: (1) broad-based bipartisan support for current educational accountability mechanisms, (2) an increase in the number of states participating, (3) creation of recent federal legislation advocating history testing that lacks impetus and funding, (4) proliferation of didactically-oriented tests, and (5) teaching and learning that is informed by high-stakes assessment, but which leads teachers to seek different means of teaching that is meaningful to their students.

SCENARIOS

Given this brief and selective outline of trends related to high-stakes history testing, what might the next 20 years bring? As a means of systematically considering the future, I offer three broad scenarios, intended to be categorical but not comprehensive. As such, these scenarios provide a heuristic analysis of high-stakes testing policy, while recognizing that significant variance will exist in all three situations. Following a brief description of each scenario, I offer an analysis of the short (less than 5 years) and long term (5 to 20 years) implications for each. The long term analyses presuppose that such a policy direction is undertaken and that its course will be redirected based on the extent to which the policy is congruent with larger social trends beyond education, or history education, for that matter.

Scenario 1—Wide Implementation of State Assessments and Creation of a National Exam in History (Or, High-Stakes Assessment on Steroids)

The expansive implementation of national and state assessments assumes the rapid growth of high-stakes assessment in history in the next five years. Though 20% of states either have or plan to have such an exit requirement and more than half of all states include some history testing, these numbers would rapidly expand as more states recognize the core academic nature of history and its significance in promoting the civic purposes of education. Such a situation would likely be stimulated in a variety of ways. Perhaps a significant national event wherein history is seen as crucial to our understanding of current events (e.g., the detonation of a nuclear device by a terrorist group in a major city) could trigger such a rapid move toward high-stakes history testing. National events might also lead to a call for more history instruction, such as a precipitous drop in participation rates of those aged 18–30 in the 2008 election, or by yet another report about what kids do not know about U.S. history. Such a report might emanate from an existing assessment instrument, such as the National Assessment for Educational Progress (NAEP), or a think-tank like the Fordham Foundation (Gaudelli, 2002b). According to Scenario 1, something of great significance would have to occur in order for the 19 nonparticipating states, the 32 nonexit requirement states, and the

federal government to include history tests, an event even more profoundly tragic than that of September 11, 2001.

If wide implementation of high-stakes history assessment occurs, a
flurry of activity to create the tests, prepare teachers and students, and
produce support materials will likely follow. We could assume, especially
given the short-term nature of such a mass movement, that the tests
would be more like their predecessors, with an abundance of multiple-
choice questions, rather than like any alternatives currently available.
Efforts to create so many items in a relatively short span of time would
likely lead to other skirmishes, as advocates for certain aspects of the master narrative, as well as those who prefer the cacophony of multicultural
or global U.S. history, would make their respective cases for inclusion and
exclusion. Those currently yearning for the spotlight of high-stakes history exams would welcome and lead the implementation, while those in
opposition would continue to raise concerns and resist, perhaps with
greater stridency than previously offered. The ensuing debate likely
would be muted, however, by the aftershock of the preceding tragedy,
much the way that the debate over war in Afghanistan and Iraq was muf-
fled in the wake of 9/11. History teachers would probably experience
some trickle down of this frenzied move toward high-stakes, as they would
be recruited to develop the instruments and all would be expected to plan
instruction around the tests. This expectation would likely lead to a
greater consensus about what gets taught and omitted from the unofficial
master narrative, dictated to some degree by the tests that are implemented.

Two results from the rapid development of high-stakes history tests
would likely emerge concomitantly with implementation: (1) an increase
of resources and attention to history curriculum and (2) a fatalistic acceptance of the policy change. As observers of high-stakes assessment assert,
what is tested indicates to some degree what will be taught (Kohn, 2002;
McNeill, 2000; van Hover, this volume). Since those associated with history instruction have a vested interest in its continuation, the increase in
resources and attention, regardless of the motivation, will be a welcomed
change. The distribution of resources may also lead, in the short term, to
fatalistic acceptance of the new policy direction, particularly since more
money will have to be spent on creating, implementing, evaluating, and
teaching toward the tests. As more resources are expended, the sense that
there is *no turning back now* will likely set in, much the same way that public discourse has turned, in the short term, with respect to the invasion
and occupation of Iraq (though lacking the same degree of saliency).

What might increase the saliency of high-stakes assessment in history
in the short term, however, is the implementation of a national exit exam,
as stipulated in the NCLB. Politically, this would likely set off (or reinvig-

orate) the federalism debate to a degree not witnessed since the early 1980s, and to an extent that a political realignment could be in the offing. As the federal government begins to project greater evaluative power into an arena like education that historically has been the nearly exclusive domain of states, fears of growing national power would raise alarms across the political spectrum. Concerns about encroaching big government may actually alter this scenario considerably. The antifederalist response to NCLB is already in evidence as Virginia's legislature voted to opt out of the stringent testing regimen, California temporarily suspended its high school exit exams for 2004 and 2005, and Alaska's Education Association voted to urge the state legislature to reject federal funding because of the laborious assessment process (Alaska: Teachers Reject, 2004; California Cancels Exit, 2003; Hilliard, 2004). So, while in the short term it is possible that all or most states would implement high-stakes history assessments, it is substantially less likely that the federal government will follow suit either with a developmental or terminal assessment.

What about the long-term viability of Scenario 1? Beyond the 5 year situation just described, the next 15 years (2010 to 2025) might look significantly different. As increasing and accumulating numbers of students may be adversely affected by the policy and those who championed the ideas initially will have left policymaking, the amount of scrutiny about high-stakes history testing will probably increase. Studies, such as McNeil's (2000) and the state cases presented in this volume, will be repeated, leading to a substantial body of scholarship about high-stakes testing, which will likely show that the apparently tightly-coupled policy of curriculum and testing is actually a loosely-coupled reality of myriad effects and nebulous dimensions. The accumulation of such studies, though easily minimized in public discourse in the short term, will be much harder to ignore over 2 decades due to the sheer weight and volume of the doubts cast. Although educational scholarship is unlikely to cause a policy rollback, it may serve to support the intuitive critique of parents skeptical about this policy direction. With this information accessible via the Internet and public access journals, a movement already evident and certainly due to increase over the next 2 decades, may be the means by which this information is employed. Although such information is unlikely to completely alter Scenario 1, perhaps a substantial modification of policy may occur, such as reconstituting the types of assessments used or the ends to which they are employed.

Since didactic pedagogy often results from high-stakes assessment, history classrooms in Scenario 1 may become increasingly fact-oriented. Such pedantic curriculum will likely result in creative and inspiring teachers fleeing the profession, or choosing another field from the outset, a trend noted by McNeil (2000) in Texas. This flight of creativity, however, may actually serve to support the continuation of high-stakes assessment as teachers left behind, will see the routinization and apparent precision that comes with standards and assessment as a blessing and advocate its continuation. Rather than creating a cadre of unwilling educators grudgingly participating in the standards movement, which illustrates many of the perspectives offered by teachers in this book, the realities of teaching may serve to filter out those individuals who would resist while enticing people attracted to the simplicity of didactic teaching toward an exam. A significant corollary effect would be the solidification of deprofessionalization gains, the extent to which they are real, made by those who seek to make teaching a job rather than a profession.

Scenario 2—Incremental Implementation of State Assessments Without National Testing (Or, More of the Same)

In Scenario 2, the current trend toward more states implementing high-stakes assessment will continue, though not at the pace of Scenario 1. Further, this scenario envisions no national test for history standards, which given the current political climate, is quite likely. If the rate of increase for states implementing high-stakes history exit exams (260% increase in 10 year period 1995–2004) is maintained, by the year 2050 all states will have such an assessment. Assuming current growth rates remain constant, it would take approximately 4 decades for nationwide (but not national) state history exit exams to be implemented. The gradualness of this trend, which is essentially a continuous replication of the status quo, may lead to a number of unanticipated events in the short and long term.

As states begin the implementation of such tests, they will invariably serve as examples to each other about how to and how not to implement the assessments. In New York, for example, where document-based questions are used, states can examine the costs and time associated with evaluating such items, and make choices about the inclusion of more open-ended questions. Most new implementation states are avoiding such items in the interest of money and time, a trend likely to continue in Scenario 2. If policymakers begin to appreciate the curricular value of such time and cost-intensive history items, however, there may be a gradual move away from the purely didactic exams and toward tests that assess the depth and contours of student understandings related to historical knowledge. Such talk may be considered pie in the sky, but such a change is not unthinkable as we move into a global society that is increasingly premised on knowledge synthesis, especially as that capacity becomes a key attribute sought by employers.

Since the change in Scenario 2 is decidedly less dramatic than either Scenario 1 or 3, the long term social response would likely be unremarkable. The continuation of bipartisan support for standards and assessment probably would remain, with periodic movements aimed at dismantling and/or fundamentally altering the policy direction. Given the projections of this scenario, most states still will not have a history exit test by the year 2020. As such, teachers who fear a potential dead-end career in a rigidly high-stakes assessment environment may choose to relocate to states that do not test and/or select locations that test in a manner which encourages critical thought, discourse, and creativity. This may lead to a more tiered system within the teaching profession nationally, as history teachers who prefer mechanistic, standards-based pedagogy locate themselves in that context and those who prefer the variety and creativity permitted by a non-standards environment venture there. Increasingly, states have begun recruiting across state lines as the looming teacher shortage unfolds in high population growth areas. The presence or absence of high-stakes testing could become a point of leverage for savvy teacher recruiters in this new environment. Such a tiered system may also lead, ironically, to the strengthening of the profession in certain areas, as candidates recognize the options available to them and make choices on that basis.

Scenario 3—Abandonment of High-Stakes Assessment by Most States (Or, a Constructivists' Dream)

Scenario 3 is what many opponents of high-stakes history testing have been suggesting will eventually happen. Referencing the pendulum-like nature of education, I have frequently heard that *this too shall pass*, despite growing evidence to the contrary. What would have to occur for high-stakes assessment in history, and in other school subjects, to be abandoned? Some suggest that a political realignment of the current bipartisan support, presumably by the Democrats, toward opposition to this policy coupled with an electoral sweep could trigger such a change. Such a shift, however, seems highly unlikely as the universe of voters who cast ballots solely on the basis of educational policy *and* who oppose standards and high-stakes testing is quite small. The bipartisan support for standards and assessment will probably continue. The only real possibility for a breakup of bipartisan support would be a groundswell of parents locally as well as nationally against exit exams. As a member of Congress for whom I interned often said, "when voters turn up the heat, Congress sees the light."

How might this heat be applied? Such a chain of events might be set into motion if policymakers cross an imaginary threshold of unacceptably high failures due to exit exams. Put another way, what percentage of students would need to fail an exit exam for high school graduation, in a given state, such that parents and students would demand an immediate end to high-stakes assessment as it is currently implemented? The NAEP exams are instructive on this point. In 2001, for example, 57% of a nationally representative sample of 29,000 students performed below basic achievement on U.S. history exams in grade 12 (National Center for Education Statistics, 2001). Assuming that such a high-stakes test were implemented in history, that approximately half of the students failed the test, and that those students were subsequently denied a high school diploma, I suspect the abandonment of high-stakes assessment would begin immediately. Indeed, one cannot even imagine such a situation coming to pass. As currently implemented, most state exams are significantly easier than NAEP and passing rates are manipulated by state education agencies to insure that widespread failure, and the subsequent loss of credibility for schools in general, does not occur. So while the abandonment of at least the current version of high-stakes assessment would be highly likely in the event of using NAEP standards, the implementation of such *rigorous* standards by states for exit exams in history is about as likely as a snowstorm in Miami during July.

The hopes of constructivists, however, may be significantly more likely in the longer term (5–20 years). Consider the predictions of some futurists about global social trends, which include: (1) a knowledge-based economy, (2) a need for cooperative, interpersonal capacity in the workforce, (3) continuation of unequal access to intellectual and cultural resources, and (4) an emphasis on self-teaching and life-long learning. If these trends manifest over the next 20 years, the viability of narrowly-conceived, high-stakes history tests may decline. There have already been reports of ambitious, computer-native students who leave high school for lucrative corporate jobs in information technology (Duffy, 2000). Given the proliferation of computer technology, such trends are likely to increase, perhaps making obsolete a high school diploma in its current form. Such radical changes, once unthinkable in the modern era, have already begun to occur as education continues to be challenged and redefined. How ornamental and irrelevant a list of 75 *need to know* historical items will appear in a transformed, information overloaded world that has completely revamped education. If these larger social trends continue, and there is little to suggest they will not, high-stakes assessment, and indeed, school as we know it, may begin to resemble the horse and buggy of the late nineteenth century in the United States—apparently indispensable in its necessity, while on the cusp of becoming an anachronism of days gone-by.

CONCLUSION

As Jim Bishop (1959) reminds us, the opaque mirror of the future is both dim and worrisome. With respect to history curriculum and high-stakes assessment, the mirror may be even more obscure, as so little is known about what has already transpired. This volume makes a significant contribution as it is the first to expressly deal with the nature and scope of high-stakes testing in this field. This work also adds to the growing body of scholarship about high-stakes assessment generally, a vital field of inquiry that has and will continue to inform a nascent public debate. The scenarios outlined herein suggest a variety of potential paths, but the unfolding reality will likely meld elements of all three situations along with other phenomena not considered at all. The future is necessarily uncertain, but its amorphous quality does not undermine its vitality in our considerations of what is being done.

Perhaps what is of most value here is not the comparisons of what might occur to what actually transpires, but rather the implicit assertion about the need to reorient our educational discourse toward what lay ahead. Despite the socially conservative nature of education, teachers and those who support them need to recall that their work is necessarily about the future, including the opaque changes on the horizon, and the children who will inherit what we have made. Elise Boulding (1988) suggests that in our increasingly global society, decisions need to be made with an eye toward the 200 year present, a constantly moving span of time that stretches 100 years back to include the eldest inhabitants of our planet and 100 years forward to prepare for the youngest inheritors of our society. While this chapter humbly attempts to consider the next 2 decades based on the preceding one, the temporal reorientation that it suggests is sorely needed in our conversations about education, and indeed, society.

Education is in many respects our society's most significant legacy. What will our children inherit with respect to high-stakes assessment, in history and elsewhere? Will they learn in schools where knowledge is treated instrumentally, as merely a means to an end? Will they be taught in such a way that their innate capacities to make sense of the world may flourish? Will they be political pawns whose education is undermined for campaign year sloganeering? Will they be afforded creative, professional teachers who will help them grow and empower them to keep on growing? These questions and many others remain. But we must recall that we have agency in shaping the future of education and society, that it is not a play whose script has already been written. Asserting what may come has certain value, so long as it does not debilitate us from considering alternative futures and working toward those uncertain ends.

REFERENCES

Alaska: Teachers Reject Education Law. (2004, February 4). *The New York Times*, p. A12.

Bishop, J. (1959). *The future*. Retrieved from http://www.quotationspage.com/subjects/the+future/

Boulding, E. (1988). *Building a global civic culture*. New York: Teachers College Press.

California cancels exit exam. (2003). *Rethinking Schools, 18*(1), 15.

Duffy, T. (2000, September 18). *Teen techies graduate with enhanced learning.* Retrieved from http://www.cnn.com/2000/TECH/computing/09/18/teen.techies.idg/index.html

Education Commission of the States. (2003). *State high school exit exams: A maturing reform.* Retrieved January 27, 2006, from http://www.ecs.org/html/offsite.asp?document=http%3A%2F%2Fwww%2Ectredpol%2Eorg%2Fhighschoolexit%2FExitAug2004%2FExitExam2004%2Epdf+

Education Week. (2001). *Quality Counts 2001: A better balance.* Retrieved from http://counts.edweek.org/sreports/qc01/articles/qc01story.cfm?slug=17toc.h20

Gaudelli, W. (2002a). High stakes assessment in social studies? No thanks. *Trends and Issues, 13*(4), 4–5.

Gaudelli, W. (2002b). U.S. kids don't know U.S. history: The NAEP study, perspectives, and presuppositions. *The Social Studies, 93*(5), 197–201.

Grant, S. G. (2003). *History lessons: Teaching, learning, and testing in U.S. high school classrooms.* Mahwah, NJ: Erlbaum.

Hill, C. (2000, December 7). Falling short of the standard, part four: High stakes testing in American education, the progress profile. *TC Record.* Retrieved from http://www.tcrecord.org/Content.asp?ContentID=10665

Hilliard, A. (2004, February). *Program keynote address.* American Association of Colleges for Teacher Education, Chicago, IL.

Kohn, A. (2002, Summer). Requesting testing. *Rethinking Schools Online, 16*(4). Retrieved from http://www.rethinkingschools.org/archive/16_04/Requ164.shtml

Manna, P. (2004). Leaving no child behind. In C. T. Cross (Ed.), *Political education* (pp. 126–143). New York: Teachers College Press.

McNeill, L. M.(2000). *Contradictions of school reform: Educational costs of standardizedtesting*. New York: Routledge.

National Center for Education Statistics. (2001). *National U.S. history achievement-levelresults, grade 12.* Retrieved January 27, 2006, from http://nces.ed.gov/nationsreportcard/ushistory/results/natachieve-g12.asp

Savage, T. V. (2003). Assessment quality social studies. *The Social Studies*, *94*(5), 201–207.

Stanley, W. B. (Ed.). (2001). Social studies: Problems and possibilities. In *Critical issues in social studies research for the 21st century* (pp. 1–14). Greenwich, CT: Information Age.

ABOUT THE AUTHORS

Jane Bolgatz is an assistant professor of social studies education at Fordham University's Graduate School of Education in New York City. Her research interests include the teaching and learning of historical thinking skills, multicultural and antiracist education, and learning in unsupervised environments. Her book, *Talking Race in the Classroom* (2005), examines how high school students and teachers talk about race and racism. Bolgatz has also published articles in *Multicultural Perspectives* and *Social Science Dockets*. Formerly, she taught secondary social studies and language arts in traditional and alternative schools in New York and Iowa.

Letitia Hochstrasser Fickel is associate professor of Secondary Education at the University of Alaska Anchorage, where her primary teaching focus she has been working with a cadre of teacher leaders to enhance the teaching and learning of history in a local school district. Currently, Fickel is principal investigator on a federally funded Title II Teacher Quality Enhancement grant designed to strengthen school-university collaborative partnerships and enhance teaching and learning. Her research interests include teacher professional development and learning in the social studies, culturally responsive teaching, and school-university collaboration.

William Gaudelli is associate professor of Secondary Social Studies Education in the Department of Teaching and Learning Principles at the University of Central Florida. His research interests include global education, democratic schools, critical media studies, and teacher development and has published numerous journal articles related to these topics. His book, *World Class: Teaching and Learning in Global Times* (2003) examines global curriculum in the practice of three high schools. Gaudelli received an EdD from Rutgers University in social studies education and a bachelor's degree in political science from Rutgers College. He taught high school for 10 years and served as an adjunct instructor at Teachers College-Columbia University for 2 years.

Jill M. Gradwell is an assistant professor and coordinator of Social Studies Education in the Department of History and Social Studies at Buffalo State College, State University of New York. She teaches both undergraduate and graduate courses in the teaching of history and research in social studies education. Her research has centered mainly on secondary teachers' perceptions of state policy changes in social studies curriculum and assessment. Currently, she is exploring the use of historical texts to teach history and is involved in a research study examining the impact of various testing prompts on students' writing of history.

S. G. Grant is associate professor of Social Studies Education in the Department of Learning and Instruction at the University at Buffalo. His research interests lie at the intersection of state curriculum and assessment policies and teachers' classroom practices, with a particular emphasis in social studies. In addition to publishing papers in both social studies and general education journals, he has published *Reforming Reading, Writing, and Mathematics: Teachers' Responses and the Prospects for Systemic Reform* (1998), *Elementary Social Studies: Constructing a Powerful Approach to Teaching and Learning* (with B. VanSledright, 2005), and *History Lessons: Teaching, Learning, and Testing in High School Classrooms* (2003).

Catherine L. Horn is an assistant professor at the University of Houston. Her work addresses issues related to high-stakes testing, higher education access, affirmative action, and diversity. Most recently she has written on the effectiveness of alternative admissions policies in creating racially or ethnically diverse student bodies. Horn coedited (with P. Gandara & G. Orfield) a special volume of *Educational Policy* (2005), which analyzed the educational access and equity crisis in California and *Higher Education and the Color Line* (2005 with G. Orfield & P. Marin), looking at the future of access and equity in U.S. higher education.

Matthew F. Pinder is a doctoral student at the University of Florida. His research focuses on issues of historical significance and worth, democratic citizenship education, and social studies teacher education. He teaches courses in secondary social studies methods and the sociohistorical foundations of American education.

Cinthia Salinas is an assistant professor at the University of Texas at Austin in the Department of Curriculum and Instruction. She currently teaches classes in secondary and multicultural education and elementary and secondary social studies teaching methods. A former Texas high school teacher and policy maker for the Texas Education Agency, she has focused her attention on the high stakes testing dialogue that dominates Texas public schools. In addition, she conducts research in the issues of migrant/immigrant social studies education.

Avner Segall is an assistant professor in the Department of Teacher Education at Michigan State University. His teaching and research combine critical theory/pedagogy and cultural studies to explore a variety of issues in teacher education and social studies education. His book, *Disturbing Practice: Reading Teacher Education as Text* was published in 2002. He is also the editor (with C. Cherryholmes & E. Heilman) of *Social Studies—The Next Generation: Re-searching in the Postmodern*.

Ann Marie Smith has taught in senior high schools and most recently, at Northern Virginia Community College, where she is associate professor of English and Reading. Currently, she is a doctoral candidate in the Department of Curriculum and Instruction at the University of Maryland, College Park, where she also teaches classes in content area reading to pre-service teachers. Smith has published in *Teaching English in the Two-Year College*. Her present research interests include the influences of state mandates on teachers and adolescent readers' responses to literature.

Stephanie van Hover is assistant professor of Social Studies Education at the Curry School of Education of the University of Virginia. She serves as the program coordinator and faculty advisor for the secondary social studies program. Her research interests include the teaching and learning of history within the context of high-stakes testing, and the instructional decision making of preservice and beginning teachers.

Kenneth E. Vogler, a former social studies teacher in Lawrence, Massachusetts, is assistant professor of Elementary Social Studies Education in the Department of Instruction and Teacher Education at the University of South Carolina. His research interests include the impact of state curriculum and assessment policies on teachers' instructional practices.

Elizabeth Anne Yeager, associate professor of social studies education in the School of Teaching and Learning at the University of Florida, is an award-winning researcher who received the Outstanding Dissertation Award in Curriculum from the Association for Supervision and Curriculum Development (ASCD), the American Educational Research Association (AERA), and the Society for the Study of Curriculum History. She currently serves as editor of *Theory and Research in Social Education*. Her research focuses on the teaching and learning of history, wise practice in the teaching of social studies, and democratic citizenship education. She has served as guest editor for a special issue of *Social Education* on teaching social studies in challenging and diverse school settings, and her most recent book is *Wise Social Studies Teaching in an Age of High Stakes Testing: Essays on Classroom Practices and Possibilities* (with O. L. Davis, Jr., 2004). She is the professor partner of Miami Senior High in Little Havana and is a former classroom teacher in Atlanta public schools.

Printed in the United States
48334LVS00001B/100-129

9 781593 114794